Precolumbian
Population
History in the
Maya Lowlands

Precolumbian Population History in the Maya Lowlands

EDITED   BY

T. Patrick Culbert
and
Don S. Rice

University of New Mexico Press
ALBUQUERQUE

Library of Congress Cataloging-in-Publication Data
Precolumbian population history in the Maya lowlands / edited by T.
  Patrick Culbert and Don S. Rice.
      p.   cm.
    Includes bibliographical references (p.) and index.
    ISBN 0-8263-1219-5
    1. Mayas—Population.   2. Demographic archaeology—Central
America.   3. Demographic archaeology—Mexico.   4. Mayas—
Antiquities.   5. Mexico—Antiquities.   6. Central America—
Antiquities.   I. Culbert, T. Patrick.   II. Rice, Don Stephen.
F1435.3.P75P74   1991
304.6'0972—dc20   90-13016
                                                              CIP

Contents

CONTENTS

Figures

Maps

Tables

Contributors

E. WYLLYS ANDREWS V
Tulane University

WENDY ASHMORE
Rutgers University

ARLEN F. CHASE
University of Central Florida

DIANE Z. CHASE
University of Central Florida

T. PATRICK CULBERT
University of Arizona

ANABEL FORD
*University of California at
Santa Barbara*

ANNCORRINE FRETER
Ohio University at Athens

ROBERT E. FRY
Purdue University

WILLIAM A. HAVILAND
University of Vermont

CONTRIBUTORS

LAURA J. KOSAKOWSKY
University of Arizona

PATRICIA A. MCANANY
Boston University

K. ANNE PYBURN
University of Indiana

DON S. RICE
University of Virginia

PRUDENCE M. RICE
University of Florida

WILLIAM M. RINGLE
Davidson University

JEREMY A. SABLOFF
University of Pittsburgh

ROBERT S. SANTLEY
University of New Mexico

MICHAEL P. SMYTH
University of Cincinnati

GAIR TOURTELLOT
University of New Mexico

B. L. TURNER II
Clark University

DAVID L. WEBSTER
Pennsylvania State University

Preface

Population research is at the heart of the transformation that has taken place within the last generation in our concept of lowland Maya civilization. When the first mapping projects of the 1940s and 1950s reported mound densities several times greater than could reasonably be expected for the low populations then postulated for the Maya, it was inevitable that the model of scattered swidden farmers inhabiting the hinterlands between vacant ceremonial centers should be challenged. That model has now become little more than a historical curiosity, as has the vague notion accompanying it that the Maya were a unique civilization.

Despite the importance of the topic, those who have undertaken research on Maya population have found it difficult to assemble the constantly increasing mass of data. Many studies are recent and remain unpublished; others are available only from preliminary reports or obscure sources. Once the sources had been assembled, laborious adjustments were often required before the data from different projects were expressed in comparable form. This intractable situation convinced us that a source book on lowland Maya population data would be a boon to Mayanists and to those working on prehistoric population in other areas.

This volume had its genesis in a session on Maya population organized by the senior editor for the 50th Annual Meeting of the Society for American Archaeology at Denver in 1985. We contacted as many Mayanists with unpublished population data as we could and received very positive responses about the utility of such a collection of material. Given the potential size of the topic and number of contributors, a very tight focus was necessary. We decided that all chapters must provide quantitative data and all must make clear the methods used and the assumptions involved in moving from raw data to population estimates. To limit the volume to a reasonable length and keep interesting but tangential issues from arising, we eschewed (*expunged* might be more accurate) such related topics as settlement patterns and ecological adaptation. This is, then, primarily a book concerned with data and method. We view it as a stepping-stone to the broader and more theoretical issues to which lowland Maya population data may lend themselves.

1 /

Historical Contexts for Population Reconstruction in the Maya Lowlands

DON S. RICE *and*

T. PATRICK CULBERT

The study of demography entails two interrelated goals: documentation of population characteristics and explanation of the causes and consequences of such characteristics. This volume explicitly focuses on the first of these efforts, the reconstruction of the size, density, and transformation of Prehispanic Maya populations from archaeologically recovered settlement remains. This compilation of gross regional population statistics for aboriginal Maya society and the systematic evaluation of methods of their estimation are critical first steps for investigation of the causal relationships among these population patterns, Maya culture, and the events of Maya history. Elucidation of these relationships requires access to biological, sociological, and economic data whose relevance is contingent on materials and interpretations brought together here but whose discussion and evaluation are beyond our current enterprise.

The following chapters take Maya studies from knowledge of a few scattered sites and implicit assumptions about demography, both easily disputed, to vast amounts of new data and explicit debate over methods and implications. Likewise, their coverage subsumes considerable ecological and sociological diversity, such that it is no longer possible to claim that any one site or area is unsubstantiated, aberrant, or without applicability to broader issues. Although there is variation, as one might anticipate in a physiographically diverse region, there is also comparability of overall population characteristics.

The volume has been compiled to make explicit the procedures and problems of a historical demography of the Maya and to establish source consistency that allows cross-checking and comparative analysis. In their discussions and conclusions the authors bring closure to some debates, while raising other issues and exposing lacunae in our methods and our knowledge about lowland Maya settlement and domestic life. In the final analysis, however, the contributors collectively provide data on the magnitude and dynamics of Maya populations, data that are unique for a world culture area.

THE LOWLAND MAYA

The tropical forests of Belize, northern Guatemala, northern Honduras, and Mexico's Yucatan Peninsula were once the homeland of a populous Prehispanic Maya society (Map 1.1) This landform of predominantly marine sediments is generally flat, ranging from sea level to several thousand feet in altitude. Karst hills provide relief in the northern Puuc region of the Yucatan Peninsula and in the central Peten of Guatemala, while the tectonic activity of the Caribbean Cocos plate has contributed to formation of the central Peten lake basins and the Maya Mountains of southern Belize. Farther south, the absolute elevations of southern Peten and northern Honduras rise, and the transition is made from marine sediments to the metamorphic igneous deposits of the Central American volcanic mountain region.

The Maya lowlands are subject to a north-to-south gradient in total annual precipitation, ranging from ca. 500 mm/year in the north to ca. 2200 mm/year in the south. Rain drains quickly through the majority of the calcareous soils and underlying limestones, and the hydrology of the lowlands is characterized by a paucity of open bodies of fresh water. Cenotes, or sinkholes, provide access to subterranean waters in Yucatan, while lakes and bajos (seasonal swamps) are major potential water sources in the Peten. Reliable perennial streams and rivers are few, and those that do exist are primarily situated on the eastern, western, and southern peripheries of the lowlands.

This geomorphological and hydrological setting supports a mosaic of tropical flora, the diversity and stature of which varies according to local physical parameters. Maya populations may have entered this forested landscape as early as 4000 B.P. (Deevey et al. 1979). The first irrefutable archaeological evidence of Maya agricultural communities is attributed to the first millennium B.C. (E. W. Andrews V and Hammond 1990; Andrews V 1990), and subsequent Maya history is largely comprised of several thousand years of population growth and expansion within the lowlands (R. E. W. Adams, ed., 1977).

Maya population is indicated by remains of masonry residential platforms and superstructures ("house mounds") of varying size and elaboration, often arranged in groups situated variably across the landscape in response to local natural and cultural conditions (Ashmore, ed., 1981). Communities of groups are often structurally diverse, but many focus on sites of monumental architecture that are thought to have housed Maya civic and ceremonial leadership. The construction of large numbers of temples and palaces, the commemoration of the rulers in carved and painted monuments, the recording of elite histories in hieroglyphic texts, and the production and consumption of labor-intensive crafts and exotic goods at these sites in the Late Classic Period (ca. A.D. 550–830) are usually considered the hallmarks of Maya civilization.

During the eighth and ninth centuries A.D. Maya civilization suffered a decline throughout much of the southern lowlands, a "collapse" manifest in a complete cessation of the architecture and arts associated with the elite class and in an apparent disappearance of much of the local population (Culbert, ed., 1973; Culbert 1988). To the north, population and political histories suffered no such setbacks, and the Postclassic Period (ca. A.D. 950–1525) witnesses considerable regional variability in settlement and organization (A. Chase and Rice 1985; Sabloff and Andrews V 1986). Only with Spanish contact and ultimate subjugation were Maya populations dramatically diminished throughout the Maya lowlands, although Indian communities and customs do survive to the present day, primarily in the Mexican states of the Yucatan Peninsula (Farriss 1985).

As Mayanists have recovered the materials of Maya history and pondered the rise and fall of Maya civilization within the tropical environment, they have not been ignorant of evolving tenets of relationship among cultural complexity, resource exploitation, and population size. Concern for the numbers and dynamics of Prehispanic Maya populations has been inextricably tied to interests in lowland ecology and aboriginal land use, the organization and complexity of Classic Maya society, and the demographic catastrophe at the close of the Classic Period in the south. Each of these topics has been a focus of historical demographic study.

HISTORICAL DEMOGRAPHY

Demographic analyses are invariably comparative, diachronic, and couched in concern for the impact of population numbers on other aspects of human life (Dupaquier 1974; Henry 1967; Hollingsworth 1969;

Willigan and Lynch 1982). At their narrowest, demographic studies describe the size and composition of populations at specific points in time and space, with these characteristics seen as products of an interplay among the dynamic processes of birth, death, and migration. In its broadest reach, demography evaluates these data and processes to establish theoretical links between formal biological properties and numbers and the sociocultural phenomena that are the substance and contexts of human history.

The goals of description, interpretation, and explanation, and the multidisciplinary perspectives they demand, have characterized the field of demography since its beginnings. Seventeenth-century academic interests in population, for example, were extensions of long-accepted efforts by monarchs to appraise the numbers and wealth of their subjects (Willigan and Lynch 1982). The need for rulers to be aware of the demographic status of their domains arose in issues of taxation, the raising of armies, and the provisioning of cities and the royal courts.

These considerations require empirical data, and it is not surprising that early investigations of demographic processes attempted to collect and critique available information. In the seventeenth century Graunt sought to compile and interpret London's "Bills of Mortality" (weekly lists of christenings and burials) for the purpose of demonstrating the need to understand then-current demographic conditions as products of past trends (1975 [1662]). Graunt's contemporaries, particularly mathematicians and actuaries, took similar interest in human birth and mortality records as a basis for determining the value of life annuities, a source of revenue for seventeenth-century European cities. The work of these and later "methodologists" focused concern on the regularities of demographic processes, particularly mortality, and led to creation and refinement of "life tables" (tables of data by which to determine average life expectancy for specific age intervals) that would reflect human demographic conditions regardless of time or place (Willigan and Lynch 1982:5–14).

While the formative work of census-data collection recognized the systematic nature of demographic patterns, interpretation and application of these data emphasized that population processes are embedded in specific cultural and historical contexts. Practitioners of the seventeenth- and eighteenth-century tradition of inquiry known as "political arithmetic" engaged in statistical description of populations in terms of material resources in an effort to distinguish the various categories of people who comprised political states (Hull 1963–64; Vilquin 1975). The goal of such analyses was to evaluate "relationships among the factors of production" with an eye toward contributing to successful statecraft (Willigan and Lynch 1982:17). Growing populations were thought to lead to increases in national wealth, provided all members were pursuing productive tasks coordinated through good government, a belief that led logically to interest in regional differences in population size and density and to consideration of the causes for increases or declines in relative population levels.

The relevance of population size to public policy and societal history has not been lost on social theorists since the days of the political arithmeticians. Investigations have turned from establishing agendas for the practice of government, however, to contemplating issues of demographic change and questioning the role of population in the development of economic heterogeneity, social stratification, and the centralization of political authority. Is population increase a constant process in human societies (Carneiro and Hilse 1966; M. Cohen 1975, 1977; cf. G. Cowgill 1975a,b)? Is population size primarily a dependent variable, dependent on the means available to support life (Malthus 1960; Marx 1967, 1974; White 1949, 1959), or an independent one that in turn promotes innovation and intensification of subsistence and nonsubsistence production (Boserup 1965)? Does population growth so contribute to changes in the material conditions of life that conflict, division of labor, and ranking occur, and if so, under what material conditions (Carneiro 1970; Durkheim 1893; Fried 1967)? To what degree can population size serve as a marker for types of social order, relative power within orders, and changes in social complexity between orders (Dobyns 1966)?

PALEODEMOGRAPHY

Questions of relationship between demographic processes and transformations in society are diachronic ones that cannot be answered from historic contexts and sources alone, and archaeologists have been particularly attendant to the potential role of populations in culture change. In order to generate estimates of prehistoric population sizes and densities, and rates of change in these, the paleodemographer must rely on the recovery and analysis of physical remains considered indicative of or sensitive to population: skeletal remains, artifacts, architecture, exploited biological resources, and environmental contexts (S. Cook 1972). The conversion of these remains to population numbers requires assessment of the quantity and distribution of the indicator being considered, together with the magnitude of association between population and that particular element at any given time (S. Cook 1972:3; Hassan 1978, 1979). The application of derived demographic data to the interpretation of the archaeological record is in turn guided by theoretical and methodological interests, and in recent years an overriding emphasis of such inquiry has been investigation of the development of complex societies.

Modern archaeological research on demographic parameters of early civilizations began in the late 1940s and 1950s and has been pursued with greatest success in Mesopotamia and highland Mexico, areas with long-standing traditions of major excavation. In both regions concern with population issues has been intimately linked to questions of the subsistence adaptations and/or the internal organization of large urban societies and to the study of settlement patterns.

In southern Mesopotamia, for example, population estimates based on survey data have been correlated with other archaeological evidence of economic activity and sociopolitical organization to demonstrate that urbanism, population aggregation, and initial state development preceded the large-scale irrigation projects hypothesized to have been a primary causal factor in the origins of government (R. M. Adams 1966, 1981; R. M. Adams and Nissen 1972; Wittfogel 1957).

In the Valley of Mexico there has been debate as to the causal factors for centralization of authority and aggregation of population at the site of Teotihuacan (Blanton 1972; Millon 1973, 1976; Parsons 1971; Sanders 1965; Sanders et al. 1970). Sanders and Price have attributed Teotihuacan's ascendancy, and its centripetal impact on the demographic history of the region, to the site's strategic location in a zone of high hydraulic potential and its control over a symbiotic regional exchange network (Price 1973; Sanders and Price 1968; Sanders et al. 1979), whereas Millon feels that the center's role as a pilgrimage center is more important than its ecological setting or control over irrigation (1973, 1976).

Similar argument has been aired over the origins of the site of Monte Alban in the Valley of Oaxaca. Blanton and his colleagues have proposed that Monte Alban was founded in response to outside threat and as a result of an administrative decision by allied leaders from varying sectors of the valley (Blanton 1978; Blanton et al. 1982). Sanders and Santley have countered, however, that the center's origin is a population density-dependent phenomenon. They reconstruct a very high agricultural and demographic potential for the site zone and hypothesize that the modern city of Oaxaca obscures from archaeologists the settlement evidence that would indicate the presence of a large population in the area before and after the founding of the city (Sanders and Santley 1978; Santley 1980).

Such demographic studies in Mesopotamia and highland Mesoamerica have been facilitated by an arid environment. These are regions of naturally diminished vegetation communities that, in turn, have been further reduced by millennia of human occupation and agriculture. Relatively clear terrain and enhanced artifact and architectural preservation have made archaeological sites easily identifiable in these zones, and surface collection is productive as a method of recovering and dating cultural materials. Moreover, sites in these regions tend to be relatively discrete, with detectable boundaries and measurable areas. Estimates of population sizes for settlements can, therefore, be derived by projecting modern densities to delimited site boundaries (Braidwood and Reed 1957) or by attributing population numbers to recovered densities of architecture and debris within site limits under the assumption that the amount of material discarded at a site varies in direct proportion to the size of the resident population (Blanton 1972; Parsons 1971). Not all regions of the world benefit from this conflation of archaeologically positive cultural and environmental factors, however.

Population research has lagged somewhat in the Maya lowlands, for example, due in part to moist tropical conditions and to attitudes about the tropical lowland environment. Although some parts of the northern Yucatan Peninsula are clear of natural vegetation as a result of long and continuous histories of human occupation, Postcolumbian populations have remained relatively sparse in much of the lowlands. As a result, dense forest vegetation obscures the landscape, and under this multistoried canopy heat and humidity degrade the recoverable archaeological record. Because surface collection is difficult, assessment of relative volumes or densities of architecture and artifacts and the dating of those materials require excavation. In addition, Prehispanic Maya settlement was generally more dispersed than in arid regions, and site boundaries are less amenable to definition.

Early disinterest in the size and characteristics of Maya populations might also be attributed to European aversions to the tropics and to forest (Haviland, personal communication 1989), and to the prevailing stereotype that tropical forests were homogeneous zones of low productivity, exploitable only through implementation of seemingly wasteful slash-and-burn or swidden agriculture. Historically, this extensive subsistence system has been deemed incapable of supporting high population densities, so the belief that the ancient Maya practiced swidden agriculture made moot questions of large resident populations and issues of demographic primacy in culture change.

It is within the context of simplistic models of environmental productivity, subsistence adaptation, and societal organization that Mayanists first pursued settlement studies and demographic reconstructions in the Maya lowlands. As a result, characteristics of agricultural systems and their carrying capacities, and discussions of societal complexity have been inextricably associated with estimates of population size and density.

AGRICULTURE, SETTLEMENT, AND POPULATION SIZE

Carnegie Institution of Washington Studies

The study of Maya historical demography first became formalized during the Carnegie Institution of Washington investigations of Maya civilization from 1930 to 1960, which included major excavations at the sites of Uaxactun, Chichen Itza, and Mayapan and anthropological and ethnohistorical research throughout the Yucatan Peninsula. The Yucatan projects investigated modern Maya production of corn through full-fallow, slash-and-burn agriculture and presumed a reliance by ancient Maya populations on similar subsistence techniques and products (Emerson 1935:12; Morley 1946:426). Caloric needs and settlement characteristics of modern Yucatan populations (Benedict and Steggerda 1936: 174, 184, 188) predicted a maximum possible density of 23 persons/km^2 for the Yucatan Peninsula (Hester 1954:108). Actual modern Maya population density figures were estimated to be ca. 12 persons/km^2, or half the potential carrying capacity of extensive milpa systems (Hester 1954:118), leaving some latitude for larger-than-modern Prehispanic populations.

In a conversation with Morley in 1921, Schufeldt proposed a much larger Prehispanic Maya occupation as a result of his encounter with multitudes of small masonry platforms and other architectural features during the cutting of thousands of acres of forest in the Peten, Guatemala , to plant milpa and grow corn to feed chicleros and mules (1950:226). Morley was apparently unimpressed at first with the idea of high population numbers and densities for the Maya lowlands, but in 1923 he published the statement that there had been continuous residential settlement throughout the Peten forests (1923:272).

In the 1930s the Carnegie Institution of Washington project at Uaxactun attempted to arrive at population size and density figures from the more tangible and archaeologically meaningful data base noted by Schufeldt: remains of aboriginal residences. This study consisted of a survey to find and record house mounds within a measured area in the vicinity of a single Maya center (Ricketson and Ricketson 1937:15–16), with the complete excavation of five such structures (Wauchope 1934). A total of 78 mounds and 50 chultunes was found in the 953,040 m^2 of inhabitable terrain within the survey cruciform, 82 structures/km^2 of inhabitable land (Ricketson and Ricketson 1937:15–16). Considering each mound a house and using an average figure of 5 persons/house, the Ricketsons projected a density of 410 persons/km^2 of inhabitable land (if all mounds had been contemporaneously occupied), or an overall density of 170 persons/km^2. The Ricketsons then assumed that only 25% of the mounds were occupied at any given time, although no justification was offered for that figure, yielding a density of 102 people/km^2 of inhabitable land, and 43 persons/km^2 of total land area.

Arbitrarily assigning a radius of 16 km from the site center as a basis for defining a Uaxactun zone (a total of 803 km^2, of which 57%, or 458 km^2, was considered inhabitable), the Ricketsons estimated a regional population of approximately 50,000 people. Although the Ricketsons accepted the predominance of maize in the prehistoric Maya diet, they rejected swidden as an unproductive system that never could have supported the ancient Maya population at its peak. They also felt that the abandonment of the Peten at the time of the Classic Maya "collapse" was due to two causes: rapid population increase and expansion, and soil erosion following implementation of intensive agricultural methods (Ricketson and Ricketson 1937:2–3).

By the end of the Carnegie Institution's field research in the late 1950s, a consensus had developed that the mass of Maya population lived in small settlements distributed around centers (J. E. S. Thompson 1954:76–81), centers that were thought to house small groups of elites or rotating ceremonial officials (Vogt 1961, 1964). Reservations by the Ricketsons and others notwithstanding, slash-and-burn agriculture was assumed to be the prevailing subsistence system. Such swidden-based communities are characteristically small, scattered, and often transitory, and it was this inherent dispersion and potential mobility that was thought to be incompatible with large and dense populations.

The apparent disjunctions among recorded mound densities, the magnitude and complexity of Maya architecture and artifacts, and the demographic attributes of swidden agriculture engendered debate, however. Opponents argued that inherent limitations of the lowland environment and the low carrying capacity of slash-and-burn agriculture were incompatible with the possibility of large Maya populations (Meggers 1954; Palerm and Wolf 1957). Others drew data from ethnographic sources and statistical experiments, respectively, to try to show that monumental structures built under Maya political aegis could have been constructed and maintained by a less-than-full time corps of slash-and-burn agriculturalists (Kaplan 1963; Erasmus 1965). U. Cowgill, on the other hand, calculated upward the accepted carrying capacity of the landscape under milpa agriculture and proposed that the system would support 58 to 77 persons/ km², with farming activities leaving blocks of leisure time for specialist activities (U. Cowgill 1962:277; cf. Reina 1967). Cowgill's figures led her to suggest that the aboriginal population of Peten never really reached the limits set by slash-and-burn agriculture, and she felt it doubtful that population size and agricultural failure were factors in the Maya collapse (1962:278–79).

Recent Settlement Studies

In the late 1950s and early 1960s new settlement surveys extended the approach taken at Uaxactun to unsampled regions and began to provide confirmation of large and dense settlement systems. W. Bullard undertook a survey of the northeast Peten in 1958, following known trails throughout the area and noting the location of mounds and features of the terrain (1960). At the site of Dos Aguadas he was able to map a 0.21 km² strip that had been cleared for petroleum exploration and found 37 house-ruin groups containing a total of 89 separate platform mounds or structures (414 structures/km²). Bullard estimated a density of 888 people/km², assuming that all structures were contemporaneously occupied. With 25% occupation of the total number of mounds at any given time, as implemented by the Ricketsons, the density would be 222 persons/km². This was five times the Ricketsons' estimate and well over the carrying capacities suggested by U. Cowgill (W. Bullard 1960:366).

During a survey in the Chontalpa, Tabasco, Mexico, in the early 1950s, Sanders reported similar structure densities from a surveyed area of 0.25 km² near the Late Classic site of Tierra Nueva (1962–63:215). Eighty house ruins were mapped, for an average density of 320 structures/km². Sanders relied on analogy to impermanent rural settlement of modern Yucatan to propose that perhaps as few as 25 to 40% of settlement remains were actually occupied at any one time. Estimating a modern regional carrying capacity of ca. 40–50 persons/km², with favorable areas reaching 100 persons/km², Sanders suggested that actual Classic Maya population densities would have been close to the maximum capacity of the system (1962–63:96–99).

Structure densities comparable to those found in the central and western zones of the southern lowlands were also recovered by the Belize River Valley Survey (Willey et al. 1965) at the site of Barton Ramie. On the basis of a total of 262 mounds mapped in the ramie clearing, a Late Classic population of 2000 for the cleared area was estimated. A total population of 6000 was projected for the river strip designated as the Baking Pot district, with a peak aboriginal population of 24,000 estimated for the Belize Valley from Cocos Bank westward and southward into Guatemala (Willey et al. 1965:576)

Similar surveys at sites in the northern Yucatan yielded even higher settlement sizes and population estimates. An intensive mapping program at Dzibilchaltun revealed 8526 structures in an area of 20 km² (426 structures/km²), and E. W. Andrews IV felt that this figure should be doubled to account for unrecovered residence remains (1965:37). Sanders also mapped structures within the walled confines of the site of Tulum and estimated approximately 7000 to 8000 persons/km² (1960). Similarly, at Mayapan 4140 structures were identified within the area delimited by the site's defensive wall, 2000 of which were considered residential, and A. L. Smith estimated a peak population for the site of between 11,000 and 12,000 (1962).

Despite increasing evidence of high aboriginal settlement densities in the Maya lowlands, many researchers remained reluctant to accept the large population sizes suggested by the settlement data (see, for example, Willey and Bullard 1965). The figures from the Peten and the Yucatan Peninsula were increasingly difficult to explain away, however, and in the early 1960s Mayanists were forced to face directly the magnitude of their data, and their methods for translating them into population figures, as a result of archaeological work at the site of Tikal, Peten, Guatemala.

In 1961 Carr and Hazard published the map of the central 9 km² of Tikal, which documented an average of 235 mounds/km². Elimination of bajo and water-storage areas gave an average density of 275 individual platforms or structures/km². An additional 7 km², peripheral to the central 9, were mapped and found to have approximately 145 mounds/km².

Based on these figures and on test excavations that allowed evaluation of structure contemporaneity and function, Haviland estimated a total population of nearly 11,000 for the 16 km² mapped, a density of occupation that appeared to preclude farming in the immediate site region (1963:521–24, 1965:429, 1970:193). Not only was there no land available in the central area to have supported the indicated population, but problems of local subsistence production were compounded by the assertion that a large segment of the measured population may not have been directly involved in subsistence cultivation (Haviland 1963, 1965). These factors, together with the still-accepted belief that slash-and-burn maize agriculture was the primary subsistence source of the Maya, were the basis for the initiation of the Tikal Sustaining Area Project in 1965.

Satterthwaite first used the term "sustaining area" in 1951 to suggest the nature of the population and immediate environment that might be expected to support a complex sociopolitical center. The hypothesis under which the Sustaining Area Project worked was that, at some distance from the site center, population densities at Tikal would drop off, and from that point outward there would be a sufficiently dispersed settlement and available arable land to compensate in subsistence terms for the high density of population in central Tikal (Haviland 1963, 1965; D. Puleston 1973:65–67, 1983).

The Tikal surveys recovered 1720 mounds and 342 chultunes in a cruciform survey area of four arms radiating from central Tikal, plus a fifth strip mapped between the northern boundary of the Tikal National Park and the site of Uaxactun. The Sustaining Area Project analyses demonstrated that the limits of the Late Classic center extended beyond the coverage of the original Tikal map, and therefore the total area and population densities for "central" Tikal were revised upward. Haviland expanded his definition of the central zone to 63 km² and defined a peripheral zone of 66 km² (1970:190). The central zone was estimated to have had an overall peak population of 40,000 (Haviland 1972a:138), or a density of 600 to 700 persons/km². Peripheral Tikal was not so densely occupied, with an estimated density of 160 persons/km² (Haviland 1970:193). Nonetheless, the Tikal settlement figures, both central and peripheral, confirmed the very high population levels reported elsewhere and contributed to major reassessments of ancient Maya subsistence production (Flannery 1982; Harrison and Turner 1978; Pohl 1985).

DON S. RICE *and* T. PATRICK CULBERT

THE PRESENT VOLUME

The Tikal project marks a threshold of sorts for this volume, one between recent history and modern research, for our contributions include a reevaluation of material from Tikal and presentations of demographic data from projects that took to the field during or after the Tikal investigations. Although the settlement and population density projections from Tikal were often treated with skepticism, even within the project itself, project results and their implications were undeniable. The introspection and debate occasioned by these data in turn called into question assumptions, procedures, and data for estimating populations. Likewise, the controversies enjoined were motivation for further field research at other venues, the results of which are here brought to bear on the fundamental problems of reconstructing the size, density, and transformation of Maya populations through time and across space.

Since the 1960s, when population became a major research issue in the Maya lowlands, there has been a steady accumulation of survey data. A primary objective of this volume is to assemble population data from recent and past research, much of it published here for the first time (see Table 1.1). Some areas have been extensively sampled. The best-known area is the central Peten, where a 50-km north-south strip between Uaxactun and Tikal has been surveyed and a 50-km east-west section along the lakes has been sampled in several locations. In the southeast zone, there are now figures for both the Copan and Quirigua areas, and an increasing number of sites in Belize have been tested. There are still major gaps in the southern lowlands, however. For the Pasion zone only Seibal and Altar de Sacrificios provide data, and not a single survey has been reported for the Usumacinta or Palenque zones. The northern lowlands are still poorly sampled, but this volume adds data for Komchen and Sayil, the latter the first Puuc site ever tested. A major lacuna is that all northern surveys have been in intrasite areas, so that we have no information about what, if any, population resided in areas away from centers.

In addition to presenting new data and population reconstructions, the authors in this volume bring methodological issues to the fore. Rather than simply accepting the standard procedure of multiplying counts of mounds by a set of correction factors to derive population estimates, they have explicitly considered sources of error and the rationale behind their calculations. The results of this careful methodological consideration are sobering; many variables are poorly controlled, and alternative assumptions may have major effects on interpretation. Nevertheless, population reconstruction is no more tenuous for the Maya lowlands than for other archaeological areas, and Mayanists seem to us to have been more assiduous than average in testing critical variables by excavation. The consideration of method indicates the directions in which future research may increase precision. It is to methodological issues that we will move first in reviewing the contents of this volume.

CALCULATING MAYA LOWLAND POPULATION

Population in the Maya lowlands has traditionally been calculated by counting small mounds, excavating a sample to determine date of use, and applying adjustments that convert numbers of mounds to numbers of people. Because most visible platforms date to the last major period of occupation, estimates for earlier populations require further adjustments.

Most of the studies in this volume based their calculations on counts of individual platforms. The excellent surface visibility at Sayil (Tourtellot et al., this volume) and large excavated samples at Copan (Webster and Freter, this volume) made it possible to use rooms rather than platforms as the basic units for those sites. At Quirigua (Ashmore, this volume), Seibal (Tourtellot, this volume), the Belize River (Ford, this volume), and peripheral Tikal (Fry, this volume), various considerations dictated the use of the patio group rather than the individual structure as the unit for calculation. McAnany (this volume) offers a radical alternative by calculating the population of Sayil on the basis of the water-storage capacity of chultunes.

Because prehistoric disturbance and rebuilding of structures were very destructive, population from periods preceding the last major occupation cannot be realistically determined from surface remains. When the detailed excavation necessary to show complete sequences of construction and occupation is lacking, some substitute indicator of earlier occupation must be accepted. Many of the studies in this volume accept the presence of sherds from a particular period as indicative of occupation. Others insist on evidence of construction or special deposits such as burials and caches before counting an occupation. Both methods are subject to the possibility of errors, as discussed in the chapters by Culbert et al., A. Chase, and D. Chase.

In all of the studies reported in this volume, dating was based on ceramics, although at Copan obsidian dating offers a more precise alternative. In most cases a sequence of ceramic complexes was used, although for some projects identification was possible only to the level of ceramic period (Late Preclassic, Early Classic, etc.). Ceramic periods are very gross temporal units, never under 200 years duration and usually 300 to 500 years. Even ceramic complexes (usually of 100–200 years duration, but sometimes longer) are so lengthy that the contemporaneity problem to be discussed in the next section arises. A related chronological issue is raised by A. Chase (this volume). A change of only 50 years in the assigned dates for the Tayasal phases resulted in a quite different population curve. There is certainly the possibility that phases in other ceramic sequences might be changed by comparable amounts, to add another factor of imprecision to population estimates.

PROBLEMS IN ESTIMATING POPULATION

That there are very substantial problems in moving from the units of observation to either relative or absolute estimates of population has long been obvious. Authors in this volume agree about the solution to some of these problems. Others provoke serious debates, the resolution of which is a critical issue for future research on Maya population. It is important that some of the issues critical for estimating population (e.g., the number of small structures that were not residential) have been specifically tested by field research. The majority of the testing, however, has taken place in a few large, long-term projects (especially Tikal, Seibal, and Copan). The extension of the test results from these sites to others rests on the assumption that key variables were constant over time and space. We are uncomfortable with this assumption, since it is only logical to expect that some factors (e.g., length of platform use) might vary between periods of light and dense population, between regions, or even between the central and peripheral areas of large sites. As is so often the case in archaeology, we must face the fact that the best inferences possible at the present may be upset when variability has been explored further.

Nonplatform and Hidden Structures

Where the structure platform is the unit of calculation, a first critical question is whether maps adequately reflect the number of such platforms that actually existed. There are several reasons for underestimation of structure counts during reconnaissance, ranging from structures that left no surface indications (Pyburn, this volume; D. Chase, this volume) to quite large structures whose remains were masked by debris from adjacent structures (Webster and Freter, this volume). A major issue raised by several authors in this volume is the possibility that a substantial upward adjustment may be necessary to allow for unmapped structures. D. Chase argues that actual structure counts at Santa Rita were 50 to 100% greater than they appear from mounded remains, and A. Chase (this volume) would add 37.4% in the Tayasal zone. Webster and Freter add 38% to the number of small structures and 50% to the number of larger structures to account for those structures that their excavation sample indicates were unmapped. Such substantial corrections would augment population estimates considerably. The Tikal authors are more conservative and add only

10% for unmapped structures, although they suggest that many early structures remain unmapped.

Almost all authors who consider this topic distinguish between "invisible" structures that left no surface indications and "hidden" structures whose surface indications were missed or not considered structures during mapping. For estimating population, the distinction makes little difference because both kinds of missed structures result in underestimation.

It is very difficult to estimate the number of unmapped structures that may exist at a site, even when excavation has been done with the question in mind. Testing a statistically significant portion of seemingly vacant terrain at a large site would be a project of enormous scope. In addition, there is every reason to believe (Pyburn 1988) that the number of unmapped structures might vary temporally and spatially within and between sites, so that a restricted sample could not safely be extended to other sites or even to other areas of the same site. Nevertheless, it is generally agreed that site maps fall short of showing the number of structures that actually existed and may at some sites fall short by quite significant amounts.

Nonresidential Structures

Even in groups that were primarily residential, some structures served other functions. Estimation of the number of nonresidential structures depends on careful excavation and artifact analysis and is possible only where extensive excavation programs were undertaken. The prototype study of the problem was Haviland's small-structure excavation program at Tikal (Haviland 1965), which resulted in his oft-quoted estimate that 16.5% of small platforms were nonresidential. The program at Copan provided an even larger sample of excavated structures. Of the single-mound, Type 1, and Type 2 groups—those most comparable to Haviland's small-structure sample—Webster and Freter suggest that 20 to 30% were not residences. D. Chase's figure for Late Postclassic structures at Santa Rita is smaller (6.6%); whether this is a function of the different date or of the area is uncertain. The consensus is that a downward adjustment between 5 and 30% should be made in small-structure counts to allow for nonresidential structures.

The Contemporaneity Issue

The contemporaneity issue is the most hotly debated and critical question in Maya population studies. The crux of the issue is whether individual house locations—once they have been established—were in continual residential use until a period of major population decline or site abandonment, or whether such locations were regularly abandoned even when population was growing or stable. The chapters by Tourtellot, Rice and Rice, and Culbert et al. in this volume spell out the contrasting viewpoints.

Early estimates of population from mound counts were made while prevailing opinion still held that Maya population was severely restricted by a dependence on swidden agriculture. Primarily for this reason, they used large contemporaneity adjustments. The Ricketsons (1937) considered only 25% of the mounds at Uaxactun to have been occupied at any single moment. W. Bullard (1960) in the Peten and Sanders (1962–63) in the Chontalpa used similar reductions. Haviland (1965, 1970), using detailed data from excavation, broke the pattern by proposing that 93% of the Tikal mounds were occupied in the Late Classic. Sanders (1973) called the Tikal data into question to start a debate that continues until the present.

Many of the arguments made in favor of frequent shifts of structure locations rest on ecological or ethnohistoric justifications. "Shifting cultivation" (Meggers 1954; Palerm and Wolf 1957) was assumed to demand frequent relocation. Now that the "myth of the milpa" (Hammond 1978) is dead, this reason for abandonment is also diminished, although the possibility of dual residence involving both permanent homes and seasonal field houses still exists (Ford 1986, this volume; Santley, this volume). Using ethnohistoric and ethnographic data, J. E. S. Thompson (1971) suggested that the Maya abandoned houses after a family member died, but Haviland (1972b) rebutted this claim with archaeological evidence indicating that although structures were often remodeled after burials, there was no evidence of abandonment. Archaeologically, Webster and Freter's obsidian dates "make it clear that there was a great deal of periodic abandonment at Copan, even in areas of high density such as the rural zone of the Copan pocket" (Webster, personal communication 1989).

Much of the support for an argument of continuous occupation of structures has been archaeological. Haviland's (1970, 1985, 1989) evidence for multiple rebuildings of structures within short ceramic intervals (rebuilding that used still-intact remnants of earlier structure) has been very influential. In addition, the architectural accretion that characterizes groups as well as structures would have been unnecessary if abandoned structures were readily available (D. Rice and P. Rice 1980). Finally, the labor investment involved in sizable substructure platforms and paved plazas seems incompatible with short-term residential use.

The contemporaneity issue has the greatest impact on comparing population between two ceramic intervals of different lengths. Whether, for example, 100 structures dated to a 100-year Late Classic phase are equivalent to 100 structures from a 400-year Preclassic phase is a question that dramatically affects interpretation of population change. The effect on absolute population estimates is less severe. Most absolute calculations involve quite short Late Classic phases that would not be radically changed by the century or longer periods of use that advocates of contemporaneity adjustments now propose.

We must also face the fact that length of occupation may have varied over time depending on the complexity of the cultural landscape and the amount of land available. In a period of high population density, space would have been at a premium and residential mobility more restricted than in intervals of low population. Few data bear on the question of changing residential mobility, although the hints of ephemeral Early Classic occupations at several sites suggest that this may have been a time of high mobility.

Disuse

The abandonment discussed in relation to the contemporaneity issue is final, or at least long-term. Another kind of abandonment, which we call *disuse,* must be considered in making population estimates. In any living community some houses will be temporarily unoccupied; presumably, the same must have been true of prehistoric communities. One can easily imagine the kinds of situations involved: a house temporarily without occupants after the last family member has died; a platform unused for a time after an old house has collapsed and before a new one is built. Without very detailed excavation, such short episodes (defined by Culbert et al. [this volume] as 10 years or less) of disuse would be impossible to detect archaeologically, but they are an obvious reality. In this volume only Webster and Freter and Culbert et al. make reductions for disuse. Both choose a figure of 10%, but this may be quite low given the 13% disuse figure reported by Ringle and Andrews (this volume) for modern Komchen and the maximum figure of 20% suggested by Sanders (1973:357).

Family Size

In calculating population, most researchers have assumed that a small structure housed a nuclear family and consequently have multiplied small structures by an estimate of the size of such a family. One of the first figures used by archaeologists for nuclear family size was 5.6 individuals, a number based on the ethnographic survey by Redfield and Villa Rojas (1934:91) of the Maya village of Chan Kom in Yucatan. This figure was used by A. L. Smith (1962) for Mayapan, Haviland (1965, 1969, 1970) for Tikal, and Tourtellot (1970) for Seibal. Sanders (1962–63; Sanders and Price

1968:163), however, suggested the lower figure of 4.0 individuals/house derived from sixteenth century Mexican census data.

In 1972 Haviland turned to ethnohistoric data from Cozumel Island, which provided a figure of 4.9 individuals/nuclear family, a figure that matched Steggarda's (1941:128) suggested family size for modern Yucatan. Rounding the figure up to 5.0, Haviland applied it (1972a:140) in later calculations of Tikal population. D. Puleston (1973:173–75) favored a higher estimate of 6.07 people/house based on Villa Roja's (1945, 1969) census figures for the X-Cacal Maya of Quintana Roo, a group that Puleston considered less acculturated and more comparable to the prehistoric Maya than the Cozumel Island group.

Even higher figures come from early postconquest accounts that single houses sometimes held several nuclear families (Hellmuth 1977). Villagutierre (1933:136, 480) describes Chol structures that housed as many as 19 to 25 individuals. Working with data on house numbers and population size for the contact-period Itza island capital of Noh Peten (Cogolludo 1842–45:II:230; J. E. S. Thompson 1951:390), D. Puleston (1973:177) calculated an average of 10 persons/house for that community.

Given the range of these estimates for family size, it is useful to have an archaeologically derived estimate for comparison. Naroll's (1962) formula that each individual will have an average of 10m² of roofed space can be applied to Maya data. Using Haviland's sample of excavated small structures from Tikal, D. Puleston (1973) calculated an average of 54.1m², which would result in a house occupancy of 5.4 individuals.

All the authors in this volume opt for figures between 4.0 and 5.6 individuals/house, although the Rices believe that the large Postclassic houses in the Peten lake district might well have come closer to the 10 individuals/house suggested by ethnohistoric data for that region.

RESULTS

We now turn to the results of the population studies reported in this volume and elsewhere in the literature, beginning with the data on structure counts and proceeding with the series of conversions that allow estimates of population density and total population.

Structure Density

Table 1.2 assembles data on structure density/km² of total land, including bajos, for the Late Classic, the period of maximum occupation at most sites. The density of the Copan urban core (1232 structures/km²) is by far the highest but includes only a small area (0.6 km²). Most other site-central areas have been between 128 and 223 structures/km², except Uaxactun and the two Belize sites (Nohmul and Lubaantun), which have about half this density. The few sites for which surveys mapped a large enough area to include a peripheral zone show lower densities in the periphery than in the site center.

Rural densities from most southern lowland sites fall between 30 and 60 structures/km². Because the foregoing figures include bajos—which at all sites were apparently uninhabited—the density differences between site centers and rural areas are partly a result of the fact that bajos make up a larger percentage of land in rural areas. The figures for inhabitable (nonbajo) land given in Table 1.1, however, show that density differences remain after the effect of bajo has been removed.

The foregoing discussion has considered only densities in the southern lowlands. Those in northern lowland sites were certainly greater. The original figure of 477 structures/km² reported for Dzibilchaltun (Kurjack 1974) has been supported by figures of 400 structures/km² at Chunchucmil (Vlacek et al. 1978) and now by 500 structures/km² for Formative Komchen (Ringle and Andrews, this volume). Sayil (Tourtellot et al., this volume) has a lower density of 220 structures/km². There are no rural surveys for the northern lowlands, but Andrews V (personal communication, 1989) believes rural densities are as high there as in the south.

There are also indications that Postclassic sites in the southern lowlands had greater structure densities than Classic sites. Santa Rita's Postclassic density of 400–712 structures/km² (D. Chase, this volume, accepting Chase's estimate of the number of invisible structures) far exceeds most Classic Period totals. A reported density of 826 structures/km² for Zacpeten in Postclassic times (Rice and Rice, this volume) supports the idea that Postclassic sites were more nucleated than Classic ones.

Population Totals

Calculating individuals/km² from structures/km² requires all the adjustments discussed in the section on method. Each researcher applies somewhat different correction formulae, but the maximum correction is about a 30% reduction. Using this adjustment will provide a conservative estimate of the number of structures in use during the Late Classic, and multiplying by five, the most commonly used figure for family size, will provide population figures. If one accepts an average of 45 structures/km² for rural areas of the central Peten, the rural population density was 180 persons/km². This is an astonishingly high figure, especially since it includes large sections of bajo without apparent population. Intrasite densities, on the other hand, were quite low in comparison with densities in many early civilizations. Most site centers had between 500 and 800 inhabitants/km², while site peripheries and smaller sites had densities about half this number. The conclusion that lowland Maya sites had lower densities than such highly nucleated sites as Teotihuacan has not been changed by the new data.

Site Boundaries

To estimate population it is necessary to define the boundaries of sites. This is not an easy matter in parts of the Maya lowlands. Among the sites covered in this volume, Copan can be delimited because the area is easily surveyed and population is confined to naturally bounded alluvial pockets. The northern lowland sites also have obvious borders. At both Sayil and Komchen, surveys located points beyond which definite residential structures no longer occurred, although chich mounds beyond the boundary cloud the picture at Sayil.

Site definition is more problematic in the Peten and Belize. Dense vegetation makes survey difficult, mounds are continuously distributed over all terrain except bajo, and although bajo provides a natural limit to populated areas, there are so many bajos of different sizes that picking which of them should be considered boundaries is not a simple matter. The traditional definition of a site as the area encompassing all major architectural groups lacks the precision necessary for population studies. The 12-km survey strips at Tikal offer a less arbitrary site definition based on the co-occurrence of bajos and earthworks with drops in mound density. Tikal, so defined, includes 120 km², a very large territory. It is unclear whether Tikal was unique or whether other sites, if investigated by equally extensive survey, might prove to be comparable. Uaxactun seems not to have had such a periphery, because population there drops off to rural densities only 2 km out from the site center (D. Puleston 1983).

Site Populations

Some of the chapters here present estimates for the maximum populations of sites (see Table 1.3 for population estimates and Table 1.6 for sources of data). Although there are regional and temporal variations, the estimates for sites of comparable times and locations are very consistent.

Webster and Freter estimate the population of the Copan urban core at 5797 to 9214 and that of the entire Copan pocket as 15,317 to 21,103, comparable to but somewhat larger than populations of the core and central areas of Peten sites. Copan differs drastically from Peten sites, however, in the size of outlying populations that would have been within its political sphere. Since population occurred only in the pockets of alluvial land along the river, the entire Copan Valley had only 18,417 to 24,828 inhabitants in an area of 162 km², only slightly more territory than the 120 km² within the borders of Tikal.

Quirigua is small in comparison with Copan. This is not surprising, because it has long been recognized that Quirigua lacked the monumental size and longevity of Copan. Nevertheless, the figures of 1183 to 1579 that Ashmore favors for the population of the 3-km² pocket of alluvial land where Quirigua is located are smaller than most would have anticipated. It could be that the political status of Quirigua as a foreign dynasty imposed from the Peten (Sharer 1989) is responsible, because several other, perhaps non-Maya, sites in the Motagua Valley are comparable in size to Quirigua (Schortman 1984).

In the Peten, population can be calculated for Tikal, Seibal, Uaxactun, Tayasal, and the lake basins. For areas of 15–16 km², the estimates for peak population are 13,275 for Tikal, 9618 for Seibal, 5936 for Uaxactun, and 10,293–15,600 for Tayasal. The Peten lake-basin pairs range from 3836 to 7262. These estimates are encouragingly similar and the variations are in the expected direction, with larger centers having the larger populations. For Tikal and Tayasal it is possible to calculate population for larger areas. Adding the additional population for the remaining 104 km² within the Tikal boundaries gives a population of 58,995 for the 120-km² site. The Tayasal-Paxcaman zone of 90 km² had 21,951–33,272 inhabitants at its peak.

At Nohmul, both the structure density and population seem very low in comparison with those of the Peten. The entire 22 km² surveyed at Nohmul would have included only 3310 occupants if calculated in the same manner as at Tikal. Santa Rita, which has the higher structure density typical for Postclassic sites, is estimated to have had a Postclassic population of 8722. This is well within the size range for Classic centers but occurs in a more delimited space (5 km²). The Late Classic Period population estimated for Santa Rita is 2438.

Northern lowland sites have higher structure densities than Classic Period sites in the south, but those reported here cover substantially less territory. The total population estimate for the 2.4-km² area of Sayil is between 4900 and 10,000. It is tentatively estimated that Komchen in the Preclassic housed between 2500 and 3000 people within 2 km², the only site for which a solid Preclassic population estimate is available.

Only for Tikal and the Sacnab-Yaxha basins are there estimates of population for larger areas than a site and its peripheries. In a circle of 10-km radius (314 km²) centered at Tikal, there would have been a population of 92,000. While there were an estimated 6252.8 people resident in the immediate Sacnab-Yaxha lake basins during the Late Classic Period, the 237-km² Thiessen polygon centered at Yaxha may have supported as many as 42,000 people. For a political realm around Tikal which included Uaxactun

on the north and the lake district on the south (a very conservative estimate of the size of a Tikal polity) there would have been 425,000 inhabitants. This figure, particularly, is far larger than anyone would have
guessed a few years ago, but several rural surveys within the proposed
Tikal realm show population at the high rural densities discussed earlier.
Unless there is some fundamental error in methods of calculating population from survey data, archaeologists must face the likelihood that maximum populations of large polities were of this order or magnitude.

Population Change Over Time

Adding the new data from this volume to that available from previous
publications provides a total of 15 sites and areas with population sequences. We present the data in Tables 1.4 and 1.5 in terms of relative
population—a measure that expresses population at each time interval as
a percentage of the maximum population. The contemporaneity problem
is particularly severe in considering population change. In Table 1.4 we
present calculations that make no contemporaneity adjustment. In Table
1.5 we have made an adjustment that assumes that structures were occupied for an average period of 150 years and then abandoned and not reoccupied. This adjusts downward the relative population for each time
interval greater than 150 years.

LATE EARLY PRECLASSIC AND EARLY MIDDLE PRECLASSIC (PRE-MAMOM).
Only a few sites give evidence of occupation during these early periods.
Most of the occurrences indicate very low population densities, usually
less than 10% of maxima.

LATE MIDDLE PRECLASSIC (MAMOM).
The Mamom horizon appears at almost all sites in the southern lowlands,
usually at densities less than 20% of the maximum. The areas with higher
densities (28–52%) are reduced to much lower figures if contemporaneity
corrections are applied.

LATE PRECLASSIC AND PROTOCLASSIC (CHICANEL).
In the Late Preclassic and Protoclassic there are large differences between
sites in estimated population. A significant portion of the differences, however, is dependent on whether or not a contemporaneity correction is
used. The unadjusted calculations in Table 1.4 indicate strong Late Preclassic population surges at sites scattered throughout the lowlands in both
central-site and rural areas (Seibal, Tayasal, the Tikal-Yaxha strip, the Belize
River valley, Barton Ramie, Pulltrouser Swamp, Becan, and Komchen). The
remaining sites have Late Preclassic populations that show only moderate

growth from earlier periods (to 14 to 34% of maxima). With the exception of Komchen, the Late Preclassic population peaks in Table 1.4 occurred during long ceramic phases that lasted several centuries. If one adjusts Late Preclassic figures to allow for noncontemporaneity (Table 1.5), the population peaks disappear, and much lower densities, usually about one-third of Late Classic maxima, result.

There are, therefore, two very different reconstructions of population curves, depending on viewpoints about the contemporaneity issue. Those who believe in continuous occupation would see a population history in which a number of sites have bimodal curves with Late Preclassic and Late Classic peaks separated by an Early Classic decline. Those who favor contemporaneity adjustments would reconstruct a more uniform pattern in which almost all sites show a steady growth to a Late Classic peak. The arguments in this volume make it clear that present data cannot resolve the debate and that contemporaneity remains a critical issue for future research.

EARLY CLASSIC (TZAKOL).

Although contemporaneity corrections also affect Early Classic population figures, they do not prevent a relatively uniform interpretation for the period. No site had its maximum population during the Early Classic. In fact, almost all Early Classic figures fall below 50% of maximum densities. The Pasion River sites show low levels of population during the latter part of the Early Classic. In the central zone, medium population levels (29–84%) at Tikal, Tayasal, Tikal-Yaxha, and Sacnab-Yaxha are juxtaposed with very low levels (8–9%) for the lakes other than Sacnab-Yaxha. In the north both Komchen and Dzibilchaltun show near-abandonment in the Early Classic following heavy Late Preclassic occupation.

Early Classic population estimates are further obscured by the fact that several sites show pervasive scatters of Early Classic ceramics that cannot be associated with visible structures. The phenomenon is so widespread (Seibal [Tourtellot, this volume], Central Tikal [Bronson n.d.], peripheral Tikal [Fry 1969], Nohmul [Pyburn, this volume]) that it seems to be an archaeological fact that suggests some difference in settlement pattern for the Early Classic. It may be that there was great mobility in settlement at this time with flimsily constructed (and rapidly abandoned?) structures that have left little archaeological evidence except for ceramics. The settlement pattern and population of the Early Classic is clearly an issue that needs careful attention in future field research.

LATE CLASSIC (TEPEU).

The majority of sites reached population maxima during the Late Classic. The sites where the Late Classic was not the time of peak population were those with heavy Terminal Classic populations or primary occupations at another time period which were so dominant that Late Classic percentages were reduced. No site in the sample had a low Late Classic occupation.

TERMINAL CLASSIC.

The Terminal Classic data show the differential effects of the Maya collapse. Despite the royal collapse at around A.D. 800, Copan population continued to be heavy for the next two centuries (Webster 1988). Both Pasion River sites reached maximum populations at this time, a fact that has long been evident. Tikal and the lake-district sites show drastic population declines in the Terminal Classic. In Belize it has been impossible to differentiate ceramics of the Terminal Classic from those of local equivalents of Tepeu 2, so no comparative figures between the two intervals are possible. Because Postclassic occupation occurs in many Belize sites, it seems likely that they did not show as severe a population decline as at most southern sites.

POSTCLASSIC.

Postclassic population was not evenly distributed across the Maya lowlands. The northern lowlands had a significant Postclassic development, and there were substantial populations in Belize and the southeast zone. There were also sites along the lakes of the central Peten. Other sites in the southern lowlands, however, show little evidence of occupation, and one must conclude that most of this area had an exceedingly low population density. Of the sites covered in this volume, only Santa Rita was primarily a Postclassic site. The northern lowland sites covered here were not primarily of Postclassic date, so we can add no new information about this important period in the history of the north.

DISCUSSION

These new data open the door to broader analyses and interpretations. The chapters of Fry, Turner, and Santley in this volume turn to both substantive and methodological questions of regional reconstruction and comparison and put the Maya data in the context of population studies in other archaeological areas.

The central area of the lowlands within a 50-km radius of Tikal is by far the most thoroughly investigated. Turner begins with this area and adds data from Calakmul and Rio Bec regions to undertake a regional reconstruction, the first that has been attempted quantitatively. He finds a single long wave of population in which growth to a Late Classic peak is followed by a decline that lasts until the Spanish Conquest and beyond. Santley notes that the Preclassic portion of this curve is exponential, suggesting that the area continued to offer room for expansion. Turner calculates the growth rate for the Preclassic to be a moderate 0.24% per annum. Although there is some variation in Early Classic population between the regions of Turner's study, they all show an increased (0.45–0.58%) growth rate in the Late Classic—a population explosion, Turner calls it. An upturn at this point in a growth curve is unexpected, and Santley suggests that it may have been due to the adoption of systems of wetland agriculture. On a smaller spatial scale, the calculations of Rice and Rice (this volume) of crude growth rates for the Peten lake basins show intraregional variation that suggests population movement in response to influences from major centers such as Yaxha and Tikal. All the lake basins, however, show the same population burst in the Late Classic and precipitous decline in the Terminal Classic.

A further characteristic distinguishing the population curve of the central area from those of other lowland Maya areas and most curves elsewhere in the world is the magnitude of the population decline after the Late Classic and the failure of population to recover. As Santley notes, the decline mirrors the growth curve that preceded it, with a rapid initial decline (Turner estimates a loss rate of 0.90% between A.D. 800 and 1000) followed by a slower downward drift. Except for long-known centers of Postclassic population in the lake district, the loss is attested in all central region surveys, at Becan, and to the south at Altar de Sacrificios and Seibal. The area affected is very large, in excess of 30,000 km². Although there was certainly a continuity of Maya culture into Postclassic centers in the southern lowlands, these data, as Turner notes, make it difficult to give credence to suggestions that the population effects of the Classic Maya collapse have been overestimated.

A single-wave population curve is not universal for the Maya lowlands, a matter that both Fry and Santley explore. A second common pattern is bimodal, at least if contemporaneity adjustments are not used, with a high Late Preclassic population followed by an Early Classic decline and then a surge to the Late Classic maximum. This pattern occurs in the unadjusted counts for the Belize and Pasion River sites and in several of the survey areas of the lake district. Fry attributes the bimodality at Belize sites to a less successful politicoeconomic integration in this peripheral area than took place at major sites in the central area. Such integration began to take effect in the Early Classic at sites such as Tikal, where population rose, while Belizean sites lagged in both development and population. As the sphere of integration widened in the Late Classic, Belize sites joined the general expansion of population. The Rices (this volume) have posited a somewhat similar explanation of Early Classic decline in the more isolated lake basins in the central area at a time when such Early Classic centers as Tikal and Yaxha continued to grow. It is less easy, however, to apply an explanation of peripherality to the Pasion River sites.

25

Santa Rita and the Tayasal-Paxcaman zone, the two areas in this volume which had heavy Postclassic populations, both show trimodal curves with Late Preclassic, Late Classic, and Postclassic peaks. There are both southern sites, and it would be unwarranted to extrapolate the curves to other regions of Postclassic occupation. A major gap in the data is the absence of a longitudinal study from any site in the northern lowlands which had a Postclassic population climax.

Finally, we turn to the question of absolute population size. The data forever dispel the notion that the Maya lowlands were sparsely populated. We must now ask whether current estimates are too high. Populations in the central areas of sites are quite consistent and not unusually high— $10,000 \pm 50\%$ for Copan, Tikal, Seibal, Santa Rita, and Sayil. What differentiates at least the well-studied central Peten from most other early civilizations is the very large territory covered by high-density rural population. Except for bajos, all land was occupied, and surveys have sampled enough territory so that one cannot reasonably posit that rural areas with low population density lie hidden somewhere. Our conservative reconstruction, based on quite consistent mound counts from several rural surveys, is 180 individuals/km², including the large stretches of bajo found in rural areas. This figure would place Maya lowland densities in the range of those in areas such as Java and China (C. Clark and Haswell 1964)—that is, among the most densely populated regions of the preindustrial world.

A potential inflationary factor in estimates (Santley, this volume; see also Ford 1986) could result from the use of some rural structures as field houses, which would duplicate structures counted in more central areas. Although there is possible support for this view in the Copan rural area (Webster and Freter, this volume), most researchers who have excavated in rural areas of the Peten believe that structures there are too substantial to be field houses.

It is very significant that, since the first population estimates from Tikal and Dzibilchaltun shocked Mayanists more than a generation ago, a constant expansion of data has consistently confirmed the results and expanded the area in which high populations occurred.

APPLICATIONS AND IMPLICATIONS

This volume is not the place to apply the information about Maya population to theoretical issues, but lest Mayanists seem even more atheoretical than they actually are, some indication of the potential applications is in order.

The long-investigated connections among population, subsistence, and environment continue to be of interest. Although the simplistic typological contrast between Mesoamerican highland irrigation and lowland swidden adaptations was a passing fancy of the early days of ecological analysis, there are still valid contrasts between Maya adaptation and those of civilizations in more arid environments. The difference between the concentration of highland populations in a few flat, fertile basins surrounded by inhospitable mountain slopes and the far more even distribution of Maya population across local ecological mosaics has important implications for cultural development. Questions about the population-subsistence balance raised by the sharp Late Classic escalation of population followed by population collapse in the southern Maya lowlands are of much more than local interest. Furthermore, the Maya data, which cover a very large area, sample both urban and rural contexts, and include some regional variation in environment, offer one of the best cases in which to test hypotheses related to the debate over whether population is better viewed as an independent or a dependent variable.

The population data assembled here are also relevant to issues involving the organization of society. The form of Maya urbanism remains a matter of interest. It is now beyond dispute that thousands of Maya lived within reasonable contact distance of site centers, but the distribution of lowland population still contrasts with that of such highly nucleated centers as Teotihuacan or Mesopotamian cities. Central-site densities among the Maya were substantially lower than in nucleated centers, but the area covered by higher-than-rural population densities was very large. The 120km² area of Tikal is six times larger than Teotihuacan, and it is likely that other major Classic sites were comparably large. In addition, very high populations were distributed continuously over rural hinterlands between sites. Such a distribution of population is different from that in many other early civilizations, a finding that has important implications for settlement patterns, economic structure, and political control.

A question destined to have increasing significance for the Maya is the relationship between population and polity, a matter of growing general theoretical interest (Blanton 1978; Blanton et al. 1982; Montmillon 1988). The recent decipherment of Maya hieroglyphic inscriptions has generated a debate about the size of Maya polities (Culbert 1988, 1989; Culbert, ed., 1989). Were such polities typically of small scale (what J. E. S. Thompson [1954] has called *city-states*) or had they begun to reach the level of regional-scale political configurations (Marcus 1976; R. E. W. Adams and Jones 1981)? Was, as one of us has argued (Culbert, 1989), the size of Maya polities (425,000 for even a minimal Tikal state) too large for a political system of small, autonomous units? Were the political fortunes of sites and regions reflected in, or caused by, variations in population? We might well

27

ask, for example, whether the population variations in Early Classic times were a response to political developments.

The foregoing are only some of the broader issues to which Maya population data relate. The data are still not complete enough to provide definitive answers for the whole Maya lowlands, but for the first time, we have enough data of regional scope so that a beginning may be made in dealing with broader issues and contexts.

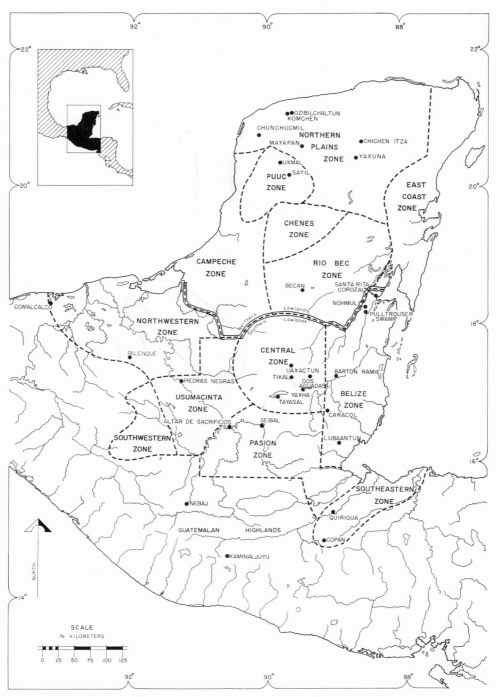

Map 1.1   The Maya lowlands: zones and sites.

Table 1.1 Surveyed Areas in the Maya Lowlands

Site	Area of Site	Area Surveyed (km²)	Total Structures/km	% of Bajo	Structures/km² Habitable Land
Copan	Urban core	0.6	1,449	0	1,449
"	Copan pocket	24.0	99	0	99
"	(urban core + pocket)	(24.6)	143	0	143
"	Rural	37.7	28	0	28
Quirigua	Central		128	0	128
Seibal	Central	1.6	275	9	436[a]
"	Periphery	0.7	144	24	244[a]
Tikal	Central 9 km²	9.0	235	20	294
"	Next 7 km²	7.0	181	41	307
"	Survey strips— inside Tikal boundary	8.5	112	42	194
"	Survey strips— rural	11.5	39	60	98
Tayasal	Central	4.0	221		
Cenote	"	0.5	214		
Peten Lakes	Macanche-Salpeten— rural	6.0	68	4	72
" "	Petenxil-Quexil—rural	5.5	39	46	72
" "	Yaxha-Sacnab—rural	10.0	59	22	75
" "	Total	21.5	56	23	74
Tikal/Yaxha	Rural	3.2	65	41	110
Belize Valley	Rural	5.0	118	0	151[b]
Nohmul	Central	4.0	58		
	Peripheral	18.0	12		
Santa Rita	Central	0.3	400	0	(400)[c]
			712		(712)[c]
Komchen	"	1.0	500	0	500
Sayil	"	2.4	220	0	220
			(324 + chich)	0	(324 + chich)
Quirigua Area					
Las Quebradas	Central	0.9	315		
Playitas	"	3.2	60		
Quebrada Grande	"	0.6	67		
Uaxactun	Central 4 km²	2.0	112	10	124
	Periphery	2.25	32	40	53
Peten Lake District					
Cante Island	Central	0.11	1,291		
Cerro Ortiz	"	1.7	63		
Muralla de Leon	"	0.13	169		
Zacpeten	"	0.23	826		
Quexil Islands	"	0.04	772		
Dos Aguadas	"	0.22	414		
Lubaantun	"	1.0	90		

Table 1.1   Surveyed Areas in the Maya Lowlands (*continued*)

Site	Area of Site	Area Surveyed (km²)	Total Structures/km	% of Bajo	Structures/km² Habitable Land
Caracol	"	2.26	300		
Becan (Turner)	Rural	1.0	80		
Becan (Thomas)	Central & periphery	3.0	222	43	389
Chunchucmil	"	6.0	400		
Dzibilchaltun	"	19.0	442		
Mayapan	"	4.2	986		

Note: See Table 1.6 for sources of data.
[a]The figures for uninhabitable land at Seibal include allowances for highly sloping land and land occupied by major architectural groups as well as for bajo.
[b]Uninhabitable land in the Belize Valley is savanna rather than bajo.
[c]The two figures for Santa Rita are based on separate survey areas. Both include allowance for "invisible" structures.

Table 1.2 Late Classic Mound Density (Including Bajos)

Site Centers

Site	Area (km²)	Structures/km²
Copan, urban core	0.6	1,232
Dzibilchaltun	19.0	398
Caracol	2.2	300
Tikal, central 9 km²	9.0	235
Seibal, central area	1.6	222
Sayil	3.4	220
Santa Rita	5.0	171[a]
Becan	3.0	171
Komchen	2.0	160
Quirigua	3.0	145
Tayasal	2.5	128
Cenote	0.5	128
Uaxactun	16.0	106
Lubaantun	1.0	90
Nohmul	4.0	58

Site Peripheries

Site	Area (km²)	Structures/km²
Tikal 9–16km²	7.0	181
Seibal	13.6	116
Tikal outside 16 km², inside boundaries	104.0	112
Copan pocket	23.4	84

Rural

Area	Structures/km²
Belize Valley	116
Tikal/Yaxha	60
Lakes Macanche-Salpeten	57
Lakes Yaxha-Sacnab	47
Lakes Quexil-Petenxil	36
Total lakes	49
Tikal (survey strips)	39
Uaxactun	30
Copan Valley outside Copan pocket	15
Nohmul	12

Note: See Table 1.6 for sources of data.
[a]Does not include an adjustment for hidden structures

Table 1.3 Populations of Sites

Site	Part of Site	Area (km²)	Population	Period
Copan	Urban core	0.6	5,797–9,464	Late Classic
Copan	Rural portion of Copan pocket	23.4	9,360–11,639	Late Classic
Copan Valley	Rural areas outside Copan pocket	476	3,010–3,725	Late Classic
Copan Valley	Total	500	18,417–24,828	Late Classic
Quirigua	Center	3	1,183–1,579	Late Classic
Seibal	Center	1.6	1,644	Late Preclassic
Seibal	Peripheries	13.6	7,974	Late Preclassic
Seibal	Total	15.2	9,618	Late Preclassic
Tikal	Central 9 km²	9	8,300	Late Classic
Tikal	Next 7 km²	7	4,975	Late Classic
Tikal	Remainder within boundaries	104	45,720	Late Classic
Tikal	Total within boundaries	120	62,000	Late Classic
Tikal	Rural within 10 km	194	29,696	Late Classic
Macanche-Salpeten Basin	Total	27.9	7,262	Late Classic
Yaxha-Sacnab Basin	Total	29.5	6,253	Late Classic
Quexil-Petenxil Basin	Total	23.5	3,836	Late Classic
All lake basins	Total	78.3	17,351	Late Classic
Yaxha Polygon	Realm	237	42,047	Late Classic
Cante Island	Whole island		410	Late Postclassic
Cerro Ortiz	Whole site		484	Middle Preclassic
Muralla de Leon	Whole site		64	Late Preclassic
Zacpeten	Whole site		546	Late Postclassic
Quexil Islands	Whole islands		102	Early Postclassic
Tayasal	Spine	8	6,861–10,400	Late Classic
Tayasal	Outer Ring	18	7,719–11,000	Late Classic
Tayasal	Periphery	64	7,371–11,172	Late Classic
Tayasal	Total	90	21,951–32,272	Late Classic
Santa Rita	Whole site	5	4,958–8,722	Late Postclassic
Nohmul	Whole site	22	3,310	Late/Terminal Classic
Komchen	Whole site	2	2,500–3,000	Late Preclassic
Sayil	Whole site	3.4	8,148–9,990	Late/Terminal Classic
Sayil (chultun estimate)	Whole site	3.4	4,900–10,000	Late/Terminal Classic

Note: See Table 1.6 for sources of data.

Table 1.4: Relative Population as Percentage of Maximum Population (Unadjusted Figures)

Period	Altar de Sacrificios	Seibal	Tikal Central	Tikal Peripheral	Tikal/Yaxha	Macanche/Salpeten	Quexil/Petenxil	Yaxha/Sacnab	Tayasal/Paxcaman	Belize River	Barton Ramie	Pulltrouser Swamp	Becan	Santa Rita Corozal	Komchen	Dzibilchaltun
Late Postclassic	28	?				10			14 / 68			27		100 / 11	6	6
Early Postclassic	100	14	4	1		19	2	8	32	21		Gap	29	40	1	5
Terminal Classic	64 / 31	85	14	20	92	29	20	11	89 / 51	50	91	91	59	54	71	100
Late Classic	19 / 39	85	100 / 95	64 / 67	100	100	100	100	45 / 38	100	100 / 76	100 / 82	100 / 74	23 / 11	0	5
Early Classic	69	34	78	100	84	8	5	46	100	50	62	73	94	34		
Late Preclassic	78	100	19 / 24 / 20	14 / 1	100	18	10	29	7	93	74 / 32	46 / 64 / 9	94 / 9	6	58 / 100	29
Middle Preclassic	17 / 11	28 / 14	4 / 0	1 / 1	41	25	34	13		52	24 / 29	18		3	6 / 0	
Early Preclassic																

Note: Screened bars indicate beginning and end of occupation. Where two or more complexes occur within a period they are separated by a dotted line. When complexes span two or more periods they are bracketed.

Table 1.5: Relative Population as Percentage of Maximum Population (Figures Adjusted for 150-Year Platform Use)

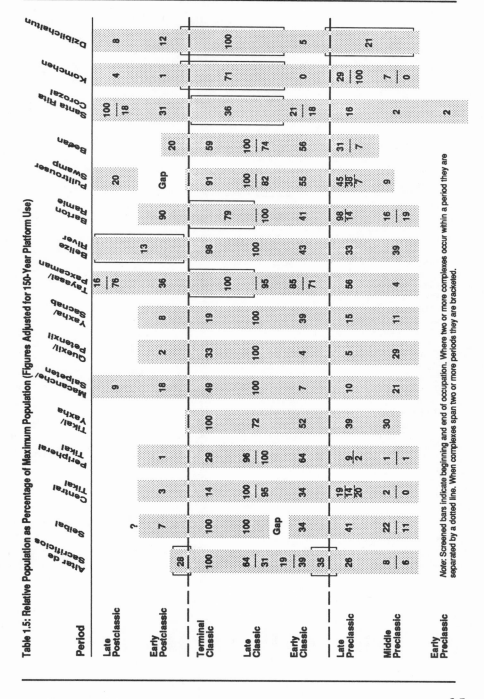

Note: Screened bars indicate beginning and end of occupation. Where two or more complexes occur within a period they are separated by a dotted line. When complexes span two or more periods they are bracketed.

Table 1.6 Sources of Population Data

Site or Area	Source
Altar de Sacrificios	Willey 1973
Barton Ramie	Fry, this volume
Becan	Turner data noted in R. E. W. Adams 1981; P. Thomas 1981
Belize Valley	Ford, this volume
Cante Island	Rice and Rice, this volume
Caracol	D. Chase et al. 1990
Cenote	A. Chase, this volume
Cerro Ortiz	Rice and Rice, this volume
Chunchucmil	Vlacek, Garza de González, and Kurjack 1978
Copan	Webster and Freter, this volume
Dos Aguadas	Bullard 1960
Dzibilchaltun	Kurjack 1974
Komchen	Ringle and Andrews V, this volume
Las Quebradas	
Lubaantun	Hammond, personal communication 1986
Macanche/Salpeten	Rice and Rice, this volume
Mayapan	A. L. Smith 1962
Muralla de Leon	Rice and Rice, this volume
Nohmul	Pyburn, this volume
Peten Lakes	Rice and Rice, this volume
Petenxil/Quexil	Rice and Rice, this volume
Playitas	
Pulltrouser Swamp	Fry, this volume
Quebrada Grande	
Quexil Islands	Rice and Rice, this volume
Quirigua	Ashmore, this volume
Santa Rita Corozal	D. Chase, this volume
Sayil	Tourtellot et al., this volume
Seibal	Tourtellot, this volume
Tayasal	A. Chase, this volume
Tikal	Culbert et al., this volume
Tikal/Yaxha	Ford 1986
Uaxactun	Puleston 1974
Yaxha/Sacnab	Rice and Rice, this volume
Zacpeten	Rice and Rice, this volume

2 /

The Demography of Late Classic Copan

Davɪᴅ Wᴇʙsᴛᴇʀ *and*

AɴɴCᴏʀʀɪɴᴇ Fʀᴇᴛᴇʀ

Two major research efforts since 1975 have produced an abundance of settlement data for the Copan region of western Honduras. The first phase of this research, begun by Gordon Willey (1975–77) and continued by Claude Baudez (1977–80), intensively surveyed an area of 24 km,[2] called the *Copan pocket,* around the Main Group (the Copan Valley in Honduras consists of five major alluvial zones, or pockets of which the Copan pocket is the largest [see Map 2.1]). Since 1980 the Phase II Copan Project, directed by William T. Sanders and David Webster, has added three more components to the already rich corpus of Copan settlement data. One consists of a set of extensive excavations in residential compounds to the northeast of the Main Group in the urban core of Copan and also in small outlying sites in the Copan pocket up to 4–5 km distant. The second component is a program of surface survey, test-pitting, and large-scale excavation outside the Copan pocket over a much larger area to capture the more distant rural dimensions of settlement variation. Finally, an ambitious obsidian hydration dating project provides detailed chronological control (Freter 1988).

Archaeological research at Copan may be conceived as a series of efforts radiating spatially from core to periphery. The early work of Maudsley, Morley, and their successors focused almost exclusively on the Main Group and a few outlying sites with impressive architecture and inscribed monuments. Willey's project began the systematic mapping and testing of the flanking residential zones of Las Sepulturas and El Bosque (Map 2.2), and under Baudez these activities were extended over most of the Copan pocket. Our Phase II project has widened the scope to include most of the Copan drainage in Honduras (Map 2.1). This history of archaeological research broadly reflects the shifting methodological emphases that typify Maya archaeology: an early preoccupation with monumental architecture, inscriptions, and reconstruction; a later concern with the systematic investigation of site cores and immediately adjacent outlying populations; and finally, efforts to reconstruct whole settlement systems and their institutional correlates.

Analysis of Phase II data is still incomplete at the time of this writing (spring 1988). In this chapter we offer a preliminary synthesis of the Phase II and earlier work and some demographic reconstructions of the Copan system as a whole, but we caution that the figures and interpretations are subject to change in subsequent reports (see Endnote). Our purpose is to reconstruct the maximum population of the Copan polity for the Late Classic Period, from A.D. 700 to 850, when the population peaked and the Copan system was at its most complex. We do not imply that population peaked and remained at the same level throughout this 150-year period, but rather that it reached its maximum at some point during this interval. This point was probably between A.D. 800 and 850 but conceivably could have been somewhat earlier during the mature Late Classic. This chapter should be read as much as a methodological exercise as for its conclusions. Any attempt to reconstruct demographic variables from archaeological data necessarily takes the form, at least in part, of a simulation, and simulations are only as good as the components used and the values attached to them. We feel fortunate that the Copan projects have provided us with a wealth of data and a breadth of perspective unparalleled to date for any major Maya polity, particularly the kind of information useful in resolving demographic issues. Our calculations rely to a large extent on field data assembled by the earlier phases of Copan research. Principal sources for these materials are Baudez (1983), Fash (1983a, b), Leventhal (1979), Willey and Leventhal (1979), and Willey et al. (1978). Although our synthesis of Copan settlement and demography draws heavily on this work, our manipulations of data and conclusions are our own.

COPAN SETTLEMENT: GENERAL CONSIDERATIONS

Although environmentally Copan may be considered part of the Maya lowlands in terms of general climate and agricultural potential (i.e., it is only 600 m above sea level), its setting is very distinctive—a well-defined river valley surrounded by extremely rugged upland terrain (Webster 1988). This topographic situation, together with the regional geology, which is much more complex than that of regions of equivalent size in the low-lands proper, produces a landscape with much greater variety of slope and soil quality than that normally associated with major lowland Maya centers. This variety has clearly conditioned both prehistoric and modern settlement systems, both of which are strongly oriented to the valley floors and to specific subregions. To paraphrase a remark once made by Chris Peebles concerning the Moundville region in Alabama, the Copan region consists of scattered islands of fertile bottomland in a vast sea of relatively unproductive uplands.

Since about 1850 extensive clearing for cash crops and pasture, as well as subsistence agriculture, has opened up large portions of the valley while still not severely damaging or destroying most archaeological sites. The situation is ideal today for survey, not only because of the accessibility of the landscape, the visibility of sites, and their generally excellent preservation, but also because the topography presents us with a well-defined cultural setting, in sharp contrast to the lack of such bounding in the lowlands farther to the northwest. Equally important is the fact that there are no other centers of remotely comparable size to Copan in the drainage or, indeed, within 70 air miles in any direction (the nearest being Quirigua in the Motagua Valley). Consequently, there is no doubt, as there would be in the northeastern Peten, about which centers rural sites relate to; if we assume that our rural sites have socioeconomic or sociopolitical affiliations with a major center, then Copan is that center.

These natural and cultural factors have provided us with a nicely compartmentalized survey universe. It is probable, though, that Copan's influence extended well beyond the Copan drainage. Nonetheless, the core population of the political domain is unquestionably within our survey area. The only exception is the unsurveyed lower Copan drainage in Guatemala, much of which was probably under the sway of Copan. Because of increasing dryness we suspect that the population of the valley falls off markedly from northeast to southwest in Guatemala. Certainly our frequent travels along the Guatemalan sections of the valley suggest much less dense settlement, and surveys immediately adjacent to the border on the Honduran side have turned up relatively light occupation compared to upriver survey zones. In this chapter we deal only with the Honduran segment of the system, which we believe includes the most numerous and important population components of the Copan polity.

THE COPAN SEQUENCE

Unlike other chapters in this volume, which present detailed diachronic analyses of settlement data, our own is largely synchronic, primarily because of the distinctive settlement history of the region. A brief summary of the whole Copan sequence, however, is necessary as background (see Figure 2.1).

There are traces of Early Preclassic occupation in the valley, as seen in ceramics recovered from burial caves in the Sesesmil drainage (Gordon 1896) and, more recently, in collections made from excavations in the Sepultura enclave by Fash (personal communication, 1980–84). By Middle Preclassic times there was a small but vigorous population in the Copan pocket. During the Late Preclassic we have only very sparse and scattered evidence for occupation at all, mostly from the Copan pocket. This is a curious anomaly, considering the earlier Middle Preclassic presence and the rapid Late Preclassic population growth and emergent political centralization generally characteristic of the Maya lowlands. A large nucleated Late Preclassic site may have been washed away by the river or may lie buried beneath the recent alluvium. Early Classic populations are light, but sometime after A.D. 400 the markers of elite Maya society begin to appear. The pace of development picks up noticeably in the Middle Classic, indicating accelerated population growth, which is still mainly confined to the Copan pocket. The core of the polity is unified by the energetic ruler Smoke Jaguar at about A.D. 650, and royal activity thereafter is concentrated in the Main Group. In the Late Classic there is a veritable population explosion, which fills in the Copan pocket and begins to spill over into the rest of the drainage, and an associated boom in construction and monument erection. Finally, elite activity on the royal level ceases rather abruptly soon after A.D. 800, although there is a considerable population of lesser elites and rural farmers in the Copan region for at least three more centuries. We now know that basic elements of the Coner ceramic phase survive, in fact, until approximately A.D. 1150–1200.

Recent surveys and excavations have dealt overwhelmingly with the Late Classic/Early Postclassic occupational phases, since material relating to them is so abundant, accessible, and well preserved. Although our perspective is obviously not entirely synchronic, it does emphasize these late phases of a mature (or disintegrating) Maya polity that, unlike the case at some other sites, has a single "pulse" of demographic and political maturity.

The Main Group

The Main Group at Copan is so well known that it warrants little discussion here (the best recent summary is Hohmann and Vogrin 1982). Although it has been extensively tested, our knowledge of its varied functions is hampered by the early emphasis on architectural reconstruction, monument discovery, and decipherment; the search for tombs and caches; and deep trenching for architectural stratigraphy. Information necessary to assess the specific functions of buildings and rooms is hence inadequate.

Essential to the interpretation of the Main Group is the identification of elite residences. R.E.W. Adams (1977b: 152) remarked that Copan, unlike Tikal or Palenque, seems to have no major palace complexes. This is certainly incorrect for the urban core as a whole and almost certainly so for the Main Group. Sanders (1989) believes that Structure 22—the so-called Temple of Meditation (Trik 1939)—is in fact a royal palace, possibly that of Rising Sun (although Fash's (1989) recent work would assign it to an earlier rule), and that the whole East Court is a private royal compound. Earlier palaces may also be present, buried under massive late constructions, and many groups remain uninvestigated. Much of the Acropolis is missing, washed away by the Copan River, so that any palaces on the east side are irretrievably lost.

What are almost certainly elite residences are situated just to the south of the Acropolis in the so-called Cementerios zone, investigated intermittently between 1891 and 1942 (Longyear 1952). Many burials, including some of the richest ever found at Copan, were recovered here. Buildings in this area are architecturally very complex and of high quality and are strikingly similar to elite residential structures recently excavated in Las Sepulturas (see below). The Cementerios zone is here considered not to be part of the Main Group, but more properly an extension of the El Bosque enclave discussed below. Our working model of the Main Group is that it was, at least from the seventh century to the beginning of the ninth century, the ruling establishment of the last five kings of Copan and should be regarded as an immense royal household, with all the associated ritual, administrative, and residential facilities this function implies.

The Urban Core: Las Sepulturas and El Bosque Enclaves

The Main Group is flanked by two heavy concentrations of structures, but not until the mapping of the Willey and Baudez projects between 1975 and 1980 were the character and extent of these settlement zones fully appreciated (Map 2.2). We designate the Main Group, together with the Sepultura and El Bosque enclaves, as the *urban core* of Copan, using the term *urban* to refer only to the comparatively high density of population in the zone. The El Bosque and Las Sepulturas enclaves cover an area of about 0.6 km² and have a total of 1035 mapped structures, (Table 2.1) so overall structure density is 1449 km²—the highest known for a Maya center. Willey and his colleagues devised a heuristic scheme for categorizing the urban core groups (Willey et al. 1978), in which they defined a series of types ranging from small, single-mound and Type 1 sites, the most numerous of all, to major Type 4 sites, which rank just below the Main Group in size and complexity, and speculated that this was essentially a residential hierarchy. We have retained this generally useful classification, with a few modifications (Freter 1988).

During the Willey project three groups in Las Sepulturas (one each from Types 1–3) were extensively tested, providing information on approximately 33 rooms and 11 buildings arranged around three plazas. Between 1980 and 1984 the Phase II project excavated approximately 77 buildings with 134 associated rooms grouped around 14 courtyards in Las Sepulturas, spanning the whole range of types. These excavations not only exposed the structures themselves but also stripped off most associated horizontal spaces. Almost one-third of the mounds at Las Sepulturas have been tested or excavated. The importance of the urban core is demonstrated not only by the density of structures, but also by the heavy concentration of sites of elite rank. Twenty-three Type 3 and 4 sites with 421 structures are in the urban zone. Since only 49 such units are known for the whole drainage, this distribution indicates a pronounced tendency for elite residential units to cluster near the household of the ruler. There is considerable variation within all classes of groups in the urban core, and especially elite ones, in terms of size, quality, function, and configuration. Abundant domestic refuse is associated with all excavated groups in Las Sepulturas, thus strikingly confirming the Harvard Project's model of ranked residences. Further support is seen in the many burials recovered from the groups: between 250 and 300 burials were found at 9N-8 alone.

The Copan Pocket Rural Zone

In the portion of the Copan pocket outside the urban core (see Fash [1983a, b] for detailed examinations of the rural pocket settlement), 736 sites with 2372 associated structures were mapped. Overall mound densities are on the order of 100 km² but are locally much higher. The site hierarchy for the outlying pocket settlement is quite different from that of the urban core (Table 2.2). In the lower ranges of the site hierarchy (single mounds, other, Types 1 and 2) there are 717 sites, which make up about 97% of the total. There are 19 sites in the elite Type 3–4 range, but these are generally smaller and less impressive than those in the urban core. Despite their outlying locations, none is more than 4–5 km from the Main Group and most are within 1–3 km. Thus of the approximately 49 known elite-level groups in the entire valley, 42, or 86%, cluster very close to the Main Group.

Rural Settlement Components

Rural settlement here refers to those components of the Copan settlement system which lie outside the Copan pocket; these areas received only slight and unsystematic attention during the Harvard/Phase I work (Baudez 1983). Vleck and Fash (1986) located 97 rural sites (mainly large ones known to informants) during a rapid survey in 1978. Because of the unsystematic nature of their work we decided to go over much of the same ground using our own procedures, with strikingly different results. In the areas where our surveys overlapped, Vleck found approximately 90 sites; we recorded 549.

We assume that Copan's core sustaining population was largely restricted to the valley of the main river and its tributaries. Accordingly, our surveys (Webster 1985) have been confined to a strip about 3.8 km wide running the length of the main valley from the Guatemalan border to the northeastern end of the Rio Amarillo pocket, and a similar strip extending for about 15 km up the major northern tributary, the Sesesmil (Map 2.1). Some survey work has also been done along the Rio Gila, the major southern tributary. These surveys were defined by available air photo imagery; Table 2.3 shows the extent of our coverage.

For the main and Sesesmil valleys our areal sample of the available photo universe is 31%, but it must be emphasized that this sample includes virtually all the productive valley floor and foothill land attractive for human settlement and agricultural land use. Those areas that remain unsurveyed are predominantly steep, remote hillsides covered with pine or occasionally tropical forest. We have surveyed large chunks of such terrain and very seldom have found sites of any kind. We estimate that 80 to 90% of the prehistoric population of the rural drainage as a whole lived in the areas covered by our survey strips, most of it in the sections actually sampled. When the rural survey is added to the Harvard/Phase I surveys, overall coverage for the drainage as a whole is about 62 km², with a total of 1425 sites with 4509 associated structures. This is a sample of a potential survey universe defined by the air photos of 134 km². We also completed an extensive test-pitting program directed by Freter during Phase II. A total of 474 test excavations (mostly in rural sites) was completed, and 38% of all rural mounds were ultimately tested. We are currently completing a similar test-pitting operation in the rural Copan pocket (see Endnote). A final set of operations in 1985–86 consisted of complete excavations (along the lines of those carried out in Las Sepulturas) of a sample of eight rural sites (Webster and Gonlin 1988). Data from these excavations provide excellent independent checks on those derived from surface survey and test-pitting and are used below in our methodology section.

Character of Rural Settlement

The most striking thing about rural settlement (Table 2.4) is the much lower site densities, and certainly population densities, than found anywhere in the Copan pocket. Overall mound densities in the pocket are about 143/km², but rural densities are only about 28/km². Of all known sites, 69%—with 76% of known structures—are in the Copan pocket. Rural settlement is heavily weighted toward sites in the lower range of the hierarchy, with elite sites very poorly represented. Virtually all sites for which we have artifact samples have Coner phase occupations. Viel (personal communication 1984) originally terminated the Late Classic Coner phase no later than A.D. 900. Our obsidian hydration dates demonstrate that general ceramic markers of this phase continue until about A.D. 1200, so that we must assume much less contemporaneity among Coner phase sites than we did earlier. Preliminary results of the obsidian research are used in our demographic reconstructions below.

METHODOLOGY

One strategy of demographic reconstruction is to use a large set of human skeletal remains from well-controlled contexts; such a set exists for Copan but is still under analysis. Another is to construct models of land use and agricultural productivity, and we have several preliminary ones for Copan. In this chapter we employ the more traditional approach of assigning population estimates to elements of the prehistoric settlement system, specifically to rooms as components of prehistoric household units. Our surveys and test-pitting programs allow us to reconstruct the numbers and configurations of structures that functioned as parts of the Copan settlement system between A.D. 700 and 850, and horizontal exposures on sites of all ranks provide estimates of associated room numbers.

We assume, according to the "principle of abundance" (Ashmore and Willey 1981: 6), that most sites are the physical expressions of prehistoric households. Certainly there are specialized structures or rooms in groups of all sizes (e.g., kitchens, shrines, storage buildings, etc.), but we regard these as integral parts of household establishments. This domestic assumption is well supported by both our test-pitting data and our extensive rural excavations. A corollary assumption is that in Maya residential groups some rooms function as primary residential space, that is, as shelters for sleeping, but also for sitting, eating, and probably for minor domestic tasks and limited storage.

Our primary goal is to model maximal population figures for the Copan system in its mature Late Classic phase (ca. A.D. 700–850). Two categories of direct evidence underlie such an effort: (1) a sample of structures on the landscape recovered in surface survey, representing some unknown but larger universe of original structures, and (2) information derived from surface collection, test-pitting, and large-scale excavation focused on some portion of that sample. Deriving actual population estimates from such a data base raises a number of methodological problems and issues, some common to Maya archaeology in general and some peculiar to Copan. Because of the importance of these issues in assessing the validity of our demographic reconstructions, they are discussed at some length below, and the solutions, or sets of alternative solutions, are specified.

EXTRAPOLATION:

The problem of extrapolation from known to unknown segments of the settlement system operates on two levels. Extrapolation must be made for differences between site configuration as known from surface inspection alone and actual site configuration (i.e., corrections for hidden or destroyed structures, for actual size and configuration of buildings as opposed to their visible elements, etc.). Such extrapolation necessitates adequate test-pitting and large-scale excavations, both of which we have carried out. Extrapolation must also be made from areas adequately surveyed to those incompletely surveyed or unsurveyed.

NONPLATFORM STRUCTURES

The presence of domestic structures not built on durable substructures could obviously skew population estimates. In our Las Sepulturas and rural excavations we have found possible traces of such structures on only a handful of occasions. We also test-pitted 30% of all the rural nonmound sites and found very sparse evidence for hidden structures. We consequently eliminate nonmound sites from the population calculations given below but have listed them in Table 2.4. Nonplatform structures appear to be so negligible in number that we make no correction for them.

HIDDEN STRUCTURES

Freter's test-pitting revealed that there were minimally 17% more platform structures present at small sites than surface inspection indicated. Large-scale rural excavations refined this figure further. Surface indications suggested 16 structures at the 8 rural sites we dug, and excavations turned up 27. Of the hidden structures, 5 were probably not in use during the major late occupations at the sites in question (that is, they had been covered by later construction, torn apart for building materials, etc.). Six hidden structures remain which seem to have been integral, functioning components of the mature occupational phases, or an increase of approximately 38% over the original 16. At small sites with low structures a significant percentage of buildings is hidden, and we thus inflate structure numbers for all sites of Type 2 rank and lower by 38%.

In elite groups the distortion is rather different. Because of the impressive scale of construction in these groups it is unlikely that major buildings are overlooked during surface inspection. Small buildings are hidden, however, either by accumulations of surface debris or by collapse from

45

nearby large structures. Such collapse also obscures structural details so that multiple buildings or building segments may appear as single structures, thus lowering the total structure counts. Our corrections for these distortions are based on complete excavations at elite groups in the Las Sepulturas enclave (Table 2.5).

We have no systematic way of controlling for the destruction or burial of whole sites by erosion or alluviation, but our surveys and excavations suggest that the problem is not serious except in local terms. The main problem area is the northern fringe of Las Sepulturas, and in the reconstruction for that area we specify the appropriate adjustments.

DISTORTIONS IN STRUCTURE SIZE AND CONFIGURATION

This issue has been touched on above. Such distortion is troublesome when accurate estimates of structure size are needed, as when using a formula relating numbers of individuals to floor space (Naroll 1962). It is also significant if there is a highly predictable relationship between structure form and function—for example, if kitchens could always be identified because of their layouts. Since our methodology depends mainly on structure and room counts, neither of these issues is of particular relevance here.

EXTRAPOLATION TO UNSURVEYED AREAS

Nonsurveyed portions of the landscape, within the photos or elsewhere, consist primarily of two classes of topography: upland pine forest on steep slopes (comprising at least 90% of the unsurveyed zone) and small, steep-sided tributary valleys with tiny concentrations of cultivable alluvium. We have, then, two extrapolation problems: first, from our 61.6 km² sample to the rest of the photo universe of 134 km², and second, from this area to the larger region of 400–500 km². For the Copan pocket, where the Harvard/Phase I surveys were virtually continuous, extrapolation presents few problems. Our correction is to add 10% to the structure counts for single-mound, Type 1 and 2 sites outside the urban core but still within the Copan pocket. For rural areas outside the Copan pocket our solution is the addition of low-rank sites (single mounds, Types 1 and 2), since it is extremely unlikely that any higher-order groups remain unlocated. We assume that 30% of rural structures remain unlocated or have been destroyed, and we inflate the structure counts for rural single-mound, Type 1 and 2 sites by this amount for areas within the photo universe. For areas outside the photo universe we add 10% to our final population figures for all sites of Type 2 status and lower.

CONTEMPORANEITY

We must correct for the presence of structures or groups of structures used exclusively before or after A.D. 700–850, which we call the mature

Late Classic Period. Here the distinctive settlement sequence of the Copan region simplifies the problem, since unlike Tikal it does not have a long history of dense population and large-scale architectural activity. Our ceramic samples and associated obsidian dates indicate that 70% of known sites show occupation between A.D. 700 and 850. This is an average figure, since sites in the Copan pocket show a higher incidence of occupation (85%) than those in rural areas (55%). Within each ceramic phase some structures were built and then abandoned, disused, or occasionally partly torn apart for building material. Based on our Las Sepulturas and rural excavations, we apply overall correction factors as shown in Table 2.6.

Situational disuse of rooms occurs because of short-term fluctuations in resident populations, which we assume at Copan were usually kinship-based and larger than nuclear families for most sites with multiple structures. The basic idea here is the familiar one that extended families experience cycles of growth and fissioning. Evidence for such situational disuse is inferential at best, and we assume that during the population maximum between A.D. 700 and 850 such disuse was lower than at any other time. For groups of all types we apply a correction figure of 10% to account for disuse of this percentage of rooms. Note that this correction could have been made by slightly reducing the average room occupation rate (see discussion below); we fell it makes the most sense to do it in this fashion.

ROOM ESTIMATES

Essential to our methodology is the ability to estimate numbers of rooms per structure. At Las Sepulturas and elsewhere in the Copan pocket most excavated platforms have at least some remaining traces of masonry superstructure elements which allow fairly straightforward estimates of rooms per structure for groups of each rank from Types 2–4; these are expressed in Table 2.7 in terms of rooms per residential structure.

Our single, well-excavated and restored Type 1 group from Las Sepulturas has an average of 1.33 rooms/residential structure. Rural Type 1 or single-mound sites very seldom show any traces of superstructures, which must have been largely of perishable materials. When such traces do survive, they almost invariably suggest only 1 room/substructure. Supporting this conclusion is the small size of rural platforms, many of which were not big enough to accommodate more than one room of reasonable size. We will use the figure of 1.33 for single-mound and Type 1 structures in the urban core. Rural Type 1 and single-mound structures, whether inside or outside the Copan pocket, will be assigned only a single room. These ratios refer to room numbers in structures that we assume to have had direct residential functions. Sites of all ranks up through Type 3 have low room/structure ratios. Only with the Type 4 units do we see an increase in room numbers, mainly due to the increased size of the substructures, which in turn reflects somewhat different uses of space by high-status individuals and groups, particularly with regard to special-purpose use and the practices of polygyny.

FUNCTION

The presence of special-function sites with no effective residential populations will obviously distort population reconstructions based on room counts. Similar distortions will occur on the level of single groups if they include specialized structures. We have very little evidence for specialized sites in the simplest levels of the hierarchy (but see Mallory 1984:177–86). Test-pitting and excavation have identified what we believe to be a valid "field-hut" signature for some rural, single-mound sites. Some sites higher in the hierarchy were apparently nonresidential, isolated ceremonial groups. Specialized structures with rooms within residential groups include shrines, kitchens, workshops, storerooms, and platforms covering tombs. Groups high in the site hierarchy include a higher proportion of such structures than groups of lower rank.

Conceptually, the two problems of special-purpose sites and special-purpose buildings within sites are quite distinct. For the purposes of demographic projections of the sort we are making, however, both involve the deletion of some percentage of rooms from a larger population and so are treated together here. Based on our extensive excavations in groups of all levels, we use the corrections presented in Table 2.8.

POPULATION UNITS

Our basic concept is what might be called a *nuclear family module*. We believe, along with most Mayanists, that Maya residential groups typically housed extended families. Such families exhibit definite cycles of growth and eventual fissioning over two to four generations, but the core elements may be conceived of as reproductively active nuclear families. Archaeologically recovered residential compounds are the residues of these cycles. Our determination of the size of the typical actively reproducing nuclear family is based on our knowledge that the population of the Copan region was growing at an extremely rapid rate between A.D. 650 and 850 and probably peaked shortly before or after A.D. 800. Long-term population growth (e.g., over several centuries) over regions of large size in complex preindustrial societies seems to allow maximal sustained doubling rates of 200 to 300 years (Sanders 1984). These are overall rates, and specific small populations in restricted areas of such regions may possibly have doubled even faster—say, every 50 to 80 years for short periods of time—but archaeological controls are usually too coarse to perceive such processes. Based on our phased settlement data, we here make the assumption that the Copan population, just before its peak, was doubling each century; this is a conservative estimate and the doubling time may well have been less. For the purpose of this simulation we are also assuming that immigration is not a major factor in regional population growth, although we suspect that there may have been a considerable influx of population at around A.D. 650–700.

The oft-cited figure of 5.6 persons/household derived from Redfield and Villa-Rojas's Chan Kom study (1934) is clearly excessive if used for nuclear families. The intrinsic rate of increase of this pioneer population was almost 3% annually, indicating a doubling time of only 23 years, far greater than we could expect for a prehistoric Maya population. Accordingly, we simulate nuclear family size using two alternate figures: 4 and 5. These certainly bracket the probable range, and the most appropriate single figure would probably be nearer 5 than 4, since the Copan population was so rapidly growing. If we were dealing with a region in which population growth was slower, the appropriate figure would be somewhere around 4.

Essentially, our reasoning is this: if we could somehow conduct a visual census of Copan at its peak, and we disregarded rooms not used primarily for residential/dormitory functions and those occupied by unmarried people or by adult couples past their reproductive prime and whose children have moved away, the average nuclear family module we would observe associated with a primary domestic room would be that of husband, wife, and 2 to 3 surviving children. This does not imply that couples, during their reproductive spans, have only 2 to 3 children who survive, but rather that at the time of the census we would observe the couple at some point during their reproductive history—that is, some children would not yet have been born and others might already have left the house permanently. The range of 4–5 is great enough also to accommodate those occasional situations in which an unmarried relative has taken up residence with a nuclear family. We originally estimated this range of nuclear family module size on the basis of general demographic modeling. Subsequent review of the ethnographic literature reinforces the suitability of the figures; nuclear family/house population estimates from both Mesoamerican ethnography and historical demography fall into this range (e.g., Nutini 1967:387–88; Eversley 1965:399). As indicated above, we have introduced a room-reduction factor to account for underoccupancy of some rooms because of the dynamism inherent in the history of the extended family groups. The two figures of 4 and 5 are applied below to all appropriate rooms in settlement units of Types 1–3. In Type 4 elite units there was probably a lower proportion of people to rooms for a variety of reasons, including the likely practice of polygyny, in which individual women and their offspring may well have had separate quarters from one another and their husbands. Rebecca Storey (personal communication, 1988) informs us that the elite group 9N-8 has a ratio of at least 2:1 of females to males among sexable individuals from burials, a striking confirmation of the practice of polygyny. Actually, in the case of the Type 4 unit we have excavated—9N-8, the most complex of them all—the room-occupancy discrepancy is probably not a serious problem, since the principal elite compound was surrounded by other conjoined plazas inhabited by people of lower rank. Other Type 4 units, however, often lack such dense appended populations. For Type 4 units in general we accordingly use room-occupancy rates of 3.5 and 4 as our range. By treating Type 4 units as elite units, we are ignoring the fact that such groups often housed residents of low rank.

The methodology outlined above provides a series of manipulations that can be applied to the raw survey data for various subregions of the Copan Valley. As an exercise we demonstrate below the set of calculations for the population range for rural Type 1 units.

Step 1. Correction for hidden structures: increase number of appropriate rural structures (711—see Table 2.4) by 38%; solution: 711 × 1.38 = 981 (all computations rounded to the nearest whole number).

Step 2. Extrapolation for unsurveyed areas within the air photo universe: increase structure counts by 30%; solution: 981 × 1.30 = 1275.

Step 3. Correct for presence of non-Coner occupation: reduce structure counts by 45%; solution: 1275 × 0.55 = 701.

Step 4. Correct for noncontemporaneity within mature Late Classic Coner phase: reduce structure counts by 20%; solution: 701 × 0.8 = 561.

Step 5. Correct for situational disuse in functioning units: reduce structure counts by 10%; solution: 561 × 0.90 = 505.

Step 6. Calculate room numbers: for rural Type 1 structures we calculate 1 room/house; solution: 505.

Step 7. Correct for specialized rooms: eliminate 20% of rooms; solution: 505 × 0.80 = 404.

Step 8. Calculate numbers of people per room, using both low estimate (4) and high estimate (5); solutions: 404 × 4 = 1616, and 404 × 5 = 2020.

Step 9 Correct for sites in unsurveyed rural areas outside photos: add 10%; solution: 1616 + 10% = 1778, and 2020 + 10% = 2222.

General Solution: Population for rural Type 1 sites ranges between 1778 and 2222.

Note that each manipulation involves slightly different calculations. It should also be emphasized that the methodology is detailed specifically for our Copan research and cannot be uncritically applied to other collections of settlement data.

DEMOGRAPHIC RECONSTRUCTIONS

These manipulations have been carried out for each subregion (Table 2.9). We also reconstruct the projected distribution of population in the several site types in terms of percentages. These percentage comparisons are based on the maximal population figures; minimal estimates would be within 1% of those given. The table also shows the estimated distribution of population among contemporaneous residential sites of different ranks, as projected from basic site numbers by using essentially the same methodology as for projecting total population.

The Main Group

Given the obvious ritual or civic nature of much of the architecture, it seems clear that there were relatively few people actually living in the Main Group during the period from A.D. 700 to 800. We here use a figure of 250 and emphasize that this is pure guesswork, although we consider it reasonable in terms of order of magnitude.

The Urban Core

The urban core includes all of the El Bosque, Cementerios, and Las Sepulturas residential zones. Applying the appropriate manipulations of our methodology to the figures in Table 2.1 yields a minimum population of 4902 and a maximum population of 5954. Unfortunately, we cannot use these figures at face value, because the urban core is one habitation zone that we know has been affected by erosion and slopewash. The total area affected by such disturbance is about 0.44 km². Since we have no way of knowing just how densely urban core habitation may have originally extended over this area, we offer two extrapolations. One assumes that 25% of the 0.44 km² area was occupied at the same density as the intact portions of the urban core and had a similar distribution of groups of the various ranks. The second extrapolation assumes 75% occupancy. When the results of these extrapolations are added to our original figures, the projected minimum population is 5797, and the maximum population is 9464. No matter where in this range the original population may have fallen, overall densities were obviously extraordinary—between 4871 and 7743 people/km² (albeit over a small area).

The Copan Pocket Rural Zone

The rural Copan pocket population is estimated to have a minimal population of 9360 and a maximum of 11,639. In making this calculation we have added 60 rooms to account for the Type 4 unit buried under the modern town. This is a conservative estimate. Although we call this outlying population "rural," much of it is very close to the urban core, and densities are far higher here than in rural zones outside the pocket. Overall densities for the rural population of the pocket itself range from approximately 407–506 people/km².

Rural Settlement Components

The rural population proper (outside the Copan pocket) is very small; we estimate a minimum population of 3010 and a maximum population of 3725. Calculating the whole rural area of the drainage in Honduras at approximately 500 km² outside the Copan pocket, we find that overall densities are tiny, only about 6 to 7.5 people/km². Effective local densities would be much higher—on the order of 20–30/km²—although there would be considerable variation locally as well.

DISCUSSION AND CONCLUSIONS

The two most striking conclusions emerging from this demographic reconstruction are the comparatively small size of the overall population of the mature Copan polity and its high degree of concentration. During its mature Late Classic phase between A.D. 700 and 850 the entire population ranged between 18,417 and 24,828, according to our calculations, which are generally geared to produce conservatively high, rather than low, results (Table 2.10). We expected to find much more rural habitation outside the Copan pocket when we began our surveys and test-pitting. During the Late Classic, and apparently in all preceding phases, the demographic weight of the polity—an estimated 85% of its entire population—was concentrated in the Copan pocket. Virtually throughout its history the regional population was strongly attracted by the agricultural potential of this zone. Even more impressive is the concentration of people in the urban core, where, along with the Main Group, we find about 38% of the entire population of the polity squeezed into an area measuring only about 1.19 km². The presence of the royal household, with all of its associated civic, ritual, economic, and administrative functions, exerted an extremely strong "pull" on major elements of the population, especially those of comparatively high status. Although the impetus for such heavy concentration of population in the urban core was probably political and social in nature, it would not have posed significant problems in terms of access to land since none of the agricultural resources of the pocket are more than a few km distant; in fact, the urban core population lived on or very close to some of the most productive parts of the Copan landscape.

The sheer overall density of the pocket population, 640–880 people/km², indicates that by A.D. 700–850 it had overshot the productive potential of the zone and severely damaged the environment in the process. Food subsidies would consequently been required from other parts of the valley, especially where multicropping was possible.

About 74% of the Copan Maya resided in groups of Type 2 status or lower, if we ignore the problematical destroyed or buried segments of the urban core. These figures are gratifyingly close to the traditional rule-of-thumb estimates commonly used by Mayanists for "commoner" or "producer" populations. Were we able to quantify the number of low-status people who resided in elite groups, the total percentage for the low-rank population would probably rise to something between 80 and 90 %. Since the frequency of elite Type 3 and 4 groups drops off markedly with distance from the Main Group, the size of the low-status component correspondingly rises, from 54% in the urban core, to 87.2% in the rural Copan pocket, and finally to 86.6% in the rural zones proper, again ignoring commoners residing in Type 3 and 4 units.

Our rural research certainly supports a major conclusion of the earlier Copan pocket surveys that there was rapid population growth beginning about A.D. 600–650 and continuing to at least A.D. 800. This growth is mainly manifested in the Copan pocket; outlying rural sites are generally later, indicating spillover into the rest of the valley as the system decentralizes. The only major shift in our perspective concerns the Postclassic. As previously noted, both subroyal elites and rural farmers continue to occupy some parts of the valley until shortly after A.D. 1200.

We find the methodological insights derived from our research as significant as the substantive conclusions. First, our ability to create a reasonably reliable reconstruction of the prehistoric Late Classic Copan population is dependent on a series of successive, integrated field and laboratory efforts, each of which enlarged and refined information from the previous phase of work. The surface surveys, both of the Copan pocket and of the rural zone, provide the basic framework for our reconstruction, but it is a framework with serious distortions. Adequate follow-up test-pitting is essential, both as a check on conclusions from the surface surveys and as an independent source of some minimal information about function and chronology. Many archaeological programs are able effectively to combine these two phases of research. At Copan we have been fortunate in that we additionally have been able to undertake extensive excavations in residential complexes on an unprecedented scale, a luxury that many projects cannot afford. This third stage of research enormously enriches the first two. One of the specific lessons we learned is that surface mapping produces only fairly reliable information about what lies below the surface at Copan. In virtually all cases our large excavations added greatly to our information about the size and orientation of buildings and the number actually present. This is particularly true for small sites but applies to Type 3 and 4 units as well. For small sites we found that test-pitting alone could partly correct some of the distortions inherent in surface data; thus Freter's efforts found about half the number of hidden structures actually present. Test-pitting turned out to be very reliable in predicting the basic range of functional and chronological information to be derived from full excavation. We are heartened that hidden nonplatform structures do not seem to be an important problem at Copan and also that even small domestic structures are usually very well preserved, despite their often unprepossessing surface appearance. The lesson here is that they amply repay excavation in many ways.

Without adequate chronological controls, demographic reconstruction would obviously be impossible. Our test-pitting and excavations have demonstrated that the overall ceramic chronology for Copan is generally accurate, except for the crucial underestimation of the duration of the Coner phase. Obsidian hydration dating, which has not been notably successful elsewhere in Mesoamerica, is working exceptionally well at Copan and is essential for some of our data manipulations. Using only ceramic chronology, we would have significantly overestimated the Late Classic population and seriously misinterpreted the nature of the Classic "collapse."

As is always the case, many sources of bias exist in our data. An important one is the imbalance between the large amount of test-pitting done in the rural parts of the valley and the relatively skimpy test-pitting done in the densely populated Copan pocket. We will shortly have the data to correct for this problem (see Endnote). Another bias is the destruction of Type 4 groups under the modern towns of Santa Rita and Copan and the incomplete mapping and testing of another, La Canteada. Although we have tried to extrapolate population figures for these centers, we will never possess adequate information about them (although work at La Canteada is possible). If we consider the purpose of this chapter to be a demographic reconstruction of the mature Copan polity in the widest sense of the word, a major bias is lack of information about that part of the dependent population which fell outside the drainage or the areas surveyed, particularly the Guatemalan component of the population. The nature of the bias is distortion of our perception of population distribution and its social, political, and economic significance, however, rather than serious distortion of overall demographic scale. Copan almost certainly did not control the Rio Copan valley all the way to its confluence with the Rio Motagua. Assuming that it dominated 30–40 km of the upper drainage in Guatemala, we would guess that we would have to increase our overall population figures by only 1000 people or so. Similarly, Copan polity outliers in the headwaters of adjacent drainages may add some other small increment to the total population when these areas are surveyed.

In all probability the overall Copan population, based on data currently in hand, was in the range of 20,000 to 25,000. Future surveys are unlikely to increase these estimates, if our methodology is used, by more than a few thousand, even if they are extended as suggested above. Even if some of our values and extrapolations are wildly off, maximum population could scarcely have ever been more than 25,000 to 30,000 people. As with all complex reconstructions, and especially those that take at least partially the form of simulations, as this one does, readers may quarrel with the values we have assigned to some of our variables. As anyone who wishes to take the time to do so will discover, however, small tinkerings with specific variable values, or especially sets of values, are likely to affect our overall figures only to a minimal degree. This is especially true of the reconstruction of the rural population component, which is small enough so that even substantial changes in our values will not affect overall estimates seriously; this is important, because it is the rural population that presents the most difficult problems of reconstruction.

In conclusion, we believe the reconstruction of the mature Late Classic Copan population given above is as reliable as present data permit. Some changes will be necessary—indeed, we anticipate making some of them ourselves. We feel, however, that our estimates are reliable in order-of-magnitude terms, both for the whole population and for its basic distribution among groups of the various types.

ENDNOTE

This version of our chapter was prepared in the spring of 1988. Since then we have carried out another phase of fieldwork designed to increase our sample of test pits and obsidian dates from rural sites in the Copan pocket. Although the surface survey of this area during Phase I was very complete, test-pitting was minimal, generating about a 1% sample of tested sites. During 1988 we completed 226 test excavations in 61 Copan pocket sites and processed 560 usable obsidian hydration dates from samples thus obtained. Of all known sites in the Copan pocket, 14.3% have now been tested and dated. Because of deadlines we decided not to incorporate this half-digested data set into the present chapter. Doing so would have involved no change in the methodology but considerable changes in population and site figures. One of the major questions we had before the 1988 work is whether the Copan pocket rural population would be heavily concentrated in the A.D. 700–850 Late Classic Period (the traditional view) or whether it, like the outlying population, would exhibit a strong Postclassic component. Our obsidian dates show that many Copan pocket sites have such components. The principal effect of this discovery is to reduce contemporaneity among pocket sites and thus for any time period to reduce population estimates. Because of the heavy concentration of people in the Copan pocket, these reductions are significant. Although final figures are not yet available, we expect that our estimate of the maximum population for the mature polity as a whole will eventually be reduced to the range of 18,000 to 20,000.

ACKNOWLEDGMENTS:

We owe a heavy debt to all the pre-Phase II researchers at Copan. Our own work has been generously supported by the Instituto Hondureño de Antropología e Historia and by three grants from the National Science Foundation (Webster and Sanders, BNS-8219421; Webster, BNS-8419933; Webster and Freter, BNS-219421). We appreciate the comments and criticisms of William T. Sanders.

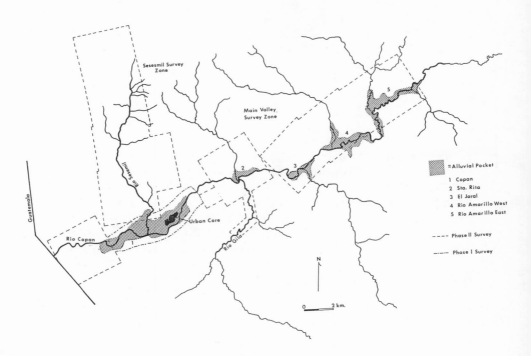

Map 2.1   The Copan Valley, with locations of survey zones and alluvial pockets.

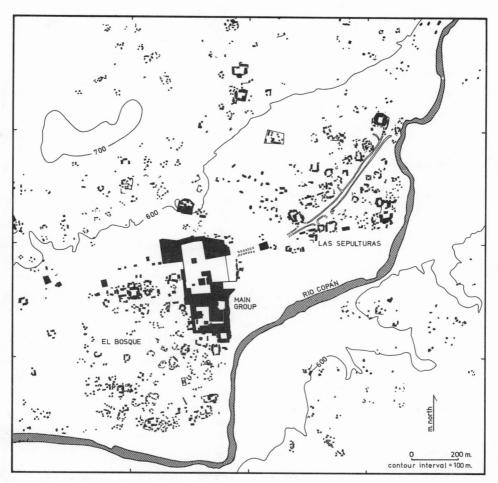

Map 2.2   The urban core at Copan.

Table 2.1 Settlement in Copan's Urban Core

Type of Site	No. of Sites	No. of Structures
single mound	21	21
1	61	227
2	33	363
3	12	171
4	11	350
5[a]	1	36
special function	1	3
Total	140	1,071

[a]The Main Group is the only site of this category.

Table 2.2 Settlement in the Rural Copan Pocket

Type of Site	No. of Sites	No. of Structures
single mound	250	251
1	386	1,340
2	78	552
3	13	172
4	6	54+
5	–	–
special function	3	3
Total	736	2,372

Table 2.3 Extent of Survey (km²)

	Main Valley	Sesesmil	Rio Gila[a]
Area of total universe defined by aerial photos	63	46.8	*
Area continuously surveyed	22.43 (35.6%)	11.72 (25%)	3.5

[a]The Rio Gila region was not sampled in the same manner as the Main and Sesesmil valleys.

Table 2.4   Settlement in the Rural Zone Outside the Copan Pocket

Type of Site	No. of Sites	No. of Structures
nonmound	148	0
single mound	174	174
1	196	711
2	25	164
3	5[a]	17
4	2[a]	—
Total	550	1066+

[a]Only two Type 4 sites are known outside the Copan pocket. One has never been cleared and mapped, and the second is under a modern town. One Type 3 site, El Raizal, falls outside our survey universe. We include all three here for completeness. In our computations in Table 2.4 we have added 8 structures for El Raizal and 40 each for the Type 4 sites. Inclusion of El Raizal brings total rural sites to 550, one more than actually listed in the survey.

Table 2.5   Summary of Correction Factors

Group	No. of Structures on Basis of Surface Mapping	No. of Structures on Basis of Excavation	Correction
9M–22A	8	15	+53%
9M–22B	4	8	+50%
9N–8	35	50	+30%

Table 2.6   Correction Factors

Region	Type 1 and lower	Type 2	Types 3 and 4
Rural	−20%	−10%	No correction
Rural pocket	− 5%	− 5%	No correction

Table 2.7   Estimate of Room Numbers/Structure

Type 2	Type 3	Type 4
1.4	1.4	3.2

Table 2.8   Corrections for Demographic Purposes

Type of Site	Correction
single mound	delete 30% of rooms (except in urban core)
1	delete 20% of rooms
2	delete 30% of rooms
3	delete 40% of rooms
4	delete 42% of rooms

Table 2.9   Settlement Data for Copan by Site Type and Location

Type of Site		Copan Urban Core	Rural Copan Pocket	Rural Copan Valley	Entire Copan Polity
Main Group	no. of sites	1	—	—	1
	% of total sites	0.7	—	—	0.1
	total est. pop.	250	—	—	250
	% of total pop.	2.6	—	—	1
4	no. of sites	11	6	2	19
	% of total sites	8	1	1	2
	total est. pop.	2,854	644	416	3,914
	% of total pop.	29.8	5.5	11	15.8
3	no. of sites	12	13	5	30
	% of total sites	8.6	2.2	2	3
	total est. pop.	1,308	850	85	2,243
	% of total pop.	13.8	7.3	2.3	9
2	no. of sites	33	69	21	123
	% of total sites	23.7	11.8	8.7	12.7
	total est. pop.	3,002	3,245	523	6,670
	% of total pop.	31.7	27.8	14	27.3
1	no. of sites	61	343	134	538
	% of total sites	43.9	58.5	55.4	55.5
	total est. pop.	1,873	5,915	2,222	10,100
	% of total pop.	19.9	50.8	59.6	40.3
single mound	no. of sites	21	153	80	256
	% of total sites	15.1	26.5	33	26.4
	total est. pop.	177	985	479	1,641
	% of total pop.	1.8	8.5	12.8	6.6

Table 2.10   Population Estimates for the Copan Polity

Region	Minimum	Maximum
Main Group	250	250
Copan urban core	5,797	9,214
Rural Copan pocket	9,360	11,639
Rural Copan valley	3,010	3,725
Total	18,417	24,828

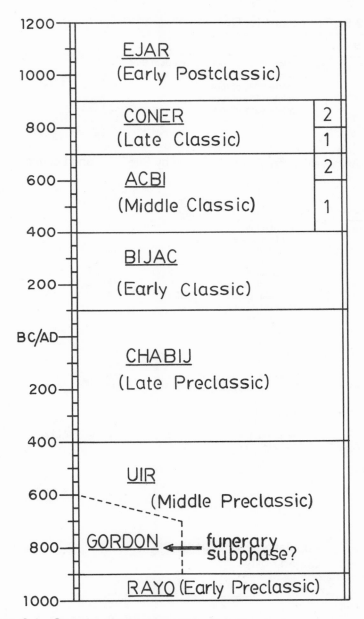

Figure 2.1   Ceramic chronology of Copan. The Coner phase
                effectively extends to ca. A.D. 1200 and subsumes the
                Ejar phase (Viel 1984, personal communication).

3 /

Ode to a Dragline: Demographic Reconstructions at Classic Quirigua

WENDY ASHMORE

The indications are that we have here the remains of two cities of different epochs. The upper one at its foundation level is about a meter below the present surface of the Motagua valley, which has been silting up gradually during past ages at a nearly uniform rate. (Hewett 1916:158)

This chapter presents evidence for reconstructing population size and density within the Classic Maya center of Quirigua. As hinted by the opening quotation, the data base for this reconstruction is somewhat different from those of most other sites discussed in the present volume. Although the approach taken is conceptually the same—a variant form of house-mound count—the deep alluvium of the settlement's location required unusual tactics for both field-data retrieval and subsequent analysis. The same alluvial conditions preclude more than generalized or speculative estimates concerning population change through time. Nevertheless, for the Late Classic, demographic characteristics of this relatively small elite center accord well with those elsewhere in the lowlands and can contribute to an overall understanding of Prehispanic Maya population parameters.

BACKGROUND

Quirigua is located on the northern floodplain of the Motagua River in the Department of Izabal, Guatemala. Although the site has been investigated sporadically since Catherwood's and Maudslay's times, data for this chapter derive solely from the work of the University of Pennsylvania's Quirigua Project of 1974–1979. Hewett's remarks notwithstanding, most earlier work had focused on the spectacular sculptures for which the site is famous, with secondary attention to minor probes of architecture within a 30-ha site core. Research by archaeologists from the University Museum, University of Pennsylvania, however, took a broader range of goals and, among other things, outlined a fuller sequence of local occupation. Settlement in the Quirigua area probably began in the Preclassic, with dynastic rule definitely established during the Early Classic, in the mid-fifth century A.D. Quirigua's final collapse as an elite center is still poorly fixed in time, but it occurred sometime after A.D. 830, in the Terminal Classic or Early Postclassic, and certainly before A.D. 1250. Between those beginning and end points, occupation is divided into a series of ceramically defined periods (Table 3.1).

Current perspectives on the full archaeological and epigraphic record, as well as models for the organization and evolution of society in Quirigua and the lower Motagua Valley generally, are available elsewhere (Sharer 1978, 1988; C. Jones and Sharer 1986; Ashmore 1980, 1984, 1986, 1988; Schortman 1980, 1984, 1986). For present purposes, suffice it to say that we believe the prosperity and power of Quirigua's Classic rulers ensued from their Peten-based expansion into the strategic setting of the lower Motagua Valley. There they successfully gained control over not only lush agricultural land, but also the critical point on the Motagua's course where multiple highland and lowland transport corridors come together, ultimately linking Copan, Kaminaljuyu, and Tikal. The same alluvial landscape that richly sustained Quirigua's ancient residents, however, proved to be rather a curse to its archaeological investigators over a millennium later.

THE SAMPLE: METHODS AND DATA

Although technically the lower Motagua Valley begins at modern Gualan, it first opens to a broad floodplain somewhat farther to the northeast, at Quirigua (Map 3.1). The Motagua's meandering has surely scoured away some traces of ancient settlement, and particularly on the northern floodplain, alluvial deposition has left most of the remainder buried under flood silts of varying thickness. These soils are generally productive (Simmons et al. 1959; Ashmore 1981a:77–85) and certainly sufficiently so to attract twentieth century exploitation by the United Fruit Company. Commercial agricultural modifications of the company and its successors have—like the river's activities—significantly affected archaeological remains on both sides of the Motagua, but since the ancient settlement of Quirigua seems to have been confined to the northern floodplain, discussion will be limited to conditions and features there.

On the northern floodplain near the current channel the average deposition rate for the last 1000 years has been 0.18–0.20 cm/yr, while ca. 2 km north from the river, it has been much lower, ca. 0.05–0.06 cm/yr (Ashmore 1981a:88–89). Such variation with distance from the channel is expectable and reflects natural processes of levee building (e.g., Leopold et al. 1964). Set in a broader hydrological context, the specific rates would be described as "moderate" and "slow," respectively, in the scale proposed by Ferring (1986:261); the higher rate is similar to the long-term average for both bed and floodplain of the Nile (Wolman and Leopold 1970:192–93). The degree of continuity of alluvial aggradation, however, remains undemonstrated (Fogel 1988), and there is positive evidence of one or more episodes of flooding within the limits of settlement during the ancient occupation.

Total deposits at Quirigua may range from a few centimeters to approximately 2 m thick, but all are aggravatingly effective at obscuring ancient settlement. They therefore posed a two-part archaeological challenge, somewhat different from those faced by Mayanists conducting settlement survey in thin-soiled karst settings: almost all architectural and other settlement traces on the northern Quirigua floodplain are ordinarily invisible, and localized variability in deposition rates have put preterminal occupation features even farther from detection. The first challenge was answered serendipitously, by commercial redevelopment of local banana cultivation in 1977, but the second—discussed below, in the context of dating—has yet to be fully resolved.

The solution to the more general problem of visibility derived from the plantation developers' need to channel surface runoff and lower the water table, an effort described colloquially as "keeping the bananas' feet dry." Achieving this end involved dragline excavation of an elaborate system of drainage ditches, most about 2 m deep and 4–5 m across at the top. These are regularly spaced at intervals of 76.2 m (250 ft) , from one center line to the next, and with few exceptions, the alignment is N24°30'-25°W, perpendicular to the fruit company rail line. The dragline cuts thereby yielded an essentially systematic (although not strictly random) sample of transects through the alluvium, in which architectural and artifactual remains were encountered and recorded. Needless to say, the few remains visible at the surface were also recorded, but the sample of most interest for demographic analyses is that from the ditches.

Ditch exposures totaled 134.4 km in length, traversing a 10.4-km² area (Maps 3.1 and 3.2) that the Quirigua Project designated the Floodplain Periphery. Within this area most features consisted of cross-sections exposed by dragline cuts, from which ditch-surface collections were taken and other observations recorded (e.g., height and length of exposure, inferred ground elevation). Fruit company engineering maps served as the base on which location and elevation data for individual archaeological features were plotted. Time-enforced limits to transit mapping of such features are shown in Ashmore 1981a: Fig. 10, p. 120, but compass, tape, and pace measurements extended survey coverage to 52.0 linear km (38.7%) of ditch exposures. (See Ashmore 1981a:114–47.)

Altogether, 275 features of varied type (structures, pavements, wells, middens, caches, etc.) were recorded (Ashmore 1981a:161–64, Table 13), in survey and limited excavations, both in and beyond the ditch exposures. For demographic reconstructions, however, the total must be disaggregated to yield sets of mutually contemporary units, and the units themselves must be warranted as appropriate indices of population numbers. Furthermore, the relation of the data sample to the settlement as a whole must be specified, including how the sample data are extrapolated to the larger frame of reference and considering the effects of suspected or known deranging factors.

Chronological Analysis

Features with evidence of multiple occupation components were not common but were notably more frequent among (1) excavated features and (2) constructions of larger overall size. For a given feature (or component), the assumption has been that the latest chronological indicator defines the feature's age; chronologically relevant material was often sparse, and not a few age determinations were based on single or a handful of sherds.

Age assessments for floodplain remains were based on several sources—ceramic associations, presence of temporally diagnostic artifacts (e.g., copper), architectural style (e.g., masonry type), radiocarbon analyses, hieroglyphic inscriptions, ground elevation, and association with other dated features. In practice, ceramic assessments were the most common (primary criterion in more than 60% of the cases in the best-controlled sample areas), and they were ultimately the basis for use of ground elevation to infer age (another 33% of cases). That is, consistent association of particular ceramics-based ages with particular elevation ranges in the ditch exposures (taking into account localized variations in elevation across the extent of the settlement) allowed subsequent inference of age by elevation when no associated ceramics were encountered.

Ages of all settlement features are expressed in terms of six Periphery Time Spans (PTS 6–1, earliest to latest). Except for PTS 1 (the period following abandonment of the site), each corresponds in time to a single ceramic complex or facet (see Table 3.1). The Hewett complex is the best defined, with Maudslay and Morley less satisfactorily represented and Catherwood still quite poorly defined (M. Bullard and Sharer 1988; Ashmore 1981a:249–64). Duration for the complexes varies, but following the procedures outlined by Culbert and his colleagues (Chapter 5), comparison across spans will correct for differential time-interval length by normalizing each to 150 years. Two other complications should be noted, however.

First, despite marked shifts in the cultural inventory sometime after A.D. 810 (Sharer 1985), there are enough material and ground-surface continuities between PTS 3 (= Hewett complex) and PTS 2 (= Morley complex) that often they cannot be conclusively distinguished from one another, especially beyond the site core. PTS 2 indices were usually accompanied by PTS 3 diagnostics (23 of 30 cases), and markers of the later period are often sparse when they are represented at all. Consequently, apparent absence of PTS 2 diagnostics does not necessarily negate use of a feature during the span, and PTS 3 and 2 are collapsed in discussion here, at least initially (see below, and Ashmore 1981a: 310–17; 1984: 381–82).

Second, PTS 4 (= Maudslay complex: late facet) is quite poorly understood but seems to have encompassed at least two significant upheavals— major flooding that destroyed or buried PTS 4 and earlier remains in at least the 3C and 1C grid areas, and establishment of a new civic core in grids 1A and 1B, the final architectural and sculptural epicenter of the settlement. Presumably, the two developments were sequential, in the order listed (reasoning is outlined elsewhere: Ashmore 1981a:285–92; 1984:377–79), but the sequence cannot be demonstrated stratigraphically or otherwise beyond dispute. Continuity of settlement may well have been disrupted on a large scale, but assignment of individual PTS 4 remains to subdivisions within the span is not currently possible.

It is important to reiterate that the time spans have been tapped to quite different degrees. Cumulative effects of levee building have buried remains to varying depths, with those closer to the active channel (or series of channels) buried more deeply across all time spans. Even where distance from the channel minimized alluvial cover, pre-PTS 3 remains are elusive. Composite profiles of ground surfaces for different periods illustrate that ditches tend to be slightly deeper in grid 3C (Figure 3.1). Consequently, that grid, and to a lesser extent its neighbors to north and east, stood the best chance of revealing remains antedating the eighth century A.D. Not surprisingly, this is precisely the area where the bulk of remains from PTS 4 and 5 have been encountered. But even these are few in number (see below), and the full areal distribution of settlement in these (let alone earlier) spans remains unknown.

Settlement Units: Counting and Converting

Scale of construction and artifact associations suggest most features encountered in the ditches were residences or parts thereof. The cross-sectional nature of the ditch transects, however, often yielded exposures of residence-related features (e.g., wells) without revealing the residences themselves. In order to incorporate this data in a systematic manner, without double-counting residential units, the operational unit for the demographic count was the patio group (Ashmore 1981b: 48–50), as represented by any plausible construction element thereof. Some evidence suggests that middens did at times occur apart from constructed areas (i.e., as if communal dumps; Ashmore 1981a:213, 338), so such features alone were not considered sufficient indication of a residence. Structures, platforms, wells, stone pavements, and disturbed construction features, however, were all considered candidates for residential remains.

It was often possible to detect coherent structure groups from ditch exposures, and each of these multifeature complexes was taken as one residential unit. Frequently, however, the dragline seems to have intersected such groups on a "corner," so that the narrow survey line embraced only a slice through a well or a cut across a pavement or structure of unknown total dimensions (e.g., Structure 1C-1:Ashmore 1980:22, Figure 9). Each of these, too, was taken as one residential unit when independence from other exposed features could be plausibly assumed. It is unlikely that any residential compounds thus encountered were large enough to appear in more than one ditch, so potential for overcounting can probably be dismissed.

Once sorted according to age, then, these units were counted and a constant factor applied to convert residence counts to population numbers. The specific procedures are detailed below, but the justification for the particular conversion figure is presented here. The usual figure used by Mayanists for demographic reconstruction is the 5.6 persons/house taken from Redfield and Villa Rojas's (1934) study of Chan Kom. At the time of that research the community was in social, cultural, and demographic transition, and for this and other reasons, the figure's appropriateness has been debated almost every time it has been used. Furthermore, we have no guarantee that persons/house ratios remained constant across space or time or social group within the Maya world. But some figure is necessary, and using a constant facilitates at least preliminary comparisons among settlements. Those used have ranged from 4 to 10.

This is not the place for a detailed review of the issue and arguments (for Quirigua see Ashmore 1981a:378–87). For the present analysis I have adopted a conversion figure of 5 persons/residential unit. Some consider this too low. I consider it conservative and justify it on the following considerations.

The best ethnographic description for possibly related peoples in this area is Wisdom's (1940) account of the Chorti Maya, who live in patio-group residential compounds. These compounds comprise multiple structures of varying size, the larger structures (one or a very few per group) being the sleeping houses. Because these structures are the most closely associable with numbers of people, they offer the most appropriate focus for demographic counts. Within the Quirigua sample, however, discrimination of structure size was seldom feasible so (as already described) the count uses groups as wholes, not individual structures. One sleeping house per residential unit is assumed as a consistent and conservative estimate. More sleeping houses per unit seem present in some Late Classic Copan patio groups (e.g., Group 9N-8; Sanders 1986) and may be at Quirigua as well (e.g., Acropolis Group 1B-1; Sharer 1978). A constant of one house per unit is, however, is preferred as most interpretively conservative.

The conversion figure of five assumes one nuclear family per sleeping house. Being derived from the lower end of the range of figures used in the Mayanist literature, it further incorporates the observation that individual structures in the southeast tend to be smaller than counterparts in the central Maya lowlands (e.g., Leventhal 1979:108). *It is claimed as no more than a provisional multiplier, aimed at yielding a conservative estimate of ancient population; other analysts can take the data outlined below and apply other conversions as deemed appropriate.*

Sample Adequacy and Extrapolation

Some final considerations and corrections are necessary before turning to the data and population reconstruction. The first involves evaluation of possible deranging factors affecting the completeness of the sample. The other refines the effective sample to minimize unevenness and maximize extrapolability.

The primary deranging factor, even in the ditch sample, is feature visibility. Readers will have noted the explicit emphasis on constructed features in Quirigua settlement analysis. These were built of combinations of stone and earth of various types and in variable proportions. But in only one ditch exposure (Structure 1A-25) was purely earthen construction observed, and even then, the traces were subtle and could easily have been missed. One presumes more such structures existed but either have not been intersected or have simply remained invisible. In this regard it should be noted that dragline work went on essentially year-round, while research was confined to the dry season. This scheduling issue is relevant because ditch walls dried out rather quickly after excavation, and erosion plus colonization by weeds obscured some of the earlier-dug cuts. Obvious, major impediments to observation of stone-built constructions and middens tended to occur in areas beyond the subsample discussed below, but the pervasive threat to more subtle settlement traces cannot be ignored. Related to this, of course, is the issue of platformless structures (Wilk and Wilhite 1982; cf. McQuarrie 1982; Pyburn, this volume), a topic of deserved concern in paleodemogrphic studies in the Maya area and elsewhere. Unless, however, these were floored with stone or retain deposits of daub from fallen walls, they would be virtually undetectable in a survey like the Quirigua ditch program. The point for both issues of visibility is that the counts given below are minimum estimates for settlement remains.

Turning to positive characteristics of the sample, the ditches were, as already stated, essentially systematic in spacing, alignment, and depth as three-dimensional transects. The sample was less satisfactorily systematic, however, with respect to representation of various time periods and intensity of recording.

The former caveat has already been noted: in areas with lower alluviation rates pre–Late Classic remains were sometimes encountered in ditch bases; in areas with higher rates no traces of these periods were detected. We simply do not know whether they exist and await discovery below the current ditch bases (and water table) in these locations, so we can do no more than speculate on areal growth or decline of the settlement between periods (see below).

The latter problem concerns investigative constraints. The most desirable spatial frame of reference for the survey was the project map grid of 500-m (0.25 km^2) squares, but not all such grids were completely traversed by ditches (see Map 3.2). Even when they were, total exposure lengths involved were not always equal. Furthermore, it was not always possible to know, during field recording, where the limits of project map grids lay with respect to fruit company ditches (for details on survey procedures, see Ashmore 1981a:118–41). Add to this the lack of time to reconnoiter and record all ditch exposures, and the result is quite uneven sampling intensity per map grid. To correct for this problem, a subsample of 11 grids was established as the control base for extrapolation.

These 11 grids (Table 3.2) maximized both total of exposures available for survey and thoroughness of actually accomplished survey and were also examined to control for edge effects of settlement dropoff (for fuller description see Ashmore 1981a:317–29). Note that the area of the site core is excluded: although the most intensively studied area of the floodplain settlement, it was not examined via systematic ditch sampling. And the grids that are included are concentrated along what we believe to have been the ancient levee, paralleling the eighth-century river course and slightly raised above the floodplain farther from that course (Map 3.2).

That the survey revealed the highest occupation densities precisely where investigative densities were greatest may be partially but is likely not entirely an artifact of research bias. The correlation between lengths of N24°30–25°W ditches examined and uncorrected number of features encountered in a given grid is fairly high ($r = .648$), and the observed distribution does not appear to differ significantly from that expected by knowing only the total number of features and the sample reconnoitered in each grid ($X^2 = 12.74$; $df = 10$; $.25 > p > .10$). Still, subjectively, there was a noticeable diminution in feature frequency farther east and north of the putative eighth-century channel. In part such decrease may be due to lessened protection from alluvial burial; I cannot quantify this effect at present, but given the excellent preservation of some relatively small features (e.g., Structure 3C-11) found within a few centimeters of the modern ground surface, the decrease is probably not attributable solely to such diminished protection. Acknowledging the foregoing, I still believe that settlement may have been densest along the prominence of the levee, unsurprising for a riverside community.

Together the 11 grids cover 2.75 km² within a settlement believed to have extended, at maximum, over about 3 km² of alluvial lands, with additional occupation on contiguous terraces west and northwest of the floodplain. Procedures for extrapolation from the controlled sample to the settlement as a whole are included in the description below.

RECONSTRUCTION FOR PTS 3/2

Table 3.2 presents the data for reconstruction of Quirigua population in PTS 3/2 combined. The analysis is slightly modified from that presented elsewhere (Ashmore 1981a:329–38, 387–90), in part by taking into account here the contemporaneity corrections suggested in Chapter 5. Discussion will proceed column by column through the table.

Column 1 lists the 11 grids in the controlled sample. Column 2 indicates total construction features, dating to PTS 3/2, encountered within the limits of each grid (plus 11-grid total and mean), counting only exposures in ditches with the regular N24°30'-25°W alignment. Because of the difficulty in distinguishing PTS 3 from PTS 2 remains, the two are lumped for this initial analysis, but a separate analysis omitting features with PTS 2 indices is offered in the succeeding section. (The reason for counting all PTS 3/2 construction features is explained below, in connection with Column 7). Column 3 lists the number of inferred residential units; the reduction from Column 2 reflects elimination of all but one feature of each patio group recorded. Column 4 indicates the ratio of residential units to construction features.

Adjustment and manipulation of data begin with Column 5. Because total length of ditch exposures varied across grids, samples were normalized to a single exposure total. Figures in Column 5 adjust the number of construction features (Column 2) for this standardized sample.

Further correction, for time span (Culbert et al., Chapter 5), appears in Column 6. Combined PTS 3/2 encompasses more than two centuries' time, but probably not much more. Quantities in Column 5 are thus reduced in Column 6 to adjust to a 150-year equivalent.

In Columns 7–9 each normalized sample is extrapolated to 100% coverage for that grid square. This was achieved by simulation of ditch sampling and by manual imposition of ditch-lines on maps of three sites, each related to Quirigua in different ways and each of which had been mapped with surveying instruments. The three sites are Tikal, Copan, and Playitas (Group I), and the complete simulation is described elsewhere (Ashmore 1981a:330–38). Basically, the procedure involved creation of a map overlay showing a set of hypothetical ditch alignments, and counting all construction features intersected by the lanes. (This overlay was the standard used subsequently to normalize ditch-length samples for Column 5, above.) To avoid problems in functional interpretation of constructions at other sites and to make the simulated ditch samples most comparable to the Quirigua sample, separate counts were made of structures and total undifferentiated construction features but not of "residences" or other functionally identified units.

For the present analysis, the most useful data come from Playitas, a large center northeast of Quirigua in the lower Motagua Valley (Schortman 1980, 1984, 1986). Preferred reliance on Playitas stems from (1) similarity to Quirigua in its alluvial setting, although apparently without the gross masking problem that plagues the other site; (2) apparently short occupation history, approximately contemporary with the period of this analysis; and (3) general similarity (though not identity) with Quirigua in architectural remains. The same grid was positioned differently over the Playitas map five times, with varying results; two trials produced identical numbers. "Success rates" (number of constructions encountered by simulated ditches/number of constructions actually present within the 0.25 km²) varied from 0.220 to 0.294 (mean "success rate" across all trials at all three sites was 0.235), and their reciprocals serve as plausible correction multipliers for extrapolating from a normalized sample to the whole grid. Since it is impossible to judge the success rate for the Quirigua sample, low (3.40), middle (4.00), and high (4.54) multipliers are used to convert the corrected figures in Column 6 to those in, respectively, Columns 7, 8, and 9.

Further multiplication of these figures by 4 expands data from each 0.25 km² (and the 11-grid mean) into constructions/km². For simplicity, only the data using the middle multiplier (Column 8) are shown, as Column 10. The result highlights variability in construction intensity in different parts of the settlement and reminds us of the hazards of relying on small samples for extrapolation.

Column 11 (again showing only data using the middle multiplier) builds on previous calculations to provide estimates of residences/km² (Column 10 × the grid-specific ratios in Column 4), and Column 12 converts these to population/km² by multiplying by 5, as justified earlier. Intergrid variability in residence and population densities/km² here reflects both variation in construction intensity and functional contrasts within the settlement (e.g., residential vs. civic areas).

Finally, Column 13 indicates population size for the entire 3-km² floodplain settlement of PTS 3/2 times, as suggested by individual grid calculations and calculation from intergrid means. The 3-km² area is delimited by falloff in construction frequencies, varying in reliability and clarity of definition from one portion of the "edge" to another (Ashmore 1981a: 301–6).

DISCUSSION AND FURTHER ANALYSES

Estimates in Table 3.2 for total population of PTS 3/2 Quirigua are somewhat lower than estimates offered previously (Ashmore 1981a, 1984), due principally to the use of the time-correction factor suggested by Culbert and his colleagues (this volume). Depending on which areal unit is used as the basis for extrapolation and which simulation-correction factor is adopted, the reconstructed population totals given here range from 427 to 2223 for the floodplain settlement during the combined span, with population density/km² ranging from 142 to 741. Acknowledging both the relative unreliability of extrapolation from any single 0.25-km² grid and the impossibility of knowing the true "success rate" of the Quirigua ditch sampling, it seems most likely the closest approximation to an ancient reality lies somewhere between the calculated extremes, perhaps in the 1000–1400 range associated with use of the intergrid mean. The intergrid variability probably reflects several factors, including functional differences (i.e., degree of "pure" residentiality) and some sampling error.

Although I believe that Table 3.2 is an appropriately conservative treatment of the data and that it corresponds most closely to the reasoning in Chapter 5, I also believe for several reasons that it undervalues Quirigua's peak population dimensions. The issue of invisible structures is pertinent here, as is the omission in calculation of the contiguous terrace settlement. Also important, however, is the effect of correcting for collapsing PTS 3 and 2 data. Although one cannot assume that absence of PTS 2 markers is a true reflection of lack of occupation at that time, only 30 of the total known 201 PTS 3/2 construction features (and only 11 of the 88 construction features in the 11-grid sample) have such markers, and using only 75% counts (i.e., to adjust to a 150-year equivalent) may have an exaggerated effect on the result. At least some attempt to assess population in PTS 3, without PTS 2, therefore seems desirable.

Eliminating the features with evidence for PTS 2 construction has a clear effect in raising all estimates. For figures analogous to those in Column 13 of Table 3.2, the range for PTS 3 population totals extends from a low of 522 with density of 174 people/km² (calculated with data from grid 3E and the low Playitas multiplier, 3.40) to a high of 2599 with density of 866 people/km² (calculated from data for grid 3C and the high Playitas multiplier, 4.54). Using the intergrid mean as a basis for calculation, the result of using the different Playitas figures would be 1183 (density 394/km²; 3.40 multiplier); 1392 (density 464/km²; 4.00 multiplier); 1579 (density 526/km²; 4.54 multiplier).

Adjusting the time span of PTS 3 to 150 years would, of course, increase figures by another 50%. The range of 3-km² population totals using intergrid means, for example, would then be 1775 (density 592/km²); 2088 (density 696/km²); 2369 (density 790/km²). Minimum and maximum estimates would be 783 (density 261/km²; 3E with 3.40 multiplier) and 3899 (density 1300/km²; 3C with 4.54 multiplier). These are certainly less conservative reconstructions, although they still necessarily omit invisible and terrace-top residences. I believe the approach of Table 3.2 is valuable, but I suspect figures in this and the previous paragraph come closer to the actual Late Classic situation.

Despite an agriculturally rich setting for the settlement, all the foregoing reconstructions place Quirigua at the small end of published estimates for Late Classic Maya centers, perhaps on a par with Seibal (Tourtellot 1970:409, 414) or even Becan (R. E. W. Adams 1981), but probably much larger than Lubaantun (Hammond 1981). Unless its invisible populace is huge, however, Quirigua is minuscule in comparison with such megacenters as Tikal (Haviland 1970, 1972a; D. Puleston 1973) and Copan, a conclusion that seems consistent with current interpretations of the Motagua center's political and economic clout. On the other hand, it seems to have been slightly larger but perhaps not more densely settled than at least some of its lower Motagua Valley competitors; one reconstruction for Playitas (using data from Group I there, plus conversion assumptions and procedures as for Quirigua in Table 3.2) suggests a population of about 1300 people in the 2.56-km² settled area, a value somewhat higher than an earlier estimate (Ashmore 1981a:390).

And what of earlier periods? Although earlier times are extremely difficult to deal with, Tables 3.3 and 3.4 present what data there are, to hazard a ballpark estimate of changes in occupation intensity between Early and Late Classic times. Only three grids are considered (1C, 3C, 5C), all of them in the 11-grid subsample and all with some evidence of pre-PTS 3 features. Features from PTS 6 are absent in the floodplain periphery, and since PTS 5 and 4 are identified with facets of the same overall ceramic complex, they are sometimes difficult to differentiate. Table 3.3 presents the uncorrected counts of features for PTS 3, PTS 4, PTS 5, and PTS 5/4 combined. Table 3.4 adjusts these figures for standardization to (1) normalized sample size of Table 3.2 and (2) 150-year equivalence. Values for PTS 5/4 combined are greater than the sum of those for PTS 5 plus PTS 4 because the former include features that cannot be reliably placed in one rather than the other.

What Tables 3.3 and 3.4 illustrate has more to do, I think, with the alluviation problem than with the magnitude of Quirigua's growth between the Early and Late Classic. For both periods the presence of a civic (i.e., nonresidential) focus in grid 3C is evident; even the "1?" Early Classic residence identified for PTS 5 might have been a ballcourt (Ashmore 1981a:865–66). But I place little confidence in inferring a nearly 30-fold increase in population between PTS 5/4 and PTS 3. Growth, yes; this period was one of marked florescence, as documented by sculptural and architectural developments in the site core (e.g., C. Jones and Sharer 1986). But we have too little access to the earlier periods to do very much, demographically, with the data at hand. Even besides the alluviation problem, there is again the invisibility issue: although PTS 5 and 4 builders certainly used stone in some of their constructions, can we presume that relative frequencies of earthen-platform and platformless structures (if greater than zero) remained equivalent in these centuries of known change? At least PTS 5 Platform 3C-1-3rd, the earliest version of a civic facility of enduring importance, may have been a purely earthen entity (Ashmore 1981a:808). And PTS 5 dynasts certainly had the wherewithal to elaborate further this civic core, as well as to erect at least two stelae in the late fifth century. These and other achievements suggest a center of more than minimal magnitude, even if the magnitude cannot be quantified. Tables 3.3 and 3.4, then, serve more to tantalize than to provide firm evidence for population trajectories.

SUMMARY AND CONCLUSIONS

The foregoing analysis of data from Classic Quirigua has yielded essentially a synchronic view of the population in the eighth and perhaps ninth centuries. Both the data base and the manipulations performed on it are somewhat different from those usually discussed for lowland Maya sites, due to the relatively unusual landscape in which Quirigua is set. Variant interpretations have been offered for the Late Classic settlement, along with the assumptions on which they are based. None is demonstrably the correct one, but together they provide a reasonable range of approximation. All estimates place Quirigua at the small end of Maya centers of the same period, and this finding is seen as consistent with other interpretations about the site's relative rank in political and economic dealings.

Many problems remain unresolved in the data and their analysis. With the necessary qualifications kept firmly in mind, however, estimates for Quirigua population may nonetheless contribute to examining overall variability in Maya demography, as well as to illuminating broader questions relating demographic characteristics to other aspects of ancient Maya life.

ACKNOWLEDGMENTS

The Quirigua Project was formed by contract between the Instituto de Antropología e Historia, Guatemala, and the University Museum, University of Pennsylvania. Financial support was provided by the University Museum (Francis Boyer Fund), the National Geographic Society, the National Science Foundation (BNS 7602185, 7624189, 7603283), the Ford Foundation, the Tikal Association, the Guatemalan Ministry of Defense, the Museum Applied Science Center for Archaeology (University Museum), the Department of Anthropology of the University of Pennsylvania, Landon T. Clay, Alfred G. Zantzinger, and John M. Keshishian. I would like to thank Robert J. Sharer, Edward M. Schortman, Patricia A. Urban, Christopher Jones, David W. Sedat, Ira L. Fogel, Don S. Rice, and T. Patrick Culbert for collaboration and consultation on various aspects of the research reported here.

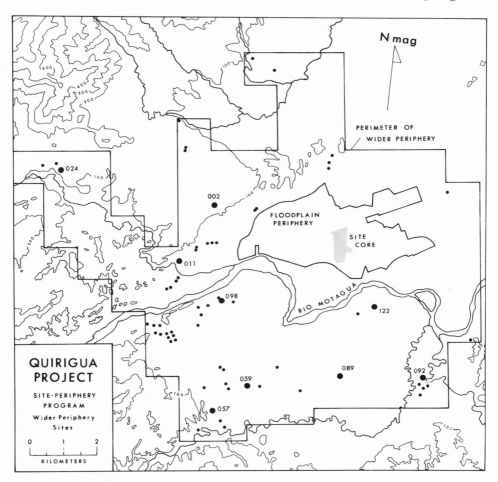

Map 3.1   Quirigua and vicinity.

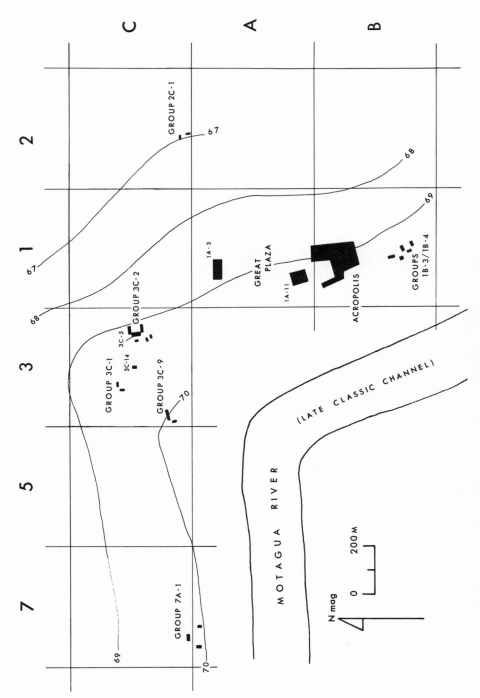

Map 3.2 Quirigua floodplain settlement. Contours are those of eighth century.

Table 3.1   Chronological Periods at Quirigua

Periphery Time Span	Ceramic Complex	Gregorian Dates
1	(none—postabandonment)	ca. A.D. 900+−1841
2	Morley	ca. A.D. 810–900+
3	Hewett	ca. A.D. 700–810
4	Maudslay (Late Facet)	ca. A.D. 600–700
5	Maudslay (Early Facet)	ca. A.D. 400–600
6	Catherwood	?–ca. A.D. 400

Note: For detailed descriptions of archaeological periodization at Quirigua see M. Bullard and Sharer (1988), Ashmore (1981a, 1984), and C. Jones et al. (1983).

Table 3.2   Quirigua Population Reconstruction For PTS 3/2

Grid (1)	Total Constructions (2)	Residential Units (3)	Residences/ Construction Features (4)	Total Constructions (Adjusted for Ditch Coverage) (5)	Total Constructions (Adjusted for Time Span) (6)
1C	15	7	0.47	19.20	14.40
1E	1	1	1.00	2.79	2.09
2A	8	4	0.50	8.72	6.54
2B	10	6	0.60	10.40	7.80
2C	3	3	1.00	4.17	3.13
3C	15	8	0.53	18.00	13.50
3E	4	3	0.75	5.12	3.84
5C	11	9	0.82	11.11	8.33
5E	3	3	1.00	6.36	4.77
7A	5	3	0.60	13.85	10.39
7C	13	8	0.62	17.55	13.16
Total	88	55		117.27	87.95
X̄	8	5	0.62	10.66	8.00

Table 3.2 Continued

Constructions /0.25 km²			Constructions/ km² (4 × Column 8) (10)	Residences per km² (Column 4 × Column 10) (11)	People/km² (5 × Column 11) (12)	Floodplain Population (3 × Column 12) (13)
Low (3.40) (7)	Middle (4.00) (8)	High (4.54) (9)				
48.96	57.60	65.38	230.40	108.29	541.45	1,624.35
7.11	8.36	9.49	33.44	33.44	167.20	501.60
22.24	26.16	29.69	104.64	52.32	261.60	784.80
26.52	31.20	35.41	124.80	74.88	374.40	1,123.20
10.64	12.52	14.21	50.08	50.08	250.40	751.20
45.90	54.00	61.29	216.00	114.48	572.40	1,717.20
13.06	15.36	17.43	61.44	46.08	230.40	691.20
28.32	33.32	37.82	133.28	109.29	546.45	1,639.35
16.22	19.08	21.66	76.32	76.32	381.60	1,144.80
35.33	41.56	47.17	166.24	99.74	498.70	1,496.10
44.74	52.64	59.75	210.56	130.55	652.75	1,958.25
27.18	31.98	36.30	127.93	81.41	407.03	1,221.10

Table 3.3 Comparisons of PTS 5 Through 3: Uncorrected Data

	PTS 3		PTS4		PTS 5		PTS 5/4	
Grid	Total Constructions	Residential Units	Total Constructions	Residential Units	Total Constructions	Residential Units	Total Constructions	Residential Units
1C	15	7	0	0	1	1	1	1
3C	15	8	1?	1?	5	1?	7	3
5C	7	6	0	0	1	1	3	3

Table 3.4 Comparisons of PTS 5 Through 3: Corrected Data

	PTS 3		PTS 4		PTS 5		PTS 5/4	
Grid	Total Constructions	Residential Units	Total Constructions	Residential Units	Total Constructions	Residential Units	Total Constructions	Residential Units
1C	28.80	13.54	0.00	0.00	0.48	0.48	0.21	0.21
3C	27.00	14.31	1.80?	1.80?	2.25	0.45	1.38	0.59
5C	10.60	9.12	0.00	0.00	0.38	0.38	0.51	0.51
Total	66.40	37.85	1.80?	1.80?	3.11	1.31	2.10	1.31
As % of PTS 3	100.00	100.00	2.71?	4.76?	4.68	3.46	3.16	3.46

Note: Data have been corrected by adjusting for both intensity of investigation (standardization of sample size) and length of time interval (PTS 4 figures multiplied by 1.50; PTS 5, by 0.75; PTS 5/4, combined, by 0.50).

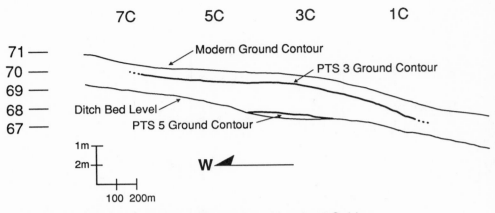

Figure 3.1 Ancient and modern ground levels at Quirigua.

4 /
Population Estimates for Preclassic and Classic Seibal, Peten

GAIR TOURTELLOT

A census of ancient population can be attempted long after the fact in numerous ways: from skeletons, artifact consumption, agronomic potential, reservoir capacity, volumetric labor/time, or direct-historic extrapolations. Elsewhere I have presented highly speculative estimates for Seibal from reservoir capacity or plaza area (Tourtellot 1982:723, 1089–91; 1988b). Here I concentrate on producing population estimates based on counts of ruin units on mapped terrain, as controlled by excavation results.

This chapter focuses on methods, how the Seibal population estimate is made, and what the methods imply for evaluating estimates from other sites. The basic form of the population calculation is the number of contemporaneous residential entities at a site multiplied by the number of people who lived in each entity. As we all know, this equation is more difficult than it may look. I shall have to lay bare the definition of the site, recognition of entities, the sampling design and its complications, identification of dwellings, periodization of occupations, demonstration of contemporaneity, selection of a family size, and the problem of standardizing durations.

The site of Seibal is located on a bluff 110 m high on the west bank of the Rio de la Pasion in the southern part of Peten, Guatemala. It had a long occupation, from about 900 B.C. to perhaps A.D. 1200, split between Preclassic and Late Classic communities. Fuller background information and maps for Seibal can be found in several publications (Willey et al. 1975; Sabloff 1975; A. L. Smith 1982).

AREA AND TERRAIN TYPES

We have direct information, from excavation or surface collections, on two different areas of Seibal. First, a 1.62-km^2 central area that includes the major civic centers and causeways adjacent to the river was defined and completely mapped (see Willey et al. 1975: Figure 2). Most of the excavated ruins were randomly selected from this area. Second, a peripheral area was surveyed, using transit and stadia, by means of a grid of transects 40 m wide along trails cut at 600-m intervals. These peripheral transects technically cover only 6.7% (0.69 km^2) of a "sampled area" of 10.3 km^2, extending approximately 2 km from the central area to the north, west, and south. However, much of the intervening and surrounding area was also mapped (see Willey et al. 1975: Figure 3), producing information on an upland area of about 15.25 km^2. For this area we rely on surface collections for chronological data, supplemented by a few excavations. Still a third, residual, area would comprise any more of the site that exists farther out or across the river—at whose dimensions we can only guess.

Figures on the types of terrain at Seibal are derived from the transects crossing the area of 11.9 km^2 formed by combining the peripheral area with the central area. Use of a grid of transects neatly cancels out upland-versus-ravine periodicities in the landscape. These transects consist of 17% steep slope and ravine terrain, 24% bajo terrain, and 59% cultivable or habitable terrain (Tourtellot 1982:Table 2). These frequencies may also characterize part of the third, nonsurveyed area as well, because the Seibal upland may extend as much as 25 km to the south and 10 km to the west to the Petexbatun Lagoons. This 250-km^2 Seibal upland may represent a mere quarter of the total sustaining area of the ancient Seibal domain (Hammond 1974a), with the low-lying terrain across the river containing hydromorphic soils perhaps once drained for cultivation (see R. E. W. Adams et al. 1981).

The actual limits of the Seibal residential area, during two cycles of expanding and contracting occupation, are defined not by the excavations, limited primarily to the central map area, but by the 229 ceramic samples collected opportunistically from treefalls across the site. Their distribution by chronological phase suggests that only at the peaks of population in the Late Preclassic and the Late Classic did the residential area of Seibal fill the surveyed area and probably extend beyond (Tourtellot 1988b).

UNITS, STRUCTURES, AND DWELLINGS

Small structures in the central area were intensively excavated in a dispro-portional, stratified, random-cluster sample that tested about 25% of the mapped, small-structure loci. Let me define these terms. These loci (the statistical clusters) are places consisting of one or several potentially do-mestic platforms, frequently arrayed in what are called patio groups and separated by distance or orientation from similar groups. It is vital to note that the sampling element was not the individual structure (building), per-haps the home of a nuclear family, but the locus consisting of one or several individual structures, perhaps the home of several families. Each locus was usually explored by numerous shallow strip trenches in search of architectural forms and functions and tested in depth by at least one pit or trench. Because excavations were not randomized over the structures and spaces comprising a unit locus, we can claim as reliably representative only the data that apply to the whole locus.

The units on the central map were classified (stratified) for random sampling according to the number of platforms shown for each locus and secondarily by form for the large number of isolated single-structure units. As it turned out, however, the number of excavated platforms at a locus often was more than the number shown on the maps (28 net struc-tures added to the 89 mapped within the selected groups). Only 50% of the units excavated on the central map had been correctly mapped and classified (Tourtellot 1976). Consequently, counts of individual structures shown on the maps will not be used as the basis for estimating site pop-ulation. Instead, the number of *units* of structures is used as the basic counting element, because very little net error was made in mapping and counting the loci of habitation selected for excavation (two added, one deleted, for a total of 41 units in the sample).

The very different reliability of counts of structures versus units is a problem for investigators who rely on mapped rather than excavated re-mains for estimating population in situations of heavy forest and deep soils: the number of surface structures may be far less significant and re-liable than the fact of occupation. Another problem is caused by the failure to discriminate between individual structures (buildings) and individual mounds concealing a substructure actually bearing several buildings, a danger particularly applicable to the "house mounds" at Barton Ramie or Altar de Sacrificios, where there are many eroded groups of platforms, not single buildings.

For the Preclassic phases of occupation at Seibal, only the loci can be counted because most excavations that exposed Preclassic floors, fills, and pottery lack adequate data on the characteristics and number of individual Preclassic structures. Consequently, I have assumed that the number of individual dwellings per unit (locus) in the Preclassic was the same as in the Late Classic, for the Preclassic loci appear to be just as extensive as (if not more extensive than) the Late Classic patio groups that often parasitized them.

Functional discrimination has been separately applied to the structures and to the units in order to obtain the counts of domestic units (loci) needed for estimating population. Regarding individual structures, considerable effort was expended on using architecture and artifacts to discriminate both formally and functionally between (1) the all-important dwellings and (2) ancillary structures such as kitchens, burial altars, and oratories, (3) basal supporting platforms and terraces, and (4) civic structures such as palaces, ballcourts, pyramid temples, ceremonial platforms, stalls, or defensive works (Tourtellot 1982:528–713).

Seibal dwellings, structures wherein people slept and lived, comprise all or most examples of seven different formal classes of platforms whose floor plans vary from simple to complex and once bore perishable buildings (Tourtellot 1988a:Figure 5.1). The excavated dwellings from these seven classes represent a projected 85.7% of all individual structures in the central probability sample of small domestic structures (from which basal and civic structures are excluded). That is, 14.3% of platforms in domestic units are ancillaries rather than dwellings (cf. 16.5% at Tikal [Haviland 1965:19]). It is these individual dwellings that we wish to count, but floor plans of the class members as mapped varied from 100 to 43% wrong, and in any case their numbers cannot be read directly off the survey maps. Instead, the average number of dwelling structures for the reliably known excavated units in the central sample is used to calculate the average number of dwellings per mapped locus. The average figure is 2.72 dwellings/domestic unit, after proper weighting for disproportional sampling.

I shall extrapolate this figure of 2.72 for dwellings/unit to units across the whole site and to the Preclassic loci. The figure represents the maximum average number of occupied dwellings; thus, its use may produce somewhat exaggerated population estimates. Excavations in three other central units and tests in seven peripheral units cannot be used as a check because they were not selected randomly and tend to be in large units (averaging 3.0 dwellings/unit), although they obtained much the same sort of chronological and functional data. Nor can we rely on counts of mapped structures, as already explained.

In regard to units, comparison suggests that some of the 41 units excavated in the central probability sample lack dwellings and must be excluded in estimating population. Five units were discarded as apparent ceremonial or defensive loci, based on an assessment of their shapes, locations, and associated artifacts. Three units were wholly Preclassic constructions still exposed on the surface. It is worth noting that each of the discarded units consists of a single isolated structure (67% of the 12 single-structure units in the sample). The actual percentage of nondomestic units that must be deducted from the total of countable units varies by temporal phase and geographical sector (Table 4.1).

What of the possibility that some dwellings (and units) are hidden, hence not counted, because of their thoroughly perishable construction, their destruction by natural processes, or inadequate recovery and recognition methods? The existence of such hidden dwellings, of course, would render still higher the bold population estimates that are constructed from fairly conservative assumptions. Six judgmental excavations deliberately searching for "hidden occupation" in gravel shows or "vacant" elevations of sorts never mapped as features produced one example each of structures or sherd concentrations pertaining to the Late Preclassic Cantutse phase and Terminal Classic Bayal phase and four examples for the Late Classic Tepejilote phase. If used as adjustment figures, these tests would add 17% to the former two phases and 67% to the Tepejilote phase. This is surely the worst case, for the sampling design is plainly suitable for demonstrating existence but not for extrapolating reliable numbers. Furthermore, these raw figures ignore other critical dimensions that must also be assessed before accepting claims to increased numbers of dwellings: identification of form, use specifically as dwellings, date, contemporaneity, areal distribution, and quantity. After defining and assessing these necessary dimensions (see Tourtellot 1982:893–908), I do not feel compelled (for reasons outlined elsewhere [Tourtellot 1983:44–45]) to adjust the population estimate for Seibal at this time.

Another problem, often overlooked, for population estimates is the possible "hiding" of population growth by the type of house construction. Although we may assume so, the addition of new buildings is not the only form of accommodation to population growth. Other documented forms include internal subdivision or lateral expansion (Tourtellot 1988a). Neither of these alternatives adds to the count of dwelling structures. Before accepting dwelling counts for a site, then, we must insist on evidence regarding the mode(s) of response to growth, whether by subdivision, expansion, or replication of dwellings. Ideally, what one should be counting is the closest attainable approximation to a basic "(family) sleeping space," perhaps a count of rooms rather than structures (see Tourtellot et al., this volume).

In the Classic Period, Seibal virtually lacks evidence for the lateral or vertical expansion of individual dwelling structures. Subdivision of dwellings, however, might have occurred in an estimated 29% of them, although based only on what I consider the flimsy evidence that interior floor platforms ("benches?") were installed in two construction stages rather than one on an estimated 29% of the excavated Seibal dwelling foundations. Nevertheless, on this basis the reader might increase the Late and Terminal Classic counts in Table 4.2 by 29%.

Periodization of excavated Seibal units was based on ceramic analysis (Sabloff 1975). Dating of individual strata and then structures was made from a careful comparison of the ceramic complexes and sherd total per lot to the stratigraphy, inferred contexts, and likelihood of intrusion.[2]

Trace amounts (one or two sherds in a lot) of excavated ceramics were rarely a problem in assigning dates, for most excavated lots had 35 or more sherds, and the strata even more. Trace quantities for "Postclassic" occupation were not enough to establish a complex or phase but were widely scattered and often associated with small platforms near old temple pyramids. Trace amounts are a problem in the Early Classic Junco Tzakol phase. Only some 1000 Early Classic sherds were found at Seibal, and the unit loci of this phase had the poorest ratio of definite construction features (stratum, pit, burial, floor, or structure) to merely ceramic shows (3:18), as indicators of occupation, for any phase in the central probability sample (Tourtellot 1982:Table 41). The count of Junco units in Table 4.1 here accepts all the traces as representing an occupation "somewhere nearby" and is singled out with a question mark. The weak Early Classic cannot be regarded as the product of an underrecovery of data, because still-earlier material was easy to find.

Identifying the complexes present in the windfall surface collections often depended on trace numbers because of small samples. Direct comparison with adjacent excavations indicated that windfall collections were rather good predictors of ceramic complexes actually present, even on deep construction, but were not to be relied on for percentage representations. These collections will be used here only to help plot the gross area of settlement of each phase (on the argument that sherds and refuse ordinarily are local).

Other significant problems in dating structures and units are encountered in the Late Preclassic and again in the later Classic. The Late Cantutse facet of the Late Preclassic Cantutse Chicanel phase is identified by Protoclassic traits that occur in very few localities at Seibal. This scarcity could be taken as evidence of a declining population (see Table 4.2). Instead, I have argued that these ceramics represent an elite functional subcomplex, not a wholly separate period, because the rare sherds are found only in excavations, were recovered mostly in the center of the site, rarely occur stratified above Early Cantutse remains, and are associated in outlying areas with loci that are independently identified as potentially elite residential loci, or what I call Very Minor Centers (Tourtellot 1982:998–1001; cf. Sabloff 1975:232). Most Very Minor Centers consist of a single Preclassic pyramid 4.6–10 m high, a single plaza, and one or two long platforms—comparable to the very simplest examples of W. Bullard's (1960) Minor Ceremonial Center site type—and are the earliest indications of ceremonial architecture and civic plazas at Seibal.

Viewed as an elite facet, Late Cantutse was probably a time of radical rearrangement of Seibal community organization: differentiation between tall residential tells and the more common Preclassic low refuse-platforms, the greatly reduced depth of Cantutse Late Preclassic versus earlier Middle Preclassic deposits in central Group A (due to new residential patterns), and the decline (and eventual paving over) of domestic remains inside Group A versus the explosive growth of Group D on its splendidly defensible hill overlooking the river (Tourtellot 1982:1002–11).

This alternative assignment—Late Cantutse overlapping with the later part of a partially contemporaneous Early Cantutse phase (whose loci often continued to be occupied in Junco times while "skipping" Late Cantutse), now extended to 570 years duration—has been included in Tables 4.1 and 4.2 as a bracketed entry, combining without duplication the counts of Early and Late Cantutse units. These combined counts produce the highest total for any "phase" at Seibal: virtually every locus has some Cantutse Preclassic evidence, but not all of them were reoccupied in the Late Classic. I have not included the many Preclassic domestic loci that probably underlie the broad plazas of Group A, whose inclusion would only increase further the remarkable number of Preclassic domestic loci.

Two Preclassic loci in the excavation sample were dated only to a general Preclassic Period. They are assigned to the Early Cantutse phase because of its high frequency in the collections.

In the windfall surface collections the number of identified Cantutse components is equivalent to the number of general Preclassic components that lack a phase assignment (42:46), and only 19 components from the late Middle Preclassic Escoba Mamom complex were found. The 46 general Preclassic collections have been assigned to Cantutse as their most probable dating and used in establishing community area by phase. This assignment perhaps reduces thereby the area the Escoba phase might otherwise have covered but has no other effect on the population estimates in Table 4.2. No windfall sherds at all were identified for the earlier Middle Preclassic Real Xe phase, nor for Late Cantutse.

The problem with material from both Late and Terminal Classic periods is that there are too many sherds, ceramic types, strata, dwellings, and units that cannot be clearly assigned to either the Tepejilote phase or the Bayal phase. These are "identified" in the small structures only by the lack of both Tepejilote and Bayal diagnostics in otherwise clearly late contexts (Sabloff 1975). The fact that a few examples of these "Late/Terminal Classic" deposits stratified beneath Bayal strata have been located suggests that these L/T materials belong either to a separate "transitional" phase or to the Tepejilote phase. The ramifications of assigning these units to either of these phases are too involved and inconclusive to consider here (Tourtellot 1982:461, 486–88, 1020–57), so both options are presented in the tables, set off by brackets.

Dates for each phase (Table 4.1) are the conventional ones assigned largely on the basis of ceramic comparisons (Sabloff 1975). It can be argued that the dates for Late Cantutse and Junco phase occupations are far too long or that occupation within their long durations was concentrated into but a short stretch, in view of the low quantities of sherds and structures, often poor qualities of evidence, cross-comparisons of ceramic modes, and position in the declining years of the Preclassic settlement trajectory (see Sabloff 1975:15; Tourtellot 1982:999, 1016).

CONTEMPORANEITY

A great amount of attention has been paid to the analysis of Late and Terminal Classic Maya lowland settlements, in good part because that is the period shown on most of our settlement maps. Consequently, lines of argument too numerous to list here prove to the satisfaction of most archaeologists that gross contemporaneity at the level of the phase did exist among most residential units at most of these settlements (see Haviland 1970; Tourtellot 1982:846–82). Nevertheless, this gross contemporaneity is still not the more essential fine contemporaneity or simultaneity that we actually assume when we estimate the number of people who were alive at a single moment.

The antidote for the probably impossible demand for evidence of simultaneity is that other can of worms, permanence. The arguments for contemporaneity of occupation during the Classic Period in the sources cited above are also general arguments for permanence of occupation. Rather than repeat these arguments as they apply to the short Late Classic phases at Seibal, where attempts to standardize counts for varying phase durations (see below) have little effect, let us look at the long Preclassic phases. Radical effects can be found there were we to accept the dubious assumptions of time standardization (when that is performed by dividing the counts from each phase by the ratio of its duration in years to the duration of the shortest phase in the site sequence, by the least common denominator, or a similar technique).

Several arguments can be advanced in defense of the permanent and cumulative development of Preclassic populations at Seibal despite the millennium involved (with 300 to 570 years per phase) and despite settlement characteristics completely absent from the Classic Period which might superficially suggest a high degree of Preclassic mobility. These characteristics include the accretion of layered tells ("basal platforms"), numerous "trace" occupations, an apparent rarity of individual building platforms, a visible expansion of the residential frontier through time, the sparsity of peripherally located Escoba loci, and the vacant areas beyond all advancing frontiers.

Counterarguments supporting the proposition that Preclassic occupation was substantially permanent and firmly rooted in place, at least at Seibal, include the following. (1) Formation processes are similar throughout, with the (domestic?) deposits 2–3 m thick beneath the South Plaza of Group A and in the peripheral basal platforms especially noteworthy. (In contrast, deposits in the 280 or so years of the combined Late and Terminal Classic phases rarely exceed 1 m even in the fill of platforms.) (2) During the Cantutse phase (570 years in length) layered deposits within single basal platforms can display up to three cycles of renewal, represented by alternating layers of sterile earth floor fill and messy occupation. (3) The ratio of construction evidences (strata, floors, or structures) to sherd evidence alone, for dated occupations in the excavated central units, first reaches parity in the Early Cantutse (24:23) and Late Cantutse (7:5) facets. This indication of the degree of permanency is equivalent to the ratio in Bayal times (22:24) when permanency is rather more demonstrable, although it falls short of the maximum ratios of 16:7 for Tepejilote and 19:6 for the problematical Late/Terminal Classic units.

(4) Not a single reliable example of phase-long abandonment of any Preclassic locus can be found in the excavations or even the windfalls with their tiny collections during the first 900 years of colonization and occupation at Seibal. (The only clear domestic abandonment layers occur after Junco and, of course, Bayal times.) This continuity appears to be very different from the interruptions reported for Preclassic Tikal settlement by Culbert et al. (this volume). (5) Most trace occupations occur outside the sectors surrounding central Groups A and C, in the contemporary frontier. (6) These two literally central sectors are the first settled ones and arguably the permanent migration centers for the growing community (their earliest occupation loci remain and regularly double in number through time, and they possessed large civic works by late Cantutse times). (7) Several isolated multiloci nodes of Escoba settlement on the frontier suggest local cycles of family growth and fission occurring in situ. (8) The first appearances of peripheral Very Minor Centers lag one phase behind the expansion of the settlement frontier and coincide with the filling in of old frontiers, plausibly as the result of either a sustainable "market demand" generated by growing numbers of people or early steps in hierarchical political control. And (9), by Cantutse times residual open space within the settlement was simply inadequate for locally viable shifting agriculture, thus falsifying the idea that the numerous loci might represent a palimpsest of house sites whose occupation had shifted in concert with the shifting of adjacent swidden fields.

A completely separate question concerning contemporaneity derives from the common observation that even within permanently inhabited settlements and households one can find disoccupied structures. Accordingly, it is advisable to make a downward adjustment in the counts of domestic units to account for some proportion that could have been disoccupied at any moment. There is no agreement on what this proportion should be at any particular period, estimates ranging up to 75% (see Tourtellot 1982:1061–62 for citations). An estimate for Seibal employing any kind of evidence for structure abandonment (e.g., gap in ceramic sequence, stone robbery, "incompleteness") indicates that possibly up to 30% of individual dwellings and perhaps 10% of units were permanently abandoned at some time during the Late and Terminal Classic phases (but before site abandonment). This evidence includes special units with defensive qualities located on the Group D hilltop which uniquely suffered high losses at the end of the Tepejilote phase, coincident with the appearance of the Bayal "invaders" (Tourtellot 1982:873; 1988a:Figure 5.3). Estimates of Seibal population here use a 90% occupancy rate for unit loci, that is, a deduction of 10% from the adjusted counts of units.[3]

Another kind of potential overcounting is the possible existence of dual residence (each family or household possessing a town house and a field house), dictated for efficiency when fields are at a great distance. Dual residence could require a sharp downward revision of unit counts in order to eliminate redundant (double-counted) personnel in our population estimates. Ways to detect it include identification of different types or qualities of construction in the two sorts of dwellings, consistent differences in size between urban and rural buildings of the same status, or evidence of seasonal occupation from associated activity sets or biological materials. No obvious differences in construction, size, or status can be established from the limited excavation in the Seibal peripheries, particularly given the predominance of elite structures in the small sample there. Furthermore, dual residence seems unlikely for the relatively small sampled area of Seibal (less than 3 km in radius), especially during the Preclassic, when for much of the time open lands were within 2 km of every house. Nevertheless, the identification of dual residence must be considered a significant problem in population and economic reconstructions where an entire sustaining area for a settlement has been mapped in some detail, as for Tikal or Copan.

FAMILY SIZE

Choice of a multiplier to represent the number of people who occupied a dwelling or a unit is a critical decision if counts are to be converted from relative population estimates to something approximating a census. I believe that 5 persons/dwelling is a reasonable average constant for the people occupying each Seibal dwelling (elsewhere I have considered the effects of employing family sizes that very according to the position of a phase within demographic trajectories [Tourtellot 1982:1074–75, 1095]). Five persons/dwelling is a relatively conservative estimate of family size—although high for *completed* family size given the observed growth rates between phases—based on biological reasonableness precedent in the Maya area, some ethnohistoric support, and the assumption that only one nuclear family occupied each dwelling building (see Tourtellot 1982:1068–74).

Five persons/dwelling accords nicely with the 10 m² of space often allowed per individual (Naroll 1962), in view of the fact that approximately 50 m² is the average size of dwelling platforms at Maya sites such as Seibal, Tikal, and Mayapan (Tourtellot 1983:37). But note that application of Naroll's actual allometric formula would produce an estimate of only 2.7 persons/dwelling, closer to what is otherwise the lowest estimate of Maya nuclear family size, Sanders's 3.3 persons (1973:329). On the other hand, a higher figure of 7.7 persons could be obtained for Maya dwellings 50 m² in area if these commodious spaces were each occupied by multiple families and Casselberry's formula (1974) for estimating the size of multifamily dwellings were applied (Tourtellot 1983:48–49). Note that at some Maya sites single rooms are only some 10 m² in area apiece and may have contained an entire family (e.g., Tourtellot et al., this volume). The oft-cited figure of 5.6 persons/Maya family is based on a faulty reading of the family statistics given in Redfield and Villa Rojas's study of Chan Kom (1934:87–91, Table 6 gives 5.1 persons/*nuclear* family; cf. R. E. W. Adams 1974).

The family size of 5 persons is equivalent to 13.6 persons/excavated Seibal unit with its average of 2.72 dwellings. A discount of 12.6% can be taken against this household figure on the argument that 1.72 of the nuclear families (at 1 family/dwelling) will be headed by a redundant 1.72 of the children of the first couple, if we assume that families residing in patio units were linked by common descent. Accordingly, our best estimate of the average number of people residing in a typical unit at Seibal becomes 11.9 people. This is a reasonable figure because numerous households of approximately this size can be reconstructed from ethnohistoric documents on the Maya and their neighbors (e.g., Hellmuth 1972b; Calnek 1972; Cook and Borah 1974; G. Jones 1979).

SEIBAL POPULATION

The numbers and factors used to estimate the population of Seibal in each phase are laid out in two tables. Table 4.1 presents the derivation of units per phase, employing the well-controlled excavated results of the stratified probability sample of central small structures. Table 4.2 projects these proportions of occupied units for each phase to the potential site area mapped.

The basis for the factors in Table 4.1 has been presented above. The first column of data presents the raw counts of occupied units. The corrected counts of units in the next column are the more reliable weighted estimates of totals, derived from the disproportional sample (see note 1). Use of excavated raw counts at other sites that did not follow an explicitly probabilistic sampling strategy are likely to be unreliable unless a very careful assessment is made of the impact, almost structure by structure, of the likely biases introduced by a more subjective or "purposeful" selection process. The estimate of occupied domestic units for each phase is obtained by multiplying the estimated number of units by the variable proportions of them that are domestic and then multiplying by the constants for occupancy rate and persons per occupied unit.

In both tables three rows are placed in brackets: Late/Terminal Classic, Late/Terminal Classic plus Tepejilote, and Early plus Late Cantutse. These are not basic phases but alternative alignments of questionable material explained in the section on periodization above.

Several additional factors in Table 4.2 are required by the complexities of the sampling design and deserve comment. Separate counts of units are maintained for the central map (column A.1) and peripheral map (A.2) areas because the central area has a mapped density that is about twice the density of the peripheral transects: 101 units/gross km^2 in the center versus 53/gross km^2 in the peripheries (Tourtellot 1982:110–19, 1079). The central area also includes a substantial deduction (B) from the count of units for the estimated number of central units that are considered functionally nondomestic, versus apparently few or none of these in the peripheries. This deduction for function also applied only to Classic times, for none of the Preclassic loci is identifiable as nondomestic (the Very Minor Centers have not been included in estimating unit counts; they are an easily discounted map element).

The numbers of units entered for the central area (A.1) is 191. This number is an extrapolation from the approximate density of 101 units/ km^2 in the central 1.9-km^2 map area of the site, as determined from the 600-m-interval transects that cross the center (thus it differs from the Table 4.1 counts, which are derived from the excavated units selected from an area of only 1.62 km^2 and are used only to determine the proportions of units per phase). The prediction of 191 central units is also very close to the 189 shown on the central map in Willey et al (1975:Figure 2).

The A.2 count (707 units) for units farther out is derived from the 53 units/gross km^2, established for the peripheral 10.3-km^2 area from the peripheral transect strips alone. This figure of 53 units/km^2 is extrapolated across the total of approximately 13.35 gross km² of peripheral land thought to be comparable to the landscape directly sampled by the peripheral transects. (This 13.35-km² area is obtained by taking the 25-km² area blocked out on the "Greater Seibal" map [Willey et al. 1975:Figure 3] and subtracting the approximate areas of the riverside floodplains on the east, the ruin-free bajo terrain near the river in the northwest, and the central 1.9 km².) These 707 units plus the 191 central ones comprise our best estimate of the total number of units (898) that would be mapped in that 15.25-km² area if the whole area were as carefully and fully mapped as on the main grid of transects at 600-m intervals (whose reliability was confirmed by numerous supplemental transect and area surveys).

An additional variable involved in calculation of map-wide (15.25 km²) population recognizes that different phases have different total residential areas. Table 4.2 variables A.1a for the central area and A.2a for the peripheral area represent the approximate proportions of their total unit counts that would have been occupied, per phase, given the documented less-than-total occupation of the mapped site area during certain phases. (This proportion is derived for each phase as the number of 0.25-km² map squares occurring within the settlement limit as documented by the distribution of excavations and windfall collections, divided by the 61 squares in the 15.25-km² area.) As can be seen, these corrections primarily affect the earliest phases dating from the initial colonization of the site.

In addition, a large correction to the Early Classic Junco total has been made, despite its broad scatter over an area of 13.0 km², on the basis of and in proportion to its uniquely weak 3:18 ratio (0.143) of construction:sherd evidence for actual occupation, as noted above. An approximately 70% reduction could also be taken from the Late Cantutse population figure in Table 4.2. The derivation of 2365 people assumes a continuous distribution of occupied places, whereas in fact Late Cantutse has a very odd distribution: it occurs in the central map area and in a few distant peripheral units, but is almost absent in between. If this 70% reduction is applied, we obtain an estimate of 790 persons, 8.3% of the combined Early and Late Cantutse total of 9618.

The column in Table 4.2 labeled Chronological Proportion (C.2) is simply the weighted number of central domestic units dated by excavation to a phase (column 6 in Table 4.1) divided by the weighted total of all central domestic units as projected from the excavation sample (153.5 domestic units on the 1.62 km² from which the probability sample was drawn). Occupancy Rate (C.3) is taken as 90% (vacancy of 10%, see above).

The number of domestic units for each phase is estimated by: $\{[(A.1 \times A.1a) - B] + (A.2 \times A.2a)\} \times C.2 \times C.3$. (Suppressed variable C.1, total mapped domestic units in the whole site area, is implicit in this equation as the sum of the expression within braces; it has no independent significance.) This equation produces an estimate of the number of domestic units in use per phase, a measure of relative population size. This quantity for each phase is then multiplied by 11.9 persons/domestic unit (constant D) to obtain a population estimate for each phase, entered in the last column of Table 4.2.

This is not the end of it, however. Recall, first, that numerous, probably domestic, Preclassic floors and structures lie buried beneath the broad plazas of Group A and could not be counted in estimating Preclassic populations. Second, elite housing in Groups A, C, and D has been largely omitted from the samples. These groups add perhaps 19 elite residential units at the center of Seibal, representing some 226 persons (19 units × 11.9 people) who could be considered the central elite population. When we add these people to the population totals from Table 4.2, the Tepejilote phase total rises to 3200 (or Tepejilote plus L/T to 7486) and Bayal to 7803. The 226 elite people would comprise about 3% of the total in either Bayal or Tepejilote cum L/T times, the same order of magnitude as the 2% R. E. W. Adams (1974) calculated for Uaxactun, but proportionately 50% higher.

TIME STANDARDIZATION

Since we know that many site maps depict ruins from several phases, is it not possible that, even after periodization of the remains by the phases in which they were occupied, we are still counting as independent cases *within* each phase some percentage of structures and units actually built and abandoned in sequence by single sets of people? Two attempts have been made to adjust Maya ruin counts per phase for these sometimes marked temporal differences by standardizing the counts according to the relative duration of the phases, producing radically lower counts for the Preclassic phases (P. Thomas 1981:109–11; Tourtellot 1982:965–69, 1092–96; technique from Dickson 1975; see Culbert et al., this volume, for an alternative technique).

The actual standardized counts per phase (equivalent to number of units per century, where the shortest phase, Bayal, lasted 100 years) that were generated in an experimental application of the technique to the Seibal counts of units appear much too low to be real (Tourtellot 1982:Table 47, Figure 136). If we assume one nuclear family per locus and do not count trace occupations, the standardized counts are approximately equivalent to only 4 people at a time during initial Xe phase colonization, 39 people during the Escoba phase (when the settlement area already contained some 250 ha), or in the range of 216–405 persons during the Late Preclassic. During this period we can project from the excavation of three Very Minor Centers that seven of them were regularly spaced and functioning (thus with only 31–58 persons to sustain each), not to mention the big civic architecture in the contemporaneous Group A center.

The crucial problem in trying to standardize comparisons between phases of varied durations, however, is the postulates that (1) longer phases subsume the operation of a greater number of relatively fixed-length cycles of such short-term processes as family fission and replacement, building construction and decay, or locus occupation and abandonment than do shorter phases (which they certainly must), and, most importantly, that (2) these processes commonly produce cycles of residential stability/mobility which are both enshrined in the built environment and substantially coincident with the minimum phase length, or any other fixed temporal yardstick, in the archaeological sequence at a settlement. The latter postulate is highly debatable.

Time-weighting (reducing) the counts of, for example, Preclassic loci derived from long phases by applying temporal yardsticks may be better than the uncorrected treatment only if one is willing to assume that *living sites (not just families) were regularly abandoned and replaced* over the shorter, intraphase, term implied by the yardstick. Counterarguments have been presented above in support of the hypothesis that Preclassic settlement loci at Seibal were in fact largely permanent and contemporaneous and therefore that the numbers of loci do not need to be reduced merely because of the length of the archaeologically defined phases during which they were occupied. Thus one consideration before applying time standardization is that the sequence to which it will be applied must first be examined for evidences that support discontinuity against permanence (cf. Fry, this volume).

Two other assumptions of time-weighting by the use of fixed temporal yardsticks need to be made explicit because, once stated, they are seen, I believe, to be questionable if not unrealistic, and surely in need of verification. One assumption is that each locus of occupation had a fixed life span. In other words, the duration of occupation for any one locus is assumed to be equivalent, for example, only to the length of the shortest phase in a sequence (100 years for Bayal), and this duration is then used as the divisor for the standardization of counts from all other longer phases. Is the approximately 100 years of the short Bayal phase at Seibal itself too long for a fixed use-life span? Or what if one phase in a long sequence could be pinned down to just 10 years? Indeed, the technique is extremely sensitive to the possible existence of functional or temporal facets within phases—Late Cantutse, for example (cf. P. Thomas's quandary at Becan, 1981:111). Also, it makes a difference if one is counting loci (places with possible transgenerational continuity) versus individual perishable dwellings, which plausibly had relatively shorter use-lives or occupation spans. Handling the presence of permanent, stone-built

dwellings, as at Tikal (Culbert et al, this volume), is an additional compli-
cation virtually absent from Seibal.

The second hidden assumption is that each locus of occupation had no
more than a single occupation per phase, no matter how long the phase.
This assumption may be a reasonable one for application of time standardization to population estimates at Becan, where there is little evidence
of successive construction within the Late Preclassic Pakluum phase (P.
Thomas 1981:110). It is manifestly false at Seibal, where some loci, as mentioned, exhibit at least three cycles of what I see as continuous construc-
tion/occupation during the single Early Cantutse phase and where
Preclassic refuse layers may well have accumulated at about the same rate
as Classic ones. (This rate was perhaps 10 cm/century, based on the Preclassic deposits often 1–2 m thick accumulated over some 1200 years versus the Late and Terminal Classic refuse/wash deposits typically 30–40 cm
thick accumulated over some 280 years.) If Preclassic occupation was instead episodic, then the refuse-accumulation rate must have been much
faster then than it was later.

If the assumptions of time standardization were accepted, then the presence of regular occupation/abandonment cycles also should lead its pro-
ponents to propose some factor more or less forcing the ancient Maya
periodically to pull up stakes and relocate, but always within a permanently occupied community—which in consequence must have seen
some interesting disputes over land tenure!

Furthermore, the application of time standardization handles the evidence for long-term trajectories of population change derived from site
sequences in a manner different from the model of continuous occupation
advocated here. These trajectories imply that the number of loci dated to
a phase could be closer to the *maximum* number of places contemporaneously occupied (with a small discount for temporarily disoccupied
units). During trajectories of population growth one would expect the
maximum number of loci occupied to occur toward the end of each constituent phase, whereas during trajectories of decline one would expect
the maximum number to occur early in the constituent phases (D. Rice
1978).

The underlying point is that population change is a dynamic process
that transcends the statics of archaeological record and the unfortunate
and unrealistic, if perhaps unavoidable, synchronistic paradigm that treats
our data only in stolid blocks of form and time often a century or more in
duration (Plog 1973; Schacht 1984). In the larger view the sole virtue of
the hypotheses of either continuous or episodic occupation is that they
are "objective" and easily reproducible, in contrast to the controversy that
must necessarily engulf any use of variable inputs of occupation spans,
mobility, and family sizes which are thought to model more realistically
the internal demographic changes that express different stages within de-

mographic growth curves or episodes of heavy immigration (Schacht 1980; for an example see Tourtellot 1982:1074–75, 1086–87).

CONCLUSIONS

By a somewhat intricate series of calculations, based on several approximations to relevant variables, we have arrived at a series of population estimates. These estimates purport to describe the trajectory of ancient population at Seibal during the slow growth of the Preclassic Period community, followed after an apparent hiatus by the explosive growth of the Late and Terminal Classic community over a much briefer span of time.

Many implications for population history, subsistence technologies, and sociopolitical organization can be drawn for additional testing, based on the apparently huge Preclassic peak, the slow but exponential internal (?) growth of the Preclassic community, the profound Early Classic nadir, the explosive migratory (?) growth of the Late Classic community, the similar size of the Middle Preclassic and Postclassic communities, the detailed changes between adjacent phases, the various possible combinations of the Cantutse and of the Late/Terminal materials, and so on. Some of these implications have been explored elsewhere (Tourtellot 1988b) in the context of more detailed analyses of the archaeological types, areas, distributions, and densities than can be presented here.

For our consideration I have also raised several points of method. These include the unreliability of counts of mapped structures alone, the need for excavation to check on the counts as well as their periodization or functional discrimination, the greater accuracy found in mapping and using places of occupation instead of individual structures, the error in combining "mounds" into a single count when some are individual structures and others are groups, the potential exaggeration involved in counting isolated single structures as dwellings, the necessity of identifying the architectural modes of accommodation to population growth, the problem of dual residence for large-scale mapping projects, and the problematical assumptions involved in standardizing counts for the varying durations of different phases.

There is no reason to expect that the population histories of different settlements were identical, considering variations in their size, hierarchical level, economy, and location as well as in our definitions of site areas and calculations. The bringing together of population estimates for Seibal and the other places in this volume will indeed permit a more refined analysis of their implications singly and conjointly. But first the presentation of the calculations involved will, it is hoped, expose, and contribute to resolving, the fundamental problems we face with sampling, periodization, standardization, and population models which color, if not seriously bias, our estimates.

ACKNOWLEGMENTS

I gratefully acknowledge the great assistance rendered me along the way by Gordon R. Willey, Jeremy A. Sabloff, and the late A. Ledyard Smith, and by the other staff and workers of the Seibal Project. Fieldwork and analysis were supported by the National Science Foundation and the J. G. Owens Fund of Harvard University. The fieldwork was conducted under permit issued by the Instituto de Antropología e Historia, Guatemala. Final revisions to this chapter, made while I was a Fellow at Dumbarton Oaks, were greatly sharpened by correspondence with the editors, although any shortcomings belong to me and not the good people acknowledged here.

NOTES

1. Raw counts of excavated units and platforms at Seibal contain one known bias and should never be used without correcting it: the probabilities of selection (sampling fractions) varied by unit class from 0.156 to 1.000. To eliminate this bias due to disproportional sampling, raw counts of excavated units or structures were multiplied by the reciprocals of their individual probabilities of selection (i.e., from 6.4 to 1.0). Summing the results by class, phase, etc., produces corrected frequencies, for the calculation of proportions and averages, which also serve as our best estimates of the absolute total numbers for each class within the designated 1.62 km².

2. For summary of the assignments made see Tourtellot (1988b). The detailed analyses and arguments are preserved in a typescript on file at the Peabody Museum of Harvard University. The lots were sent to the Museo Nacional (IDAEH) in Guatemala City.

3. Although units rather than structures are being used, for reasons already stated, note that the two rates are equivalent because the three-times-higher disoccupation rate for dwellings is approximately convertible into the lower rate for units (since units average nearly three dwellings apiece). Accordingly, no adjustment will be made to the figure of 2.72 contemporaneous dwellings/unit.

Table 4.1 Seibal Population Factors

Phase	Dates	Raw Count of Units	Weighted Count of Units	Domestic Proportion	Estimated Domestic Units
Postclassic	A.D. 930–	7	18.7	1.00	18.7
Bayal	830–930	48	130.1	.95	123.6
[Late/Terminal Classic		26	69.7	1.00	69.7]
[Late/Terminal Classic + Tepejilote		53	130.9	.90	117.8]
Tepejilote Hiatus	650–830	27	61.2	.79	48.3
Junco	270–500	23	51.8?	.88	45.6
Late Cantutse	0–270	12	42.1	1.00	42.1
[Early + Late Cantutse		58	153.5	1.00	153.5]
Early Cantutse	300–0 B.C.	50	125.8	1.00	125.8
Escoba	600–300	21	42.8	1.00	42.8
Real Xe	900–300	9	21.2	1.00	21.2

Table 4.2 Population Estimates for Seibal (15.25-km² Sampled Area)

Phase	Central Units			Peripheral Units		Chronological Proportion	Occupancy Rate	Domestic Units/Phase	Persons/ Unit	Population
	A.1	A.1a	B	A.2	A.2a	C.2	C.3		D	
Postclassic	191	1	0?	707	1?	0.122	0.9	98.6	11.9	1,173?
Bayal	191	1	20.2	707	1	0.806	0.9	636.8	11.9	7,577
[Late/Terminal Classic	191	1	0	707	1	0.454	0.9	366.9	11.9	4,366]
[Late/Terminal Classic + Tepejilote	191	1	16.5	707	1	0.769	0.9	610.1	11.9	7,260]
Tepejilote Hiatus	191	1	16.5	707	1	0.315	0.9	249.9	11.9	2,974
Junco	191	0.143	6.4	707	0.143	0.296	0.9	32.5	11.9	387
Late Cantutse	191	1	0	707	1?	0.274	0.9	221.4	11.9	2,635?
[Early + Late Cantutse	191	1	0	707	1	1.000	0.9	808.2	11.9	9,618]
Early Cantutse	191	0.842	0	707	0.255	0.820	0.9	251.7	11.9	2,995
Escoba	191	0.421	0	707	0.127	0.279	0.9	42.7	11.9	508
Real	191	0.263	0	707	0	0.133	0.9	6.2	11.9	74

5 /

The Population of Tikal, Guatemala

T. Patrick Culbert,

Laura J. Kosakowsky,

Robert E. Fry, *and*

William A. Haviland

The Tikal Project, conducted by the University of Pennsylvania between 1956 and 1970, provided an unusual amount of data relevant to the question of prehistoric population. The results from Tikal, in fact, were the precipitating factor in the general acceptance by archaeologists of considerably higher population densities in the southern Maya lowlands than had been suspected earlier.

One of the first tasks undertaken by the Tikal Project (Coe and Haviland 1982:23–24) was the preparation of a map of a 16-km² zone centered on the Great Plaza (Carr and Hazard 1961). Later, a map made by the Tikal Sustaining Area Project of survey strips extending 10 km beyond the central map added an additional 20 km² that helped define central and peripheral Tikal and established site boundaries. (D. Puleston 1983:24–25, Figures 20–22). These maps provided information on structure density in Tikal and the surrounding rural area. Small-structure excavations under the direction of Haviland (1965, 1969, 1970, 1985, 1988, 1989) confirmed the residential nature of most such structures and gave evidence of development and change in domestic groups. Work in the more elaborate Group 7F-1 (Haviland 1981) confirmed the residential nature of at least some large-range structures, lending support to Harrison's (1970, 1986) conclusions about residence in the Central Acropolis. Testing of small-structure groups in the outlying survey strips by Fry (1969) provided a statistically controlled base lacking in the more disparate testing within the 16-km² central mapped area. Finally, a multitude of test pits and excavation programs in all parts of the site provided additional data relevant to population from structures of all sizes.

Reconstructions drawn from various segments of these data have already been presented in a number of sources (Culbert 1973, 1977; Haviland 1965, 1969, 1970, 1972a, b, 1985; D. Puleston 1974). This publication, however, is the first to include data from all operations of the Tikal Project. The authors have not achieved unanimity about all the factors involved in estimating population, but we will outline the divergences that remain in our interpretations.

METHODOLOGY

Units of Analysis

The individual structure was used as the unit of analysis for data from central Tikal, although we recognize that final structures often provide little information about the location and number of earlier structures in a group. The amount of excavation for individual structures varied from a single test pit to complete excavation. All lots in or associated with each structure, including those from plazas and chultunes were summed to give a demographic profile. Even if no architectural remains could be associated with a particular time period (a common occurrence for earlier periods), the presence of even a few sherds was considered to constitute occupation for the period involved.

The procedures used by Fry in the 10-km survey strips to the north and south differed from those used in central Tikal. The sampling unit was the patio group rather than the individual structure. Each survey strip was divided into three sampling universes based on distance from central Tikal, and one-third of the patio groups within each of the sampling universes was then selected randomly. Test pits were placed in midden deposits outside of structures, with the location for each pit chosen on the basis of posthole tests for sherd quantity (Fry 1972).

Dating

The dates of occupation for each unit were based on ceramic analyses performed by Culbert for central Tikal and by Fry for the sustaining area (Table 5.1). Two levels of precision were possible: dating by period (e.g.,

Late Preclassic, Early Classic, etc.) and dating by ceramic complex. Distinctions between periods involved abundant and easily recognized ceramic markers and could be achieved for almost any sample. Such dating, however, lacked the precision desirable for our study. We therefore base our analysis on a division by ceramic complex, a procedure that necessitated apportioning between complexes those samples for which only period dating was possible. This was done in a proportion determined by the relative frequency of the complexes in samples where dating by complex was possible. One-third of the Late Classic samples and one-half of the Preclassic samples had only period dates. The Early Classic and Terminal Classic periods contained only a single complex each, so that period and complex identification were identical.

Potential Sources of Error

Complete excavation of residential groups can give very accurate sequences of construction and occupation (Haviland 1981, 1985, 1989). Because budgetary constraints prohibit full excavation of enough groups to provide population estimates for a large site, however, archaeologists must turn to the less precise data from test-pitting. A review of the Tikal data leads us to conclude that a full sequence of all construction events cannot be reliably reconstructed from test pits. Consequently, we have chosen to accept the presence of even small quantities of ceramics as indicating occupation at a particular locus. This section will be concerned with the potential errors inherent in this procedure. The data from a sizable sample of small structures excavated in detail (Haviland 1981, 1985, 1989) aids us in evaluating the likely severity of the various kinds of error. A consideration of errors cannot be divorced from archaeological context. Whether samples were obtained from excavation in structure fill or from outside structure walls and whether they pertain to the last period of occupation in a group or to an earlier one are questions that affect the expectable errors.

Material in structure fill was almost invariably moved by the Maya, so that its original location is unknown. Both artifactual (sherds of a single vessel from different locations) and stratigraphic data from Tikal strongly indicate that the fill of small structures was usually obtained from within the local patio group rather than from more distant locations. Such was not necessarily the case for large structures, for which the amount of fill needed and the size of labor forces involved made transportation of fill from some distance more likely. Mayanists frequently refer to tests outside of platform walls as tests in "midden," a very loose use of the term because there is usually little guarantee that the material actually represents in situ refuse. Careful excavation reveals that slumped fill, occupation refuse, and postabandonment debris all occur in such locations, often in very compli-cated mixtures (Haviland 1985, 1989). In addition, some periods of occu-pation refuse may have been removed for use elsewhere. The position of samples in relation to structures is important, but it is not a simple di-chotomy of fill versus midden.

There is a strong contrast between the contexts of archaeological re-mains of the final period of a group's occupation and those of earlier periods. Debris from the final occupation is usually abundant and much of it may represent deposits still in situ. Architecture from the final occu-pation is easier to investigate than that of earlier periods. Remains from earlier periods have been subjected to all the disruptive processes asso-ciated with continuing construction and occupation: movement, removal, and mixing of refuse; and reuse, rebuilding, and destruction of earlier construction levels. Final periods of occupation are subject to different kinds of error in assessing population than earlier periods.

FINAL OCCUPATION.

Samples from structure fill and from outside structure walls may err in different ways in assessing late population of a group. Fill samples may lack ceramics from a final period of occupation. In Haviland's (1985, 1989) sample of thoroughly excavated small structures, there are several cases in which the latest sherd in fill is earlier than the date of last construction (as determined from burials or stratigraphy). Even more numerous are instances in which occupation of a structure continued into a ceramic interval later than the last construction. Such events would represent a serious problem if analysis were confined to fill samples alone or if oc-cupation were judged solely on the basis of construction levels. If, how-ever, surface levels above construction are included and even small quantities of sherds accepted as indicative of occupation (the procedures used in our analysis), the possibility that a final period of occupation would be totally unrepresented is remote. We conclude, therefore, that there is little danger that the last period of occupation is underestimated in our study.

Overestimation of the final period of occupation is a serious potential problem for complexes not sealed by construction. At a time after con-struction in a group had ceased but while some structures were still oc-cupied, refuse would accumulate because it was no longer being reused as fill for new construction. The refuse might be dumped around struc-tures that had already been abandoned, as Haviland's data (e.g., 1985:59–61) indicate sometimes happened. The process of late dumping around an abandoned structure is unlikely to be detected in test pits, and a spu-rious late period of occupation could be attributed to such a structure. Such errors would usually affect the Imix complex, the time of final oc-cupation of most small-structure groups. We have no way of estimating how many Imix occupations derived from test-pit data may be spurious. But in Haviland's sample of small structures for which the final date of occupation is secure, 90% of the structures had Imix complex occupations, a figure so high that it allows little room for overestimation to be a serious factor in the test-pit sample.

EARLY OCCUPATION.

The Maya practice of demolishing old structures and moving material from one location to another introduces a considerable potential for error in estimating early populations. Two slightly variant processes might result in *overestimation* of early-period occupation. One would be the deliberate importation of fill in beginning a new structure. If, for example, a structure was begun at a new location in Imix times and the fill imported contained some Ik ceramics, our procedures would attribute a false Ik occupation to the locus. It was common in the excavation of small structures at Tikal to encounter fill samples with sherds that predated any securely identifiable construction. We have no way of knowing how many such cases involved imported fill, but it is comforting that such early fill material was often associated with very fragmentary walls or floors that might have been the remains of early in situ construction. Nevertheless, this is probably the least controlled of our possible sources of error.

A second process that could result in overestimation of early occupation in either fill or midden samples would be the widespread dispersal of early material through a variety of natural and cultural events. What had originally been a single locus of early occupation within a group might then appear in association with several later structures and be counted as multiple cases of occupation. Data from fully excavated small-structure groups at Tikal, however, suggest that such wide dispersion was not a typical process. The excavations show that, when groups had early loci of occupation, the early material was usually found concentrated in one or a few deposits rather than spread over a large area.

Test pits can also *underestimate* early periods of occupation. When a small early locus is buried under larger later construction, test pits can easily miss the early levels. In addition, it is possible that occupation debris from an early period was sometimes so effectively removed by the Maya that nothing of it remains (see Haviland [1985:19–20] for a case in point). Although one cannot eliminate the danger of underestimating early population, our procedure of accepting even small amounts of sherds as indicative of occupation guards somewhat against underestimation. To test for evidence of underestimation of early periods in test-pitting operations, we compared a sample of 157 locations yielding 10 or fewer excavation lots against 67 structures that provided more than 10 lots. In general, structures with few excavation lots would have been tested with only a single test pit, whereas those with a greater number would have been subject to more thorough excavation. If we assume that the demographic histories of the two samples were the same, differences between the two could be the result of the errors just discussed. In the sample of structures with 10 or fewer lots, 94% showed Late Classic occupation, 63% showed Early Classic, and 31% had Preclassic remains. Comparable figures for the more completely excavated samples are 100% with Late Classic occupation, 69% with Early Classic, and 40% with Preclassic. These data suggest that limited testing misses a fraction of the occupations of any time level, with a slightly greater chance of missing Preclassic than Classic occupation. The differences are not very great, however, and are certainly no greater than several other kinds of imprecision inherent in making population estimates from anything other than complete excavation.

Our discussion has been directed primarily to the possibility of error in estimating population through test-pitting of small structures. The potential problems, especially in the interpretation of fill samples, are even greater when large structures are involved. In fact, however, so few of the large structures in the Tikal sample were examined by the use of limited test-pitting operations that the effect on our population estimates would not be very large even if error rates were significantly higher.

The foregoing comments have been intended to indicate the serious sources of error inherent in estimating population on the basis of ceramics recovered from limited test-pitting. Haviland's (1985, 1989) data from much more detailed excavation of small structures demonstrate that almost all the imaginable errors do, in fact, occur and give some indication of their frequency. None of the possible errors occurs in the majority of cases, and some kinds of error, if they occur randomly, would cancel out overestimations by underestimations. It would be foolish to claim that our procedures of estimating population have great precision, but changes through time are often so drastic that we are confident that at least the general outline of population change is reliable.

The Contemporary Issue

A final methodological question that must be discussed is contemporaneity. Population estimates cannot be made without an assumption about contemporaneity, and the assumption chosen has a drastic effect on the results. The heart of the issue is the question of how long an individual residential location (here equated with the site of a single house structure) was occupied. If the period of occupation was short, adjustments must be made in calculating both absolute and relative population. If, for example, a location was used for only 25 years and then abandoned, a single family would leave evidence of occupation in four locations within a 100-year interval, 12 locations within 300 years, and so on. In calculating absolute population for a ceramic interval that lasted 100 years, the counts of locations would have to be divided by four to correct for the multiple locations occupied by each family during the interval. To deal with relative populations and compare the figures for a ceramic phase of 100 years with those from another 300 years, the counts for the longer phase would have to be divided by three to make the counts comparable. Mayanists disagree profoundly about how long locations were occupied and, consequently, about what, if any, adjustments must be made. Individual positions fall between two extremes that we will consider in the next section.

MODELS OF STRUCTURE USE

To be precise about terms, the unit of occupation considered here is the individual residential location. Archaeologically, what we identify is a structure platform or just ceramics assumed to indicate occupation. By continuous occupation of a location, we mean occupation with no long gaps (no longer than 10 years). If several structures were built sequently at the same location, even if there were radical change in size, form, or axis, the structures are considered a continuous occupation if there were no such gaps. Locations abandoned for more than 10 years and then reoccupied are considered to represent separate occupations.

One polar view of this process, the *continuous occupation model*, posits that once a location has been occupied it will be used without interruption until a period of major population decline or total site abandonment. Thus, in a phase with increasing population, the number of locations (structures) occupied will accumulate, and at the end of the phase, all of the structures built during that or earlier phases will be simultaneously occupied. Calculating the population at the end of the phase involves no more than multiplying the count of residences by a people/structure figure. Comparing the populations at the ends of two different phases can be done by simply comparing counts regardless of phase length.

The other polar extreme, the *cyclical abandonment model*, assumes that locations had finite periods of occupation, even during periods of population increase. At no point during a phase would all locations be occupied simultaneously, because by the end of a phase some of the locations occupied at the beginning would already have been abandoned. Calculating population at any point in time involves adjustments for phase length, average period of structure use, and the frequency with which locations were reoccupied. The comparison of population between two phases of different length would be affected because more abandonments would occur during a longer phase.

The models differ drastically enough so that they should be differentiable in the archaeological data. At Tikal, where there was a steady growth in population from the Middle Preclassic through the Late Classic, all structures should have been occupied during the Imix complex population peak if the continuous use model were correct. If locations were abandoned after short intervals, on the other hand, the majority should have been abandoned (or abandoned and reoccupied) by that time. Not surprisingly, the Tikal data do not fit either extreme. In the sample of 218 small structures tested (both mapped and "invisible"), 4 showed no occupation after a period of Preclassic use, 8 were abandoned after the Manik phase, and 24 after Ik. In addition, 20 tested structures show a gap in occupation of at least one ceramic interval, suggesting lengthy abandonment and reoccupation. Haviland cautions that some of these cases may be the result of removal of deposits from structures that were, indeed, occupied during intervals of seeming abandonment. Nevertheless, abandonment certainly occurred at Tikal, but it was not the predominant factor that would be expected if use-life of platforms had been very short.

We are not agreed among ourselves about the need for or amount of a contemporaneity adjustment with the Tikal data. Culbert and Kosakowsky, who earlier (1985) suggested abandonment after fewer than 100 years, now believe a 150-year average use-life more likely and would adjust accordingly. Fry, for his test pits, distinguishes on the amount of artifacts between structures occupied for brief periods, for which he uses a 100-year adjustment, and others occupied much longer, for which he makes no adjustment. Haviland, although his small-structure excavations demonstrate frequent rebuilding, argues that rebuildings followed demolition so rapidly that what we call abandonments did not occur. The example of Group 2G-1 (Haviland 1988) demonstrates this sort of rapid modification; archaeologically, the lack of sterile layers, incorporation of old architecture into new construction, and avoidance of old burials (whose locations were evidently remembered) when houses were rebuilt all imply the absence of significant time gaps between constructions. In no case is a dwelling, once truly abandoned, known to have been reoccupied. Furthermore, if others in the same group continued in use, then the abandoned one was normally at least partially razed and burned, either beneath new construction (such as a plaza) or by trash discarded from some nearby building. Hence, rarely would abandoned houses be visible to confound counts of others still being lived in. Given our disagreement, we present the Tikal data in two formats: one without contemporaneity adjustment and one based on an average 150-year use of each location. Fry's method of calculation is used in his chapter in this volume.

The contemporaneity issue is a strong reminder that the calculation of population is a complicated procedure depending on variables that are very poorly controlled. In addition, we must anticipate that such variables as length of platform use might vary with size of structures, over time, from central to peripheral areas of a single site, and from one site or region to another. Pyburn's date from Nohmul (1988) show enormous variability in features such as nonplatform occupations over time. Fry (1969) and Haviland (1989) have both suggested that population in rural areas near Tikal may have been more mobile (i.e., quicker to abandon platforms) than population near the site center.

The Small-Structure Set

In the analysis we divided our sample into three sets based on size of structure as judged from the site map. Since the size of Tikal structures covers a continuous range with no gaps, the use of a threefold division was arbitrary. We tried to be strict about assigning structures to the small-structure category, so that the sample would include only what most Mayanists would define as small structures or "house mounds." We begin our discussion with small structures, the basis of most lowland population estimates. There were 218 small structures in the central 16-km² sample and 93 in the sustaining area testing program.

Small-Structure Results

Tables 5.1 and 5.2 present the counts of structures by ceramic complex. The cases reported for each complex already include the apportionment into complexes of those samples that could be dated only by period. Table 5.1 presents complex counts without adjustment; that is, it reflects the continuous occupation model that assumes all structures dated to a complex were occupied simultaneously at the end (or population peak) of the complex. Table 5.2 adjusts counts for those complexes that exceed in length the 150-year average occupation span accepted in this study for use with the cyclical abandonment model. The final column in each table presents relative population, a measure derived by setting structure counts for the most heavily populated complex equal to 100% and calculating other complex counts as a percentage of this total.

Although the use of a contemporaneity adjustment makes a significant difference for some time intervals, the general curve of population is very similar for both the central area and Fry's sustaining area sample. Eb complex population was very low. The Tzec complex was both more common and more widespread in the central area but was not encountered in the sustaining area sample. The Late Preclassic was a time of population growth but never to figures that much exceeded 20% of the eventual maximum. In central Tikal there seems to have been relative stability in population through the three Late Preclassic complexes. Only the Cauac complex was represented in the sustaining area sample, but the absence of the other two complexes may be a result of difficulty in identifying them ceramically in small samples.

The Early Classic Manik complex was marked by continued population growth but was the time interval most affected by a contemporaneity adjustment. In unadjusted figures, Manik population was high—78% of the maximum in the central 16 km² and the period of peak population in Fry's outlying tests. If adjusted for contemporaneity, the figures are much lower—33% and 50% of maximum for the two areas, respectively. Early Classic estimates are further complicated by Bronson's (1968) data from tests in areas of Tikal without visible structures. By far the largest number of structures discovered in these areas dated to the Early Classic. In addition, Manik complex sherds were ubiquitous in Bronson's tests in comparison with those of the Preclassic and Late Classic, which tended to be clustered in certain areas rather than dispersed. If the wide scatter of Early Classic sherds was the result of occupation of structures that leave little archaeological evidence, the total number of Early Classic occupation loci would have been raised very substantially. On the other hand, such ephemeral structures without platforms might have been rapidly abandoned and need a high contemporaneity adjustment. We must admit that our estimate of Early Classic population at Tikal is unusually dependent on factors that are poorly controlled.

The Late Classic Ik and Imix complexes saw very high population. If one accepts a contemporaneity adjustment for the Manik complex, the Ik and Imix were a time of rapid population expansion to a maximum. Which of the complexes was of highest frequency depends on area and contemporaneity adjustment, but the differences between the two are too small to have any significant. The Terminal Classic Eznab complex was a time of population collapse in small structures in all areas of the site, with a population loss in excess of 80%. Postclassic remains are represented only in tiny amounts.

Medium- and Large-Structure Results

For larger structures, we classified all pyramidal structures as "ceremonial" and consider here only range and other structures that were potentially residential. The classification is based on the size and form of final structures, and we recognize that there is no guarantee that earlier buildings at the same loci were of the same size and use. For medium and large structures, we are in agreement that no contemporaneity adjustment is necessary. The results are presented in Table 5.3

Medium-size residential structures show a pattern of occupation very similar to that for small structures. Manik occupation in medium structures is slightly higher, even if contemporaneity adjustments are not made for the small-structure data. Eznab figures are also higher for medium structures, probably as a result of the use of some vaulted buildings for Eznab occupation. The figures for large residential structures are different. There is an unexplained high frequency in the Cauac complex compared to the frequency for smaller structures, and the peak number of cases was reached in the Manik complex (although by only a small margin over the Late Classic periods). There was substantial occupation of large residential structures in Eznab times, reflecting the already well-known pattern of Terminal Classic use of vaulted range structures for occupation (Culbert 1973).

ABSOLUTE POPULATION

Although Haviland (1965, 1969, 1972a) has previously calculated absolute population figures for Tikal, the figures need updating in light of more precise estimates now possible. The calculations here are based on counts of structures/km² derived from the 16-km² map of Carr and Hazard (1961) and the maps of outlying survey strips done by the Tikal Sustaining Area Project (D. Puleston 1983). Given figures for structures/km², the first step in calculating absolute population at its peak during the Imix complex is to correct for mapped structures that were not in use in Imix times. We are not entirely agreed on the magnitude for this correction. Haviland (1989) believes that 99% of mapped structures had Imix occupation. Culbert argues for a smaller figure. Of the total sample of tested small structures (Table 5.2), 19% had no Imix ceramics. This is too high a figure to use for a correction, however. Some of the cases without Imix ceramics were hidden structures that do not appear on the site map. Others were chultun samples, where the lack of a ceramic interval may mean that the chultun was covered at the time rather than that there was no occupation at a neighboring structure. Given these factors, Culbert posits that 10% of mapped structures lacked Imix occupation. We will use a compromise figure of 5% as the number of mapped structures that lacked Imix occupation.

A second adjustment is necessary to correct for mapped structures that were not residential. Thanks to Haviland's small-structure excavations, we have a reliable estimate for nonresidential structures. In his excavated sample Haviland (1965:19) found that 16.5% of the structures served other than residential uses. Although the sample was located entirely within central Tikal, we extend it to outlying areas since it is likely that such structures as kitchens and family shrines were a part of domestic life everywhere.

Finally, we must consider how many residences have left no surface indications obvious enough to be included as mounds on the Tikal map site. Tests of five areas of "vacant terrain"—areas without mapped structures—were done by Bronson in 1966 (Bronson 1968). The sample areas covered a total of 2 ha, of which about 0.1% was actually excavated. A variety of evident residential features was discovered, including low stone-walled platforms and floors laid directly on the ground surface.

Of concern here is how many unmapped residences existed in Imix times, the period for which we make absolute population estimates. In discussing Late Classic population, Bronson (1968:107–9) suggests three possible classes of unmapped structures: (1) platformless structures built directly on the ground; (2) low platforms missed or not considered structures by mappers in "vacant terrain"; and (3) similar low platforms within the confines of mapped groups. Within the central 9 km² of the Tikal map, he estimates that there might be 300 platformless structures, 650 structures in vacant terrain, and 600 structures hidden within mapped groups. These estimates would almost double the number of structures in the central 9 km², although Bronson suggests an increase of 50% might be more realistic.

Given recent evidence for unmapped ("invisible") structures at Santa Rita (D. Chase, this volume), Nohmul (Pyburn, this volume), and Pull-trouser Swamp, (Harrison, personal communication 1988), Bronson's suggestions deserve serious consideration. Haviland's (1985, 1989) data from excavated small-structure groups, however, suggest that Bronson's estimate of an additional 30% unmapped structures within mapped groups is far too high. Haviland's research showed that 4 mounds mapped as "structures" within tested groups were natural features, and 5 structures were found that did not appear on the map (a net gain of 1 structure). Since 118 structures were tested, an almost insignificant increase of 0.8% is indicated. Furthermore, none of the unmapped structures found was of Imix date, so there would be no addition to the figures used for absolute population estimates. Additional vacant-terrain investigations undertaken by Haviland, Puleston, Jones, and Chowning showed that, although some indication of unmapped structures was encountered with great frequency, almost none of the structures was of Late Classic date.

The fact that unmapped residential features (both "visible" and "hidden") occur with some frequence at Tikal is undeniable, but estimating their number remains very difficult. Bronson's test areas were very small, and the scope of a project to obtain a significant sample of vacant terrain is staggering. In addition, there is evidence that the number of unmapped structures may vary significantly from one part of the site to another. For example, an area south of Temple 4 which is devoid of mapped structures seems to have been a location in which a whole residential neighborhood was removed to provide fill for the temple construction. Finally, some quite visible structures were simply missed during the mapping process.

Seven such structures were discovered in the central 9-km² map and more (for which we make an adjustment below) in the more rapidly mapped outer 7 km². Admitting the lack of any firm basis for a quantitative estimate of unmapped structures for the Imix complex, we would guess that an addition between 5% and 25% of mapped structures seems most sensible. We will use an addition of 10% in the calculations of population that follow, although Haviland considers this adjustment too large.

Another adjustment is necessary to allow for the fact that at any given moment some platforms in a community must have been temporarily unoccupied, as, for example, when an old house had become unusable and nobody had gotten around to building a new one. That disoccupation is a universal phenomenon is evident from modern data, but there is no way of determining its magnitude at a prehistoric site. We will adopt an arbitrary reduction of 10%, a figure used by other participants in this volume who deal with the issue.

To adjust the raw counts of mounds, therefore, we will add 10% to account for various kinds of hidden structures and make deductions of 5% for non-Imix structures, 16.5% for nonresidential platforms, and 10% for disoccupation. These adjustments, totaling a reduction of 21.5%, will be applied to mound counts from the site map to reach an estimated number of residences occupied at the point of maximum population during Imix times. This figure will be multiplied by five, the figure we accept for number of individuals per family (Haviland 1972a) to produce absolute population estimates.

The Boundaries of Tikal

Tikal is one of the few lowland Maya sites for which we can speak of site limits determined by archaeological evidence (D. Puleston 1983). The four radial survey strips show that structure density drops off sharply a few km from the site center. On the east and west the dropoff correlates with the start of large bajos, but the drop in density to north and south occurs in areas where high ground was still available for habitation. To the north the number of structures declines 4.6 km from the center, at the location of the earthworks (D. Puleston 1983), which appear to be a border-marking mechanism. On the south, density drops off between 6 and 7 km from the center, about where a second earthworks may have been (D. Puleston 1983). An area of 120 km² is defined by the combination of lower-structure density, earthworks, and bajo (map 5.1). This is what we consider the site of Tikal.

Population Reconstruction

In reconstructing the absolute population for Imix phase Tikal, we will work outward from the site center. The central 9 km² of the Carr and Hazard (1961) map was done with plane table and alidade. Although some errors have been discovered in the years since the map was completed, they do not suggest any great inaccuracy in the total count of mounds. The 9km² contain 235 structures/km². (This figure and those that follow give mound density in terms of total territory, including bajo. Densities in the higher terrain where most structures were located were greater.) The surrounding 7 km² of the Carr and Hazard map was done by pacing and rapid reconnaissance. Remapping of some of this area by the Sustaining Area Project indicates that about 25% of the mounds were missed in the original reconnaissance. We consequently use a figure of 181 structures/km² for the outer 7 km² of the site map rather than the 145 structures/km² suggested by Carr and Hazard(1961). The remaining 104 km² within the boundaries of Tikal include 112 mounds/km², a figure based on the radial survey strips of the Sustaining Area Project (D. Puleston 1983).

Making the deduction of 21.5% explained earlier and multiplying by the figure of five for people/structure, the central 9 km² would have included 8300 inhabitants (922/km²). The next 7 km² would have contained 4975 people (711/km²), and the remaining 104 km² would have added 45,720 people (440/km²), a grand total for Tikal of 58,995 residents. These calculations do not include any allowance for the people who inhabited the large range structures at the site. Pending final analysis by Harrison (1970), we estimate that this would have added several thousand more and conclude that our best estimate for the maximum population of Tikal is 62,000. This estimate will need further revision when final analysis of range structures and some groups of medium size has been completed.

What of the surrounding rural areas that would have been part of the economic and political structure of Tikal? For areas outside the Tikal boundaries, the radial survey strips indicate a density of 39 mounds/km². This figure is probably too low for an overall rural density because the survey strips intersected an atypically large amount of bajo to the west and north. The unrepresentative nature of the 39 structures/km² figure is also suggested by other central Peten surveys, for which rural densities average about 60 structures/km² (Culbert 1988). Rather than introducing an artificial figure, however, we will use 39 structures/km² as a minimal density for rural Tikal.

We will consider first the Tikal rural area, defined as the area closer to Tikal than to any other major site and therefore almost certain to have been part of Tikal's zone of subsistence and political interaction. A very conservative estimate of the rural area includes a circle of 10-km radius centered at Tikal, a distance suggested by Fry's (1974, 1979) study of ceramic production. The circle includes 314 km²; 120 km² within the Tikal boundaries and 194 km² of rural area. At 39 structures/km² (equivalent to 153 people/km²), this area would add an additional 29,696 people to the 62,000 in Tikal itself for a sum of approximately 92,000. If a more liberal rural area with 12-km radius is adopted, the figure would rise to a total close to 120,000.

Finally, we will estimate the population within the area Tikal probably controlled politically. A recent School of American Research seminar (Culbert, ed., 1989) that integrated data from archaeology with that from hieroglyphic inscriptions attested to the serious disagreement over the size of Maya political units. Nevertheless, it is possible to outline a minimal Tikal political realm about which there is good agreement: a realm of 25-km radius (half or less the distance to such possibly independent sites as Naranjo, Xultun, and El Peru). Such a realm would include an area of 1963 km². Since this area includes other surveyed areas (Ford, 1986; Rice and Rice, this volume) with considerably higher structure densities than the low 39/km² for rural Tikal, we will use a structure density of 50 mounds (196 people)/km² in calculating the population. Using the figures for Tikal and its rural area already presented and adding estimates for the remainder of the 1963 km² realm indicates a minimal Tikal state with a population in excess of 425,000. That the Maya did not have a scattered, low-density population is now clear, but the magnitude of population does not strike home until figures are calculated for large areas such as the Tikal state.

CONCLUSIONS

There are many advantages to having data accumulated over 15 years of survey and excavation. The Tikal data provide unusually good control of some of the variables that affect population reconstruction, but they also show that there are many sources of error that still cannot be controlled. Nevertheless, the general magnitude of both relative and absolute population at Tikal and its surrounding area is clear. The site showed an overall growth curve from the first occupation in the Middle Preclassic through the Late Classic Imix phase. The growth trend was interrupted by periods of stability in the Late Preclassic and again in the Late Classic. The Terminal Classic was a period of drastic decline in both Tikal and the surrounding rural area, and the Postclassic saw almost no population in the vicinity. At its maximum Tikal had a population in excess of 60,000, and rural population added another 30,000 to the numbers of those who must have been in economic dependence on the site. Tikal was certainly the largest Classic site for which we have population figures and was substantially larger than most other sites discussed in this volume.

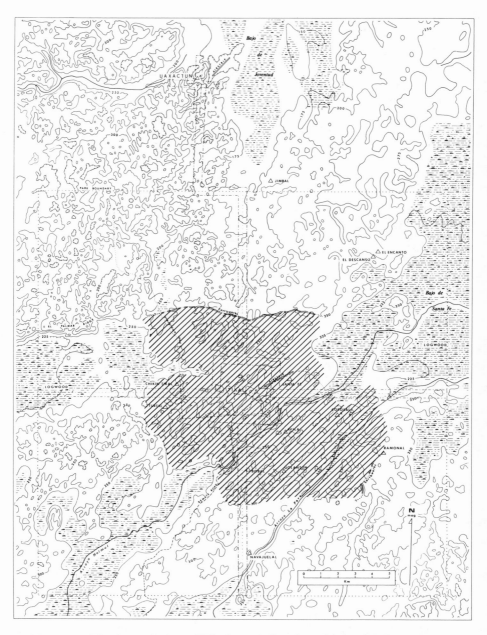

Map 5.1 The boundaries of Tikal, as defined on the basis of structure density and location of earthworks and bajos. Area within diagonal striping constitutes Tikal. Unevenly dashed areas are bajos. (From D. Puleston 1983: Figure 20)

Table 5.1 Small-Structure Counts and Relative Population by Ceramic Complex

Period	Complex	Dates	Cases		% of Total Tests		Relative Population (% of Maximum Cases)	
			Central Tikal	Sustaining Area	Central Tikal (N = 218)	Sustaining Area (N = 93)	Central Tikal (N = 176)	Sustaining Area (N = 80)
Postclassic	Caban	A.D. 930–1130(?)	8	1	3.7	1.1	4.5	1.2
Terminal Classic	Eznab	A.D. 830–930(?)	25	15	11.5	16.1	14.2	18.8
Late Classic	Imix	A.D. 700–830[a]	176	69	80.7	74.2	100.0	83.8
Late Classic	Ik	A.D. 600–700	167	70	76.6	75.3	94.9	87.5
Early Classic	Manik	A.D. 250–600	138	80	63.3	86.0	78.4	100.0
Late Preclassic	Cimi	A.D. 150–250	33	0	15.1	0.0	18.8	0.0
Late Preclassic	Cauac	100 B.C.–A.D. 150	42	15	19.3	16.1	23.9	18.8
Late Preclassic	Chuen	250–100 B.C.	35	0	16.1	0.0	19.9	0.0
Middle Preclassic	Tzec	500–250 B.C.	7	0	3.2	0.0	4.0	0.0
Middle Preclassic	Eb	750–500 B.C.	0	0	0.0	0.0	0.0	0.0

[a]Haviland (personal communication 1986) and C. Jones (personal communication 1987) prefer a date of A.D. 889 for the end of the Imix complex.

Table 5.2 Relative Population of Small Structures, Adjusted for 150-Year Average Occupation

Complex	Years	Adjustment Factor	Cases		Adjusted Cases		Relative Population	
			Central Tikal	Sustaining Area	Central Tikal	Sustaining Area	Central Tikal (N = 176)	Sustaining Area (N = 70)
Caban	200	15/20	8	1	6	1	3.4	1.4
Eznab	100	1/1	25	15	25	15	14.2	21.4
Imix	130	1/1	176	69	176	69	100.0	98.6
Ik	100	1/1	167	70	167	70	94.9	100.0
Manik	350	15/35	138	80	59	35	33.5	50.0
Cimi	100	1/1	33	0	33	0	18.8	0.0
Cauac	250	15/25	42	15	25	9	14.2	12.9
Chuen	150	1/1	35	0	35	0	19.9	0.0
Tzec	250	15/25	7	0	4	0	2.3	0.0
Eb	250	15/25	0	0	0	0	0.0	0.0

Table 5.3   Medium and Large Residential Structures in Central Tikal

Complex	Cases		% of Total Tests		Relative Population (% of Maximum Cases)	
	Medium	Large	Medium ($N = 72$)	Large ($N = 78$)	Medium ($N = 64$)	Large ($N = 69$)
Caban	0	0	0	0	0	0
Eznab	15	43	20.8	55.1	23.4	62.3
Imix	64	67	88.9	85.9	100.0	97.1
Ik	59	66	81.9	84.6	92.2	95.7
Manik	56	69	77.8	88.5	87.5	100.0
Cimi	10	10	13.9	12.8	15.6	14.5
Cauac	10	28	13.9	35.9	15.6	40.6
Chuen	10	12	13.9	15.4	15.6	17.4
Tzec	0	3	0	3.8	0	4.3
Eb	2	1	2.8	1.3	3.1	1.4

6 /

Population Size and Population Change in the Central Peten Lakes Region, Guatemala

DON S. RICE *and*

PRUDENCE M. RICE

This chapter summarizes settlement data from archaeological surveys of six lake basins in the central part of the Department of El Peten, Guatemala, with speculations on the implications of these data for settlement dynamics and the sizes of Maya populations from the Preclassic through Postclassic periods. Some of these reconstructions have been presented elsewhere, but we wish to update our analyses, review our methods of calculating population, and compare population size and change among the basins.

CENTRAL PETEN LAKES REGION SURVEYS

The data reported here were generated by a research program focused on an east-west "chain" of lakes in Guatemala, an area of karsted and dolomitized limestone overlain by tropical deciduous forest. This region witnessed continued occupation by Maya populations from Middle Preclassic times (beginning ca. 1000 B.C.), through Classic (ca. A.D. 300–900) and Postclassic (ca. A.D. 900–1525) periods, up to Spanish contact in A.D. 1525 and final conquest in 1697.

Between 1972 and 1981 a series of related research endeavors, united under the title "The Central Peten Historical Ecology Project," involved archaeological and ecological studies of the cultural and natural histories of the lake region (Deevey 1978, 1984; Deevey and D. Rice 1980; Deevey et al. 1979, 1980, 1983; D. Rice and P. Rice 1983, 1984a; D. Rice et al. 1985). Archaeological surveys were coordinated with biological and paleolimnological analyses in order to investigate human impact on tropical resources by correlating changing settlement characteristics with the measurable effects of environmental perturbations.

The objective of the archaeological research was to document aboriginal settlement characteristics, landscape modification, and demographic history (here meaning relative settlement/population size and growth characteristics) around six of the central Peten lakes. The surveys took place in the hydrological basins of Lakes Sacnab and Yaxha, Macanche and Salpeten, and Quexil and Petenxil (Map 6.1), the paired lakes lying in conjoined basins or sharing to a degree geological and physiographic characteristics.

RESEARCH DESIGN

The archaeological survey of the lake basins consisted of two facets: systematic mapping of settlement remains and a test-excavation program to provide chronological data for use in the interpretation of settlement patterning. A form of multistage probability sampling was employed for both placement of survey units and selection of structures for test excavation (see D. Rice and P. Rice 1980, 1982a, 1982b for amplified discussions of procedures).

The survey units chosen were transects 500 m wide and minimally 2 km long. The length and number of mapped units per lake varied according to the size of the basin, with the goal being to sample approximately 25% of the directly adjacent biological and geochemical catchment region contributing to the paleolimnological record. The discovery and location of settlement remains within all transect units were achieved by a variant of the pace-and-map technique developed at Tikal (Fry 1969:44). Survey attention was also judgmentally directed toward islands and peninsulas in the lakes, because of the affinity of Postclassic populations for these areas, and toward specific known sites. Seven nontransect areas were mapped and tested: Cante Island (Topoxte), in Lake Yaxha; Cerro Ortiz and adjacent intersite area, Macanche Island, and Muralla de Leon at Lake Macanche; Zacpeten, on the peninsula in Lake Salpeten, and Ixlu, on the isthmus between Lakes Salpeten and Peten-Itza; and the two islands in Lake Quexil (see Map 6.1).

Test excavation involved limited testing of residential and adjunct construction, with the individual mound as the unit in random sampling.

Twenty-five percent of the mound loci on each transect were selected for excavation; structures chosen were sampled by means of 1 x 2m test pits, expanded when necessary. Test pits were placed into structures, rather than around the mounds, since the objective was to date constructions. It was felt that this strategy offered greater probability of recovering datable materials relevant to the history of settlement and mound-rebuilding activities (Willey et al. 1965:155), although perhaps at the cost of recovering more complete artifact complexes obtainable from hidden deposits (Fry 1969:57).

A major goal of the test-pitting program was to provide chronological control in the interpretation of settlement data. Analyses of chronologically significant materials, primarily pottery, were based on sequences established at other sites in the Maya lowlands. In general, it was relatively easy to distinguish broad temporal phases, such as Middle Preclassic, Late Preclassic, Early Classic, Late Classic, and Postclassic, but finer subdivisions occasionally suffered from an insufficient quantity of diagnostics (P. Rice 1979a, 1979b, 1987). Therefore, we rely here on dating by period, and report settlement and population dynamics within a period framework (Figure 6.1).

Estimates of population sizes and densities for the Preclassic through Late Classic trajectory are based on the results of work solely within the transects. Postclassic occupation, which was substantial in the lakes region, was largely situated on rather inaccessible, naturally defensible terrain not sampled by our transects, however, and we use both transect and nontransect data to project Postclassic population figures, as well as to discuss the Terminal Classic transition.

SETTLEMENT DATA AND TRENDS

A total of 1211 discrete mounds, dispersed among 368 spatially distinct loci, was mapped within the 20 transects surveyed in the six basins (Table 6.1). Of these, 284 (23.5%) were sampled by "telephone-booth"-style test excavations. An additional 60 occupation loci were so sampled at nontransect locations. For each sampled location, an "occupation" was counted when a construction episode could be identified and dated. In addition, most of the surface remains of the mounds were datable to either the Late Classic or the Postclassic Periods. Our excavation strategy allowed us to characterize only the cumulative occupation history as reflected in vertical construction profiles; it was not sufficient to characterize architectural form or function, regardless of period of occupation.

Table 6.2 shows the numbers and percentages of structure loci built or modified in the basins from the Middle Preclassic through the Late Postclassic periods. Differences are immediately apparent for the Middle Pre-classic Period, when 32% of all mounds tested in the Quexil-Petenxil basins show construction, as compared to 21% at Macanche-Salpeten and 10% at Sacnab-Yaxha. In the Late Preclassic Period, occupation percentages range from 23 at Sacnab-Yaxha to 9 at Quexil-Petenxil. It is in the Early Classic Period when the greatest disjunction among basin-pairs occurs. Thirty-six percent of the sampled mounds at Sacnab-Yaxha show construc-tion activity, whereas at the other lakes construction declines further, to only 6.5% at Macanche-Salpeten and 4.5% at Quexil-Petenxil.

Published reports indicate that a number of lowland Maya Late Preclas-sic centers in other zones ceased to be occupied during the Early Classic Period—Becan (R. E. W. Adams 1977a), Cerros (Freidel et al. 1982), Mira-dor (Dahlin 1984; Matheny 1986), Nohmul (Hammond 1981), and Seibal (Sabloff 1975) among them—and the distribution of Early Classic centers and population may have been restricted to a few isolated regions, one of which is northeast Peten (Dahlin et al. 1987; Willey and Mathews 1985). Lincoln (1985) has suggested, however, that archaeologists have failed to recognize both the longevity of Late Preclassic ceramic complexes and the restricted (i.e., elite) contexts of ceramic complexes by which the Early Classic Period has traditionally been identified. Mayanists have thereby created scenarios of Early Classic abandonments where none really oc-curred (see also R. E. W. Adams 1971 and A. Chase 1979, 1983 for discus-sions of the difficulty of identifying Early Classic occupation).

At least three considerations lead us to believe that the Early Classic occupation at Quexil-Petenxil and Macanche-Salpeten was truncated. First, the sample size is sufficiently large to yield evidence of Early Classic con-struction in domestic contexts, if it existed. Second, of the 58 obsidian artifacts from those lakes that were hydration dated only 3 have dates fall-ing in the Early Classic range (P. Rice 1986b.). Finally, granulometric stud-ies of sediment cores from Lakes Macanche and Quexil suggest a relaxation of human activity in these basins (Binford 1983). Agricultural activities in the region are indicated by the species composition of pollen rain in these core sections, but there appears to have been little architec-tural manipulation of the local landscapes during the Early Classic Period.

All three lake pairs have comparable Late Classic occupation percent-ages: 80 at Sacnab-Yaxha, 84 at Macanche-Salpeten, and 93 at Quexil-Pe-tenxil. The relative equality is also found within pairs, the greatest disparity being at Sacnab (68%) and Yaxha (84%), where the center of Yaxha dominated the cultural landscape. The end of the Classic Period sees uniform decline in settlement throughout the basins, to occupation percentages ranging from 24 at Macanche-Salpeten to 9 at Sacnab-Yaxha.

As suggested by Culbert et al. (this volume), Terminal Classic occupa-tion may be underrepresented in our recovered materials from Classic contexts. The Terminal Classic Period was short-lived, and apparently pop-ulations tended to use existing architecture without modification, rather than to remodel extensively or construct buildings anew. Artifacts diagnostic of this closing phase of Classic occupation were not, therefore, often incorporated into construction core, but rather lie accessible only on living surfaces or in middens. As result, variable test-excavation strategies or loci may produce different quantities of Terminal Classic material (see also Ford, this volume; Fry 1969).

We did identify some Terminal Classic construction, as well as Terminal Classic materials on Late Classic constructions, and we also found Terminal Classic pottery mixed with Postclassic sherds in construction core of Postclassic architecture at both transect and nontransect locations (see D. Rice 1986, 1988; D. Rice and P. Rice 1984b; P. Rice 1986a, 1987; P. Rice and D. Rice 1985 for details on architectural contexts and interpretations). Postclassic settlement is itself reduced in size and restricted in area, however, and is not necessarily the best indicator of Terminal Classic distributions or densities.

The Early and Late Postclassic periods see a continued transition in structure locations, with an inverse relation between mainland construction in basins and settlement on the more isolated islands and peninsulas. The overall incidence of transect occupation drops 40% from the Terminal Classic to Early Postclassic periods, falling to 2% at Quexil-Petenxil, 7% at Sacnab-Yaxha, and 16% at Macanche-Salpeten. In contrast, 86% of the structures sampled on the Quexil Islands experienced construction during the period, as did 47% on Yaxha's Cante Island (the site of Topoxte); 25% of mounds in Macanche's walled site of Muralla de Leon, Macanche Island; and 44% of the loci at Zacpeten. There was no indication of Late Postclassic transect settlement at either Sacnab-Yaxha or Quexil-Petenxil, although the Cante and Quexil islands continued to be heavily occupied. Approximately 9% of the sampled transect structures in the Macanche-Salpeten basins yielded Late Postclassic materials, while occupation continued at Muralla de Leon, Macanche Island, and Zacpeten.

Culbert et al.'s argument (this volume) regarding the "visibility" of Terminal Classic populations to a test-excavation methodology that samples only construction core can be extended to the Late Postclassic case. If Postclassic populations were not investing substantially in new or remodeled mainland domestic architecture, and they were not followed by later populations that incorporated available trash into construction, then Late Postclassic numbers may well be underestimated when a "construction" definition of "occupation" is used (D. Rice 1986, 1988).

SETTLEMENT DENSITIES

Occupation percentages can be used to estimate the average density of structures occupied per km^2, per time period (Table 6.3). Variability in structure densities reflects in part regional social and political dynamics, but it is also conditioned by the structure of basin environments. Average densities should not be confused with structure densities per unit of inhabitable terrain (land suitable for the placement of residential structures) or with economic densities related to landscape or differential productive value (D. Rice 1978).

Overall density projects population against all terrain. Modern perceptions of "inhabitable" and "productive value" are conditioned by twentieth-century natural science, but the Maya provided more functional definitions of inhabitable land by rather consistently avoiding particular areas as sites for construction of domiciles, regardless of their use of those areas for nonresidential purposes. Thus, extremely steep and/or broken terrain and low flat zones of poor drainage, or bajo, were avoided as locales of human settlement.

In the Sacnab-Yaxha basins, for example, 22.3% of the 10 km² surveyed is bajo and presumed uninhabitable, or unsuitable for the placement of residences (Table 6.1). The average overall structure density of 58.6 structures/km² is therefore equivalent to 75.4 structures/km² of inhabitable land. At Quexil-Pentenxil, where 46.4% of the 5.5 km² of transects is low-lying hydromorphic soil, structure density/km² of inhabitable terrain is 72.5. Only at Macanche-Salpeten, where 4.2% of the transect area is considered uninhabitable because of steepness, are overall structure densities and structure densities/km² of inhabitable land approximately equal, at 68.5 and 71.5.

POPULATION CENSUS

To arrive at estimates of actual population sizes and densities, we must calculate or assume four values: the quantity of the variable on which the estimate is based; the time-frame for that variable; the turnover rate, or life expectancy, of the variable; and the magnitude of association between actual population and the variable at any given time (S. Cook 1972:30). As is common among archaeologists in the Maya area, we rely on residential mound counts and text-excavation-derived chronologies as a foundation for such estimates. In selecting the individual structure as the basis for calculations, we acknowledge that the number of mapped structures in a group may be only an approximation of the total number of platforms in that group (see Tourtellot's caution, this volume). The few instances of "hidden" structures that we encountered in the basin surveys were thought to be Preclassic in date (D. Rice 1978; see also Bronson 1968 and Haviland 1989 for discussion of similar findings at Tikal). Since there is no way to determine how many of these structures are undiscovered, we can only assume that their effect on population estimates would be relatively small.

Once the number of structures has been determined, it remains to decide exactly how many of those structures were residential rather than specialized domestic, civic, or ceremonial adjuncts. Because our text-excavation strategy was not directed toward evaluating structure function, we are forced to rely on other determinations. On the basis of complete excavation of 24 structures at Tikal, and extensive testing of many others, Haviland estimated that approximately 16% of all mounds were nonresidential (1970:193), a figure not out of line with the estimate of 14.3% by Tourtellot for Seibal (Tourtellot, this volume; for discussion of more variable figures see also Ford 1986; D. Chase, this volume; McAnany, this volume; and Webster and Freter, this volume). We accept the correction factor of 16% as a basis for eliminating those Preclassic-through-Late Classic structures not used for habitation, although we acknowledge that the percentage undoubtedly varied through time and across space (Santley, this volume).

We do not rely on a correction factor for Terminal Classic and Postclassic structure functions. The characteristics and contexts of Terminal Classic occupation (Culbert 1973:67–69; Fry 1969; D. Rice 1986) suggest that populations were making little or no investment in civic, religious, and/or other adjunct architecture, and we assume that all Terminal Classic loci identified were residential. Postclassic structures, on the other hand, are distinctive in form, limited in variation, and relatively unencumbered by multiple reconstructions, and ethnohistoric sources described activities within sites and particular classes of architecture (D. Rice 1986, 1988; D. Rice and P. Rice 1984b; P. Rice 1986a, 1987; P. Rice and D. Rice 1985). We believe that we can identify temples, shrines, oratorios, large open halls, and so on, and have removed them from consideration when discussing population numbers.

Once we have obtained an estimate for the total number of residences, the duration of residence habitation must be assessed in terms of artifact complexes defined by the archaeologist. The large blocks of time represented by these complexes call into question the most debated variable of Maya population estimates—the turnover rate of residential structures within any given ceramic phase. The problem is one of determining the degree of continuous occupation of structures and thus the percentage of contemporaneously occupied structures during any given period. In the "continuous occupation" versus "cyclical abandonment" debate (see Culbert et al., this volume; Tourtellot, this volume) we come down in favor of continuous occupation, although we do not deny the likelihood of periodic short-term, perhaps even generational, disuse of residential structures.

Available settlement data from the lake basins do not suggest the kind of "entrenched" system described for Copan (Santley, this volume; Webster and Freter, this volume), with "rural" residences occupied on an impermanent basis and "urban" residences more permanently so. We have identified construction histories that indicate periodic abandonment or disuse, followed by later reoccupation of structures (D. Rice and P. Rice 1980). Likewise, our test-excavation profiles have revealed multiple reconstructions of structures within periods. Such abandonments, reoccupations, and modifications were not specific to particular periods, geographic zones, or classes or sizes of architecture, however, making it difficult to attempt to generalize about use-life of structures (as in Culbert et al., this volume).

The incidence of reconstructions reinforces our feeling that the evidence for long-standing occupation at residential loci is strong (see Haviland 1970; Tourtellot, this volume, for similar arguments). We therefore do not feel that periodic disuse negates the hypothesis of long-term use of structures. In previous discussions we have tried to accommodate the dynamics of settlement by projecting population figures for the close of periods (D. Rice 1978). This assumes the development of communities through time and also assumes maximum contemporaneity of occupation for all structures constructed during a period, by the close of that period.

With the number of occupied structures per phase determined, it is necessary to estimate the number of inhabitants for each occupied structure. The raw data for this estimate come from ethnographic and ethnohistoric population records of house and household size, and the alternatives are many. Here we opt, as we have in the past (D. Rice 1978), for D. Puleston's (1973) application of Naroll's (1962) projections of optimal individual requirements for dwelling floor space to Haviland's small-structure data from Tikal (1963), and Puleston's resulting average of 5.4 inhabitants/structure.

It is difficult to believe that residential numbers were unvarying through time and space, or within communities, however, and we are particularly concerned with the application of a 5.4-person house size of Postclassic contexts. Ethnohistoric data have provided a range of 7 to 25 persons/house (Cogolludo 1842–45:II:230; Haviland 1972a:137; Hellmuth 1977; J. E. S. Thompson 1951:390; Villagutierre 1933:136, 480). Postclassic settlements also differed from that of earlier periods in the basins, and structures were generally larger than earlier counterparts (D. Rice 1988). Although larger structure area can be attributable to factors other than the number of house occupants (Netting et al. 1985; Wilk and Ashmore, eds., 1988; Santley, this volume), we would not be surprised if the modal house size was likewise greater, perhaps on the order of the 10 persons/house that D. Puleston calculated from ethnohistoric data for the Postclassic Itza community of Noh Peten (1973:177).

Table 6.4 presents population densities for the lakes area, based on survey transects. The Preclassic-Classic population figures are calculated by assuming that all the structures occupied during any period were contemporaneously occupied by the end of that period, by multiplying the mound-density figures for each period (Table 6.3) by a factor of 84% to eliminate nonresidential units, and then by multiplying by the figure of 5.4 persons. Terminal Classic and Postclassic estimates are made in similar fashion, but without the 84% correction factor, and projections for the Postclassic periods in Table 6.6 employ both 5.4-person and 10.0-person household sizes.

Total population for nontransect sites surveyed (Table 6.5) is estimated by similar means but is based on total structures occupied per period (Table 6.2), rather than structure densities.

Population densities per km² of inhabitable land and nontransect population numbers provide the bases for estimating total populations within the basins. The densities (Table 6.4) are multiplied by the amount of inhabitable land projected for each basin, and population figures for nontransect sites (Table 6.5) are factored in, to arrive at basin and basin-pair totals (Table 6.6).

As with measures of occupation percentage, structure density, and population density, the Sacnab-Yaxha basins experienced consistent increases in total population through the Classic Period, from 815.7 persons for the Middle Preclassic Period to 6252.8 persons for the Late Classic. The Macanche-Salpeten and Quexil-Petenxil catchments suffer the now-familiar Late Preclassic and Early Classic variability and disjunctions, then jump to total populations of 7261.7 and 3836.3 persons, respectively, for the Late Classic Period. Postclassic totals are also highest in the Macanche-Salpeten basins, with 3568.3 residents projected for the Early Postclassic Period and 2323.6 persons for the Late Postclassic Period (10-person household sizes).

The survey transects sampled catchments that approximate the actual drainages, but it is highly unlikely that these surveyed zones conform well to the areas of ancient Maya communities or political units. Unfortunately, estimating population sizes for these social groupings requires boundary definitions that are difficult to make given the data we have in hand. We have previously accepted a Thiessen polygon, centered on the site of Yaxha, as a model of the limits of the "sustaining area" for this center (Hammond 1974a), however, and although nearest-neighbor site data for the Macanche-Salpeten and Quexil-Petenxil basins are incomplete, making construction of similar polygons for these pairs pointless, it is possible to suggest a total population for the Sacnab-Yaxha unit.

The Sacnab-Yaxha polygon is 237 km² in area, approximately 30% of which consists of swamp forest and swamp thicket, leaving some 167 km² of inhabitable landscape (D. Rice 1978:40–41, Figure 4.2). A resident population can be estimated based on the projected population densities per km² of inhabitable terrain (Table 6.4), together with counts for the To-poxte Islands (as with Cante Island, Table 6.5) and for the population of Yaxha itself. Yaxha presents some problems because, though the site has been extensively mapped (Hellmuth 1972a), little excavation or functional classification of architecture has been undertaken. Subjective evaluation of the published site map suggests that a minimum of 107 of the 426 numbered structures are potential candidates for residences. Without ex-cavation we can suggest site numbers (and polygon numbers) only for the Late Classic Period. Although monumental architecture and elite contexts call into question assumptions about structure function and household demographics, we continue to use the 84% correction factor and 5.4 per-son/house figure. A minimum Late Classic residential elite population at the site is thus calculated to be 483 people, or slightly more than 1% of the 42,047.5-person Late Classic population estimated for the hypothetical sustaining area as a whole. Although the absolute number and percentage of elites may seem low, it is interesting that R. E. W. Adams has arrived at similar orders of magnitude and ratios for Uaxactun using very different methods of population estimation (1974).

AVERAGE ANNUAL CRUDE GROWTH RATES

These estimates of lake-basin population densities and totals are depen-dent on the particular positions we have taken on issues of contempor-aneity of habitation, use-life and reuse cycles of structures, structure function, and modal house size. If any or all of our assumptions and ac-cepted values are significantly altered, then population densities and totals will change, as will the implications of those numbers for discussion of population and social or environmental change. If such alterations are applied uniformly to the survey data, however, the growth curves for settlement and population through time should remain the same.

Table 6.7 provides the crude annual growth rates for each period for each of the lake-basin pairs. These rates were determined using total pop-ulation estimates per time period for each pair (Table 6.6) to ensure in-clusion of nontransect data, particularly for the Terminal Classic through Late Postclassic. Calculations can be made using either the two formulae for computing average annual growth rates:

$$N_t = N_0(1 + r)^t \text{ (G. Cowgill 1975a) or } N_t = N_0 e^{rt} \text{ (Hassan 1978),}$$

where N_0 is the initial population at the beginning of a period (or the end of the preceding period), N_t is the population at the end of the period, t is the elapsed time of the period, r is the rate of growth, and e is the base of natural logarithms, here 2.718. The resulting rates are averages, and the real growth rates must have fluctuated considerably in response to random and nonrandom biological, cultural, and environmental changes (Ammerman 1975; Bronson 1975; Hassan 1978).

To determine growth rates during the Middle Preclassic Period, we accept a starting date of ca. 700 B.C. as a zero population point. This conforms to both the beginning date given the Eb complex at Tikal (Culbert 1977) and the cluster of obsidian hydration dates obtained for obsidian artifacts from secure Middle Preclassic contexts in the lake basins (P. Rice 1986b). Our survey data could not track archaeologically the obvious build-up of population during the Middle Preclassic, so calculation of growth rates for the period presents the problem of determining an initial seed population. The size of that seed population obviously has a dramatic influence on subsequent growth. We assume that initial colonization of the basins took place over several centuries, until stable local breeding populations were established, but that in-migration is hopelessly difficult to posit quantitatively. Therefore, we arbitrarily began the period with our 5.4 persons for a single house in each basin and calculated growth rates accordingly.

After initial colonization and settlement expansion during the Middle Preclassic Period, the Sacnab-Yaxha basins experienced steady, slightly accelerating growth through the Late Preclassic and Early Classic, while the Macanche-Salpeten and Quexil-Petenxil basin pairs suffered decline. If average growth rates could be assumed legitimate measures of annual loss during each of those periods, a very unlikely assumption, yearly losses during those 550 years would be on the order of 2.34 persons lost/annum from the Macanche-Salpeten basins at the beginning of the Late Preclassic Period to 1.24/annum lost by the end of the Early Classic, and 3.23 to 0.43 persons/annum lost from the Quexil-Petenxil basins.

If, indeed, there were relatively fewer people resident in these basins during the Early Classic Period, what might have brought about such a transformation? The major variability in social and natural resources within the lakes region lies in the distribution of major centers and in lake sizes and volumes, soil characteristics, and the presence of bajos in the vicinity of Sacnab-Yaxha. It is difficult, however, to identify stresses that might differentially call these resources into play.

Paleoecologists are equivocal about the identification of climatic fluctuations in lake cores from central Peten (U. Cowgill and Hutchinson 1966; Deevey et al. 1979; Vaughan et al. 1985), but any climatic change might be expected to affect the lacustrine landscapes of the central Peten uniformly. Paleolimnological data also do not appear to indicate marked differences in rates of chemical and biological transport between Lakes Sacnab-Yaxha and the more western pairs (Brenner, personal communication 1986), and the dramatic reestablishment of settlement in all basins during the Late Classic Period likewise suggests that any earlier human-induced environmental degradation had no long-standing impact.

The close of the Late Preclassic Period in Peten is associated with construction of defensive earthworks at Tikal (D. Puleston and Callender 1967) and perhaps Muralla de Leon at Macanche (D. Rice and P. Rice 1981), suggesting an element of civil strife in the Late Preclassic-Early Classic transition which might affect basin populations differentially. The ascendancy of the site of Yaxha in the lakes region in the Early Classic is marked by Cycle 8 (A.D. 238–435) and early Cycle 9 (A.D. 435–534) carved monuments, extensive architectural activity, and sustained basin occupation. The site had its own emblem glyph by this time, and Mathews (1985:31) has suggested that Yaxha was one of several independent polities during Cycle 8, although one with possible affiliations to Tikal (Marcus 1976). While Early Classic settlement densities are low at Macanche-Salpeten and Quexil-Petenxil, Yaxha and Tikal experienced settlement growth and nucleation (Fry 1969; Culbert et al., this volume), and these opposing trends may not be unrelated.

Migrations and population redistributions, particularly during periods of political transformation and urbanization, can lead to increases or decreases of local population sizes without pronounced changes in rates of birth or death (R. M. Adams 1972; R. M. Adams and Nissen 1972). Given that population losses in the Macanche-Salpeten and Quexil-Pentenxil zones are contemporaneous with population increases in the vicinities of sites such as Yaxha and Tikal, it is intriguing to consider that Late Preclassic and Early Classic residential declines in the former basin pairs might reflect the strong influence of out-migration, in addition to effects of natality and mortality. The rise of centralized authority and the coalescence of control and management of resources at major centers may have contributed to demographic flux in more "rural" zones without such major centers. That is to say, Tikal, and Yaxha may have attracted population from some surrounding territories, for reasons of higher agricultural potential or assured hydrological resources in times of stress or perhaps effective political persuasion and/or coercion.

All basin pairs experience dramatic growth in the Late Classic Period, ranging from 0.26%/annum at Sacnab-Yaxha to 1.03%/annum at Quexil-Petenxil. The presence of the center of Yaxha does not appear to have had an accelerating effect on local growth rates, relative to those at basin pairs with less impressive evidence of elite organization. The rates at Macanche-Salpeten and Quexil-Petenxil undoubtedly reflect in-migration, but we have no indication of its timing or magnitude or of possible zones of population contribution.

The Late Classic crude average annual growth rates from the three basin pairs are quite dramatic, both in terms of previous population levels in the lakes region and compared to rates projected for peak population periods elsewhere in Mesoamerica. For example, Hassan has estimated the annual rates of population growth at Ixtapalapa, Mexico, to have been 0.59% and 0.39% during two periods of rapid population growth occurring between 1200 B.C. and A.D. 1520, and the annual growth rate at Kamin-aljuyu, Guatemala, from 800–500 B.C. to A.D. 500–700 is projected to have averaged 0.10% (Hassan 1973; 1978:69; original data from Blanton 1972 and Sanders 1974).

One of us recently implied that the Terminal Classic demographic transition in the lake basins may not have seemed that catastrophic to local populations experiencing the "collapse" (D. Rice 1986, 1988), but the rates of decline belie that naive thought. Losses ranged from 0.74%/annum at Macanche-Salpeten to 1.90%/annum at Sacnab-Yaxha. Estimated average rates of change would have the Sacnab-Yaxha basins losing 118.8 to 11.82 persons/annum, while the Macanche-Salpeten basins would lose 53.66 to 22.05 persons and Quexil-Petenxil 44.12 to 11.06 persons/annum. If we assume that Terminal Classic populations are for the most part archaeo-logically visible, and our measures relatively accurate, then in the absence of evidence for Terminal Classic substantial colonization and densities elsewhere, we suggest that the losses in the lake basins are attributable to an imbalance between birth and death rates, rather than to out-migration.

The Sacnab-Yaxha and Macanche-Salpeten basin pairs experienced a mi-nor resurgence of population during the Early Postclassic Period. Given the dramatic change in settlement patterns in the Postclassic periods, how-ever, these rises may be due in large part to redistribution of remnant postcollapse populations. The Late Postclassic Period sees variable but consistent declines in all three basin pairs. Unfortunately, there is at pre-sent no way to rationalize these population fluctuations with speculations about large Maya populations around Lake Peten-Itza at the time of Span-ish contact (J. E. S. Thompson 1951), except to suggest that Late Postclassic families were not investing in imperishable household architecture. For purposes of computing crude annual growth rates we end the Late Post-classic Period with the Spanish presence in Yucatan in 1525, even though the Itza Maya of central Peten were not completely subjugated until 1697.

The average annual growth rates for populations in the basin pairs from 700 B.C. to A.D. 830, the end of the Late Classic Period, are, for Sacnab-Yaxha, 0.46%, a doubling time of 151 years; for Macanche-Salpeten, 0.47% a dou-bling time of 148 years; and for Quexil-Petenxil, 0.43%, a doubling time of 162 years. Alternatively, given the difficulty of reconstructing the de-mography of initial Middle Preclassic colonization, if we compute overall growth once Middle Preclassic settlements are established, the average annual population growth rates for the period 250 B.C.-A.D. 830 are, for Sacnab-Yaxha, 0.19%, a doubling time of 365 years; for Macanche-Salpeten, 0.12%, a doubling time of 578 years; and for Quexil-Petenxil, 0.10%, a doubling time of 693 years. These latter rates are all within the 0.10-0.20% range of annual growth rates which G. Cowgill calculated to be common overall regional trends spanning a millennium or more for preindustrial societies (1975b).

Although Middle Preclassic to Late Classic average annual growth rates are comparable for the three basin pairs, and are comparable to rates from the south-central lowlands as a whole (Santley, this volume: Figure 16.3; Turner, this volume), the population projections thus far discussed do indicate variable population histories. These are substantiated by the crude growth rates for individual periods and by the semilog graphed population curves for the basin pairs (Figure 6.2). The latter adds no new quantitative information, but the shapes of the curves deserve brief attention.

Constructed from a limited number of measurable data points, the Sacnab-Yaxha growth curve best approximates log-linear exponential increase, with steady growth at a relatively uniform rate (Pressat 1972; D. Rice 1978; Wilson and Bossert 1971). In this pattern the basin pair is apparently not unlike the Tikal, Calakmul, or Rio Bec regions (Culbert et al., this volume; Fry, this volume; Santley, this volume; Turner, this volume). In these zones as well, moderate growth is sustained, with stable exponential rates during the Preclassic and Early Classic periods and increased growth peaking in the Late Classic Period, then subsequent rapid population loss (Santley, this volume).

The Macanche-Salpeten and Quexil-Petenxil curves better fit a logistic population model of fluctuations in growth followed by attenuated collapse (Odum 1971; Pressat 1972; Santley, this volume; Whittaker 1975), however, as do apparently the Pulltrouser Swamp area and the Belize River valley (Fry, this volume; Santley, this volume). For human populations this pattern involves colonization followed by cycles of growth and decline, and results in what Santley refers to as "sawtooth" growth curves. The pattern is often associated with growing populations reaching or overshooting the carrying capacity of their natural and/or social environment, suffering a rapid loss, then recovering, often with innovations in subsistence technology and/or social organization. Although neither the central Peten's carrying capacity nor the biotic potential (maximum possible rate of growth) for Maya populations has been adequately demonstrated, communities were undoubtedly subject to degradation of resources, crop losses, competition, and/or predation, each of which could have temporary or long-standing negative impact on growth (Santley, this volume; Willey and Shimkin 1973).

The variability in slopes of the growth curves reflect differences in the relative balance of natality, mortality, and migration for the basin pairs. Biological characteristics of the resident populations being equal, the variation in population history from subregion to subregion suggests in particular that migration and cultural factors are influencing relative population figures (Santley and Rose 1979). In this context the two patterns of overall growth are provocative. Santley (this volume) has proposed that differences in resources or agricultural potential may be responsible for whether a region follows an exponential or a logistic growth pattern. He suggests further that the sawtooth effect is character-istic of zones where raised-field agriculture is practiced and/or where there is access to riverine habitats, while the exponential profile is more characteristic of landlocked areas where agriculture is dominated by dry-land technologies.

With respect to environmental contexts and characteristics, the central Peten lakes do not conform to these expectations, however. The lake-basin pairs all share access to potable water and lacustrine resources, but the only basins with access to riparian or upland bajo zones are Sacnab and Yaxha. Tikal has similar access to upland bajos. It is the Sacnab-Yaxha basin pair, however, that manifests exponential growth. Macanche-Salpeten and Quexil-Petenxil have little potential for hydraulic agriculture of any kind, yet they more closely conform to the logistic pattern.

The one independent variable that does appear to correlate with the variability of growth curves, both in the lakes-region samples and in the other lowland zones discussed by Santley, is the presence or absence of major civic-ceremonial centers. Those regions that exhibit patterns of ex-ponential growth—Tikal, Calakmul, Rio Bec, and Sacnab-Yaxha—all have major centers at their core, whereas those of the sawtoothed logistic pat-tern do not. That there is monumental architecture in the Macanche-Salpeten and Quexil-Petenxil basins, or in the Pulltrouser Swamp region or Belize River Valley, is indisputable. The orders of magnitude are consid-erably different, however.

In the central Peten lakes region the lake-basin pair with the presence of a large civic-ceremonial center, that is, the Sacnab-Yaxha basin pair, does not have the largest population in the Late Classic Period. Instead the high-est population total occurs in the Macanche-Salpeten basins, characterized also by the highest percentage of inhabitable terrain. The presence of the Yaxha site may have been a catalyst for higher settlement density per km^2 of inhabitable land on the shores of Lake Yaxha (Tables 6.3, 6.4), but there do appear to have been some logical limits to maximum local population sizes in the Late Classic. With the exception of tiny Lake Petenxil, total Late Classic numbers at all lakes are generally equivalent.

Although Yaxha's impact on peak population size may have been slight, we speculate that, perhaps as at Tikal, Calakmul, and other major centers with considerable longevity, the presence of a strong centralized authority in the Sacnab-Yaxha had a modifying or stabilizing influence on local pop-ulation histories. Perhaps as a result of control and management of re-sources, entrepreneurial initiatives, alliances, and so on, these centers provided a buffer against the stresses that would have negatively in-fluenced more rural populations. Success in "spatial energy averaging" (Tainter 1988:170) would in turn promote population growth and/or aggregation. In the absence of such a strong local organization or buffer, the populations of Macanche-Salpeten and Quexil-Petenxil may have been more vulnerable to the vagaries of climate and disruptions of production, as well as to the politics of the larger centers within the region, and thus their numbers could have been more prone to fluctuation.

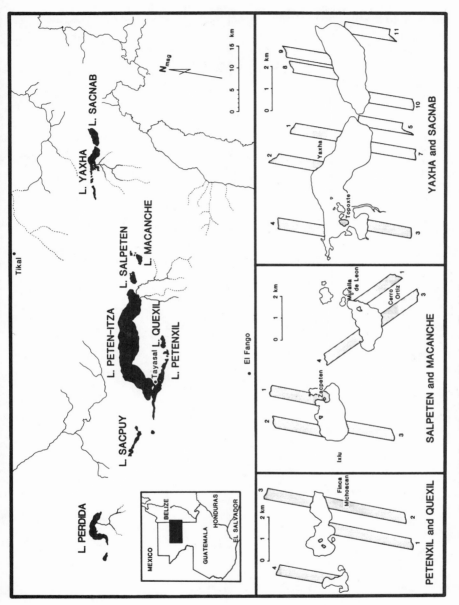

Map 6.1   The Central Peten Historical Ecology Project survey transect and site locations.

Table 6.1 Transect Survey Data

Lake/Site	Total Area Surveyed (km²)	Inhabitable Area Surveyed (km²)	Total Structures Mapped	Overall Structure Density (/km²)	Structure Density in Inhabitable Terrain (/km²)	Total Structures Test Excavated No./%
SACNAB-YAXHA						
Sacnab	4	3.625	161	40.3	44.4	40/24.8
Yaxha	6	4.15	425	70.8	102.4	108/25.4
Basin Pair	10	7.775	586	58.6	75.4	148/25.3
Cante Island	0.11		142	1,290.9		19/13.4
MACANCHE-SALPETEN						
Macanche	3	3.0	248	82.7	82.7	53/21.4
Salpeten	3	2.75	163	54.3	59.3	39/23.9
Basin pair	6	5.75	411	68.5	71.5	92/22.4
Cerro Ortiz Area	1.7		107	62.9		7/6.5
Macanche Island	0.05		1	20.0		1/100
Muralla de Leon	0.13		22	169.2		8/36/4
Zacpeten	0.23		190	826.1		18/9.5
QUEXIL-PETENXIL						
Quexil	4.5	1.95	163	36.2	83.6	35/21.5
Petenxil	1	1	51	51	51	9/17.6
Basin Pair	5.5	2.95	214	38.9	72.5	44/20.1
Quexil Islands	0.036		26	722.2		7/26.9
All mainland transects	21.5	16.475	1,211	56.3	73.5	284/23.5

Table 6.2 Number and Percentage of Sampled Structures Occupied: Middle Preclassic–Late Postclassic

Lake/Site	Middle Preclassic No./%	Late Preclassic No./%	Early Classic No./%	Late Classic No./%	Terminal Classic No./%	Early Postclassic No./%	Late Postclassic No./%
SACNAB-YAXHA							
Sacnab	6/15.0	9/22.5	18/45.0	27/67.5	1/2.5	0/0	0/0
Yaxha	9/8.3	25/23.2	36/33.3	91/84.3	12/11.1	10/9.3	0/0
Basin pair	15/10.1	34/22.9	54/36.4	118/79.7	13/9.3	10/6.8	0/0
Cante Island	0/0	1/5.3	2/10.5	3/15.8	0/0	9/47.4	14/73.7
MACANCHE-SALPETEN							
Macanche	12/22.6	13/24.5	3/5.7	41/77.4	7/13.2	11/20.8	7/13.2
Salpeten	7/17.9	1/2.6	3/7.7	36/92.3	15/38.5	4/10.3	1/2.6
Basin pair	19/20.7	14/15.2	6/6.5	77/83.7	22/23.9	15/16.3	8/8.7
Cerro Ortiz Area	7/100	2/28.6	1/14.3	5/71.4	2/28.6	2/28.6	0/0
Macanche Island	0/0	0/0	0/0	1/100	1/100	1/100	1/100
Muralla de Leon	0/0	6/75.0	0/0	2/25.0	0/0	2/25.0	2/25.0
Zacpeten	0/0	0/0	1/5.6	4/22.2	7/38.9	8/44.4	13/72.2
QUEXIL-PETENXIL							
Quexil	14/40.0	4/11.4	1/2.9	32/91.4	5/14.3	1/2.9	0/0
Petenxil	0/0	0/0	1/11/1	9/100	3/33/3	0/0	0/0
Basin pair	14/31.8	4/9.1	2/4.5	41/93.2	8/18.2	1/2.3	0.0
Quexil Islands	1/14.3	1/14.3	2/28.6	3/42.9	5/71.4	6/85.7	4/57.1
All mainland transects	48/16.9	52/18.3	62/21.8	246/86.6	43/15.1	26/9.2	8/2.8

Table 6.3 Transect Structure Densities by Time Period

Lake/Site	Middle Preclassic OT/IL (/km²)	Lake Preclassic OT/IL (/km²)	Early Classic OT/IL (/km²)	Late Classic OT/IL (/km²)	Terminal Classic OT/IL (/km²)	Early Postclassic OT/IL (/km²)	Late Postclassic OT/IL (/km²)
SACNAB-YAXHA							
Sacnab	6.0/6.7	9.1/10.0	18.1/20.0	27.2/30.0	1.0/1.1	0.0/0.0	0.0/0.0
Yaxha	5.9/8.5	16.4/23.0	23.6/37.3	59.7/86.3	7.9/11.4	6.6/9.5	0.0/0.0
Basin pair	5.9/7.6	13.4/17.3	21.3/27.4	46.7/60.1	5.5/7.0	4.0/5.1	0.0/0.0
MACANCHE-SALPETEN							
Macanche	18.7/18.7	20.3/20.3	4.7/4.7	64.0/64.0	10.9/10.9	17.2/17.2	10.9/10.9
Salpeten	9.7/10.6	1.4/1.5	4.2/4.6	50.1/54.7	20.9/22.8	5.6/6.1	1.4/1.5
Basin pair	12.3/14.8	10.4/10.9	4.5/4.7	57.3/59.9	16.4/17.1	11.2/11.7	5.6/6.2
QUEXIL-PETENXIL							
Quexil	14.5/33.4	4.1/9.5	1.0/2.4	33.1/76.4	5.2/12.0	1.0/2.4	0.0/0.0
Petenxil	0.0/0.0	0.0/0.0	5.6/5.6	51.0/51.0	17.0/17.0	0.0/0.0	0.0/0.0
Basin pair	12.4/23.1	3.5/6.6	1.8/1.8	36.3/67.6	7.1/13.2	.9/1.7	0.0/0.0
All mainland transects	9.5/12.4	10.3/13.5	12.3/16.0	48.8/63.7	8.5/11.1	5.2/6.8	1.6/2.1

Note: OT = overall terrain; IL = inhabitable land

Table 6.4   Transect Population Densities by Time Period

Lake/Site	Middle Preclassic OT/IL (/km²)	Late Preclassic OT/IL (/km²)	Early Classic OT/IL (/km²)	Late Classic OT/IL (/km²)	Terminal Classic OT/IL (/km²)	Early Postclassic OT/IL (/km²)	Late Postclassic OT/IL (/km²)
SACNAB-YAXHA							
Sacnab	27.2/30.4	41.3/45.4	82.1/90.7	123.136.1	5.4/5.9	0.0/0.0	0.0/0.0
Yaxha	26.8/38.6	74.4/104.3	107.0/169.2	270.8/391.5	42.7/61.6	35.6/51.3	0.0/0.0
Basin pair	26.8/34.5	60.8/78.5	96.6/124.3	211.8/272.6	29.7/37.8	21.5/27.5	0.0/0.0
MACANCHE-SALPETEN							
Macanche	84.8/84.8	92.1/92.1	21.3/21.3	290.3/290.3	58.9/58.9	92.9/92.9	58.9/58.9
Salpeten	44.7/48.1	6.4/6.8	19.1/20.9	227.3/248.1	112.9/123.1	30.2/32.9	7.6/8.1
Basin pair	55.8/67.1	47.2/49.4	20.4/21.3	249.9/271.7	88.6/92.3	60.5/63.2	30.2/33.5
QUEXIL-PETENXIL							
Quexil	65.8/151.5	18.6/43.1	4.5/10.9	150.1/346.6	28.1/64.8	5.4/13.0	0.0/0.0
Petenxil	0.0/0.0	0.0/0.0	25.4/25.4	231.3/231.3	91.8/91.8	0.0/0.0	0.0/0.0
Basin pair	56.2/104.8	15.9/29.9	8.2/15.0	164.7/307.1	38.3/71.3	4.9/9.2	0.0/0.0
All mainland transects	43.1/56.2	46.7/61.2	55.8/72.6	221.4/288.9	45.9/59.9	28.1/36.7	8.6/11.3

Note: OT = overall terrain; IL = inhabitable land

Table 6.5 Nontransect Population Estimates by Time Period

Site	Middle Preclassic	Late Preclassic	Early Classic	Late Classic	Terminal Classic	Early Postclassic	Late Postclassic
Cante Island	0.0	34.1	67.6	101.8	0.0	263.6	409.9
Cerro Ortiz area	484.4	138.8	69.4	346.5	165.3	165.3	0.0
Macanche Island	0.0	0.0	0.0	5.4	5.4	5.4	5.4
Muralla de Leon	0.0	63.5	0.0	23.8	0.0	21.6	21.6
Zacpeten	0.0	0.0	48.3	191.3	294.1	335.7	545.8
Quexil Islands	16.9	16.9	33.7	50.6	84.8	101.8	67.8

Table 6.6 Estimated Total Basin Populations by Time Period

Lake/Site	Middle Preclassic	Late Preclassic	Early Classic	Late Classic	Terminal Classic	Early Postclassic 5.4-person household/ 10-person household	Late Postclassic 5.4-person household/ 10-person household
SACNAB-YAXHA							
Sacnab	484.9	724.1	1,446.7	2,170.8	94.1	0.0/0.0	0.0/0.0
Yaxha	330.8	975.6	1,611.9	4,082.0	527.9	1,030.8/1,906.9	919.3/1,700.7
Basin pair	815.7	1,699.7	3,058.6	6,252.8	622.0	1,030.8/1,906.9	919.3/1,700.7
MACANCHE-SALPETEN							
Macanche	1,284.1	1,070.8	270.3	3,113.2	726.1	1,068.3/1,976.4	581.0/1,074.9
Salpeten	767.2	108.5	381.7	4,148.5	2,257.5	860.5/1,591.9	675.0/1,248.8
Basin pair	2,051.3	1,179.3	652.0	7,261.7	2,983.6	1,928.8/3,568.3	1,256.0/2,323.6
QUEXIL-PETENXIL							
Quexil	1,319.8	387.6	127.4	3,031.4	642.1	213.6/395.2	67.8/125.4
Petenxil	0.0	0.0	88.4	804.9	319.5	0.0/0.0	0.0/0.0
Basin pair	1,319.8	387.6	215.8	3836.3	961.6	213.6/395.2	67.8/125.4

Table 6.7 Average Annual Crude Growth Rates by Time Period (%)

Basin Pair	Middle Preclassic (700–250 B.C.)	Late Preclassic (250 B.C.– A.D. 250)	Early Classic (A.D. 250– 550)	Late Classic (A.D. 550– 830)	Terminal Classic (A.D. 830– 950)	Early Postclassic (A.D. 950– 1200)	Late Postclassic (A.D. 1200– 1525)
Sacnab-Yaxha	1.12	0.15	0.20	0.26	−1.90	0.45	−0.04
Macanche-Salpeten	1.33	−0.11	−0.20	0.87	−0.74	0.07	−0.13
Quexil-Petenxil	1.23	−0.25	−0.20	1.03	1.15	−0.36	−0.35

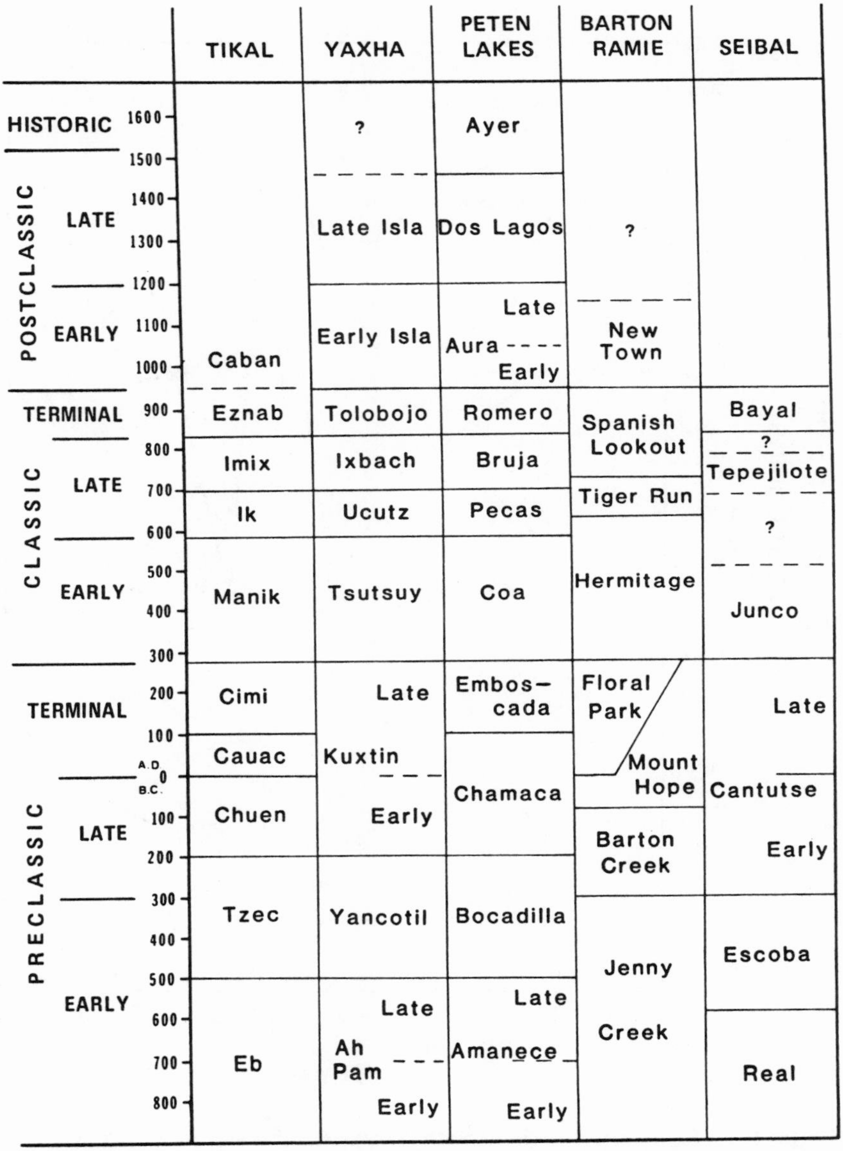

		TIKAL	YAXHA	PETEN LAKES	BARTON RAMIE	SEIBAL
HISTORIC	1600		?	Ayer		
	1500					
POSTCLASSIC · LATE	1400		Late Isla	Dos Lagos	?	
	1300					
	1200					
POSTCLASSIC · EARLY	1100	Caban	Early Isla	Late Aura - - - - Early	New Town	
	1000					
CLASSIC · TERMINAL	900	Eznab	Tolobojo	Romero	Spanish Lookout	Bayal
	800	Imix	Ixbach	Bruja		? Tepejilote
CLASSIC · LATE	700				Tiger Run	
	600	Ik	Ucutz	Pecas		?
	500				Hermitage	
CLASSIC · EARLY	400	Manik	Tsutsuy	Coa		Junco
	300					
PRECLASSIC · TERMINAL	200	Cimi	Late	Emboscada	Floral Park	Late
	100	Cauac	Kuxtin		Mount Hope	Cantutse
	A.D. 0 B.C.			Chamaca		
PRECLASSIC · LATE	100	Chuen	Early		Barton Creek	Early
	200					
	300	Tzec	Yancotil	Bocadilla	Jenny Creek	Escoba
	400					
	500			Late		
PRECLASSIC · EARLY	600		Late			
	700	Eb	Ah Pam	Amanece		Real
	800		Early	Early		

Figure 6.1   Chronological framework for the Peten lakes analyses.

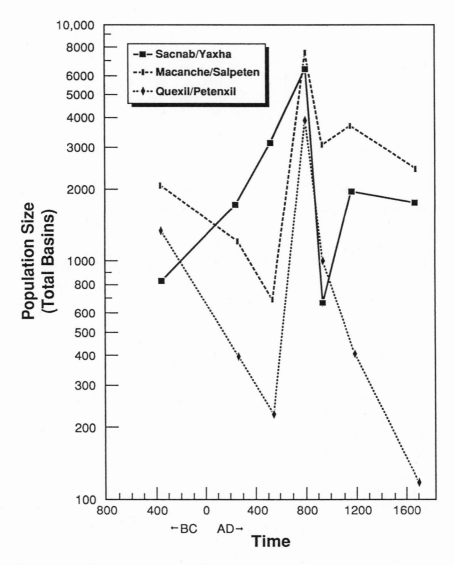

Figure 6.2 Semilogarithmic growth curves for the Peten lake-basin
pairs.

7 /

Maya Archaeology and Population Estimates in the Tayasal-Paxcaman Zone, Peten, Guatemala

ARLEN F. CHASE

The Carnegie Institution of Washington evinced the first interest in the Tayasal-Paxcaman Zone. Sylvanus G. Morley, director of Carnegie's Maya program, was convinced that Tayasal was one of three key sites for understanding Maya prehistory (Kidder 1950:1). Morley believed Uaxactum would provide data on the Preclassic and Classic periods, Chichen Itza on the shift from the Classic to Postclassic, and Tayasal on the latest Maya. Thus, from early on, Tayasal was viewed as critical for understanding late Maya prehistory, largely because of the belief that the site was the capital of the last independent Maya kingdom of the Itza, who were finally conquered by the Spaniards in A.D. 1697 (see D. Chase and A. Chase 1986b).

Archaeologists who have worked in the Lake Peten area (Map 7.1) went there primarily to find Postclassic remains (post–A.D. 950 for the Tayasal-Paxcaman Zone), but evidence of earlier occupation proved to be far more plentiful (A. Chase 1979, 1983, 1985a, 1985b). In the early 1920s Morley's excavation program at Tayasal was halted after two years when it became clear that it was uncovering almost exclusively Classic remains. In the 1950s George Cowgill (1963) succeeded in finding Postclassic remains on Flores and on the shores of Lake Peten. Fueled by Cowgill's success, a University of Pennsylvania expedition excavated at various sites on the

Tayasal Peninsula in search of Postclassic remains in 1971. Because large-scale Postclassic architecture was not encountered, however, a decision was made to conclude excavations after the first season; a 1977 season tied up loose ends.

The 1971 and 1977 research defined an area of settlement known as the Tayasal-Paxcaman Zone (A. Chase 1983:6–12). This zone of approximately 90 km² was concentrated on the uplands of the peninsular spine. The entire peninsular spine between the northern and southern arms of Lake Peten was found to exhibit almost continuous settlement. Although different settlement nodes could be recognized (such as Tayasal, Cenote, and Paxcaman), archaeological evidence for habitation was continuous between these nodes, albeit not as dense as within the centers themselves. However, because distinct nodes or epicenters existed on this spine which could be considered "sites," the entire area was designated a "settlement zone."

Even a cursory view of the prehistoric occupation within this zone reveals that the specific population history of any given site differs from that of its neighbors. The spatial distribution of settlement for any given temporal frame is likely to follow similar rules and patterns, but these guidelines vary from one spatial frame to another. The population also appears to have moved freely over time. Yet when viewed collectively, it seems to have grown continually within the zone until the onset of the Postclassic Period. The data also make it clear that sampling schemes focusing only on mounded constructions and higher terrain are likely to misjudge the actual population history.

METHODOLOGICAL CONSIDERATIONS AND DATA BASE

Although the problems of interpreting excavations are apparent in all aspects of archaeological reconstruction, they are critical in demographic work, where small variations in temporal assessment or functional assignment may drastically change population totals. Other important questions arise with regard to archaeological interpretation and the potential equivalencies among different kinds of data. What constitutes a unit of demographic presence: a building itself or a modification of it; a primary deposit consisting of refuse or a cache or a burial? Or can material from fill indicate demographic presence? (See Coe and Haviland 1966 for problems in associating fill and people at Barton Ramie, Belize.) How do these units compare with others garnered from areal clearing or excavation of special deposits? How specific or gross a unit are we talking about? The answers to these questions produce dissension over whether such a data base can be used as a source of cultural, behavioral, spatial, or temporal information.

Regardless of the excavation strategy, not all excavations completely uncover constructions; structures are often sampled by test pit, trench, and/ or areal excavation. Usually only a small portion of a building or platform is exposed or has its temporal dimensions defined. If only a fraction of a building is sampled, it is quite possible that the excavations may present a skewed representation of dates of construction and function(s). However, such partial samples generally form the building blocks for wider interpretations concerning chronology and demography or function and process. These statements certainly hold true for the Tayasal-Paxcaman Zone. For this reason, it is necessary critically to review the data base with respect to the temporal fames used and the spatial units recorded.

Timeframes

Analysis of the Tayasal materials from 1977 through 1983 resulted in the establishment of a tentative chronological framework for the zone, originally cross-dated to other preexisting sequences in the Peten. The phase dates presented here are slightly realigned (Table 7.1); this realignment is based on further analysis of the Tayasal pottery, on the viewing of other central Peten collections, and on firsthand knowledge of well-dated contexts from Santa Rita Corozal (D. Chase 1982; D. Chase and A. Chase 1986a, 1988) and Caracol (A. Chase and D. Chase 1987a, 1987b). Although this realignment is usually in the neighborhood of only plus or minus 50 years, it presents an entirely different demographic curve for the sites of Cenote and Tayasal and, by extension, the entire zone.

Under the original temporal frame established for the zone (in which Hoxchunchan was dated A.D. 400–600 and Pakoc A.D. 600–700; see Table 7.1 for revised dating), both Tayasal and Cenote would appear to have experienced Early Classic Hoxchunchan declines in their populations, but with the shift of 50 years to the succeeding Pakoc phase in the adjusted timeframe, a smooth demographic development is seen from the Late Preclassic through the Terminal Classic periods in the zone. This suggests that the population depression during the Early Classic claimed for other Peten sites (Willey 1977:394–97) may be a product of excavation methodology *and* temporal assignation. It should be further noted that, at least for the Tayasal-Paxcaman Zone, the use of an 11.3.0.0.0 correlation (see A. Chase 1986: 117–21) to interpret the data would also eliminate the severe drop in population now seen during the Early Postclassic Chilcob phase. It is quite evident that even slight changes in the temporal frame can produce drastic revisions in demographic profiles.

Dating, Contemporaneity, Occupation, and Context

A problem in the construction of any population history is the establishment of contemporaneity. Population reconstructions for Maya sites with long histories of occupation are useless unless an assessment can be made as to which of the defined units of the site were used and inhabited at the same time. Most Maya buildings are constructed of what is colloquially known as "fill"—material placed in the core of a structure to provide a firm, flat foundation for a platform that raises the building mass above ground level. Much archaeological interpretation in the Maya area is based indirectly on this core material, particularly when special deposits such as burials, caches, or primary refuse are missing. However, dating or any other interpretation of excavated construction core requires careful evaluation of the activities that led to its deposition. Such an assessment is problematic because Maya fill may result from a single effort or from accretionary efforts and may be carried in from almost anywhere at the site. Thus, the fill, though always somewhat earlier in date than the construction that encases it, frequently includes items of mixed or uncertain associations, especially if earlier constructions or dump sites are raided for building materials. In small excavation samples, particularly those generated by test pits, it is often extremely difficult to assess such context. Mistakes here can lead to errors in interpretation and, if such a sample contributes to the larger picture, to errors in site or regional synthesis.

The Tayasal-Paxcaman Zone has a large number of primary deposits directly associated with pottery vessels, allowing the construction of a tightly seriated sequence (A. Chase 1983:Table 3). Thus many of the loci used in the construction of the tables presented here were assessed on more than the simple presence and absence of sherd materials. Rather, the inference of occupation was derived from the dating of actual construction or use-related events recovered from the excavations. Optimally, occupation was established based on the recovery of special deposits consisting of caches, burials, or refuse; this was possible in 6 out of 8 Cenote investigations and 30 out of 99 Tayasal investigations. In the other excavations occupation was established through the use of stratigraphy, seriation, and spatial considerations.

The use of these techniques at Tayasal, however, calls for a cautionary note. Without the careful consideration of context, it would have appeared that Late Preclassic occupation of the zone was extremely heavy—for at least a half-dozen constructions dating to the Middle Postclassic Period contained only large Preclassic sherd materials in their cores. Based on sherd counts alone, these could be interpreted as Preclassic constructions reoccupied during the Postclassic Period. Contextual analysis, however, made clear that these constructions were entirely Postclassic and that Postclassic peoples were mining earlier loci, not necessarily close by, for fill (cf. A. Chase 1983:696).

Apart from determining when something was built, other problems exist in any excavation sample. For instance, how long was a structure occupied? The Tayasal-Paxcaman data suggest that an answer would have to be based on both time period and kind of construction. As a rule of thumb, it appears that the more effort expended on any particular locus, the longer that locus was generally occupied. Many well-constructed loci exhibit a long history of occupation. As no natural earth occurs in any of these loci, it is usually predicated that they were occupied continually. In particular, because of the labor invested, it is likely that well-plastered constructions were occupied longer than unplastered or poorly plastered buildings. Thus, units of time approaching 100 or 150 years are acceptable figures for the occupation of better-built buildings, whether continually or cyclically lived in. The flimsily constructed buildings generally representative of nonmounded constructions, and especially characteristic of the Postclassic, were probably occupied for no longer than 50 years. This interpretation is based not only on the available building materials, but also on the general lack of rebuilding found in Postclassic constructions and on the uniformity in associated ceramic deposits. Nevertheless, to attempt to make different use-life predictions within the same time era based on the various kinds of buildings is exceedingly difficult or even fruitless without more extensive excavation. It is, however, interesting to note that, if all buildings are held constant, the general demographic curves in the Tayasal-Paxcaman Zone are not significantly altered whether the occupation span is considered to be uniformly 50, 100, 150, or 200 years.

One further issue needs to be raised—the existence of "invisible con- structions" (Bronson 1968; D. Chase, this volume; Pyburn, this volume). These undoubtedly exist in the Tayasal-Paxcaman Zone. Based on the excavation sample, they are numerous, but it is not easy to give a quantitative estimate. Part of this difficulty is due to the research design used in the epicenters of the mounded Classic Period sites. The 1971 excavations focused on mounded constructions on the mainland spine centers without sampling vacant areas. However, when vacant areas were sampled along the lakeshore of Tayasal, every test pit dug revealed some evidence of occupation. Thus, estimating a figure for the Tayasal-Paxcaman Zone which may account for the unmapped invisible construction is problematic. It is also difficult to tell if the percentage of invisible constructions differs for each time period. I have always believed, however, that the mounded constructions visible in the Tayasal-Paxcaman area were not the residences of the poorest inhabitants of the zone. For purposes of population reconstruction, a figure of 37.4% invisible constructions might be proffered; this figure is based arbitrarily on the overall percentage of nonmounded structures found and investigated at the site of Tayasal. Nevertheless, this figure could just as easily be doubled based on the same data.

Settlement Data

The Pennsylvania Tayasal Project mapped a variety of settlement concentrations and excavated numerous Postclassic remains as well as a far larger amount of earlier materials. Besides Cenote, Tayasal, and Nima, the mainland sites of Yachul, Chaltun Grande, Chaja, Michoacan, Tres Naciones, and Paxcaman (north) were mapped during 1971 or 1977, and the islands in Lake Quexil and Lake Peten were mapped during 1977. The 1971 excavations focused on Cenote, Tayasal, and Nima (Map 7.1). Seven structures were intensively excavated at Cenote, and data from an eighth construction were recovered in 1977 (A. Chase 1983:85–354). Information pertaining to 99 constructions is extant for Tayasal. Twenty-six of these constructions were investigated by trenching, partial areal stripping, or some combination of these two techniques; the rest were sampled by means of test pits (A. Chase 1983:355–1057). Two additional structures were tested at Nima (A. Chase 1983:1098–1139), one with a slightly expanded test pit and the other with a small trench. A total of 51 burials, representing 56 individuals, was recovered by the Pennsylvania Project; 8 additional burials representing 8 individuals (all Late Classic Hobo) were recovered by the Guthe excavations (A. Chase 1983: Table 37).

Cenote

Excavations into seven different structures were undertaken in 1971 at Cenote; all involved trenching, areal stripping, or some combination of the two. In 1977 information was recorded concerning a looted building in which an early Late Classic (Pakoc) burial had been encountered. Taken collectively (Table 7.2), the Cenote excavations reveal an epicenter that must have blossomed after the Late Preclassic and presumably dominated the Tayasal Peninsula in the Early Classic era, only to be overtaken by Tayasal itself during the Late Classic. Perhaps significantly, the Cenote data demonstrate a smooth development out of the Late Preclassic into and through the Early Classic without any disruption of population. Additionally, Protoclassic ceramic modes are clearly evident from the earlier part of the Early Classic; these modes do not appear to be intrusive to the zone but apparently are part of a ceramic continuum (A. Chase and D. Chase 1983, 1987c:53) and indicate that there was no population replacement in the Tayasal-Paxcaman Zone during this era. The site yielded no Postclassic material.

Mapping at Cenote showed a total of 107 structures in an area of approximately 0.5 km². Most of these remains were easily visible in the savanna; additional structures exist in the surrounding bush. Although Cenote was definitely a primary node of settlement in the Tayasal-Paxcaman Zone and exhibits sizable constructions, its overall mapped density of structures is quite low. Even if one were to assume that the site was twice its mapped size, this would indicate a density of only 214 structures/km²—not large by any calculation. Cenote's maximum population during the early part of the Late Classic Period could only have been in the neighborhood of 1200 (see below for mode of calculation).

Tayasal

After it was realized that Postclassic remains were not to be found at Cenote, excavations were emphatically shifted to Tayasal, a site heavily occupied throughout most of its prehistory (Table 7.2). Initial excavations focused on the mounded structures found on the peninsular spine. With very few exceptions, the remains here proved to be earlier than Postclassic. As a result, excavations were again refocused, this time to vacant-terrain areas along the Tayasal lakeshore. Here an extensive and widely scattered test-pit program encountered, in a majority of the tests, the Postclassic remains that were being sought, suggesting that almost any semi-level area along the lakeshore was once a locus of late occupation.

The Tayasal excavations are interesting for several reasons. Approximately 25% of the 399 mapped structures have been investigated by a single test pit, multiple test pits, trenches, or some combination of areal stripping and trenching (Table 7.3). These different sampling methods demonstrate, first, that all Early Classic (Yaxcheel and Hoxchunchan) and early Late Classic (Pakoc) occupation is less likely to be encountered in a single test pit than in any other form of excavation; this finding suggests that single test pits would likely underrepresent these time periods (at least for Tayasal). Second, because excavations took place in both mounded and nonmounded constructions (Table 7.4), these same time periods are likely to be underrepresented in nonmounded constructions (at least along the Tayasal lakeshore). Third, the data clearly show that excavations into mounded constructions to the exclusion of vacant-terrain investigations would likely significantly misrepresent the amount of Postclassic settlement. Finally, the data demonstrate that locational factors enter into the excavation sample. A consideration of those structures excavated on the peninsular spine as compared to those excavated along the lakeshore (Table 7.5) shows an inverse relationship between Early Classic/early Late Classic and all Postclassic constructions. Structures dating to Yaxcheel, Hoxchunchan, and Pakoc times tended to be on the higher peninsular spine, whereas Postclassic constructions tended to be near the lakeshore; excavation samples excluding one or the other locale would severely misrepresent the overall occupational history of the site. Interestingly, no matter how the sample is broken down, Tayasal exhibits widespread Late Preclassic and late Late Classic settlement both on the peninsular spine and on the shores of Lake Peten.

Mapping at Tayasal revealed a total of 399 structures over an area of approximately 2.5 km². Because only about 40% of this mapped area was intensively recorded and the other 60% was merely surveyed for the larger constructions, the actual structure total for the 2.5 km² is probably in the neighborhood of 532 structures (assuming that 25% of the structures are still to be mapped). If we assume that Tayasal is approximately 5 km² in size, we find that mapping will likely reveal a total of about 1,064 structures. With a 60% occupation rate at any one time (a figure extrapolated from actual excavation percentages for Hobo times, when population was at a maximum at Tayasal), this would mean a total population of 3064 to 3575, without any correction factor for vacant terrain. Correcting for vacant terrain would significantly raise the overall Tayasal population (again, based on Tayasal excavation percentages, anywhere from 37.4 to 75% and maybe higher), yielding totals ranging from 4210 to 6256 for the Late Classic Hobo era.

Nima

In a final expansion of the successful Tayasal testing program, text excavations were made in two small mounds at Nima, on the northwest corner of the Tayasal Peninsula. These two investigations recovered stratified remains suggesting the existence of a continuous sequence from the Late Classic through the Middle Postclassic. Surface collections make it clear that the area had been used not only for habitation, but also as burial ground from the Late Preclassic era through the Late Postclassic Period (Table 7.2). Mapping at Nima revealed only three mounded structures. Density figures derived from both Nima and Tres Naciones suggest that the outlying sites in the Tayasal-Paxcaman Zone approached a density of only approximately 30 constructions/km².

ABSOLUTE POPULATION IN THE TAYASAL-PAXCAMAN ZONE

Although it is clear that population centers shifted over time within the Tayasal-Paxcaman Zone, it is likely that a sizable population existed within the region at any one time (Table 7.2). Thus, while Cenote may have been in "decline" during the later part of the Late Classic era, Tayasal was "booming" and much of the area between Tayasal and Paxcaman was probably densely settled. Similarly, while Cenote was booming during the Early Classic era, Tayasal was densely settled but not quite in control of its future. Inverse relationships in settlement and population may therefore be seen at different sites within the zone over time.

In an attempt to get at absolute population numbers for the zone, the area has been tentatively subdivided into two types of natural regions: those likely to be heavily occupied and those less likely to be occupied. The densest settlement in the Tayasal-Paxcaman Zone corresponds with areas of higher topography and poorer soils (A. Chase 1983:1225–27). This part of the peninsula, the Tayasal spine, encompasses a region of about 8 km². A region of lesser settlement rings the spine, occupying an estimated 18 km². The remaining 64 km² represent a region of lower terrain that slopes into Lake Peten to the north and the south and into a marshy area to the east.

In order to calculate maximum settlement figures, it is necessary to estimate first how many structures are present within the Tayasal-Paxcaman Zone (Table 7.6). Mapping tended to concentrate in nodal areas. On the peninsular spine an area of slightly over 4 km² was mapped, yielding a density of 221.08 structures/km². If we assume that there are 8 km² at this structure density, a total of 1768.64 structures would exist for the upland region. The next densest area of settlement, surrounding the spine, is estimated (for the purposes of absolute population considerations) as being half as densely occupied as the spine. This 18-km² region thus yields a total structure count of 1989.72. By far the largest area of the Tayasal-Paxcaman Zone, the 64 km² of low terrain, was not densely occupied. Here only 1920 structures are estimated to exist based on the mapped totals of only 30 structures/km² found in the lakeside sites of Nima and Tres Naciones. Thus, the approximately 90-km² Tayasal-Paxcaman Zone probably houses a grand total of 5678 mappable structures.

Based on the fact that only 56.57% of the structures sampled at Tayasal yielded materials from the Late Classic Hobo, when the zone reached its zenith in terms of overall habitation, it is estimated that only 60% of the predicted mappable buildings were constructed or used during the Late Classic era, yielding a total of 3407 buildings. Because the exclusion of 40% of the sample is probably large, this total is assumed to represent habitation units and can be multiplied by a figure ranging from 4.8 (Wilk 1984:Table 9.2) to 5.6 (Redfield and Villa Rojas 1934; cf. Haviland 1970) inhabitants/structure to yield a population figure of 16,354 to 19,079 for the entire zone. This figure, however, is considered low, even though no correction has been applied for nonresidential buildings. It is likely that a high number of invisible constructions exist in the Tayasal-Paxcaman Zone. Based on the Tayasal sample of nonmounded constructions, these invisible constructions minimally comprise 37.4% of the overall sample and are likely to be double this figure. Thus, the overall population estimate for the zone presumably needs to be increased by anywhere from 37.4 to 75% of the total mapped structures.

Based on the figures above, the actual absolute population in the Tayasal-Paxcaman Zone is estimated to have ranged from a low of 21,951 to a high of 33,272. Such an estimate is within the realm of reason. For the zone as a whole, this means an overall density of 250 to 341 individuals/km². For the more densely settled spine, the population occupying the high ground would have ranged from 6861 (858/km²) to 10,400 (1300/km²). For the less densely settled area between the spine and the lakeside, the population would have ranged from 7719 (429/km²) to 11,700 (650/km²). The sparsely inhabited 64-km² area would have held between 7371 (115/km²) and 11,172 (174/km²) individuals.

INTERPRETATIONS AND CONCLUSIONS

From the standpoint of prehistoric population history, the Tayasal-Paxcaman Zone data are interesting for several reasons. They generally represent a smooth development from the Preclassic to Postclassic with a slight depression between the Classic and Postclassic periods, according to current interpretations of this timeframe. The Early Classic Period in the zone does not show any loss of population, but rather appears continuous, with preceding periods indicating an ever-increasing population through the end of the Late Classic. However, this picture could be altered with only slight temporal adjustments to the parameters given to the various phases. In this light, a cautionary note must be sounded concerning simple acceptance of interpretations of cultural decline and abandonment at various sites during the Early Classic.

An additional caution must be added to our understanding of the Early Postclassic Period. As reconstructed for the Tayasal-Paxcaman Zone (Table 7.2), there is a drop in population during the Early Postclassic in the neighborhood of 60%. Although this is drastic, it is not the almost complete exodus seen at the sites of Tikal and Uaxactun. It must be noted, however, that if the current correlation is ever altered in favor of another, this population depression would be eliminated (see A. Chase 1986:120–21). Regardless of the temporal scheme, by the Middle Postclassic the population of the Tayasal-Paxcaman Zone is again approaching its Classic Period limits. In contrast, the later Postclassic settlement pattern has shifted dramatically in the zone, for no longer is the peninsular ridge being occupied nor are large constructions being built; instead, smaller, often invisible, house platforms are being massed in the low-lying terrain around the shores of Lake Peten (A. Chase 1979, 1983, 1985a, 1985b).

That such population shifts occurred earlier in prehistory can be seen in the data from Cenote, Nima, and Tayasal. No single primate center emerges over time within the zone. Cenote clearly peaks during Yaxcheel (Protoclassic or early Early Classic), Hoxchunchan (later Early Classic), and Pakoc (early Late Classic) times whereas epicentral Tayasal peaks during Pakoc and Hobo (later Late Classic and Terminal Classic) times and lakeshore Tayasal peaks during Cocahmut (Middle Postclassic) times. Thus, differential settlement is distinctly visible in the broader temporal patterns within the Tayasal-Paxcaman Zone.

Even on a synchronic level the settlement of the zone cannot be understood by reference to a single site nor could a simple archaeological testing program define the zone's prehistory; rather, a broad perspective combined with an intensive excavation program is needed to garner data important to the overall region. Additionally, excavations in areas devoid of mounds are imperative, as many of the Postclassic structures at Tayasal are not visible on the ground surface. Thus, an excavation program concentrating only on mounds or raised structures would totally miss and misinterpret the Postclassic settlement system of the Tayasal-Paxcaman Zone. The vacant-terrain excavation undertaken by the 1971 Pennsylvania Project centered on the shore of Lake Peten and the steeper terrain between the lake and the peninsular spine; a similar program on the spine might encounter other hidden spatial patterns pertaining to earlier temporal horizons of the zone (based on data gathered for Tikal by Bronson 1968). An assessment of the Tayasal data, however, makes it clear that archaeological programs, at least in the southern lowlands, that ignore vacant terrain likely will misjudge both the temporal and spatial aspects of Maya settlements. Likewise, excavations within different topographic areas will augment and change the view of population history. Different excavation strategies additionally affect the recovery of relevant data. Finally, by viewing the Tayasal-Paxcaman Zone as a whole, we gain a better perspective on its component parts and are able to place each within its correct milieu, thus permitting a more accurate interpretation of regional dynamics.

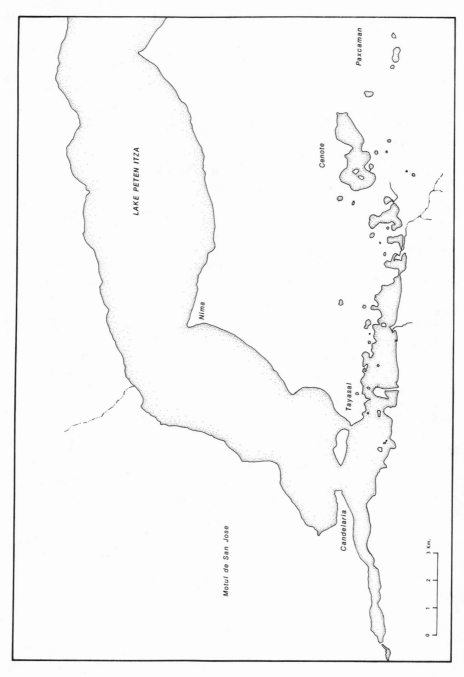

Map 7.1 The Tayasal-Paxcaman Zone.

Table 7.1   Tayasal-Paxcaman Zone: Dates for the
             Ceramic Complexes

Period	Complex	Dates
Middle Preclassic	Chunzalam	750–250 B.C.
Late Preclassic	Kax	250 B.C.–A.D. 250
early Early Classic	Yaxcheel	A.D. 250–400
late Early Classic	Hoxchunchan	A.D. 400–550
early Late Classic	Pakoc	A.D. 550–700
late Late Classic	Hobo	A.D. 700–950
Early Postclassic	Chilcob	A.D. 950–1200
Middle Postclassic	Cocahmut	A.D. 1200–1450
Late Postclassic	Kauil	A.D. 1450–1700
Historic	—	A.D. 1700–1850

Table 7.2 Tayasal-Paxcaman Zone: Occupation Adjusted for 100-Year Average Use-Life

Complex	Number of Cases			Adjustment Factor	Adjusted Cases			Relative Population		
	Tayasal (N = 99)	Cenote (N = 8)	Total[a] (N = 109)		Tayasal	Cenote	Total	Tayasal	Cenote	Total
Chunzalam	4	1	5	1/5	0.8	0.2	1.0	4	4	4
Kax	69	3	71	1/5	13.8	0.6	14.2	62	11	56
Yaxcheel	21	6	27	1/5	14.0	4.0	18.0	63	76	71
Hoxchunchan	25	7	32	1/1.5	16.7	4.7	21.3	75	89	85
Pakoc	26	8	36[a]	1/1.5	17.3	5.3	24.0	77	100	95
Hobo	56	5	63[a]	1/2.5	22.4	2.0	25.2	100	38	100
Chilcob	21	0	23[a]	1/2.5	8.4	0	9.2	38	0	37
Cocahmut	46	0	48[a]	1/2.5	18.4	0	19.2	82	0	76
Kauil	10	0	10	1/2.5	4.0	0	4.0	18	0	16

[a]Includes two excavations at Nima

Table 7.3   Tayasal: Amount of Excavation and Frequency of Period by Excavation Type

Period	Test Pit (N = 62)		Multiple Test (N = 11)		Trench (N = 17)		Areal/Trench (N = 9)		All Structure Excavations (N = 99)	
	Number	%	Number	%	Number	%	Number	%	Number	%
Chunzalam	2	3.23	1	9.09	1	5.88	0	0	4	4.04
Kax	48	77.42	9	81.82	11	64.71	1	11.11	69	69.70
Yaxcheel	9	14.52	3	27.27	9	52.94	0	0	21	21.21
Hoxchunchan	9	14.52	2	18.18	10	58.82	4	44.44	25	25.25
Pakoc	11	16.13	4	36.36	8	47.06	3	33.33	26	26.26
Hobo	29	46.77	8	72.73	12	70.59	7	77.78	56	56.57
Chilcob	11	16.13	2	18.18	6	35.29	2	22.22	21	21.21
Cocahmut	25	40.32	11	100.00	6	35.29	4	44.44	48	48.48
Kauil	2	3.23	1	9.09	5	29.41	2	22.22	10	10.10

Table 7.4 Tayasal: Excavations in Mounded and
           Nonmounded Constructions

Period	Nonmounded (N = 37)		Mounded (N = 62)	
	Number	%	Number	%
Chunzalam	2	5.40	2	3.20
Kax	27	72.97	42	67.74
Yaxcheel	7	18.92	14	22.58
Hoxchunchan	4	10.81	21	33.87
Pakoc	4	10.81	22	35.48
Hobo	21	56.76	35	56.45
Chilcob	12	32.43	9	14.52
Cocalhmut	27	72.97	19	30.64
Kauil	6	16.22	4	6.45

Table 7.5 Tayasal: Excavations by Location

Period	Tayasal Spine (N = 31)		Lakeside (N = 68)	
	Number	%	Number	%
Chunzalam	2	6.45	2	2.94
Kax	15	48.39	54	79.41
Yaxcheel	10	32.26	11	16.18
Hoxchunchan	13	41.94	12	17.65
Pakoc	13	41.94	13	19.18
Hobo	22	70.97	34	50.00
Chilcob	5	16.13	16	23.53
Cocahmut	4	12.90	42	61.76
Kauil	1	3.23	10	14.71

Table 7.6   Tayasal-Paxcaman Zone: Mapped
Structures and Structure Density by Site

Site	Mapped Structures	Mapped Area (km²)	Structure Density (structures/km²)
Islands			
Islote Grande	2	0.02364	84.60
Piedra Rajada	1	0.001	1,000.00
Santa Barbara	14	0.0282	496.45
Pedregales	3	0.02	150.00
Lepet	6	0.385	15.58
Flores	—	0.131	—
Quexil (2)	24	0.04	600.00
All island structures (excluding Flores)	50	0.49784	100.43
Mainland			
Nima	3	0.10	30.00
Yachul	101	0.346	291.90
Chaltun Grande	138	0.365	378.00
Chaja	36	0.06	600.00
Tres Naciones	12	0.40	30.00
Michoacan	65	0.1558	417.20
Paxcaman	63	0.1848	340.90
Cenote	107	0.50	214.00
Tayasal	399	2.50	159.60
All mainland structures	924	4.6116	200.36
Spine structures	909	4.1116	221.08
Lakeside (excluding Tayasal)	15	0.50	30.00
Entire Zone (mapped)	974	5.10944	190.63

8 /

Maya Settlement in the Belize River Area: Variations in Residence Patterns of the Central Maya Lowlands

ANABEL FORD

Research in the central Maya lowlands (Map 8.1) has revealed variations in settlement distribution and chronology which correspond to broad hydrographic areas within the lowlands: the interior core area around the center of Tikal, the southern lakes area running from Lake Peten Itza east to Lake Yaxha, and the rivers fringing the area on the east and west. It is increasingly apparent that these local variations need to be understood before the regional Maya development can be explained. The Belize River Archaeological Settlement Survey (BRASS) was specifically designed to gather local settlement and resource data within the valley area along the Belize River and north into the interior. These data will be used to reconstruct the local Belize River area developments and for comparison with the growing body of data from the lakes and core areas. Taken together, these interregional comparisons will provide a basis for understanding variability in the central Maya lowlands.

The archaeology of the Belize River area promises to cast light on Maya development in several important ways. Evidence suggests that the upper Belize Valley was one of the first areas to be occupied within the central lowlands and, as a geographical link from the Caribbean to the interior, served as an avenue of entrance into the core area (O. Puleston and D.

Puleston 1971, 1972). The valley is situated in a logistically advantageous locale at the terminus of the navigable portion of the river and within 60 km of the core area around Tikal. From the excavations at Barton Ramie in the upper Belize River area, occupation appears to have been relatively continuous throughout the course of prehistory, bracketing the rise and decline of the Classic Period Maya (Willey et al. 1965; Gifford 1976). It is on this base that the BRASS project was initiated.

BELIZE RIVER ARCHAEOLOGICAL SETTLEMENT SURVEY

Settlement and Environment

The upper Belize River area can be characterized geographically as (1) the open undulating valley and savanna east of the confluence of the eastern and western branch of the Belize River and (2) the constricted valley foot-hills and uplands to the west (Map 8). The soils of these zones have been classified for the area (Wright et al. 1959; Jenkins et al. 1976) and are locally described for the project (Fedick 1989). Broadly speaking, there are several soil zones important to ancient Maya settlement: the fertile alluvial soils of the valley and well-drained soils of the uplands, the moderately fertile foothills, poorly drained swamps soils interspersed in the uplands and foothills, and the poor soils of the savannas.

The open valley on the east is composed of a floodplain and low rolling hills north of the plain and scattered Pleistocene savannas inland from the river. The valley includes modern flood zones, recent alluvial terraces, and older alluvial deposits (Fedick 1985, 1989). Much of the northern interior of this area is savanna, currently supporting oak, palmetto, and grasses. The savanna is composed of poorly drained, infertile Pleistocene subsoils. Relief is minimal in this eastern zone. Elevation at the river averages about 60 m above sea level and rises only another 50 m within 5 km of the river.

The western mountains, ascending more than 300 m above the river valley, are a sharp contrast to the rolling terrain of the east. There is much variability within this zone. The limestone foothills rise steeply to the crests (ca. 5 km from the river), but beyond they spread into a hilly upland plateau with alternating gentle and steep areas. This upland region is dominated by fertile, well-drained soils, which are associated with upland forests, interspersed with moderately drained areas associated with transitional upland swamps and some poorly drained swamp soils.

The BRASS project was designed to investigate settlement patterns within these environments and with respect to the river and the administrative centers. To accomplish these objectives, survey transects were located so as to pass through each of the identified environments. They were oriented to crosscut the valley and bisect an identified administrative center (see Map 8.2).

Three survey transects were selected, two 5 km long, designated Bacab Na and Yaxox, and one 10 km long, designated El Pilar. The eastern Bacab Na Transect covers the open valley and interior savanna zone and bisects the 1-courtyard center of Bacab Na, 0.75 km north of the river at an elevation of 80 m. The middle Yaxox Transect traverses the flanks of the uplands and bisects the relatively large center of Yaxox, in the foothills, which has 5 courtyards. Yaxox is situated 1.3 km north of the river at an elevation of 100 m. The western El Pilar Transect covers the constricted valley, foothills, and upland zones. It includes two centers: Alta Vista and El Pilar. Alta Vista is a 2-courtyard center in the foothills overlooking the valley, 2.1 km from the river at an elevation of 167 m. El Pilar, an extensive, 15-courtyard center well within the upland zone, is located at the northern end of the transect, 10 km from the river at 250 m elevation.

The settlement survey was undertaken in two five-month seasons (1983, 1984) and encompassed five major activities: (1) transit mapping of the four centers, (2) establishment of the two 5-km baselines and the one 10-km baseline to serve as the axes of the transects, (3) settlement survey of 125 m on each side of the baseline, (4) mapping of all cultural remains within the 250-m-wide transect, and (5) test excavation of a 12.5% stratified random sample of residential units (48 total) based on distance from the transect origin point. The 1986 season focused on acquiring data on the chronology of the four centers.

The settlement survey involved the systematic surface coverage of the entire area of the transects. Individuals were positioned 10 to 20 m apart, depending on the vegetation (burned fields, pasture lands, and various stages of forest), and all areas were traversed to record topography, vegetation, and cultural remains. In addition, all soil zones were defined by soil test pits and samples collected from residential unit excavations (Fedick 1985, 1989). Following the surface survey, a mapping crew returned to highlighted areas of potential cultural significance. All superficial remains, including stone foundations with associated cultural debris and midden scatters, were recorded and positioned relative to the baseline.

A total of 500 ha was covered in the transect settlement survey. The cultural remains mapped within the three transects included 535 structures grouped into 342 residential units, several midden scatters, cultunes (storage pits in the limestone bedrock), limestone quarries, and chert quarries. Residential units were defined by rubble and mounded debris representing ancient structural remains. Units were designated as solitary structures when no other structures were within 10 m and/or no formal arrangement of structures was discerned. Such single-structure residential units include the numerous small foundations recorded in the uplands as well as the large "tell-like" platform units of the valley (e.g., those of Barton Ramie and Bacab Na). When structures were formally arranged around an interior space, or courtyard, or they were loosely arranged in close proximity to each other, they were grouped into a residential unit composed of two or more structures. The proportions of the different environmental zones and the corresponding settlement densities are presented in Table 8.1.

Excavations focused on residential units (total = 342). Mapped units were numbered and grouped by eights, based on distance from the river, and one residential unit in a group of eight was selected (12.5%) for the testing phase. The subsurface testing phase included examination of 48 residential unit middens, or ancient trash deposits, located adjacent to the randomly selected residential units. Five residential units were tested in the Bacab Na Transect, 15 from the Yaxox Transect, and 29 from the El Pilar Transect. These tested units composed the sample of residential settlement in the Belize River area.

Test excavations concentrated on midden deposits around the selected residential unit. The deposits were located by probing with a posthole digger immediately around structural remains (cf. Fry 1972). Posthole tests revealing the greatest amount of midden debris were selected for the expanded one-by-one-m test-unit excavations. The number of test units selected varied from one to three, based on the extent of the identified middens. The main purpose of this effort was to obtain temporally diagnostic ceramics for dating the occupation areas. Diagnostic sherd densities are relatively high, averaging 54 pieces/excavation site and from 10 to 15/ period represented at a site. Other midden debris (chert tools and manufacturing by-products, obsidian, other ceramic artifacts, grinding implements, etc.) was also recovered to help in reconstructing the various domestic activities at each site (see Ford and Olson 1989). In addition to the random sample, tests were made at an identified chert quarry and tool-production site, 2.5 km north of the river, adjacent to the Yaxox Transect and a biface production site adjacent to the center of El Pilar (see Map 8.2).

Preliminary investigations at the four centers of Bacab Na, Yaxox, Alta Vista, and El Pilar were initiated in 1986 to acquire data on the chronological sequence using looter's trench exposures and plaza test pits. Investigations included excavations of four test pits at Bacab Na, two test pits and three looter's trench column samples at Yaxox, three test pits and three looter's trench column samples at Alta Vista, and ten test pits and eight looter's trench column samples at El Pilar.

Belize River Area Chronology

The chronological data from the BRASS project follow a variation of the expected occupation pattern for the lowland area (Table 8.2). Growth is clear from the Middle Preclassic to the Late Preclassic, when occupation nearly doubles. Although residential settlement is well dispersed within the valley and upland zones for the entire Preclassic, there is a subtle difference between the occupations of the two zones. In the Middle Preclassic not only did the valley have a higher percentage of occupied sites, but the intensity of use, as reflected in sherd densities, differs by zone: the overall sherd density/m^3 of excavated middens in the valley is four times that of the upland zone. This difference narrows in the Late Preclassic, when most of the sites are occupied. Still, the valley contains a slightly higher percentage of occupied sites and a sherd density two times greater than that of the upland zone. In the foothills, settlement increased and the sherd density is comparable to that of the valley.

The Early Classic shows an enigmatic decline in the number of sites occupied and a distribution pattern similar to that of the Middle Preclassic. Sherd densities of residential middens are equally low in all zones. This decline appears to be quite different from the situation at Barton Ramie, where most sites occupied in the Late Preclassic continued to be occupied in the Early Classic. Settlement in the BRASS area concentrates at El Pilar, 10 km from the river, in the uplands. The Early Classic distribution may indicate a reorientation of more permanent settlement away from the marginal agricultural zones in the uplands toward centers and into the valley proper, where Barton Ramie is located.

These interpretations must be considered tentatively. It may be that our understanding of the Early Classic materials, which is limited to ceramic forms dominant in the core area around Tikal and Uaxactun, does not extend into the Belize River area (cf. Lincoln 1985). Data on the formal composition of the BRASS Early Classic ceramic assemblage is illustrative. Few forms are represented in this collection, and basal-flange bowls make up 65% of the assemblage. The low proportion of any Early Classic diagnostic in the BRASS collection, the restricted distribution among the residential units of the area, and the emphasis on the special, and often decorated, serving forms of the basal-flange bowl suggests a problem with the local relative dating of this period.

It is not difficult to distinguish the Late Classic time markers in the Belize River area. Ceramic distribution shows marked growth in the Late Classic, with 98% of sites occupied. This growth appears to correlate with the major building activity at centers in the area. The increase in occupation during the Late Classic corresponds to the data from all surrounding areas of the central Maya lowlands.

Evidence suggests heavy occupation in the Late Classic in all zones of the Belize River area. Nevertheless, sherd densities in excavated middens, indicating frequency of site use, vary among the zones. There is relative homogeneity in the sherd densities of valley sites but considerable variability in the sherd densities of upland sites. In the uplands the largest sites exhibit the highest sherd densities and the smallest sites the lowest. Considerable variation among sites also exists in the foothills, but unlike the case in the uplands, the highest sherd densities are found among the smallest sites.

The expected decline in settlement during the Terminal Classic and Postclassic periods is exhibited in the BRASS data. Only 48% of the tested sites exhibit occupation during the Terminal Classic, about half that of the Late Classic Period. The majority of the settlement concentrates in the uplands and around El Pilar. Postclassic occupation is even less than that of the Terminal Classic, dropping to 21% of the site total. Within the BRASS study area, occupation during the Postclassic is higher in the uplands than in the valley and the lowest in the foothills.

The data on the chronologies of the centers indicate that their construction spans the entire length of the development of the Belize River area. Some evidence suggests that initial constructions may have begun in the last phase of the Middle Preclassic at El Pilar and Alta Vista. There is considerable evidence of major building efforts in the Late Preclassic, and several major construction phases during that period are clear at El Pilar, Alta Vista, and Yaxox. Discrete Early Classic diagnostics are scarce, found only at El Pilar and Yaxox, and always occur with Late Preclassic materials. Early Classic markers are almost exclusively the basal-flange bowls. This limited evidence of Early Classic material corresponds with the settlement occupation data for this period (also based on the distribution of the diagnostic basal-flange bowls). It appears that the more general distribution of utilitarian forms associated with the Early Classic Period at Tikal is not present in the Belize River area. Further, the co-occurrence of traditional Preclassic material in all constructions with Early Classic materials suggests the continuance of Preclassic forms into the Early Classic in this area (cf. Lincoln 1985). For example, test excavation at the main temple of Barton Ramie in March 1988 corroborates the construction-fill data from the BRASS centers by demonstrating a long Late Preclassic building sequence on which is superimposed construction fill containing Late Preclassic utility vessels and Early Classic basal-flange bowls.

Late Classic construction is evident at all the centers and is the only construction at Bacab Na. Evidence of building in the Late Classic Period is not as extensive as in the Late Preclassic, especially at El Pilar, where some areas appear to have no Late Classic construction at all. Terminal Classic construction has been found at El Pilar, Yaxox, and possibly Bacab Na. Although Postclassic construction has been tentatively identified at Yaxox, it is clear that no major constructions were undertaken after the Terminal Classic Period.

The Regional Setting

Major cultural development of the central Maya lowlands began in the interior core area around Tikal, the last area to be settled. Because areas such as the Belize Valley were peripheral to the developments of the core area, they would be expected to exhibit overall lower settlement densities and less concentration of wealth in comparison to the core area. Although the full analysis of the BRASS data is still underway, the preliminary results generally corroborate the peripheral status of the Belize River area. The picture of the area's developments, however, is complex in that there is evidence of considerable early development by the Late Preclassic Period. Moreover, in the Late Classic there is a differentiation among the upland, foothill, and valley zones, as was seen with the chronological data discussed above.

A general comparison of the Belize River area with the lake and core areas provides insights into the settlement variations in terms of both structure density (structures/km²) and the comparison and size of residential units. The Belize River area exhibits a relatively high settlement or structure density when compared with densities of the lakes and core areas (Table 8.3). Taken at face value, this could argue for a higher population density in the Belize River area, but residential unit composition, in terms of the number of structures per residential unit, and unit size and volume as calculated in labor investment (cf. Arnold and Ford 1980) need to be considered before such a conclusion can be drawn.

The Classic Period Maya residential unit has been typified as a compound of several structures, often facing a defined courtyard area (e.g., Ashmore 1981b:49). Although such may be the standard in the core area, where 70% of all residential units are made up of two or more structures and only 30% are solitary structures (Ford 1986:43–58), this is not the case in the Belize River area. On the average, 68% of all residential units in the Belize River area (including all zones) are solitary structures (Table 8.4).

This difference in settlement composition is equally evident in the construction-labor investment of residential units (Arnold and Ford 1980). Construction-labor investment was calculated based on an estimate of labor involved in the building of all components of a residential unit. The labor investment total for each residential unit provides a relative means for comparison among residential units within the central Maya lowlands. All mapped structures were considered individually and then combined in cases where they were grouped as a residential unit. The average Belize River area residential labor investment is less than one-half the average of the core area, and the highest labor investment in the Belize River area is one-third that of the core area (Table 8.5). This difference is largely due to the higher average number of structures per residential unit and more complex residential unit composition characteristic of the core area as compared with the Belize River area.

Residential unit labor investments have been ranked based on their distribution at the center of Tikal (Ford and Arnold 1982) and in the Tikal-Yaxha intersite area (Ford 1986:83–87). If we accept that family size correlates with house size and wealth in agricultural societies (McGuire 1983; Netting 1982; M. Smith 1987; among others), these labor ranks provide a general indicator of residential status and aid in understanding relative differences among areas of the lowlands. The ranks for the core area from low to high are as follows:

1:0–500 construction labor-days
2:501–2000 labor-days
3:2001–6500 labor-days
4:6501–11,000 labor-days
5:11,001–20,000 labor-days

Comparison between the core and riverine areas reveals dramatic differences in residential composition and wealth at the residential level. The highest labor-investment ranks drop out as one moves from the core to the Belize River area. These disparities in overall wealth of residents point to important differences in basic residential organization between the core area and the Belize River area. Although the Belize River area has relatively high structure densities (see Tables 8.2 and 8.3), the structures are significantly smaller and residential units much simpler in composition than those found in the core area. The high percentage of solitary structures compared to residential structure compounds points to a fundamental difference in the organization of the domestic unit, and the low labor ranks in comparison to those of the core area support the position of the area's status as peripheral in the Late Classic Period. Clearly, settlement comparisons examining only settlement or structure densities mask the important variability that may exist within the Maya lowland area.

The Local Setting

Much of the same variation seen in the comparison of the core area with the Belize River area can be found within the Belize River area itself. Variation in settlement densities can be seen from the western uplands to the eastern valley zone (Table 8.1). Settlement density decreases from west to east. The upland zones have higher structure densities than the valley—

for every two structures recorded in the uplands, one was recorded in the valley—and there was no settlement recorded in the eastern inland savanna zone.

The difference between the uplands and valley zones, including Barton Ramie, extends to residential unit composition, that is, the number of structures per unit. Though most of the residential units in the entire Belize River area are single solitary structures, they make up less than two-thirds of the residential units within the uplands but nearly all residential units within the Bacab Na Transect and Barton Ramie area (Table 8.1). These distinctions among the survey areas can also be seen in the average number of structures per unit (Table 8.6). This pattern is associated with the different environments.

Both the valley and the uplands were important agricultural zones for the ancient Maya, yet residential settlements of the two zones differed greatly. The average number of structures per unit suggests that the residential units of the valley are simpler than those of the uplands, but they are significantly larger than single-structure units of the uplands. The difference between the upland and valley settlement can be seen in the average construction-labor investments in residences of the area (Table 8.6). The upland zone has a lower overall labor-investment average than the valley.

As argued above, the average labor investments reflect the relative distribution of wealth among the zones. There is greater wealth differentiation in the uplands than in the valley. Wealth distribution in the upland zone, as determined by labor investments, includes many small residential units and few large residential units. This is the type of distribution noted for the core area around Tikal and in the Tikal-Yaxha area. The distribution of labor ranks is very different in the valley, where more than half the residential units fall in ranks 2 and 3. Even though settlement densities are lower in the eastern open valley in which the Bacab Na transect and Barton Ramie area are located, wealth ranks, as interpreted from labor investment, are more evenly distributed than in the uplands or foothills. Given the general size of valley residential units and their associated midden densities, it seems likely that residential settlement in the valley had greater continuity and homogeneity of use than residential settlement of other zones.

Settlement density in the upland area, based on structure counts, is greater than in the foothills or valley. Nevertheless, residential unit composition and sherd densities of the middens suggest an unequal intensity of use among residential units of this zone. The larger residential units, composed of two or more structures, often formally arranged around a courtyard, concentrate in specific zones in the uplands—for example, adjacent to the center of El Pilar. These large units have the highest sherd densities of the one. Most other zones have small residential units and low sherd densities. This variety among residential units of the uplands implies different domestic uses, such as permanent home base and temporary field residence.

The foothill zone is typified by moderate agricultural potential as compared with the valley and uplands (see Fedick 1989). Despite the relatively poor agricultural production quality of the zone, there was significant occupation in the Late Classic. There is reason to believe that residents in this zone could not have been self-sufficient agriculturally (see Fedick 1989). The area, however, is characterized by very high sherd densities occurring at small sites. In addition, there is evidence of chert-tool production in the zone (Ford and Olson 1989). Collections from this zone differ from the collections of the other zones and could indicate a level of residential cottage industry in chert and pottery.

Hierarchical Ordering of the Belize River Area

Separation of the zones evident in the examination of residential settlement density, size, and composition can also be seen in differences in the administrative centers recorded and mapped by the BRASS project. There is little differentiation among the valley and foothill centers of Yaxox, Alta Vista, and Bacab Na. All fall within the expected range of the lowest hierarchical levels, based on R. E. W. Adams and Jones's (1981) courtyard count, and are consistent with the ranks of other Belize Valley centers (R. E. W. Adams and Jones 1981:Table 1). The upland center of El Pilar is a dramatic contrast to valley centers and ranks equal to most major centers of the core area around Tikal.

Residential settlement density and composition in the vicinity (1 km) of El Pilar have much in common with the core area (Table 8.7), with high residential unit labor investments (average 1705 construction labor-days) and few solitary structures (27%) in comparison to the overall area (see Tables 8.4 and 8.6). Further settlement density around El Pilar is 292 structures/km². This pattern of settlement aggregation around centers is noted in the core area and not in the Belize Valley proper, as discussed below.

Valley and foothill centers do not appear to have the same relationship to the surrounding settlement as does the center of El Pilar. The average settlement density in the overall Yaxox, Bacab Na, and Barton Ramie areas corresponds to the density within 1 km of the center. The center of Alta Vista differs from other centers. Settlement density around Alta Vista is two times as great as the overall valley settlement density. Alta Vista is situated on a plateau of the limestone foothills. The terrain south toward the river is steep and would not be useful for settlement. This may account for the high settlement in the area.

IMPLICATIONS OF SETTLEMENT VARIABILITY IN THE
CENTRAL MAYA LOWLANDS

Residential structure densities are a means of making general comparisons within the Maya region. These data have been useful in understanding relative population distribution but mask variations that may exist in
settlement form and composition. Settlement in the Belize River area is a
good illustration of this point. The area has relatively high settlement densities, comparable to those of the core area, but overall size and composition of the Belize River area residences are not at all equivalent to those
of the core area. This variability among residential units in the central
Maya lowlands suggests significant organizational differences minimally at
the domestic level and probably at the administrative level.

The comparisons among the core, lakes, and Belize River areas of the
central lowlands have demonstrated variability in residential units which
needs to be pursued in greater depth. This diversity is also evident in
settlement patterns of the Belize River area. Far from homogeneous, settlement of the area appears to vary according to general environmental zone
and corresponding agricultural potential.

Fundamental settlement pattern differences among the upland, foothills,
and valley zones suggest basic differences in economic and community
organization which may be generalized to the entire central lowland region. It appears that the upland zone of the Belize River area has more in
common with the core area both in hierarchical organization and in residential unit composition than does the valley zone. Clues to the possible
distinctions in economic and community organization may reside in examination of the potential adaptive strategies of the different environmental zones and in the organizational ties they have with the core area in the
Late Classic Period. These issues have implications for our interpretation
of demographic patterns in the entire lowland area.

ACKNOWLEDGMENTS
I gratefully acknowledge the assistance of the University Research Expeditions Program (UREP) of the University of California and the Fulbright
Commission, as well as private individuals for their partial support of the
BRASS fieldwork. The fieldwork would not have been possible without the
gracious assistance and interest of the Belize Department of Archaeology.
I also wish to thank my field crews and UREP volunteers of the 1983, 1984,
and 1986 seasons and the students who volunteered as laboratory assistants after each season.

177

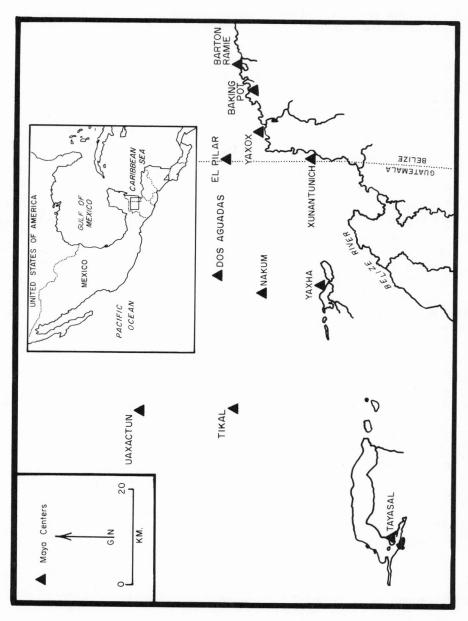

Map 8.1   Major centers of the central Maya lowlands.

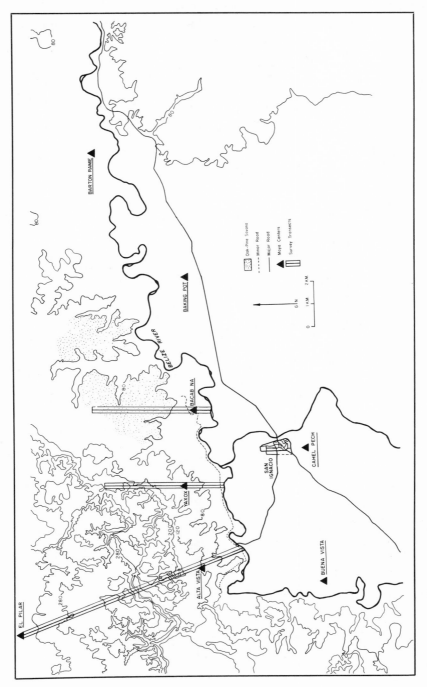

Map 8.2 Belize River area.

Table 8.1   Distribution of Environmental Zones
and Settlement Density in the
Belize River Archaeological
Settlement Survey

Environmental Soil Zone	Proportion of Terrain (%)	Structures/km²
Valley Alluvial Soil Zone (67 ha)	13	102
Fertile Upland Soil Zone (118 ha)	24	200
Shallow Foothill Soil Zone (173 ha)	35	114
Poorly Drained Soil Zone (55 ha)	11	0
Pleistocene Savanna Subsoil Zone (87 ha)	10	0

Table 8.2   Percentages of Residential Units with Occupation
by Period in the Belize River Archaeological
Settlement Survey

Zone	Middle Preclassic	Late Preclassic	Early Classic	Late Classic	Terminal Classic	Postclassic
Total area	51	91	49	98	48	21
Valley	56	88	55	100	42	20
Foothills	52	100	47	100	42	16
Uplands	45	85	45	90	66	33

Table 8.3   Structure Density by Area

	Tikal Center	Tikal-Yaxha	Yaxha Center	Yaxha Sacnab	Belize River
Structures/km²	200	110	105	59	118

Sources: The Tikal data are based on the Carr and Hazard (1961) map of Tikal, the Tikal-Yaxha data are based on the Tikal-Yaxha Intersite transect (Ford 1986), the data for Yaxha are based on Operation 2 of the Yaxha-Sacnab surveys (D. Rice 1976), the data for the lake area are based on the Yaxha-Sacnab survey (D. Rice 1976), and the Belize River area data are based on the Belize River Archaeological Settlement Survey and Barton Ramie (Willey et al. 1965).

Table 8.4   Percentages of Solitary Structures
by Area

Tikal Area	Belize Uplands	Belize Foothills	Belize Valley	Barton Ramie
30	64	69	85	98

Table 8.5   Residential Unit Labor Investment by Area

	Belize River Area	Tikal-Yaxha Area	Tikal Center
Average labor investment	997	2,085	2,793
Highest labor investment	6,500	9,000	19,500

Table 8.6   Residential Unit Composition in the Belize River Area

	Uplands	Foothills	Valley
Average no. of structures/unit	1.6	1.4	1.2
Mean Labor investment (labor-days)	688	673	1,144
Greatest Labor investment (labor-days)	5,299	3,322	6,112

Table 8.7   Residential Unit Composition by Area

	Barton Ramie	El Pilar Center	Tikal-Yaxha	Tikal Center
Average no. of structures/unit	1.0	2.3	2.4	2.8

9 /
Settlement Patterns at Nohmul: Preliminary Results of Four Excavation Seasons

K. Anne Pyburn

K. Anne Pyburn

Site Description

Nohmul is located in northern Belize about 10 km north of Orange Walk Town on a low, undulating, limestone ridge. The Rio Hondo forms the site's western boundary and offers a water route into the central lowlands via its tributaries, such as the Rio Azul, which passes the site of the same name, and the Rio Bravo, which originates within 75 km of Tikal. To the north, the Hondo is a waterway to the sea and prehistoric seaports such as Santa Rita and Cerros.

Settlement is continuous but uneven from Nohmul's central precinct to the Hondo River, 3.5 km west, and east 10 km to Pulltrouser Swamp, where the landscape is a maze of prehistoric raised fields. Nohmul is also bounded on the north and northeast by swamps densely packed with relict fields. North of these swamps, settlement is continuous to the small site of San Victor, about 5 km from Nohmul's central acropolis. Similarly, some 4 km south of Nohmul's central precinct, Nohmul's settlement merges with the settlement of the small site of San Luis. Farther south along the Hondo (approximately 11 km from Nohmul's center) is Albion Island, another locus of prehistoric fields.

Nohmul is the largest site in northern Belize, both in terms of courtyard count (R. E. W. Adams 1982) and areal extent (Hammond et al. 1985). From 1 km north of site center to the site's northern edge along the raised fields, the land is currently used to pasture cattle. Consequently, many prehistoric features are exposed and were mapped as early as 1972 (Hammond et al. 1973). There is no obvious patterning in the distribution of these features, aside from their tendency to occur on ridgetops. Excluding those in the site's central precinct, most visible mounds range from about 10 to 50 m in diameter, and from 1 to 5 m or more in height.

Visibility of the southern portion of the site (about 60% of the total site area) is limited by sugarcane. Although larger mounds are not sown, when surrounded by mature cane even these are visible only from above. Southern areas exposed and mapped during cane harvests in 1982, 1983, 1985, and 1986 suggest a distribution similar to that visible in the north sector.

All Nohmul's larger mounds have been trenched by looters, and several mound groups have been bulldozed for road fill (Hammond 1982). In spite of this disturbance, Nohmul has fared much better than many north Belize sites (Sidrys 1983) and still contains a relatively intact occupation sequence. Large areas of the north sector have escaped extensive deep plowing, owing to the protective ownership of the Belizean Sugar Industry, but this protection ended in 1986 when the land was sold to private citizens.

Nohmul was first reported in 1897 by Gann, who excavated in the central precinct and returned in 1936 (reported in Gann and Gann 1939) to expand his operations into some of the larger plazuela groups. Gann recovered mostly Late and Terminal Classic material. In 1940 illegal destruction of a large mound northeast of site center along the Douglas-San Pablo Road uncovered ceramics in the Floral Park (A.D. 250–300) style in a series of chambers. A small portion of this material was recovered (Anderson and Cook 1944).

In 1973 the British Museum-Cambridge University Corozal Project, directed by Norman Hammond, mapped the two main groups of the central precinct and their connecting sacbe and did some mapping of the northern settlement. In 1974 the project test-trenched the plaza of the central acropolis, focusing on a set of Yucatecan-style structures, and did some preliminary settlement testing in the northern sector (Wilk et al. 1975). This work showed that the site was occupied from at least the Middle Preclassic to the Early Postclassic and had a Yucatecan-influenced component in the Terminal Classic (D. Chase and A. Chase 1982; D. Chase and Hammond 1982).

GOALS AND STRATEGIES

The goal of the Nohmul settlement study was to delineate 2500 years of Maya settlement in the 35-km² occupation area in order to reconstruct changes in community pattern. The occupation of Nohmul spans the critical phases of Maya cultural evolution, including the adoption of intensive agricultural techniques and the rise and decline of complex society. Although Nohmul is unlikely to have been the origin point of these developments, its long occupation and likely participation in the wider spheres of Maya interaction make the site a prime candidate for the study of processes of cultural evolution. Nohmul is the largest site in northern Belize (R. E. W. Adams 1982; Hammond 1983), has a particularly strategic ecological setting, and contrasts in size and architectural style with contemporary sites in the Maya lowlands. This unique set of characteristics suggests that Nohmul may be crucial to understanding the working of specific historical processes at the regional level.

The strategy of the Nohmul Settlement Pattern Project was to obtain a representative sample of cultural features via extensive test-pitting followed by intensive areal excavation of selected features. Test-pitting outlined large-scale changes in Nohmul's settlement configuration along several axes of variation, such as size and location in relation to natural and other cultural features. Imminent destruction of the site due to land sale supported the decision for broad coverage. At the same time, more intensive excavation was required to investigate the function of certain features so that generalizations about occupational density and building function would be possible.

Settlement excavation was done in concert with development of the Nohmul Project site map, and comparison of subsurface findings with the surveyors' interpretations of surface features was used to develop daily field strategies. The research design was continuously modified to accommodate important findings at the site, as well as in response to the literature, which was augmented considerably during the five-year span of the project. The sampling strategy, for example, underwent several stages of development, beginning with a generalized approach in 1982 and ending with a narrowly problem-focused excavation in 1986.

SAMPLING

The inadequacy of a pre-excavation mound typology based on volumetric and formal assessments of mounds (for discussion of this method see Hammond 1975; Hester et al. 1982; Pendergast 1981; Scarborough and Robertson 1986; Sidrys 1983; Willey et al. 1965) is very apparent at Nohmul, where visible mounds in the settlement are not easily separable into types. Platform mounds of varying heights and diameters support one to five structures of a variety of sizes and shapes. Consequently, an attempt was made to sample structural variation along several continua. To sample the range from site center to raised-field boundaries, excavations were placed at km intervals from site center to swamp edge. Testing in the raised fields themselves was done by Hammond (Hammond et al. 1985). At each interval, ranges of structural variation in size (largest to smallest by volume, platform size, height, etc.), in association with other cultural features (grouped or isolated, large with small, with and without platforms, etc.) and with natural features (ridgetop, bajo, river), were tested. This approach tests (rather than assumes) whether structures with similarities in visible characteristics actually do have similar occupation histories and functions (see Tourtellot 1983 for a discussion of the issue of pre-excavation mound typologies).

So much has been said about the dispersed nature of Maya settlement that the assumption that all Maya structures (in the lowlands) were built on platforms and are still visible above ground as mounds has become a methodological axiom. Archaeologists in other parts of the world have not accepted such shortcuts, and a variety of compensating techniques has been developed (Fish et al. 1987; Plog 1968; Plog et al. 1978; Schiffer et al. 1978). This issue became central to the Nohmul Settlement Pattern Project.

Evidence from several sites in the lowlands indicates that not all Maya occupation is represented by visible mounds (Bronson 1968; Cliff 1982; Harrison, personal communication 1988; Kurjack 1974; Wilk and Wilhite 1989). From the start of the second season of settlement testing at Nohmul (1983), artifact concentrations and buried surfaces were discovered in posthole tests of nonmound areas. Consequently, systematic posthole testing to locate "invisible" features became part of the research design. Paralleling the treatment of visible mounds, an attempt was made to determine the range of variation in invisible features in relation to visible features. Subsurface features were systematically recorded and frequently tested.

EXCAVATION PLACEMENT

The placement of 1 × 1-m pits in relation to visible features was investigated in 1985. Some Mayanists recommend excavation through mounds (Tourtellot 1983); others prefer to excavate associated middens (Fry 1972). Because of the well-known Maya proclivity for redepositing midden material in structural fill, sealed deposits can provide only *terminus post quem* dates. Also, excavations through structures tend to be very deep and time-consuming. In a method following Fry (1972) and D. Puleston (1974), middens associated with structures were located with postholes and then tested with 1 × 1-m pits. More 1 × 1-m pits were then dug through the structures associated with the tested middens to provide comparative data. If comparable chronological information was provided, substituting midden tests would save time. More importantly, middens are more likely to yield functional information about associated structures than the redeposited fill of the structures themselves.

Test results are not yet quantified, but they suggest that through-mound excavations produce a wider range of ceramic dates for two reasons. Structural fill is usually from intentionally collected middens and is protected from the elements. Consequently, the haphazard collection of pottery in fill dates occupation in the general area, not just the structure itself, and is more identifiable because it is better preserved. Middens, on the other hand, are frequently above earlier middens and offer a soft matrix that is disturbed by scavengers and rodents. Almost invariably, platform-associated middens were inextricably mixed with eroded platform fill, consequently presenting the same mixing problems as the fill layers themselves but yielding much more poorly preserved sherds. For strictly chronological information, fill layers seem to be better, if we bear in mind that the last occupation of the structure cannot be incorporated in a sample of structural fill, and other periods of occupation may not be. For functional interpretations, investigators must attempt to separate earlier middens and platform fill from platform-associated middens. For middens associated with nonplatform structures, these problems are greatly reduced.

EXCAVATION SITE

The next decision concerned the size of the excavations. This choice is invariably a trade-off between broad coverage and recovery of detail. Since the goals of the project included an understanding of both the synchronic functioning and the diachronic development of Nohmul, both extensive and intensive excavation were necessary.

Extensive testing, aimed mostly at defining density and chronological ranges of settlement in different parts of the site, was accomplished with postholes and 1 × 1-m pits. The relative efficiency of different sized sampling units was considered in the 1983 excavations. For example, 2 × 2-m pits were compared with 1 × 2-m pits and 1 × 1-m pits for information output per hour of labor (S. Cohen 1986). The 2 × 2s yielded more information than smaller pits, but information increase was not commensurate with increased excavation cost. For chronological information 1 × 1-m pits were by far the best, since even 2 × 2s rarely added to the chronological information produced by a 1 × 1.

The need to define building function required that the size of the excavations be varied. Two features were excavated intensively: a Terminal

Classic platform group and a Terminal Classic nonplatform occupation. Architectural detail and artifactual associations were examined to make a comparison between a relatively well known style of habitation—the plazuela group—and an almost unknown style of occupation—a ground-surface construction. The plazuela group excavations exposed 26 m² of a single occupation and associated features, and the nonmound occupation exposed 33.5 m² of occupation and associated hearths and middens. Several other excavations ranged in size from 1 × 1.5 m to 3 × 4 m. These were mostly the result of a need to define anomalies or determine the function of unexpectedly common features that were not visible above ground. In some cases narrow trenches up to 12 m long were dug to determine the size of such features.

Identifying the function of nonmounded features is especially important for the reconstruction of population density, since it has been suggested that nonplatform constructions were limited-activity areas and not permanent occupations. Clearly, only permanent occupations should be included in density calculations. The number and length of periods of reoccupation of visible features must also figure in these estimates.

In all, 76 test pits and several hundred postholes were excavated. Forty-three pits were dug directly through visible mounds, uncovering a total of 60 m² of architecture. Twelve 1-m² pits were dug on the outside edges of platforms in areas where postholes revealed sherd concentrations. Twenty-one separate excavations were placed in areas without surface indications. These excavations uncovered an area of 107 m².

Preliminary Results

The earliest evidence for occupation at Nohmul comes from the latter part of the Early Preclassic Period (Bladen phase: 1000–750 B.C.). Data from this period are found mainly in an occupation area about 1.5 km northwest of Nohmul's central acropolis which probably predates the central acropolis by at least 1000 years. Excavations to the north and west of the Bladen discoveries have yielded a disproportionate amount of Floral Park (A.D. 250–300) ceramics, supporting the hypothesis that early occupation of the site area was mostly in the northern precinct. Late Preclassic ceramics are ubiquitous but are apparently less abundant at greater distances from site center.

All excavation collections examined contain Late Preclassic (300 B.C.–A.D. 250), Late Classic (A.D. 650–800), and Terminal Classic Early Postclassic (A.D. 800–1000) artifacts (these last-named dates are combined pending clarification of the ceramic chronology now underway by Laura J. Kosakowsky). This finding supports work done at other north Belize sites, where artifacts from these periods are abundant but material from intervening periods is sparse. The same pattern is followed by the Nohmul surface collections (Hammond et al. 1987; Muyskins 1985; Robin 1985).

Most Preclassic artifacts were recovered from midden fill used in very large Late Preclassic buildings or smaller, later buildings. A scarcity of Preclassic domestic architecture has been noted at several sites in northern Belize: Barton Ramie (Willey et al. 1965), Albion Island (Pohl, personal communication, 1988), and even in the central Maya lowlands at Seibal (Tourtellot 1983). Late Preclassic monumental architecture exists in the central precincts of all these sites, except Albion Island; only settlement-area excavations fail to produce Late Preclassic buildings.

Several reasons for this shortage of early buildings may be cited. First, and most obviously, older buildings are more likely to be deeply buried (Tourtellot 1983; Cliff 1982; Willey et al. 1965; and Pohl, personal communication 1987). The possible Late Preclassic structure encountered in Nohmul test excavation T03 (described in Hammond et al. 1985), for example, was below more than 2 m of debris and later architecture. On the other hand, structures of organic materials not built on platforms are completely gone. Furthermore, evidence for perpetual prehistoric recycling of fill materials, frequently including shaped stones from earlier structures, is prevalent at all Maya sites.

The earliest buildings in an area would have no earlier sherds to incorporate in construction layers, making them hard to date. The structure in excavation T03, for example, remains "possibly" Late Preclassic, since it had few associated artifacts. Moreover, small test pits typical of settlement-pattern work are statistically unlikely to encounter deeply buried buildings *and* their associated middens.

A number of excavations at Nohmul yielded evidence of occupation directly on bedrock (Wilk et al. 1975; Pyburn 1986). Bedrock features are usually buried; reused as garbage of burial pits; difficult to date, since they have no construction layers; lacking evidence of any superstructure; and affected by erosion due to exposure and groundwater. Bedrock modification ranges from simple leveling of the surface to the construction of deep pits. These pits often contain burials or quantities of shells from edible snails (*Pomacea flagellata*) in the fill above bedrock hearths lined with Preclassic sherds (Pyburn 1989). The pits may be the result of quarrying, but careful leveling and prepared hearths denote some additional function.

Progressing through time, Early Classic artifacts are not as common as those from earlier and later periods. This may be partly a result of the fact that the Early Classic is only 350 years long, in comparison to the 600-year span of the Late Preclassic (Culbert, personal communication 1988). There is some confusion about divisions between later ceramic phases. Kosa-kowsky and Valdez (1982) have suggested that Terminal Preclassic ceram-ics may have remained stylish in northern Belize for much longer than elsewhere in the lowlands, overlapping with both Floral Park and Early Classic styles.

Another possibility is suggested by the Early Classic ceramics (Culbert, personal communication, 1988) from a nonplatform occupation in Noh-mul's northern precinct. As with earlier periods, buried or ephemeral oc-cupations may account for some of the apparent drop in artifact density during the Early Classic, since most tests are in mounds (Pyburn 1988). One of Wilk's 1974 excavations uncovered a bedrock hearth that was ten-tatively identified as Early Classic (although it may have been earlier but was associated with later garbage [Wilk et al. 1975]). The fact that most visible platforms seem to contain Late Preclassic artifacts and Late Classic (or later) constructions, may indicate a change in residence style during the Early Classic. The resemblance between Late Classic and Preclassic sherds (Pring 1977) may echo a return to earlier construction loci as well. This is not to deny the possibility that a population decline occurred at Nohmul in the Early Classic, but to suggest that many factors may affect population visibility.

Most structures and artifacts from Nohmul date to the Late and Terminal Classic periods. Late and Terminal Classic domestic structures include reused earlier buildings, single-phase platform constructions 1 to 3 m tall, and ground-surface constructions associated with middens, hearths, and burials. Monumental architecture used in later periods is mostly a reoc-cupation of structures built earlier. This is the reverse of the situation in the Preclassic, for which many monumental or large-scale buildings have been found, but few ordinary domestic structures.

There was significant reoccupation of the central precinct during the Postclassic Period. The Terminal Classic ballcourt was used as a platform for domestic structures, and incensario fragments have been recovered from the surface of several large buildings. However, very little material from this time has been identified in settlement collections. An exception was found 4 km north of Nohmul's central precinct, where an isolated Postclassic structure (Structure 682) some 3 m tall shared a low platform with a much smaller structure. No other structures are visible from Struc-ture 682, which is located in the edge of a swamp containing evidence of extensive prehistoric fields. Its situation is in striking contrast to that de-scribed by D. Rice (1988) for Postclassic occupations in the central Peten lakes region. Postclassic settlements in the central Peten tend to be ex-tremely nucleated and in defensible locations (e.g., islands). Platform structures often were arranged within C- or L-shaped walls. The apparent isolation of this large building suggests that nonplatform structures were situated nearby.

"INVISIBLE" OCCUPATION

Five hundred m west of this Postclassic structure is an area of dense, non-platform, "invisible" occupation. Preliminary analysis suggests a Preclassic to Terminal Classic occupation. Two Early Classic and two Late Classic marl floors 10 to 25 cm thick with associated domestic debris, burials, and hearths were exposed. At least four other structures (as yet undated) were located in this area. Three were almost entirely lacking in associated artifacts, but two could be identified as floors because they consisted of white marl that contrasts with a leveled black A horizon.

Much of the evidence for nonplatform occupation at Nohmul is concentrated in this single "neighborhood," which begins immediately south of an area of prehistoric fields, about 4 km north of Nohmul's central acropolis. The exact dimensions of the nonplatform settlement area are unknown, since testing was limited by time and money to 21 separate excavations uncovering 107 m², but all known buildings are within a space that is ½ km long and ¼ km wide. The nearest platform structures are on the opposite side of a swamp that holds standing water in rainy weather. Like most platforms, all known nonplatform structures are situated along ridges in adequately drained areas.

NOHMUL DEMOGRAPHY

The surveyed area of Nohmul is bounded by swamps to the north and northeast and by the Rio Hondo to the west. The steady decline in visible structures which occurs between site center and these natural features suggests that they were actual site boundaries (see Figure 9.1). Visible structures also decline in number to the east of site center, but the surveyed area is bounded on this side by modern habitations, so actual site boundaries are unknown. (The completed site map has been published in Hammond et al. 1988.)

The southern site boundary is poorly defined because survey was stopped by impenetrable cane fields and limits to time and money. Settlement in this direction is continuous with the settlement of the site of San Luis. It would be possible to extrapolate the mound density of the unknown area from the areas surveyed, but natural boundaries may exert different pressures on residence pattern than the proximity of other populations or simple distance from site center. Consequently, density estimates will be confined to areas surveyed, without implying that all features pertinent to the occupation of Nohmul are included.

Of Nohmul's possible 35-km² area, about 22 km² were mapped. If each platform on the map is counted separately, whether grouped with others on a large basal platform or isolated, the Nohmul map shows a total of 700 separate, visible structures. The distribution of these structures is depicted in Figure 9.1, which shows visible architecture to be densest in the site center, with a heavily settled "corridor" running north toward San Victor and an increased density near the Hondo, where Pring and Hammond identified a "port" mound in 1975. Some of the falloff in structures to the east may result from disturbance by modern inhabitants of the village of San Jose.

As already described, invisible occupation exists at Nohmul and is dense in some areas of the site. For reasons elaborated below, this kind of occupation is not expected to occur uniformly all over Nohmul, and its extent currently remains undemonstrated. Only eight floors have been identified with absolute certainty, and only four of them are securely dated to the Late Classic. When the final data analysis is complete, a larger number will be estimated, but for the time being the total structure count for Late Classic Nohmul will simply be increased by four to include known invisible structures.

A standard set of procedures is often used to turn mound counts into population estimates. These procedures may be more or less elaborated depending, in part, on how much is known about a particular site, but they always include four operations:

1. A percentage is added for features that were missed because they were either outside the survey or hidden by alluviation or vegetation.
2. A percentage is subtracted for features that were not houses and so do not represent population increments.
3. The total is divided by the number of chronological periods and/ or generations spanned by the occupation.
4. The total is multiplied by a standard figure for family size.

Count reductions for nonresidential structures at other sites range from 16% (Haviland 1965; 1970) to 10% (Webster and Freter, this volume). Since percentages at the larger end of the scale are commonly used, a 16% reduction will be accepted for Nohmul. The result will be a conservative population estimate.

At this stage of analysis only estimates for Nohmul's period of population maximum are reliable. All central area and settlement excavations at Nohmul, except two (Hammond et al. 1985), and 70% of surface collections that have been examined (a total of 87) yielded Late Classic ceramics (Kosakowsky, personal communication 1988). Surface collections are biased toward more recent occupation, except in cases where they are produced by looters. In such cases surface collections are likely to contain much earlier material and may not relate to the final occupation of the disturbed area. It is reasonable to assume that all Nohmul's 700 visible features were in use during the Late Classic (A.D. 650–800). This is probably also true for the Terminal Classic/Early Postclassic Period and possibly the Terminal Preclassic Period, both of which are represented in 100% of the excavations. Nonetheless, neither is as strongly represented as the Late Classic in the surface collections that have been examined, so population reconstruction for these periods will require more information than is available at this stage of analysis.

Most structures show considerable evidence of remodeling, so that the use-life of each platform was probably considerably longer than that of the perishable superstructure. There are only two known instances of Nohmul platform groups (a group of two or more platforms built on a shared basal platform), including a structure dating to a period preceding the occupation of the rest of the group (Hammond et al. 1985). These are the only excavations that failed to produce Late or Terminal Classic artifacts, and an argument has been advanced for the possible special sacredness of these structures (Hammond, personal communication 1986).

These findings suggest that unused structures were not common during later periods, either because they were in demand for habitations or because building materials were readily scavenged for new constructions. Late Classic ceramics do occur in the fill layers of Late Classic buildings. All visible structures will be assumed to have been occupied continuously during the Late Classic.

Estimates of family size for lowland sites are almost invariably derived from ethnographic studies of recent lowland populations. Most estimates have drawn on the 5.6 figure provided by Redfield and Villa Rojas for Chan Kom in 1934, or on Naroll's (1962) correlation between floor area and family size. Some authors have considered these estimates too high or too low (e.g., R. E. W. Adams 1974; Ringle 1985; Tourtellot 1983) but continue to base their extrapolations on the family sizes of relatively modern occupants of the Maya area. Since the differing origin of the ethnographic analogy employed is the primary reason for different estimates, not differences in archaeological data, 5.6 can be accepted as a median figure.

Application of this model to Nohmul data results in the following estimate: $700 + 4 - 16\% \times 5.6 = 3310$. The mapped area is slightly under 22 km^2, so the population density of Nohmul works out to about 150 people/km^2, a figure significantly lower than that proposed for most sites in the lowland core. This is especially interesting in light of the fact that Nohmul is associated with a considerable quantity of raised fields, presumably indicating intensive agriculture and the production of a large surplus for such a small population.

There is some suggestion that a significant portion of Nohmul's inhabitants is not included in mound counts. Much of the evidence for invisible occupation at Nohmul is also available from other sites (including Tikal, [Bronson 1968]). If all invisible lowland features could be detected, it is possible that the absolute population counts would change, while the relative population sizes of different cities remained constant.

Nohmul is different from other sites in the central lowlands. Its population was either smaller or much more given to perishable structures. Its monumental architecture is large but not flamboyant—no roof combs, no architectural masks. Most ceramic periods include imitations of tradewares but few pieces that actually came from afar (Hammond et al. 1987), even though the site is situated on an arterial river that connects the central lowlands to the sea. On the other hand, imported obsidian is surprisingly abundant; few excavations failed to turn up broken blades, and one completely excavated Late Classic midden produced 40 blades. The Postclassic workshop in site center yielded hundreds.

These facts suggest that there is something different about Nohmul's economic structure in comparison to that of core sites. The findings also bring out some important points about the foregoing analysis. The absolute population density of some portion of a settlement has very limited utility. Population density per se is not directly correlated with subsistence, social or political complexity, or urbanism. A dense permanent population suggests intensive agriculture, but such an argument is unnecessary because we can see raised fields and terraces all over the lowlands.

The correlation between density and social complexity depends on the unit of analysis. Hainline-Underwood (1964, 1965) found an inverse relationship between social stratification and the population density of Micronesian islands; Cordy (1986) found that the level of social stratification on the same islands was highly correlated with absolute population counts of individual polities, of which each island has several. Despite his best efforts, Carneiro (1967) was forced to admit that the correlation he saw between population density and social complexity broke down when applied to societies with multiple communities. Units of analysis like "most of Nohmul," "visible structures," or "central Tikal" truncate the range of variation in density which is characteristic of complex societies and urbanism. More importantly, they ignore the probability that in multicommunity societies population density, especially that of a single site or an arbitrary portion of a single site, does not correlate in any simple way with social complexity or give any indication of the economic factors underlying settlement distribution. Wealthy people often use space as a form of conspicuous consumption, while poor people are not allowed to build their small mounds or shacks anywhere they wish, even in preindustrial societies.

On the other hand, variations in density, family size, and habitation style are directly related to the economic and cultural systems of complex societies. For example, family size is correlated (but not always directly) with differences in wealth in many cultures (Netting 1982). Population density estimates based on uniform family sizes, extrapolated to encompass unsurveyed areas and combined with the conviction that all Maya cultural features, even ancillary structures, were built on platforms, obscure the essential variation that is key to the social structural and economic systems we wish to understand.

CONCLUSION

Nohmul has approximately 700 visible structures. Current data suggest that almost all these were occupied in the Late and Terminal Classic periods. Evidence for earlier periods is more equivocal, but further analysis is likely to suggest a Late Preclassic occupation well over half the size of that existing at the end of the Classic. Intermediate and later periods made a lesser impact on the archaeological record of Nohmul. Completion of the artifact analysis will refine these estimates and clarify the role of nonplatform structures in Nohmul's settlement.

Nohmul's apparently low population density implies that the site may have been channeling produce from its raised fields, via inland rivers such as the Hondo, into the more densely occupied central Peten. Other north Belize sites certainly produced surpluses; both San Esteban and Colha were manufacturing huge quantities of lithic tools, some of which were exported directly, while many were undoubtedly used to produce other goods for export (Wilk 1975, 1976). Nohmul's relatively large size and strategic location on the Hondo River suggest that smaller production sites may have marketed some of their produce through Nohmul. On the simplest level of analysis, the inhabitants of Nohmul seem to have had access to more food and goods than they needed.

That nonplatform occupation might have added significantly to Nohmul's population density does not necessarily change the conclusion that it produced for export. The possible division of Nohmul's residents into a nucleus of elaborate architecture and a densely populated neighborhood separated from the area of platform-based structures and bordering agricultural fields suggests that Nohmul's agricultural surplus was not directly produced by the labor of the people inhabiting the platforms. In fact, this may be a rare glimpse of a class of prehistoric Maya that did not own the products of its labor.

Such aspects of social structure, although not commonly recognized for the Maya, are well known from the records of prehistoric cities elsewhere in the world. The existence of a class structure is more important for interpreting Nohmul's settlement and its role in the larger sphere of Maya economics than are regularizing assumptions about population density and carrying capacity. Although work is still in progress to treat a number of methodological issues addressed in the Nohmul excavations, it is not premature to suggest that some apparent problems of Maya culture history may be solved by methodological improvements.

ACKNOWLEDGMENTS

Every phase of the work presented here has benefited from the criticism and encouragement of Richard R. Wilk and T. Patrick Culbert. The research was funded by National Geographic Society grants to the Nohmul Project (Norman Hammond, director) and by University of Arizona Commins, Fulton, and Tinker Foundation grants. Any errors are my own.

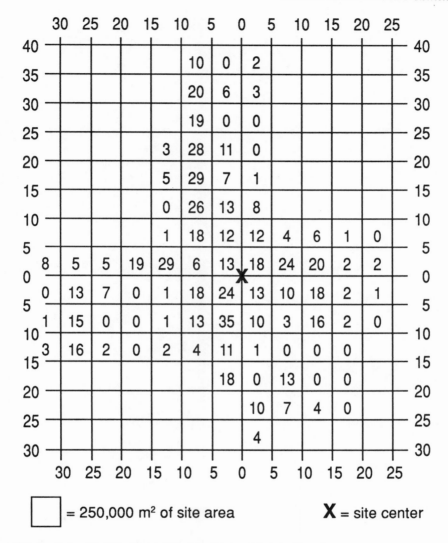

Figure 9.1   Distribution of Nohmul mound densities by count.

10 /

The Invisible Maya: Population History and Archaeology at Santa Rita Corozal

DIANE Z. CHASE

The archaeological site of Santa Rita Corozal is located in northern Belize on a bluff overlooking Chetumal Bay, halfway between the Hondo and New rivers. The archaeological ruins both lie under and encircle Corozal Town, Belize's third-largest modern community. Santa Rita Corozal has been continuously occupied from the Early Preclassic Period (ca. 1200 B.C.) through the present day (D. Chase 1981, 1985, 1986; D. Chase and A. Chase 1986a, 1986b, 1988:10–11). This history of occupation alone makes it an excellent site from which to view changing population dynamics. Santa Rita Corozal is also an interesting demographic case because most of its constructions are virtually invisible on the surface. Rather than the tall, raised constructions common in the Maya lowlands, many of the buildings at Santa Rita Corozal were only slightly raised or not elevated at all above the surrounding terrain. Today such buildings are indicated only by the line-of-stone foundations that occasionally protrude above the ground surface. The site thus offers a cautionary note for those who would attempt population reconstructions without intensive and area-wide excavation in "vacant terrain." Beyond these factors, the Santa Rita Corozal population reconstructions are somewhat unusual because they use only data with clear contextual evidence for occupation and because the demographic reconstructions can be roughly cross-checked with ethnohistoric data.

Santa Rita Corozal is best known for its late-facet Late Postclassic (A.D. 1300–1530) occupation, primarily brought to light by the early work of Gann (1900, 1918) but also through the efforts of later researchers (Green 1973; Pring 1973; Sidrys 1976, 1983) and the Corozal Postclassic Project (D. Chase 1981, 1982; D. and A. Chase 1986a, 1988). During this Late Post-classic era, it is believed, the site served as the capital of the Maya territory of Chetumal (J. E. S. Thompson 1972:6; D. Chase 1982:12–15, 571–73; D. and A. Chase 1986b:19, 1988:65–68). Late Postclassic occupation at Santa Rita Corozal is extensive, and material remains from this era are abundant and varied. Thus, this site provides a rare opportunity to view archaeolog-ically a very late (indeed, a protohistoric) Maya community. While the Late Postclassic occupation was clearly a prominent one, earlier time periods, especially the late Preclassic and Early Classic, also manifest significant activity. Even though there is nearly continuous habitation of the Santa Rita area from 1200 B.C. to the present, population densities, kinds of con-structions, artifactual remains, and cultural affiliations clearly change over time (see A. Chase and D. Chase 1987c; D. Chase and A. Chase 1986a, 1988).

Reconstruction of Population History at Santa Rita Corozal

The Corozal Postclassic Project was developed to answer specific ques-tions concerning Late Postclassic Maya society; thus, excavation at Santa Rita Corozal was intentionally geared toward the discovery of late-facet Late Postclassic remains (A.D. 1300–1531). For this period, there is at first a close correspondence between Santa Rita Corozal and the site of Maya-pan, to the north in Yucatan, particularly in terms of nonmonumental ar-chitecture and pottery. Santa Rita Corozal, however, was still occupied and prospering following the fall of Mayapan ca. A.D. and was not abandoned until the arrival of the Spaniard Davila in A.D. 1531.

During the four field seasons of excavation by the Corozal Postclassic Project (D. Chase 1982, 1985, 1986; D. Chase and A. Chase 1986a, 1988), investigations were aimed at testing examples of six defined structure types (D. Chase 1986:Figure 10.2) in an effort to understand the site's so-cial composition. Investigations were undertaken in approximately 20% of the mapped and extant constructions (a total of 43 structures) and were specifically designed to exploit locales that were most likely to produce heavy Late Postclassic occupation. Most of this research involved areal stripping and deeper penetration of selected structures or areas, rather than simple test probes. Whenever possible, at least 50%, and often 100%, of the selected structures was exposed. Test excavations, generally 1.5 × 1.5 m, were expanded to areal exposures in all but two cases. Each structure was also axially trenched to ascertain its construction sequence and to identify related special deposits. Some structures were excavated solely by 1.5-m-wide trench. This research design and excavation methodology led to the discovery of deposits and construction activity from all known periods. Excavations frequently were stopped intentionally prior to the extensive exposure of early levels, but smaller excavations to bedrock were almost always conducted. It is not surprising, therefore, that most of the special deposits and constructions recovered in Corozal Postclassic Project investigations were Late Postclassic. Yet, the deeper cuts and areal tests that encountered earlier remains make it possible to estimate earlier population (Table 10.1).

Assessing the total extent and population of Santa Rita Corozal from surface remains is problematic. Most of the excavations that produced evidence of significant Late Postclassic occupation found associated structures composed merely of line-of-stone foundations; many of these buildings were impossible to see before excavation, as there was no surface mounding or protruding base wall (for similar constructions in Tayasal see A. Chase 1983:565–66, 768, 786, 816, 828). A similar situation has been noted for a variety of other lowland Maya sites (see, for example, E. W. Andrews IV 1965; Kurjack 1974; Bronson 1968; A. Chase, this volume; Pyburn, this volume). Because of the large number of these "hidden" or "invisible" structures, population counts based solely on visible mounds at Santa Rita Corozal would considerably underestimate the actual number of structures and individuals at the site. Thus, tables in this chapter include at least minimal allowances for invisible structures; although these allowances may seem large to some researchers, the Santa Rita Corozal data clearly indicate that minimally 25% and more likely 50% of Maya structures are invisible to the archaeologist. Significantly, the term *invisible building* within this discussion implies constructions with actual building foundations revealed after excavation. Another potential class of invisible building includes those with no stone foundation; these may have added greatly to structure and population totals, but there is no simple way to account for them. No adjustment has been made for buildings with no foundations, as all clearing excavations in nonbulldozed areas provided at least some evidence of floors or foundations.

The high proportion of invisible structures estimated for Santa Rita Corozal may be partially attributable to the large amount of areal stripping that was undertaken. It became possible after seven years of work at the site to predict fairly accurately where invisible constructions would be found. It also became apparent that certain parts of Santa Rita Corozal were literally covered with hidden constructions that areal excavation would have revealed but that mapping alone could not record, even when area were cleared of growth. Not only did excavations in apparently vacant areas produce evidence of construction and occupation, but areas with only one mapped structure generally were transformed into groups of at least four buildings following detailed excavation. In many cases areal stripping also revealed a hidden construction with little in the way of associated artifactual material. In these cases dating was possible because of the larger sample of artifacts present in the area-wide clearing or the deposits encountered in deeper cuts; sherd densities recovered in probes would not have adequately mirrored the presence of such constructions. Four seasons of excavation, however, made it abundantly evident that at least as many structures are hidden at Santa Rita Corozal as could be recorded from surface mapping. These constructions are not only Postclassic in date. Sometimes they reveal a series of temporally stratified constructions even though nothing was visible on the ground surface. Interestingly, the nineteenth-century population at Santa Rita Corozal, although widespread, is even more invisible than that of the Late Postclassic Maya, as architecture datable to this era lacks the base walls used during the Postclassic Period. In many cases historic occupation can only be inferred based on the large amount of reconstructable refuse found in areal clearing. Unless one can show that Santa Rita Corozal is a unique site, a conclusion not supported by the data, then a similarly high percentage of hidden constructions must exist at most other sites in the southern Maya lowlands.

The data from Santa Rita Corozal suggest other problems for techniques commonly used by archaeologists to make population reconstructions. Not only are many of the constructions invisible prior to excavation, but surface sherds were found to be either absent or misleading in suggesting the date of materials below the ground. In addition, excavations frequently revealed that fill sherds were significantly earlier than the actual date of a construction based on sealed special deposits such as burials or caches, a situation potentially leading to incorrect dating; only large-scale areal stripping and/or the recovery of associated special deposits allowed secure dates to be established for various constructions. Because of these problems, dating in the tables in this chapter was based on archaeological remains that were well defined contextually, such as the contents of primary deposits like refuse dumps, burials, or caches; dating was not predicated solely on the presence or absence of sherds from particular temporal eras. If sherds alone had been used, percentages of occupation for each period would have increased substantially, as nearly all excavations produced isolated sherds from more than one period.

Other problems inherent in the creation of population histories for any site are the establishment of the base unit (most often a house or household) from which to extrapolate population size and the determination of the contemporaneity of occupation within a single phase. The basic unit for many population studies is the household, but what defines a household archaeologically and how many people could be expected to live in each one? At Santa Rita Corozal nearly all excavated constructions contained artifacts suggestive of domestic residence. Only 6.6% of the investigated constructions suggested either ritual or administrative use, exclusive of residential use. No evidence was found for separate kitchens or outbuildings; perhaps such buildings did not have stone foundations at Santa Rita Corozal. Many archaeologists use a 5.6 person/household figure in the Maya area (cf. Ashmore 1981b:65), even though there are ethnohistoric references indicating figures as high as 10, 25, or 100 people/protohistoric household (Hellmuth 1977:438). Given the problems of the assignation of specific function(s) to buildings, the difficulty of defining what is a house, and the varying estimates of people per household, the Santa Rita Corozal population estimates were made using a high percentage of buildings (all but the 6.6% known to be nonresidential) but a low number of individuals per household (5.6), even though these figures are not without their own problems (for discussion of figures for people per household see Ashmore 1981b:65 and Kurjack 1974:94; for estimates of residential buildings see Haviland 1965:19 [Tikal], and A. L. Smith 1962:265 and Pollock 1962:15 [Mayapan]). Although there is variation in building size, this was not used as a factor in calculating population for two reasons: first, it is clear that most Postclassic multiroom constructions at Santa Rita served more than simply a "residential" function, and second, it is believed that the exercise of population reconstruction already has enough problematic variables without the addition of yet another, seemingly insoluble one.

Although contemporaneity is extremely important for any population reconstruction, it, too, is a difficult problem to tackle. Dating at Maya sites is generally limited to the delineation of phases of time that vary from 100 to 600 years in length. If little or no ceramic change is definable within a phase, it becomes virtually impossible to state which buildings were occupied at any one point in time. Arguments based on the presence of rebuilding at a single locus are likewise problematic, as there are no absolute associations between amount of construction/modification and length of time that such efforts may have taken. Secure dating of either carbon or phase seriation also did little to provide clues toward the use-life of single constructions and subsequent rebuilding efforts, at least at Santa Rita Corozal. Until archaeological techniques for dating become more precise, any estimate of the number of years buildings were generally used is likely to be a gross estimate at best. To allow comparisons of population histories among sites in the Maya area, however, a tentative approximation of structure use-life must be made (see Culbert et al., this volume); even if such an estimate is incorrect, its definition permits intersite comparison of the various computations. For Late Postclassic Santa Rita Corozal, it is my belief that most constructions were occupied contemporaneously, at least 60–70% at any one point in time. There is substantial rebuilding activity on the majority of constructions, and all evidence indicates that the site reached its zenith just prior to 1531. For the 230-year time period assigned for the late facet of the Late Postclassic Period at

Santa Rita Corozal, this would indicate a use-life of roughly 150 years for each building. This use-life has been arbitrarily extended to lesser-known, earlier time periods.

Perhaps the greatest problem in attempting to define the full extent of the Maya occupation of Santa Rita Corozal is that associated with the extensive site destruction. Because of modern housing efforts in Corozal Town and also to natural erosion of the land directly near the bay, significant portions of the settlement of Santa Rita Corozal are difficult to evaluate. Therefore, to some extent estimates of settlement must be extrapolated from areas in which destruction is less evident.

Although determining the population peaks and ebbs at Santa Rita Corozal is not a difficult task given the archaeological data base, establishment of population numbers for temporal eras at the site is difficult, not only for all the usual reasons, but also because of the specific problems caused by site destruction and the difficulty in the surface assessment of invisible occupation. Nevertheless, several lines of evidence can be used to reconstruct diachronically the prehistoric population history of the site. In Santa Rita's case, perhaps the best way to proceed is to compare the results of archaeological evidence gained from mapping and excavation with that garnered from historic information concerning the site's population.

THE POPULATION OF PROTOHHISTORIC SANTA RITA COROZAL

Santa Rita Corozal is located within the ethnohistoric Maya province of Chetumal. As noted earlier, the site was most likely the capital of that territory. Chetumal was selected as the location for the Spanish settlement of Villa Real and was occupied for 18 months before being abandoned in 1532. In spite of this occupation, the only estimates for the number of houses at Chetumal comes from an account by a Spaniard, G. Fernandez de Oviedo y Valdez, who never actually visited the Maya center. He described the area as containing 2000 houses surrounded by rich fields (1851–55:32–36). If one assumes that Oviedo's estimate is correct and that he is identifying houses and not solely buildings, then a figure of 5.6 persons/house would indicate a contact-era population of more than 11,200. If one lessens this estimate by 6.66% to account for the potential inclusion of nonresidential buildings, the population estimate (10,461) for early historic Chetumal would still be greater than the modern population of Corozal Town, listed as 6899 in 1983 (Government Information Services 1983).

Merely counting the absolute number of constructions at Santa Rita Corozal to double-check Oviedo's numbers is problematic, given the site destruction and the abundance of invisible structures. However, estimates of density of construction in certain sectors of the site are possible. Mapping has suggested that the most dense Late Postclassic occupation was in a 2.526-km² area in the center of Santa Rita Corozal; this was surrounded by an area of slightly lower density occupation (estimated at 50% of the core) incorporating at least an additional 2.5 km² as well as pockets of settlement in other areas such as along the bay.

In order to estimate the Late Postclassic population size at Santa Rita Corozal, a series of calculations was made based on structure counts from two segments of the site—the South Intermediate and the Northeast sectors. Each sector was found to mirror the other in derived population and structure counts. Within each sector, an approximately 200-m² area had been intensively excavated and tested and a broader area (500 m²) had been mapped as well as possible. Calculations in the two sectors can be based on both spatial areas (see Map 10.1 for the South Intermediate sector).

Buildings were counted in each of two spatial units (see Table 10.2), and a calculation was then made of structures/km². Based on archaeological work in both the Northeast and South Intermediate sectors of the site, estimates were made of the percentage of invisible structures likely to be missing in each of these areas—minimally gauged at 50% and 100% of the current counts, respectively. With these figures corrected, calculations of structures/km² were made as an extension of the 200-m² figure and the lower 500-m² figure. An adjusted proportion of non-Postclassic structures, determined based on excavations in each area, was eliminated from the sample. This number was further decreased by 6.66% to account for purely administrative or ritual constructions. It was estimated that 66.22% of Postclassic buildings were coeval in their use. A figure of 5.6 persons/household was used, in spite of certain ethnohistoric evidence that there may have been larger numbers in single households, in an effort to under-, rather than over-, estimate population. Based on these calculations, the total projected population for the 5-km² area of Late Postclassic Santa Rita Corozal would have ranged from 8722 to 4958. It should be noted, however, that these figures are minima, as the site area was most likely larger; even so, they are remarkably close to the population numbers of contemporary Corozal Town, but slightly lower than that derived from Oviedo's description of Chetumal (Chactemal). Of the two calculations, I favor the higher figure, established for the more intensively excavated areas. However, a median population figure of 6840 for late-facet Late Postclassic Santa Rita Corozal is used as the basis for making the calculations in Table 10.1.

These late Postclassic population calculations for Santa Ritz Corozal also bear some comparison to its northern sister site of Mayapan in the Yucatan Peninsula of Mexico. Mayapan was a Late Postclassic Maya capital city and the primate Late Postclassic center in the northern lowlands. It was the seat of unity or joint government for the lowland Maya provinces until its destruction around A.D. 1450 (Pollock 1962:1, 4). Mapping at Mayapan indicated the existence of 4015 structures within a 4.2-km² area inside the wall (A. L. Smith 1962:173). Of these, at least 2100 were presumed to be residences (A. L. Smith 1962:265). These figures were used to project a population of 11,000 to 12,000 (Pollock 1962:15).

There are, however, several reasons to believe that Late Postclassic Mayapan may have had a larger number of inhabitants. First, the estimate of only 2100 residences out of the total of 4000 structures may be too low; it is a much lower proportion than that suggested for Late Postclassic Santa Rita Corozal or for the earlier Classic Period at other well-investigated sites (Haviland 1965:19). Second, and perhaps more significant, it is quite possible that Mayapan also contained invisible constructions. Work at other sites in the Yucatan Peninsula has indicated the predominance of such constructions (E. W. Andrews IV 1965:37; Kurjack 1974:29, 94) as did our own at Santa Rita Corozal. A. L. Smith (1962:265) noted that "about one-third of the estimated 2100 dwellings at Mayapan are not associated with other structures." If the Santa Rita experience that single-surface structures were almost invariably associated with invisible structures could be extrapolated to Mayapan, then minimally 700 other residences probably existed based on Smith's own figures, thus yielding a low population figure of 15,680. However, the greater density of mapped structures at Mayapan suggests that the percentage of invisible constructions at this site might not be as high. If one increases the percentage of domestic structures at Mayapan solely by decreasing the estimate for mapped nonresidential structures from roughly 50% to 6.66%, as found at Santa Rita, and then assumes the same figure of 5.6 individuals/dwelling, then the population within the walled area of Mayapan would have been at least 20,988.

That a larger population existed at Mayapan than at Santa Rita Corozal is to be expected, given Mayapan's position as the capital of a confederation of provinces and not just of one territory. The relative density of mapped construction at Mayapan, prior to any estimates for invisible construction, is roughly double that of the mapped 500-m² estimated structure density at Santa Rita Corozal of 400 and is 34% higher than that of the mapped density estimate for the 200-m² area projected at 712.5. This apparently indicates that the vacant-terrain estimates employed at Santa Rita provide densities well within the realm of those extant during the Postclassic Period at other major centers and that, if anything, the Santa Rita Corozal estimates may be too low.

POPULATION TRENDS OVER TIME

The relative population history (see Table 10.1) covers all time periods at Santa Rita Corozal and was determined following the procedures outlined by Culbert and Kosakowsky (1985), which compensate for differing lengths of time in each archaeological phase. As mentioned previously, dating at Santa Rita Corozal is based on assessments of primary deposits. For comparative purposes, Table 10.1, based on excavation data, is complemented by Table 10.3, which was compiled exclusively from burial data. A comparison of information from structures and burials should reveal the reliability of either sample. In contrast to the population history garnered from structural data, the burial data appear to overemphasize the Preclassic population and underestimate the Protoclassic and Terminal Classic occupation. Part of the difference is surely due to divergent burial practice(s) following the Preclassic and Classic periods. Indeed, the transition from Classic to Postclassic is still not adequately defined even in well-excavated northern Belize (A. Chase and D. Chase 1985). The overestimation of the Late Preclassic population based on burials is easily understood, especially if one realizes that the same settlement locales were used during the Preclassic and Postclassic periods (A. Chase 1979, 1985b, this volume).

The Santa Rita Corozal data and computations suggest a relatively stable population from Late Preclassic to Early Postclassic times, followed by a dramatic increase of population during the Late Postclassic. These estimates, however, cannot be taken completely at face value; sampling is a consideration for the number of Early and Middle Preclassic constructions, which probably could have been increased, at least slightly, had the excavations continued in the Southwest Sector of the site. Also neglected by the tables is the evidence for monumental construction activity, particularly during the Early Classic Period. It is perhaps significant that the population had expanded to its Classic Period limits prior to the construction of massive architecture in the Structure 7 locus, although excavation suggests it is quite likely that lower-lying constructions are buried there. The data also have ramifications for our conceptions of how many people are necessary to maintain "complex society" and massive architecture, for they suggest that a relatively small Early Classic population was capable of a great deal of visible construction. Interestingly, the Santa Rita Corozal structural data do not show the dip in Early Classic population that has been suggested for some southern lowland sites (Willey et al. 1975:41; Willey 1977:395–96; see also Sidrys 1983:397–99).

That the Late Postclassic is the most heavily populated period of occupation at Santa Rita Corozal is readily apparent from the data. This situation contrasts greatly with the evidence from most southern lowland sites, which indicates depopulation during the Postclassic. Although part of this large population may be simply attributable to the location of Santa Rita Corozal near the bay and rivers, it is also possible that research strategies focusing on large mounded Classic sites are partly responsible for this discrepancy.

CONCLUSIONS

Work at Santa Rita Corozal provides several important lessons for those studying settlement patterns and population reconstructions. Most of the excavations undertaken at this site were in areas that would be called vacant terrain, where there was no mounding or artifact scatter on the surface to indicate construction below. Nevertheless, the excavations frequently produced evidence of multiple-room, elite residences with remnants of base walls and spectacular cache and burial deposits dating to the Late Postclassic Period (D. Chase 1982; D. and A. Chase 1986b, 1988:54–61). Significantly, many of these structures rested on earlier, often non–Postclassic constructions and deposits that would never have been encountered had the excavations been geared toward the traditionally conceived Maya raised constructions. These earlier buildings were also not temporary or lower-class houses but were well-cut and finished stone construction; when penetrated, they have produced substantial numbers of special deposits.

Not only is architecture frequently invisible on the surface at Santa Rita Corozal, but surface indications of pottery only rarely suggest the date of occupation below. In addition, certain constructions would have been incorrectly dated had there been a reliance on temporal determination based on sherds in construction fill; these often were found to predate significantly building activities when sealed primary deposits were encountered. Finally, some Postclassic buildings—little more than buried lines of stone—were not associated with large amounts of debris and would have been missed had an excavation strategy other than large-scale areal stripping been used. Thus, Santa Rita Corozal serves as a reminder that surface indications alone are of extremely limited use in reconstructing past cultural activity for any multiphase site and that investigations concentrating on areal clearing and the recovery of primary remains of buildings, refuse, burials, or caches are obviously the most reliable way to provide direct evidence of prehistoric occupation.

It is extremely important to note that Santa Rita Corozal is situated on a bluff and not in a river valley or other low area; thus, silting is not a factor in obscuring prehistoric remains. The extent of hidden structures encountered has important implications for other Maya sites in nonriverine locations and suggests that the visible occupation at these sites may also represent only about 50% of the actual prehistoric occupation.

Despite the problems of destruction and invisibility, the prehistoric population reconstructions for Santa Rita Corozal proved to be roughly equivalent to the population of modern Corozal Town and slightly less than secondary ethnohistoric guesses of population levels. Without such a cross-check and substantial area-wide excavation, however, the problem of invisible structures might well have precluded any reliable population estimates (see Kurjack 1974:94). Even given the problems inherent in demographic reconstruction, the data from Santa Rita Corozal suggest a different trajectory than that found at many other Maya sites, in that there appears to have been a relatively stable and low number of inhabitants at the site until the onset of the Late Postclassic Period—at which point, by all accounts, Santa Rita Corozal's population increased substantially.

ACKNOWLEDGMENTS

The author wishes to thank the editors of this volume and A. Chase for their comments on an earlier version of this chapter. Work at Santa Rita Corozal was supported by a variety of sources, including grants from Sigma Xi, the Explorer's Club, and the University Museum and Anthropology Department of the University of Pennsylvania for the 1979 and 1980 field seasons, and grants BNS-8318531 and BNS-8509304 from the National Science Foundation and additional support from the University of Pennsylvania and the University of Central Florida for the 1984 and 1985 seasons.

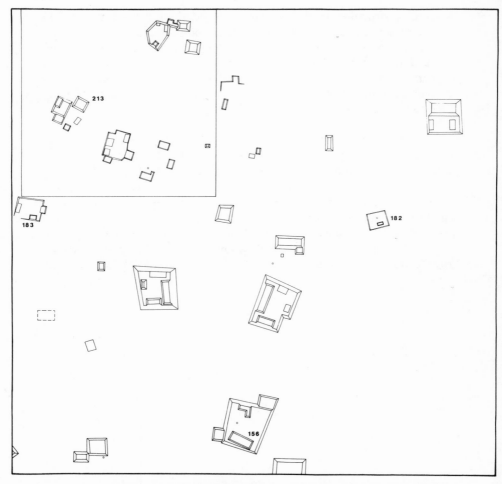

Map 10.1   Structures in the South Intermediate Sector of Santa Rita
Corozal used for population estimates. Inset is 200m²;
larger area is 500m².

Table 10.1 Santa Rita Corozal Occupation: Securely Datable
Investigations and Estimated Population Counts

Period	Cases (N = 43)	Adjustment	Adjusted Cases	Relative Population-% (Adj. cases = 22.83)	Estimated Population
Early Preclassic 1200–900 B.C.	1	15/30	0.50	2.19	150
Middle Preclassic 900–300 B.C.	2	15/60	0.50	2.19	150
Late Preclassic 300 B.C.–A.D. 200	12	15/50	3.60	15.77	1,079
Protoclassic A.D. 200–300	4	15/10	6.00	26.28	1,798
Early Classic A.D. 300–550	8	15/25	4.80	21.02	1,438
Late Classic A.D. 550–900	19	15/35	8.14	35.65	2,438
Terminal Classic/ Early Postclassic A.D. 900–1200	14	15/30	7.00	30.66	2,097
Early-facet Late Postclassic A.D. 1200–1300	4	15/10	6.00	26.28	1,798
Late-facet Late Postclassic A.D. 1300–1530	35	15/23	22.83	100.00	6,840

Note: All 43 structure loci produced some evidence of late-facet Late Postclassic artifact or sherd material; in eight cases, however, it was determined that this material was not clearly representative of any direct occupation, thus resulting in 35 securely assessed Postclassic occupation loci.

Table 10.2   Structure and Population Counts for
Late Postclassic Santa Rita Corozal

	200 m² Area	500 m² Area
Buildings in Surveyed Area	19	50
Structures/km²	475	200
Proportion Missing	50%	100%
Estimated Total Structures/km²	712.5	400
Non-Postclassic Occupation/Sector	1/15	1/15
Estimated Non-Postclassic Structure/km²	47.5	26.7
Postclassic Structures km²	665.0	373.3
Buildings in 2.526-km² Center	1,680	943
Proportion of Buildings Purely Administrative/Ritual	1/19	2/50
Number of Buildings Purely Administrative/Ritual	88	38
Central Postclassic Residences	1,592	905
Coeval (65.22%)ᵃ Postclassic Residences	1,038.3	590.2
Population at 5.6 Persons/Building	5,814.5	3,305.3
Population in Additional 2.5-m² Area at 50% of Central Area Population	2,907.3	1,652.7
Total Postclassic Population in 5-km Area	8,721.8	4,958.0

[a]The 65.22% figure is based on a life span of 150 years for each building and a span of 230 years for the late-facet Late Postclassic period at Santa Rita Corozal.

Table 10.3 Santa Rita Corozal Occupation (Based on Securely Dated Burials)

Period	Burials	Individuals	Adjustment (based on life span of 50 years)	Adjusted Cases	Relative Population (Adjusted cases = 13.91)
Early Preclassic 1200–900 B.C.	4	4	5/30	0.67	4.82
Middle Preclassic 900–300 B.C	5	5	5/60	0.42	3.02
Late Preclassic 300 B.C.–A.D. 200	32	34	5/50	3.40	24.44
Protoclassic A.D. 200–300	4	4	5/10	2.00	14.38
Early Classic A.D. 300–550	13	14	5/25	2.80	20.13
Late Classic A.D. 550–900	28	29	5/35	4.14	29.76
Terminal Classic/ Early Postclassic A.D. 900–1200	6	6	5/30	1.00	7.19
Early-facet Late Postclassic A.D. 1200–1300	4	5	5/10	2.50	17.97
Late-facet Late Postclassic A.D. 1300–1530	38	64	5/23	13.91	100.00

11 /

The Demography of Komchen, An Early Maya Town in Northern Yucatan

WILLIAM M. RINGLE

and E. WYLLYS

ANDREWS V

The architectural remains of the early Maya, both domestic and ceremonial, are often covered by structures of the Classic Period or are buried under the surface and invisible. The ideal site at which to investigate the settlement patterns and demography of this period would be one that was occupied during the entire Formative sequence, was situated in an area where soil formation was minimal, and was abandoned just before the beginning of the Classic Period. It would be a site that saw no occupation in later years and that had not been extensively disturbed.

Komchen, a large Formative site in northwest Yucatan first investigated by the Dzibilchaltun Project in 1959, promised to have most of these characteristics, although its largest buildings had been robbed of stone in the early 1950s and some were mere shells. We surveyed and excavated at Komchen during the first five months of 1980, mapping half the site, testing 162 platforms, and investigating the largest building in more detail. The result is a unique study of the growth and decline of an early Maya town in the millennium before the Classic Period (Andrews V et al. 1984; Ringle and Andrews V 1988; Ringle 1985).

THE SETTING OF KOMCHEN

Komchen is located about 16 km north of Merida and 19 km south of the Gulf Coast. This sector of Yucatan is characterized by a very thin cover of mostly tzekel lithosols (nearly 50% of the surface is exposed bedrock) and by low annual rainfall of about 650–700 mm. Soils are poorer and rainfall is lower to the north and west. The slight soil cover (usually 10 cm or less) did, however, make for excellent surface visibility, and numerous small rock scatters (chich piles) were recorded which would undoubtedly have been invisible at more southerly sites. This also made the site limits relatively easy to define.

Because northwest Yucatan is the most recently emerged portion of the peninsula, karst solution features are small and the topography is unrelievedly flat. The water table is, however, only 3 to 3.5 m below the surface. Our survey located some 25 prehistoric wells, many still functional, and four small cenotes, so that lack of drinking water was probably never a problem.

The present vegetation is secondary scrub or thorn forest (Thien et al. 1982). This was probably true even in Formative times, since regeneration of the climax vegetation would have been slowed by low rainfall, the poor nutritive qualities of the soil, and the considerable clearing necessary to support the population levels indicated by archaeological remains. Because of poor soils and low rainfall, the chief agricultural activity until recently has been henequen cultivation, and milpa yields are far lower than elsewhere on the peninsula.

The rich coastal resources of the fringing mangrove swamp and the open gulf were, however, but a half-day's journey away. This inland band paralleling the coast and just within the limits of agriculture was a prime focus of prehistoric settlement (Map 11.1). Garza and Kurjack (1981) note that the zone in which Komchen lies, transitional between the largely uninhabited tzekel zone closer to the coast and the interior henequen zone, was one of the most densely populated areas in Prehispanic times.

THE SETTLEMENT SAMPLE

We mapped a total of 98 ha in 1980 (Map 11.2), which we estimate to have been about 45% of the entire site. The chief component of our sample was the 78-ha west transect, measuring 1200 m E-W by 650 m N-S. This transect encompassed all the public architecture of the site center and extended westward to the limits of settlement. The later ruins of Dzibilchaltun and modern activity had disturbed the site to the north, south, and east of this transect, but we did cut three brechas 100 m wide in those directions to establish the limits of Komchen.

A total of 505 structures, 380 of which were from the west transect, was found within the 98-ha sample. Remains consisted almost entirely of stone platforms or chich piles. The major exceptions were five large (and badly gutted) mounds that were undoubtedly public structures. Four of these were grouped around a plaza 80 by 160 m (Map 11.3), and the fifth (Structure 2501, referred to as Structure 450 in reports on the Dzibilchaltun Project) was linked to this group by a sacbe. All were several times larger than the next largest platforms.

The 500 presumably nonpublic structures were classified into two broad groups, Type 1 and Type 2. Type 2 structures had a surface area of 40 m² or more and usually had retaining walls of dry-laid, roughly cut stone. Type 1 structures were smaller than 40 m² and included all the chich piles. Most lacked retaining walls and were irregular in outline (Map 11.4). In many cases it was not obvious whether these were natural or cultural features. The fact that 77% of the 70 excavated Type 1 structures contained sherds and that no sherds were found in four test pits placed as controls within the site limits but off structures suggests that Type 1 structures are of human construction, and we believe they are the remains of small, low, gravel platforms supporting perishable buildings. We also found very few house-foundation walls, and those we tested all postdated the Formative Period. We thus have no direct means of calculating the number of Formative houses at Komchen.

Our excavation program was confined almost exclusively to the west transect, in which we test-pitted 40% (152) of the structures. They were stratified by their distance to the center of the main plaza, and random 40% samples were chosen from each 100-m-wide north-south strip in the transect. An additional 10 structures were also excavated, including intensive clearing and trenching of the most conspicuously placed public structure, Structure 21J1 (referred to as Structure 500 in reports on the Dzibilchaltun Project). These investigations were intended to date structures rather than investigate structure usage, so nearly all excavations were 2-m by 2-m pits carried to bedrock.

STRUCTURE FUNCTION

We have little hesitation in assigning a domestic function to all our Type 2 (over 40 m²) structures. Most of these were less than 1.5 m high, and the few substantial secondary platforms atop the basal platforms usually proved to be later additions. There were no formal groupings of platforms that might suggest a ritual function, although there was a preference for an orientation rotated slightly clockwise of the cardinal points. The clearest direct evidence of domestic use was the frequent presence of large, limestone metates. Some platforms had eight or more of these, and structures with two to four were common.

The functions of Type 1 structures are less clear. On the one hand, most lack metates or any other direct evidence of domestic use. As is the case at Sayil, however, many chich piles were located far from major structures and predominated in the site peripheries, suggesting that they cannot all be classified as outbuildings. A few did have associated metates and even burials, so these were almost certainly residences.

Our estimate of the fraction of Type 1 structures that were dwellings is based on a consideration of each structure's size and its proximity to larger platforms. If it was small and was close to a larger structure or a structure of more obviously residential nature, it is classified as an outbuilding, whereas if it was isolated and larger than about 15 m², it is considered a dwelling (see Table 11.1 for modern and archaeological examples of Maya house floor areas). On this basis, 45% of the Type 1 structures would be considered dwellings.

This is admittedly an estimate, and a larger percentage of these small platforms may have been residential. The predominance of these small structures in a wide belt around the outskirts of the community suggests that there at least most did serve as dwelling platforms. Houses and house platforms of the periphery were therefore often simpler (Table 11.2), contained fewer persons, and represented less investment in construction time than those closer to the site center.

Data from mapped and excavated houses at Dzibilchaltun and surrounding Formative sites also indicate that quite small platforms may have supported residences. Most apsidal houses at Dzibilchaltun, essentially all of which date to the Classic Period, covered an area of only 15–30 m² ("5–7 m long and 2.5–4.5 m wide"), probably averaging slightly more than 20 m² (see Table 11.1), with occasional larger variants over 50 m² (Kurjack 1974:54). Five Formative superstructures from the Mirador and Xculul groups averaged 13.5 m², with the largest, from the Xculul phase, covering about 16 m². This early sample, small as it is, prompts us to regard with caution our classification of Type 1 platforms under 15 m² as outbuildings, especially since stone robbing and the general wear and tear of 2000 years has obviously left many chich piles smaller and less regularly shaped than they once were.

ESTIMATING THE SIZE OF KOMCHEN

We judged the site limits had been reached when no structures were found within a 100-m-long stretch of a transect, and we inspected an area beyond the end of each transect to assure ourselves that the area was in fact vacant. The only exception to the predominance of small chich piles in the site peripheries was to the east, where we found Classic Period structures that clearly were part of the much larger settlement that extended out from Dzibilchaltun, the center of which lay 6 km southeast.

Komchen was roughly circular (Map 11.2). Settlement extended an average distance of 890 m from a point in the main plaza we designated as the site center; the average diameter was 1740 m along the E-W and N-S axes if the most distant structures are used. This definition results in a site area of 2.4 km². Our sample of 0.98 km² thus covered just over 40% of Komchen, in its maximal definition. For reasons given below, however, the area of Formative Komchen was probably closer to 2 km².

Because the west transect actually extended 300 m east of the main plaza, and because the site is highly nucleated, the zone in which most of the Type 2 structures occurred was much more heavily sampled than were the peripheries. More than 87% of the Type 2 platforms mapped lie within 600 m of the site center, and 57.9% of this concentric zone was surveyed (Table 11.3). We therefore are reasonably confident about our estimate of the number of structures within this inner zone.

Coverage of the region beyond 600 m from the site center dropped to just a few percent (Table 11.2). Settlement extended to the north farther than in the other directions, and most of it probably dates to the Classic Period. Only six structures beyond 800 m from the center were tested, and none proved to have Formative occupations. A conservative estimate of the size of Formative Komchen would thus be about 1600 m in diameter and approximately 2 km² in area.

To compensate for the low areal coverage of this outlying area, and to produce samples of a reasonable size for calculation of structure frequencies for the entire site, we divided the site into concentric zones 200 m wide. The fraction of each zone surveyed and the number of structures within the zone were then used to project settlement density. Comparable calculations using zones 100 m wide gave similar results.

A total of just over 1000 structures is estimated for the area within 800 m of the site center (the Formative limits of the site) (Table 11.2). We also found an additional 77 structures beyond at distances of up to 1250 m, although the percentage of this area actually surveyed was low. As mentioned, the sample in this area is probably badly skewed by later Classic settlement, and a projection of these figures would nearly double the total number of structures. To arrive at our total, we used our data for the ring of 800–900 m, where we have a 14.2% sample, and added the 309 projected structures. Since beyond this only 2.6% of the area was surveyed, we simply rounded this total to the next hundred (1400 total) to avoid a spurious impression of precision.

Phase projections for Type 1 and Type 2 structures were then made using the frequencies of dated structure within each 200-m-wide circular zone. The Formative phase structure totals in Table 11.4 are slightly more than the values that would be expected from a simple projection of the excavated totals, because the size or condition of the sherd sample permitted some structures to be assigned only a general Formative date. In such cases, fixed fractions of these platforms were assigned to the Late Nabanche and Xculul periods, based on the relative frequencies of excavated platforms firmly dated to the two phases.

These figures indicate there are about 5.8 structures/ha overall at Komchen, and 5 structures/ha within the Formative limits. Even if only Type 2 platforms are considered, the density is about 2.3 structures/ha, a value considerably in excess of residential density at most Peten sites and exceeded or equaled only by published settlement samples from Coba (Folan et al. 1983; Gallareta N. 1984), Dzibilchaltun (Kurjack 1974, 1979; Stuart et al. 1979), Mayapan (Pollock et al. 1962), and perhaps Becan (P. Thomas 1981).

CHRONOLOGY: DATING THE KOMCHEN PLATFORMS

The architectural remains at Komchen are dated primarily by potsherds found on, inside, and below. About 41.4% of the 69,962 excavated were classified to the level of ceramic type. The resulting ceramic sequence is based both on recurrent superposition of these types (and sometimes on their mutually exclusive horizontal distributions) and by comparison with sequences defined at other lowland Maya sites, especially Dzibilchaltun. Dating of the types and modes, and thereby the ceramic complexes of which they formed a part, depended on dates assigned to them at other sites and on 10 radiocarbon dates. Most of the dates were reasonably close to what we would have expected and internally consistent, but they clustered toward the latter part of the Formative occupation.

The most difficult problem we had in assigning dates to the 162 excavated structures was that many platforms contained few or no sherds. As can be seen in Tables 11.5 and 11.6, this particularly affected the small (Type 1) platforms, nearly a third of which had no identifiable ceramics. A further problem was that 58.2% of the 608 excavation lots had between 1 and 20 typed sherds, and 42.9% contained fewer than 10 sherds, as did 49 (30.3%) of the structures (most of these, also, were very small platforms located toward the outskirts of the site). The reliability of the dates assigned on the basis of ceramic content is therefore not constant, but we may place the greatest confidence in dates given to the larger and more important buildings, which contained more sherds.

The construction and occupation history of each platform was considered individually with attention to architectural stratigraphy and the number of identifiable sherds. The dates of structures with few typed sherds are recorded as probable only, although this caveat does not appear in our tables of excavation data or in the tabular projections from these data to the entire site. In general, although we made no hard and fast rule, about 10 typed sherds dating to a given phase, without later admixture, were sufficient to date the construction securely to this span. A smaller number often resulted in a probable assignment only.

Determination of periods of reoccupation and rebuilding was even more troublesome. It was difficult to ascertain how many sherds distinguished chance deposition from genuine occupations, and the intrusion of later ceramic materials into the fill of earlier platforms often gave us pause and vexed us sorely. Here we established a rule: if 5% of the sherds from a lot could be dated to a later phase than the bulk of the pottery, we assigned the platform a reoccupation. We made two exceptions: (1) if five or more sherds dated to a phase later than the period of construction, we assigned a reoccupation, no matter how small a percentage these represented; and (2) no reoccupation was ever based on a single sherd.

The weak points in the data and in our methods of dating the 162 excavated structures at Komchen should be apparent. Since we extrapolate from this number to the larger sample of 308 structures in the main transect and the 505 structures surveyed, and then project the subtotals to the grand total of about 1000 or 1100 platforms composing Formative Komchen, any misinterpretation or bias in the original counts has also been magnified. We believe, nevertheless, that the large excavated sample (42% of the platforms in the main transect and 15% of the total number of structures at Komchen) is almost certain to have yielded valid results that mask the minor effects of what are undoubtedly a number of individual errors. A 10%, or perhaps even a 20%, random, stratified excavation sample of platforms in the main transect (40 or 80 structures) would not have produced enough securely dated units to permit confident extrapolation to the entire site.

A DEMOGRAPHIC HISTORY OF KOMCHEN

Early Nabanche Phase (ca. 650–450 B.C.)

No structural remains are known from Komchen during the late Middle Formative, which represents the earliest known occupation of the northern Maya area, although a few soil horizons under excavated platforms contained only Early Nabanche sherds. Although the earliest low platforms and stone house walls at the El Mirador group of Formative ruins, about 5 km to the south (Andrews IV and Andrews V 1980:21–41, 287–88), date to Early Nabanche, all structures of this time at Komchen must have been of pole and thatch, built directly on the surface or on the most minimal of foundations.

Occupation was nevertheless substantial during these early years. Early Nabanche pottery is a major component of the fill of most platforms at the site. It is typologically identical to the earliest ceramics recovered from sealed structural contexts in the El Mirador group, probably dating as early as 650 B.C. (Andrews V 1986), and it developed into the local pottery of the Later Formative Period. As the extremely common black Ucu and unslipped Achiotes ceramic groups form part of both the Early and the Late Nabanche complexes, and as the latter is also the unslipped pottery of the intervening Ek complex, it is possible only to estimate the number of sherds in these three complexes. We believe that about 25 to 30% of the total number of typed sherds belong to the Middle Formative Early Nabanche complex and 40 to 45% to the Late Nabanche complex.

Ek Phase (ca. 450–350 B.C.)

The Ek ceramic complex was intrusive at Komchen, possibly from sites about 100 km to the south, along the northern edge of the hilly Puuc zone. Its appearance coincided with what we consider to be the beginning of the Late Formative Period and the first known platform construction at the site.

Ek ceramics appear in about 30 platforms, but only 4 of these (Structures 15R2, 18J2, 21J1, and 22N1) contained Ek structures free of Late Nabanche sherds. Ek living surfaces, packed with cultural debris, underlay the huge Structure 23F1 on the central plaza and Structure 18J2, about 150 m west of Structure 21J1. Ek phase occupation and construction were concentrated in areas that remained important throughout the Formative Period. Two Ek platforms were the first stages in what became the largest buildings at the site, and the central plaza appears to have been delineated at least in part by Ek inhabitants. Since Ek phase pottery seems not to have been of local origin, but rather to have been a tradition intrusive onto the northern plains from the Puuc zone, we think the approximately simultaneous beginning of permanent, formally arranged architecture may not have stemmed purely from local Middle Formative antecedents at Komchen.

Diagnostic Ek pottery constitutes just over 4% of the Komchen total, but as the unslipped Achiotes group averages about 50% of uncontaminated Ek lots and is not uncommon in other lots, 6% is probably closer to the actual frequency of Ek pottery. This small proportion of Ek material may indicate that the 100-year span assigned to the phase is too long.

Late Nabanche Phase (ca. 350–150 B.C.)

This phase marked the peak of population and building activity at Komchen. Our 2 × 2-m excavation units do not allow us to estimate the size of buried structures, but it is clear that well over half the architecture at the site dates to this time. All five large platforms around the central plaza, and Structure 2501 to the north, were either started or enlarged, usually in several stages, during these years.

Of 162 tested structures, 131 contained sherds of the Nabanche complex, and at least 73 (including identifiable stages of mounds constructed during more than one phase) were built during the Nabanche phase. This is about half the total number of excavated structures that could be dated, and we therefore estimate that about half of the 22 structures that could not be dated are Nabanche.

The late facet of Nabanche is defined at Komchen first by the presence of the red Sierra group and later by the appearance of the variegated buff Chacah group, as well as several changes in form and decoration in other ceramic groups. Because Joventud Red evolves gradually into Sierra Red, it is often impossible to distinguish these groups, and any method of dating that relies on this distinction will be imprecise. Of the 73 excavated constructions dated to Nabanche, however, 61 contained Sierra group sherds. Since no structures at Komchen are known to date to Early Nabanche, probably all 73 date to the Late Formative facet of this phase, rather than to the Middle Formative. Late ceramic features allow 19 of these to be assigned to the second half of Late Nabanche. We estimate that 40 to 45% of the total number of shreds at Komchen date to Late Nabanche. As noted above, this uncertainty results from the persistence of Achiotes Unslipped and Ucu Black as major groups from the Middle into the Late Formative.

Xculul Phase (ca. 150 B.C.–A.D. 250)

Forty-two structures date to the Xculul phase, which according to our present understanding of the sequence lasted almost as long as the Nabanche phase. Thirty-one were new platforms where none existed before, and 11 were reoccupations or enlargements of Nabanche structures. This is only slightly more than half the number of Nabanche buildings. Expenditure on architecture was probably even less than this figure would indicate, given the high percentage of reoccupations. The relatively small amount of Xculul ceramics, just 15% of the total, reinforces this impression of decline.

Structures of all sizes were well represented in Late Nabanche, but in Xculul, along with a clear drop in population, there was a concentration of occupation on larger platforms. Although Type 1 platforms constituted 33% of the excavated Nabanche sample, they were only 17% of the Xculul sample.

It is difficult to know just how much was added to the large, ceremonial platforms around the central plaza, because so much has been removed for modern building material. Although presumably all of them saw some use, only Structures 21J1 and 25O1 appear to have been enlarged. Excavations in the others did not produce Xculul sherds. The causeway between 21J1 and 25O1 dates to Xculul, however, and both of these platform complexes saw major refurbishing and expansion. No large public or elite buildings were started in this final Formative phase.

The final centuries of the Formative Period are weakly represented at Komchen, although a modest occupation and some late additions to Structure 21J1 probably date to the Protoclassic (ca. A.D. 150–250). A number of Protoclassic vessel forms and modes that appeared in the latest construction levels of Structure 226, excavated by the Dzibilchaltun project and about 3 km to the southwest in the Xculul group, are rare or absent at Komchen. Late constructions contained 39 sherds of the Protoclassic orange Aguacate ceramic group.

Piim Phase (ca. A.D. 250–600)

No certain occupation can be documented for the Early Classic (Early Period I, in the northern lowland terminology). Six sherds are possibly related to Balanza Black, an Early Classic lowland type, but these probably form part of the late Xculul complex with which they occur. No Early Classic ceramics were identified. Aguila Orange and Dos Arroyos Orange Polychrome, so common at Edzna, are absent. Xanaba Red of the Xculul complex, which Brainerd (1958:49–50) placed in both the Formative and Early Regional (Early Classic) periods, calling it Flaky Redware, may have continued to be made in post-Formative times in far northern Yucatan, but no evidence to date from Komchen or from the earlier Dzibilchaltun Project substantiates this. The archaeological record in this zone indicates clearly that the end of the Formative Period witnessed a dramatic demographic decline that lasted until the Late Classic Period.

Copo Phase (ca. A.D. 600–1000)

During the Late and Terminal Classic periods (Early Period II and Pure Florescent) Komchen was reoccupied, perhaps as a small satellite community of nearby Dzibilchaltun, sprawling over the crumbling remains of a once-powerful early Maya town. At the center of the Late Classic village, about 150 m east of Structure 21J1, the Maya built a small platform (Struc-

ture 18J1) for a crude, uncarved stela. Ceramics suggest that this late occupation occurred in the years from about A.D. 700 to 900, rather than
covering the full 400 years assigned to Copo in the standard northern
chronology chart.

Twenty-four new platforms (about 15% of the total) were built in Copo,
and 28 older ones were reoccupied, as compared to 42 platforms occupied during the Xculul phase. An important difference, however, is that
during Xculul, most occupations were new constructions, whereas in
Copo more than half were reoccupations of old platforms. New Copo platforms also tended to be smaller than Formative constructions. Only 8.9%
of the excavated ceramics are Copo, compared with 15% for Xculul. We
think that this figure more accurately reflects the level of Late Classic population than does the number of platforms on which Copo sherds were
found.

Zipche and Chechem Phases (ca. A.D. 1000–1540)

The final half-millennium before the Spanish conquest, like a similar span
before the Late Classic fluorescence, saw Komchen revert to ruin. The
Early Postclassic Zipche phase (Modified Florescent Period) is represented
by only a single sherd of Silho Orange and 10 of Xcanchakan Black-on-
cream (the latter of which also was manufactured in the early Chechem
phase) and possibly one small rectangular house foundation near the center of the site. The diminishing population at the center of Dzibilchaltun
during these years left few traces in the far more ancient ruins to the
northwest.

The Late Postclassic Chechem phase (Decadent Period) saw a slight re-
awakening of interest in the old platforms at Komchen, as was true at
Dzibilchaltun, the El Mirador ruin group, and many other sites in northern
Yucatan. Two minuscule shrines were built atop old platforms, one beside
Structure 21J1 at the north end of the central plaza; superficial debris of
unslipped, painted, and modeled censer sherds attest to the reuse of two
other platforms. Eighty-seven sherds are assigned to the Chechem complex.

PHASE LENGTHS AND RELATIVE POPULATION DENSITIES

Culture phases at Komchen, defined by changes in the ceramic complexes
and by radiocarbon dates, with attention paid to traditional divisions of
lowland Maya sequence, are of different durations. The question arises
whether to weight structure frequencies according to the length of these
phases to arrive at a more accurate estimate of occupation history.

Culbert and Kosakowsky (1985) suggest that at Tikal large structures were occupied continuously but small structures were not. They therefore weight the number of small buildings by phase length and use unmodified frequencies of large ones. At Komchen, Type 1 platforms, covering fewer than 40 m², may well have been so easily constructed that they were abandoned from time to time, for reasons such as the death of the senior male or decay and collapse of the house. Type 2 platforms we think would not usually have been abandoned, because they represent far more effort and in fact often show evidence of continued construction and occupation, as well as multiple burials in their fill.

The result of adjusting the number of structure occupations per phase to a standard number of years affects the population totals for only two phases, Terminal Formative Xculul, which lasted about 400 years, and Late Postclassic Chechem, which lasted about 300 years, compared with 200 years each for Early Nabanche, Late Nabanche, and Copo. The Chechem sample is so small (four structures) that the change is meaningless, and because only 17% of Xculul platforms are Type 1, the total downward adjustment for this phase is only 8% (seven structures). The Ek phase lasted only about 100 years, half as long as Early and Late Nabanche, but as no small platforms are recorded for the span, no adjustment was required.

Any adjustment that tries to equalize the number of structures occupied by weighting totals of Type 1 platforms for phase length, therefore, has no significant effect. Since some Type 1 platforms almost certainly were for outbuildings, rather than houses, and since they are so small that fewer individuals would have been living on them than on the larger platforms (see below), they affect population estimates less than do Type 2 platforms.

A second way to approach more accurate estimates of relative population densities by phase is to weight the total amount of nonarchitectural remains (in this case, the number of potsherds) by phase length. Again, we standardized each sample to a duration of 200 years. The two resulting changes were that Ek pottery increased from about 6 to 12%, and Xculul ceramics decreased from 15 to 7.5% of the total. If these changes have any significance, it is that weighting the ceramic totals shows more cultural debris in pre-Xculul times while strengthening the impression of a decline in population in the Xculul phase.

ESTIMATING THE FORMATIVE POPULATION

Since we recovered no evidence of Formative houses per se, we cannot follow the usual practice of estimating population by multiplying the number of houses by an assumed average number of inhabitants per dwelling. If, however, platforms are considered the habitation units of households of extended families, an equally plausible estimate may be made.

We possess few reliable data on the size of Precolumbian residential units. Such units were for the most part subject to Spanish resettlement policy in the sixteenth century and were subdivided into nuclear families in order to increase the number of tribute-paying households. A few early Colonial censuses have nevertheless survived which suggest that precontact residential patterns were still in use (Table 11.7), and scattered comments in other early documents support these figures. Fray Lorenzo de Bienvenida, for instance, wrote in 1548 that "there is hardly a house which contains only a single citizen [*vecino*]. On the contrary, every house has two, three, four, five, and still more; and among them is one paterfamilias who is the head of the house" (quoted in Roys et al. 1940:197). These documents imply that average household sizes varied greatly, ranging from 7.5 to 11 persons, certainly larger than most nuclear families. Other early sources record only the number of tributaries, or vecinos, and Roys et al (1959) suggest that there were 4 persons for every vecino. Data from the Tixchel area indicate an average of 3.25 tributaries, or about 13 persons/household (Scholes and Roys 1948:471). The *Relación de Ek Balam* (de la Garza et al. 1983:II:135–36) indicates that the large contact town of Chuacah had 250 houses and about 600 to 700 vecinos, or 2.4 to 2.8 vecinos/house. If the above figure of 4 persons/vecino is used, a household size of 9.6 to 11.2 persons is indicated for Chuacah, in agreement with some of the other census data.

Exactly how far back in time we may project such figures is uncertain, but it is clear that the Formative platforms of Komchen were the precursors of Classic platforms that often supported several house foundations. Thus, we have employed an average figure of 11 persons/Type 2 platform, the equivalent of 2 nuclear families. Since the average area of Type 2 platforms is greater than 240 m², and since most apsidal house foundations at Dzibilchaltun covered between 15 and 30 m² (Kurjack 1974:54), we believe an estimate of 2 nuclear families/Type 2 platform is cautious. Type 1 structures classed as dwellings were assumed to have housed nuclear families, couples, or solitary individuals, with an average value of 4 persons/ structure. If we use these figures with the estimated number of structures for each period, a maximum population of about 4050 is indicated for Late Nabanche and about 1850 for Xculul. Factors diminishing these estimates are discussed below.

Another method of estimating the number of occupants per platform is by analogy with better-preserved Classic Period platforms that bear preserved house foundations. In many cases platform size correlates quite well with the number of houses per structure. We compared the platform areas and the number of rooms or house foundations they supported at

Dzibilchaltun ($N = 347$, Stuart et al. 1979), Sayil ($N = 30$, Sabloff et al. 1984), and Coba ($N = 66$, Folan et al. 1983). At Sayil and Dzibilchaltun, platform area proved a good indicator of the number of superstructures ($r = .84–.92$), but somewhat less so at Coba ($r = .73$). The regression equations resulting from the data were:

Dzibilchaltun
(no. of houses) $= 0.829 + (0.0040 \times$ platform area $[m^2])$
Sayil
(number of rooms) $= -0.173 + (0.0073 \times$ platform area $[m^2])$

We applied these formulae to the Komchen platform data. In calculating the average Komchen platform size for a given phase, only platforms whose last construction dated to this span were used. This resulted in average Type 2 platform areas of 267 m^2 for the Late Nabanche phase, 428.7 m^2 for Xculul, and 211.4 m^2 for Copo. If we apply these values to the Dzibilchaltun equation, an average Late Nabanche platform would have supported 1.897 houses and a Xculul platform would have supported 2.544 houses. The Sayil formula would yield 1.776 and 2.957 houses, respectively. Assuming 289 Late Nabanche and 152 Xculul Type platforms, 5.6 persons/house, and 4 people/Type 1 structure, we estimate the following values:

Late Nabanche phase
Dzibilchaltun formula: $289 \times 1.897 \times 5.6 + 216 \times 4 = 3934$
Sayil formula: $289 \times 1.776 \times 5.6 + 216 \times 4 = 3738$
Xculul phase
Dzibilchaltun formula: $152 \times 2.544 \times 5.6 + 46 \times 4 = 2349$
Sayil formula: $152 \times 2.957 \times 5.6 + 46 \times 4 = 2700$

These values are in rough agreement with the previous method, but both almost certainly overestimate the true population, for several reasons. The effect of unequal phase lengths, discussed in the previous section, was not large. Of greater consequence, however, is the assumption in the above calculations that Type 1 structures were residences, although some fraction were probably outbuildings. Haviland (1965) has estimated that 16% of structures at Tikal were residential outbuildings. At Komchen, no more than 50% of Type 1 structures are located near larger platforms, so that even the most conservative calculation would result in a reduction of no more than 100 small houses, or 500 persons, during the Late Nabanche phase.

All the structures dated to a given phase were not simultaneously occupied. Estimates for the degree of contemporaneity vary from about 55% for Coba (Folan et al. 1983) to 95% for Late Classic Tikal (Haviland 1972a).

Shuman's (1974) map of modern Komchen shows 13% of the houses to be abandoned. We see little hope of arriving at any fixed number applicable to all archaeological cases, for occupancy must have varied with the local economy, the density of the surrounding population, and political conditions. Smaller platforms were probably abandoned more readily than larger Type 2 platforms. Given the density of the surrounding rural population, we doubt that a value as low as 55% is applicable to Komchen.

Another factor is the small sample size associated with the fringing areas of the site and the dating problems resulting from small sample sizes and eroded sherds. If only those structures dated to Late Nabanche were used in Table 11.5, our total projection of Type 1 structures for that phase would be reduced by perhaps 45 and our Type 2 total by 33.

Artifact frequencies have sometimes been used to estimate Formative populations, although the problems associated with this method are formidable. Nevertheless, artifact counts may provide a valuable corrective to demographic estimates based on house-mound counts. As indicated above, our criterion of assigning an occupation to the latest phase for which there were five or more sherds seems to overestimate the number of Copo platforms. In contrast, Copo sherds represented only about 8.9% of the total, indicating that occupation during this phase was relatively slight and dispersed.

Taking all these factors into account, we suggest a population of about 2500–3000 for the Late Nabanche phase and 1000–1500 for the Xculul phase. This figure is substantial for a pre-urban center in any part of the world and clearly foreshadows the pattern of dense settlement seen in northern Yucatan during the Late and Terminal Classic periods.

THE REGIONAL SETTLEMENT HIERARCHY

Our knowledge of the distribution of the Formative population outside Komchen itself is limited but sufficient to demonstrate that by the Late Nabanche phase settlements varied considerably in size and complexity. Komchen was by no means the sole center in the region with public architecture, although it was clearly the largest. Sites such as Tamanche (Kurjack and Garza T. 1981:301) and El Mirador (Andrews IV and Andrews V 1980:21–40) are examples of sites occupying the next level down in the Formative settlement hierarchy. Below are sites lacking large public structures or formal plazas. The Xculul group, near the center of Classic Dzibilchaltun (Andrews IV and Andrews V 1980:58–68), and San Antonio Dziskal (16Qd(4)-55), 6 km to the SSW (personal observations), are typical of this class of sites.

Our best evidence on Formative rural population levels outside

Komchen comes from an adjoining 19 km² surveyed by the Dzibilchaltun Project (Kurjack 1974, 1979; Stuart et al. 1979). Kurjack (1974:Table 5) indicates that 53 of 366 excavated structures had Formative sherds (the Formative occupations were not further subdivided chronologically, but Kurjack and John C. Cottier inform us that the bulk of the pottery was of the Nabanche complex, both Early and Late). Thirty-seven of the 139 tested platforms (26.6%) were assigned to the Formative Period. If we apply this proportion to the 5786 basal platforms (5090 small ones and 696 large ones) mapped at Dzibilchaltun (Kurjack 1974:Table 3), we arrive at a very high Formative settlement level of 9.7 large platforms and 71.26 small platforms/km². This estimate is based on an excavated sample of only 2.4% of the total number of platforms.

Even if adjusted downward by the relative ratios for Late Nabanche and Xculul platforms at Komchen, these levels are close to or exceed some estimates of the population density capable of being supported by modern swidden agriculture. The probable explanation is that smaller residences were changed fairly frequently during the Formative Period. Nevertheless, Komchen does not seem to have exerted a centripetal force on the rural population, and levels of population seem to have been high throughout the area.

IMPLICATIONS OF THE DEMOGRAPHIC RECORD

The archaeological data from Komchen provide the first detailed information on an early Maya population center in the northern Maya lowlands, beginning about 650 B.C. with the earliest solid evidence for occupation of the north and continuing until the end of the Formative, when the site was abandoned.

What is most striking about Komchen is that its peak, in terms of population, amount of construction, and no doubt political and economic influence, was reached between 350 and 150 B.C. The beginning of this relatively rapid surge can be placed at about 450 or 400 B.C. Many sites in the southern Maya lowlands, and no doubt also in the north, had far eclipsed Komchen by the end of the Formative Period, but this northern community, with its formal plaza and massive platforms, appears to have developed as early as large towns with public architecture and extensive domestic architecture in the Peten. Cerros, in northern Belize, the only other Formative Maya site lacking significant Classic overburden whose settlement pattern is known, probably does not predate the Xculul phase in the north, and the majority of its occupation appears to fall within the last centuries before the Classic Period, when Komchen had entered its decline (Scarborough 1980; Robertson-Freidel 1980). That Komchen developed so early in a dry zone with shallow soils that are less productive than those in most areas occupied by the Maya is all the more striking.

It is also clear that by the first half of the Late Formative Period the northern Maya had a complex settlement hierarchy of at least three levels. The size of Komchen and the fact that smaller ceremonial centers were within a few hours' walk indicates that Komchen was something more than an overgrown village. More than one factor must have contributed to the early evolution of an internally differentiated society dwelling in a large town with massive formal architecture (Ringle 1985; Freidel 1978, 1979; Ball 1977a). Crop failure, resulting from drought, insects, or other causes, was probably common in this area throughout Maya history, as it was in late Prehispanic times. The development of managerial elites in the largest population centers may have helped ameliorate agricultural disasters by creating the mechanisms necessary for the regional distribution of foodstuffs.

Located near the northern limit of cultivable land, Komchen was well situated to participate in commerce along the coast of the peninsula and to share in the collection and distribution of salt (A. Andrews 1983) from the flats behind the coast. Our excavations, however, recovered very little in the way of trade goods such as jade, obsidian, and pottery, and it is clear that the site was not a trade or redistribution center for foreign goods (cf. Freidel 1978).

Komchen was a highly nucleated community, with about 1000 platforms of varying sizes in the 2.0 km² that we define as the Formative site. Although its population cannot be precisely known, we estimate between 2500 and 3000 persons, or 1250–1500/km², lived at the site during the Late Nabanche phase. The density of architecture and population is equal to that of Dzibilchaltun, exceeding that of southern Maya sites, and clearly sets the pattern of dense population and nucleated sites which characterizes northern Yucatan throughout the Prehispanic record, culminating in Mayapan and other late sites (Kurjack and Garza T. 1981; Tozzer 1941).

A further point is that our population estimate is similar to those for some of the larger contact-period towns. At that time, political power was highly fragmented, and petty cacicazgos were the rule rather than the exception. This was probably similar to the Late Formative situation, when political institutions, communication routes, or trade networks likely had not evolved to the point of permitting settlements much larger than Komchen.

One difference between Komchen and its Classic Period neighbor is that the clusters or groups of architecture at Dzibilchaltun, usually separated from each other by zones with far fewer buildings and sometimes connected to the center of the site by causeways, do not appear at

Komchen. We do not know if the earlier site lacks these divisions because it is so much smaller, in effect forming one huge cluster, or because it is earlier, predating the formation of large, perhaps originally kin-based, residential units within northern sites.

After about A.D. 250 or 300 Komchen was abandoned for the next four centuries. This pattern of Early Classic abandonment, common but by no means universal in the Maya lowlands, starts much earlier at Komchen than at other sites where it has been recorded. Although the Terminal Formative Xculul phase saw a good deal of residential and public construction, this period represented a clear decline from Late Nabanche, both in the amount of building and in population density. The gradual abandonment of the site began around 150 B.C., about 300 or 400 years before the Formative collapse occurred in most other lowland areas.

The early dating of the Komchen Formative collapse strengthens the arguments that it was by no means a unitary phenomenon throughout the Maya area and that climatological factors are not likely to have been the root cause of these disruptions. Like the Late Classic collapse, which took 150 years, and the shorter Middle Classic hiatus, the Late Formative decline seems to have been a complex series of events whose interrelationships are obscure. In northwest Yucatan we suspect that the local hierarchy of sites, which had evolved since the first occupation by agricultural groups about 700–600 B.C. and among which Komchen was preeminent, was disrupted by the growth of more powerful political spheres based farther inland at such sites as Acanceh, Ake, and Izamal.

ACKNOWLEDGEMENTS

The 1980 excavations at Komchen were a joint project of the Middle American Research Institute, Tulane University, and the Centro Regional del Sureste of the Instituto Nacional de Antropología e Historia. The fieldwork was funded by the National Science Foundation (award BNS-7912960). We are indebted to many colleagues in Mexico and the United States who have participated in this research, especially to Norberto González Crespo, co-principal investigator and at that time director of the Centro Regional del Sureste, and to Edward B. Kurjack, who surveyed at Komchen in the late 1960s after the end of the Dzibilchaltun Project and who in the early 1970s urged Andrews to continue there. Our gratitude to these two friends is deep.

With us in the field were Philip J. Barnes, Alfredo Barrera Rubio, Tomás Gallareta Negrón, Susan D. Gillespie, Carlos Pérez Alvarez, Marí José Roche, Kathy Rowland, Georgia Schneider, and Patty Andrews. They made it a good season.

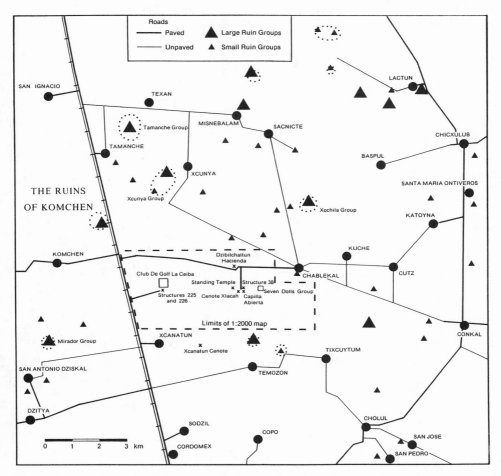

Map 11.1   Archaeological sites and modern communities near
Komchen and Dzibilchaltun, northwest Yucatan. (From
Kurjack: (Figure 8; in Stuart et al. 1979)

233

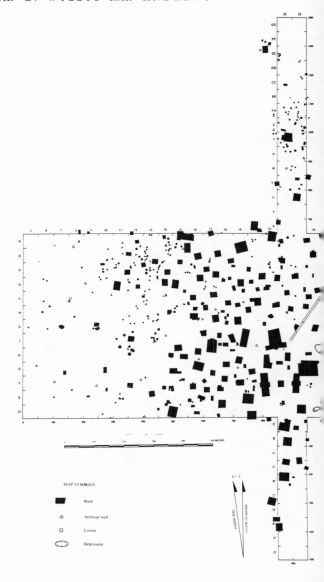

Map 11.2   The ruins of Komchen.

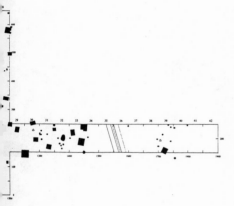

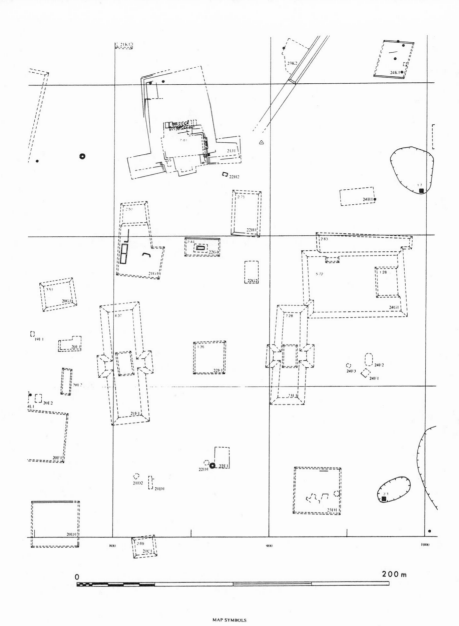

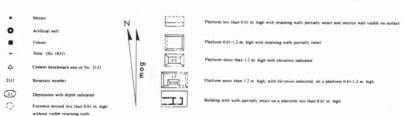

- Metate
- Artificial well
- Cenote
- Stela (Str 18J1)
- △ Cement benchmark east of Str. 21J1
- 21J1 Structure number
- Depression with depth indicated
- Formless mound less than 0.61 m. high without visible retaining walls

Platform less than 0.61 m. high with retaining walls partially intact and interior wall visible on surface

Platform 0.61-1.2 m. high with retaining walls partially intact

Platform more than 1.2 m. high with elevation indicated

Platform more than 1.2 m. high, with elevation indicated, on a platform 0.61-1.2 m. high

Building with walls partially intact on a platform less than 0.61 m. high

Map 11.3 The Central plaza, Komchen.

236

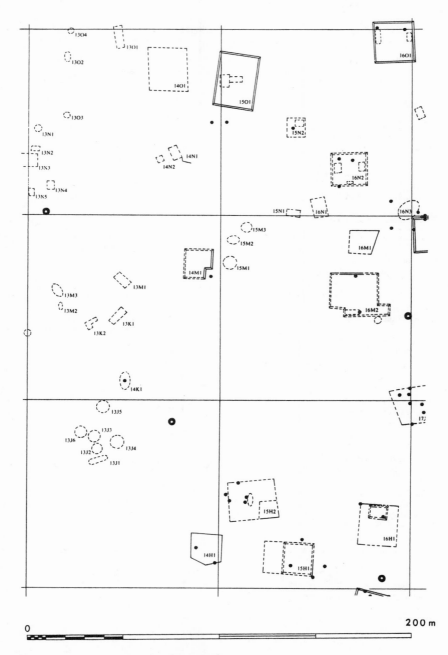

Map 11.4   A western portion of Komchen.

Table 11.1 Maya House Floor Areas

Location	Size (m²)	Source
Modern Examples		
Tizimin, Yucatan	31.2	Wauchope 1938
Chan Kom, Yucatan	54.2	"
Lerma, Campeche	44.1	"
Piste, Yucatan	23.9	"
Telchac Pueblo, Yucatan	48.5	"
San Lucas Toliman, Guatemala	17.8	"
Santiago Atitlan, Guatemala	12.1	"
San Pedro de Laguna, Guatemala	28.1	"
San Sebastian, Guatemala	18.4	"
San Cristobal, Guatemala	38.1	"
X-Cacal, Quintana Roo	60.0	Villa Rojas 1945
Archaeological Examples		
Mirador Group, Yucatan		Andrews IV and Andrews V 1980
(Early Nabanche phase)		
Structure 605 Period 1Ba	11.4	
Period 2A	13.8	
Period 2B	12.2	
Period 2E	14.4	
Dzibilchaltun, Yucatan		Andrews IV and Andrews V 1980
Xculul Group (Xculul phase)		
Structure 226, Period 7	15.9	
Single-room apsidal (Copo phase)		Kurjack 1974
Structure 736	23.4	
Structure 3605	27.1	
Structure 3610	24.4	
Structure 3721	20.1	
Single-room rectangular (Copo phase)		
Structure 730	19.6	
Structure 777	19.3	
Average single-room Copo house	22.3	
Isla Cozumel, Quintana Roo		Freidel and Sabloff 1984
(house definition)	> 20.0	
Cuello, Belize		Hammond 1977
Swasey house 1	28.0	
Swasey house 2	50.0	
Becan, Campeche		
Structure XXVII (Late Formative)	13.0	Ball and Andrews V 1978
small farmsteads (8 examples)	8.5–20	Eaton 1975
average small farmsteads	13.4	"
storehouses (2 examples)	4.4–7	"
large farmstead	36.2	"

Table 11.2 Projections of Structure-Type Frequencies by 200-m Rings at Komchen

Radius of Ring (m)	Area Surveyed (m²)	% of Ring Surveyed	Survey Sample Structure Counts		Total Projected Structure Counts	
			Type 1	Types 2 & 3	Type 1	Types 2 & 3
0–200	122,195	97.24	10	40	10	41
200–400	266,643	70.73	21	110	30	156
400–600	263,534	41.94	90	76	214	181
600–800	187,851	21.36	60	21	281	98
Subtotal[a]	842,223	41.89	181	247	535	476
800–900	76,029	14.24	35	9	246	63
900–1250	63,748	2.61	30	3	53	27
Total	980,000	19.96	246	259	834	566

[a]Because of the small sample sizes and limited areas sampled, the projected structure counts for the zones from 900 to 1250 m are not considered reliable. Most structures encountered beyond 900 m, especially to the north and east, probably date to the Late Classic Period. We have therefore defined Formative Komchen as extending about 800 m from the center, since Formative remains beyond that distance are scarce. This radius yields a total projected structure count of 1011. If we extend the radius of the Formative site to 850 m, thereby including all structures in the west transect, an additional 80 structures are projected, for a grand total of 1091. We believe this is a more reasonable estimate to use than the 1400 structures arrived at by including all the Classic Period remains out to 900 m.

Table 11.3 Distance of Mapped and Dated Structures from the Center of Komchen

Radius (m)	No Sherds Found	Sherds Unidentified	Late Nabanche	Xculul	Formative	Copo	Untested	Total
			Type 1 Platforms (area < 40 m²)					
0–100	0	0	0	0	0	0	0	1
100–200	0	0	3	0	3	0	6	9
200–300	0	0	1	0	3	0	1	3
300–400	0	0	3	2	7	3	10	18
400–500	1	0	5	4	10	2	24	37
500–600	8	0	7	1	9	3	33	53
600–700	6	4	5	0	7	0	25	42
700–800	1	0	0	0	0	1	16	18
800–900	0	2	0	0	1	1	31	35
900–1000	0	0	0	0	0	0	17	17
1000–1100	0	0	0	0	0	0	8	8
1100–1200	0	0	0	0	0	0	5	5
1200–1250	0	0	0	0	0	0	0	0
Total	16	6	24	7	40	10	176	246
			Type 2 and Type 3 Platforms (area > 40 m²)[a]					
0–100	0	0	7	3	8	4	1	10
100–200	0	0	3	3	6	3	22	30
200–300	0	0	14	11	19	12	28	50
300–400	0	0	11	12	20	11	35	60
400–500	0	0	0	4	5	4	31	38
500–600	0	0	9	2	10	4	26	38
600–700	0	0	4	0	5	2	11	16
700–800	0	0	1	0	2	0	3	5
800–900	0	0	0	0	0	2	7	9
900–1000	0	0	0	0	0	0	0	0
1000–1100	0	0	0	0	0	0	1	1
1100–1200	0	0	0	0	0	0	2	2
1200–1250	0	0	0	0	0	0	0	0
Total	0	0	49	35	75	42	166	259

[a]There were 5 Type 3 platforms, 4 in the 0–100-m ring and 1 in the 500–600-m ring.

Table 11.4   Projections of Dated Structure Frequencies at Komchen

Phase/Sample	0–200 m	200–400 m	400–600 m	600–800 m	800 m–	Total
	Type 1 Platforms					
Nabanche excavated	3	4	12	5	0	24
" projected	8	17[a]	91[a]	100[a]	[b]	216+
Xculul excavated	0	2	5	0	0	7
" projected	0	8[a]	38[a]	0	0	46
Formative excavated	3	10	19	7	1	40
" projected	8	32	103	99	[b]	242+
Copo excavated	0	3	5	1	1	10
" projected	0	10	34	14	[b]	58+
Total excavated	4	10	33	19	4	70
" mapped	10	21	90	60	65	246
" projected	10	32	226	272	314	854
	Type 2 and 3 Platforms					
Nabanche excavated	10	25	9	5	0	49
" projected	24	83	94[a]	93[a]	0	294
Xculul excavated	6	23	6	0	0	35
" projected	13	77	62[a]	0	0	152
Formative excavated	15	39	15	7	0	76
" projected	35	130	146	93	0	404
Copo excavated	7	23	8	2	2	42
" projected	17	77	78	27	[b]	199+
Total excavated	17	47	19	7	2	92
" mapped	40	110	76	21	12	259
" projected	41	157	185	93	70	546

Note: Projected values are calculated by dividing the number of excavated structures dated to a phase by the total number of structures excavated in that 200-m ring and multiplying the result by the total number of structures projected for that 200-m concentric ring ("Total projected"), which is calculated by comparing the area of a concentric ring to the area of the ring actually surveyed (see Tables 11.2 and 11.3).
[a]Includes a proportional contribution from structures dated only to the Formative.
[b]Excavated samples were too small to warrant confident projections.

Table 11.5 Komchen Structure Occupation by Phase

Phase	Type 1			Type 2			Type 3			Total		
	Constructed	Reoccupied	Total	Constructed	Reoccupied	Total	Constructed	Reoccupied	Total	Constructed	Reoccupied	Total
No sherds	0	0	16	0	0	0	0	0	0	0	0	16
Unidentified	0	0	6	0	0	0	0	0	0	0	0	6
Early Nabanche	0	0	0	0	0	0	0	0	0	0	0	0
Ek	0	0	0	4	0	4	0	0	0	4	0	4
Late Nabanche	24	0	24	44	0	44	5	0	5	73	0	73
Xculul	7	0	7	24	8	32	0	3	3	31	11	42
Formative	38	0	38	70	0	70	5	0	5	113	0	113
Copo	9	1	10	15	26	41	0	1	1	24	28	52
Zipche	0	0	0	0	0	0	0	1	1	0	1	1
Chechem	1	0	1	0	3	3	0	0	0	1	3	4
Total			70			87			5			162

Note: Phase totals include those structures dated to subdivision of these larger units.

Table 11.6 Komchen Structure Counts by Phase and Size

Total Period/Sample	Type 1 Platform Size			
	< 15 m²	< 25 m²	< 40 m²	Types 1, 2, 3
	Excavated			
Ek	0	0	0	4
Nabanche	9	18	24	73
Xculul	3	6	7	42
Formative total	9	18	26	114
Copo	2	5	10	52
Zipche	0	0	0	1
Chechem	1	0	0	4
Eroded sherds only	3	4	6	6
No sherds found	10	15	16	16
Total excavated sample	32	54	70	162
	Mapped			
West transect mapped	74	127	164	380
Total mapped	116	195	246	505

Note: Totals in above columns are cumulative; for example, values in the < 40 m² column include all structures with areas less than 40 m². In the west transect there are 160 excavated platforms; in the north transect, 2.

Table 11.7 Maya Household Sizes

Location	Year	Persons/ household
Xcacal, Q.R.	1945	6.3
Temaza	1579	9.35
Pencuyut, Yucatan	1583	8.42
Tizimin-Boxchen, Yucatan	1583	9.89
Dzonotchuil	1583	8.66
Tecay	1583	7.48
Tixcacauche	1583	8.32
Cozumel Island, Q.R.	1570	11.43
Chinautla, Guatemala	1727	
Barrio 1		11.17
Barrio 2		13.58
Barrio 3		10.48
Barrio 4		7.19
Chinautla average		10.97
Southwestern Campeche	1615	
Ichbalche		7.20
Tzuctok		8.00
Chunhaz		4.50
Chacuitzil		8.48
Ichmachich		9.00
Southwestern Campeche average		7.04

Sources: Roys et al. 1940 (Cozumel), 1959 (Yucatan and Quintana Roo); Reina et al. 1984 (Chinautla); Villa Rojas 1945 (Xcacal, Q.R.); Weeks 1988 (southwestern Campeche).

12 /

Room Counts and Population Estimation for Terminal Classic Sayil in the Puuc Region, Yucatan, Mexico

GAIR TOURTELLOT,

JEREMY A. SABLOFF,

and MICHAEL P.

SMYTH

Despite the current lack of excavation, we can offer a tentative population estimate for Sayil because it is apparently a large-size example of that class of archaeological settlement known as a single-period site. This inference is based not only on the previous work of the Ceramic and Architectural Surveys conducted by H. B. Roberts and H. E. D. Pollock for the Carnegie Institution of Washington (Brainerd 1958; Pollock 1980) and rescue efforts by archaeologists of the Instituto Nacional de Antropología e Historia in Merida (Barrera Rubio et al. 1983), but also on the results of style datings and limited test excavations conducted by our research team from the University of New Mexico, and its collaborators, during the 1983–85 Sayil Archaeological Mapping Project (Sabloff et al. 1985; Tourtellot et al. 1988).

We have mapped thousands of remains at the northern lowland site of Sayil (Map 12.1), in the Puuc region of Yucatan, Campeche, remains whose remarkable clarity of exposed surface plans stands in sharp and exciting contrast to the frequently buried and obscure plans of structures at deep-soil sites farther south. From these mapped structures we can offer a preliminary assessment of residential construction, room counts, and population during the Terminal Classic

Period at Sayil, even in advance of extensive, problem-oriented excavations.[1]

INTRODUCTION

As a background to understanding the first comprehensive data set collected from one of the archaeologically neglected but architecturally famous Puuc sites, we will review the goals and methods of the Sayil Project. We have just completed the first phase of a long-term study of a large Puuc site, for which we wish to (1) determine the nature of the adaptation of the former inhabitants to land and scarce water in the little-known, seasonally desiccated Puuc environment; (2) classify and assign functions to the full range of features and structures of a community occupied during the short floresence of Puuc occupation and development; (3) codify the internal social and political organization of that community; and (4) delimit the organization of Sayil and its relations to sites near and far at a critical time in the growth of ancient Maya civilization, when the Puuc apogee contrasts with decline in many other lowland regions (Sabloff et al. 1984).

This phase of research at Sayil has concentrated on the preparation of the first detailed comprehensive map of a major Puuc site, Sayil having been picked as an appropriate and manageable example of a Puuc site of Rank 2 (Garza T. and Kurjack 1980; Sabloff et al. 1984:4–5). Sayil is situated at the northern end of a shallow valley on the edge of the Bolonchen physiographic province (Wilson 1980). It lies just south of the finest Puuc soils associated with major sites such as Uxmal, Kabah, and Yaxhom. Local relief varies from the flat central-valley floor—where the causeway and multistory civic constructions of the site core are placed—to rolling limestone outcrops that bear most of the residential structures, to several rings of cone-karst (haystack) hills up to 40 m in height.

A fourfold field strategy was followed in order to map a substantially complete record of surface features, some of them probably natural (such as sinks and potholes), but most of them arguably artificial and ranging from quarries and spreads of cobbles (chich mounds) to water cisterns (chultunes), platforms, foundations, and stone buildings.

The first step was the progressive cutting of a grid of survey lines (brechas) through the often dense grass and scrub forest covering the relatively undisturbed site in various stages of secondary regrowth from a former condition of extensive swidden agriculture. The interval between brechas was 200 m, in parallel sets of transects each 200 m wide (100 m to either side of the main brecha) by 500 to 1600 m long, with cross-brechas every 100 m, forming a grid of squares each 1 ha in area, as one basis for field control and spatial analysis.

The second step was the examination and sketch mapping of each ha square after its definition by the surrounding brechas. The sketch of each square, showing the general location of natural and cultural features, served as a guide for planning the actual mapping.

The third step was detailed mapping of each ha by crews of archaeologists and workers using a theodolite or transit, occasionally supplemented with tape and compass. Square by square, they cleared, examined, and mapped the terrain and cultural features onto Mylar sheets mounted on portable drafting boards, using a series of quasi-conventionalized feature representations at an initial scale of 1:500. As the fourth step, the crews immediately encoded each mapped feature onto standard forms that were later used for data entry and basic computer-aided analyses. The 23 variables coded include, location, terrain, feature type, construction details, building details, room count, surface artifacts, and planimetered area. A formatted printout of these encoded features will be published along with the 1:1000 site maps.

SITE COVERAGE

Unlike the situation for most Maya sites, at Sayil we have a good idea of exactly what amount of space the ancient settlement occupied. Map 12.2 schematically depicts the areas we have recently mapped intensively, a supplemental area adequately mapped previously by Edwin M. Shook in 1934–35 for the Carnegie Institution of Washington (Pollock 1980:Figure 164), and the location of the rather sharply defined settlement limits.

The "urban limit" to the site indicated on Map 12.2 is most directly recognized in the field by the cessation of a series of features and construction details as one moves out from the site core. Within the compass of our survey transects but beyond this border, one rarely finds stone buildings, platforms, or other constructions employing masonry. What one may find outside (as well as for some distance inside) the limit are hundreds of chich mounds scattered across hills and outcrops. These mounds may represent floor foundations for long-perished buildings, for excavations in five examples from *inside* the borders showed that at least those five were laced throughout with potsherds (see Sabloff et al. 1985:36–43, 70–73). Nevertheless, two of the most obvious markers of domestic occupation within the urban limit, chultunes and stone basins (trough metates?), are, respectively, *totally* or *almost totally absent beyond the border*. We think that the absence of the masonry constructions, *to-*

247

gether with the absence of these two quintessentially domestic markers commonly associated with buildings, gives us a powerful argument for at least a very significant change in the residential character of the community, if not its outer limit. (It may also prove significant that there are few potsherds visible on cleared surfaces beyond the border, in contrast to most areas within it.)

We have also found indications of a feature type that may have marked this same border in a positive, formal, and even ritual fashion. Four piles of stone rubble are tentatively identified as the remains of small, isolated, two-tiered pyramids, each built of rough or poorly shaped boulders. One pyramid is located on the border directly south of the site core, and three others are located on or close to the border east of the site core. One of the latter, directly east of site center, is a two-tiered, west-facing, round pyramid placed on a square, basal platform. No similar rubble pyramids have yet been recognized or mapped on either the northern or western borders (Tourtellot et al. 1988).

Well beyond the border indicated on Map 12.2, we know there are occasional clusters of masonry structures with chultunes and other domestic impedimenta. The known examples closest to Sayil, Chac (Rank 4 in size) and the Column Group, are also indicated on the map (see Sabloff et al. 1985:63–64, Figure 13). We have examined some of the terrain between Sayil and Chac, where it is exposed under modern milpa clearings, and are fairly confident that there is little in the way of masonry construction or ceramics in the intervening area, although there are again quite a few chich mounds. These "satellites" are not included here as part of Sayil.

Based on these data, we believe the probable built-up community area for ancient Sayil extended over approximately 3.45 km². The proportion of that community area that we have mapped and processed up to this writing is represented in Map 12.2 by the shaded areas.[2] This archaeologically known area covers 2.44 km², or 70.72% of the community within the limits as specified.

All terrain at Sayil appears to have suitable soils and topography for cultivation by complex and varied swidden and garden techniques. All types of terrain at Sayil show evidences of human residence: the flat central valley, marginal outcrops, hilltops, and slopes (except for a small proportion that are very steep). If there is any bias in terrain selection it was toward the flat valley bottom or "lowland" (rugged in detail along its margins) rather than any upland landscape. There are no bajos. Indeed, there is absolutely no surface water anywhere near Sayil. We believe this lack of water was one of the primary reasons for putting most ancient residences on top of the rugged marginal outcrops, where water cisterns for the collection of the highly seasonal rainfall could be dug into the conveniently exposed bedrock (Sabloff et al. 1985:73–75).

CLASSIFICATION OF FEATURES

We already have a good idea of the sorts of features we are going to count in order to derive a population estimate for Sayril, in advance of excavation, not only because of the many previous studies by Mayanists devoted to identifying dwellings and other functional types (e.g., Wauchope 1938; A. L. Smith 1962; Haviland 1963; Willey et al. 1965; Stenholm 1973; Tourtellot 1983), but also because of the splendid clarity of preserved structure plans at Sayil due to the thin soils and short period of occupation.

At present we have identified and classified more than 34 different types of feature at Sayil, of which at least 29 are cultural. The most likely ancient residential features consist of six structure types that are either buildings containing rooms or the likely foundations for such buildings. Excluded from further consideration here are features that have other, special, nondomestic, or wholly enigmatic uses: for example, basal platforms, pyramids, ring (doughnut) structures, and depressions. Also excluded are all features we think are recent: (see Sabloff et al. 1985:32–36).

The six structure types that offer the most promise as ancient dwellings are foundation-brace buildings (with stone building [superstructure] walls that are no more than half-height) and both vaulted and nonvaulted stone buildings with full-height walls. Foundation braces almost always consist of a single straight row of rooms, each room about 3 m² and having its own entrance. Stone buildings have more varied plans, the larger examples occasionally including "apartments" of two or three connected rooms with a single common exit. Other feature types potentially in the pool of residences include bare platforms (lacking surface evidence of superstructural walls or features), a few levelings (small areas of fill without visible retaining walls but attached to recognizable buildings), and the numerically dominant chich mounds.

These feature types are a reasonable place to start an estimation of population because of their designs and plans, their frequent clustering together atop basal platforms, and common association with chultunes and stone basins (metates?), all of these generally considered hallmarks of domestic settlement in the northern lowlands (Folan 1969; Kurjack 1974; Kurjack and Garza T. 1981; Folan et al. 1983). We are aware that not all structures with domestic uses were necessarily used as dwellings (covered sleeping and living areas), nor were all rooms within such domestic buildings necessarily used primarily as dwellings rather than for ancillary purposes like storage. We are even considering the possibility of sliding scales of building or room usages whereby the particular use depended on what other sorts and sequences of structures were present in the same cluster of features.[3]

We currently envision a labor/energy continuum of these potential dwelling types from (a) perishable houses on bare platforms and perhaps on levelings and chich mounds (and even on some large building plinths or basal platforms), to (b) foundation braces whose upper walls and roofs were perishable, to (c) nonvaulted stone buildings, and culminating in (d) vaulted stone buildings. These four levels of architectural distinction are readily visible in the types of surface remains they left behind, and they correspond to scales of materials and skills, and perhaps to status and use. The preliminary frequency distribution of these levels in the mapped area is also suggestive: as many as about 541 perishable buildings, 362 foundation braces, and 214 stone buildings.

The major problem is represented by the numerous chich mounds, for only a small percentage of them rest on basal platforms or in association with the other types. Although those can tentatively be accepted as foundations, most have a marked affinity for rock outcrops and look suspiciously like the expected natural outcome of bedrock corrosion in a karstic landscape. Also, as mentioned above, most chiches occur in the outer reaches of the settlement, a pattern seen elsewhere in the Yucatan (E. W. Andrews V et al. 1984). Our definition of chich mounds differs in a perhaps significant formal respect from the thousands of similar spreads of cobble "fill" classified at other sites as bona fide "platforms" (Kurjack 1974; Ringle 1985). We have not classified features with chich material as examples of (bare) platforms unless the remains of an actual rock retaining wall are visible. Operating conservatively, if we find that a loose stone feature lacks any indication of a retaining wall, we identify it initially only as a stone pile or chich, depending on the size and working of the stone. Our excavations did not turn up any indication that the chich mounds ever had such walls. In recognition of this suite of problems, chich mounds have been treated separately in the counts that follow.

Another potential problem cannot be intelligently discussed until we have accomplished some of our many planned, extensive, horizontal excavations of extramural locations at Sayil. This is the problem of the possible existence and numbers of entirely perishable buildings that have left no currently recognized surface signature. The problem is particularly severe in the present context only if, as has not been generally demonstrated, any such "invisible" buildings were contemporaneous with the rest, *and* were used as dwellings rather than ancillaries, *and* were permanently occupied by discrete persons not already countable from the already visible remains (e.g., were not field houses, seclusion huts, sweat baths, or dormitories for age-mates). The former presence of any invisible remains meeting these criteria would obviously require an addition to the population calculations below.

CONTEMPORANEITY

There is evidence from previously studied architectural styles and ceramic dating that Sayil is essentially a single-period site where, therefore, all remains can be considered grossly contemporaneous. Further studies along both these lines as part of the Sayil Archaeological Project so far largely confirm the earlier results, although it must be stressed that a "single period" of major occupation at Sayil still covers a span of approximately two centuries.

Boucher (1984) made a complete type: variety analysis of 6107 potsherds recovered from our exploratory excavations into five chiches at Sayil. The significant finding of her study is that 97.74% of the pottery is Terminal Classic (Cehpech Horizon). Construction dates for the chiches are all Cehpech, virtually eliminating the possibility that chiches simply belonged to a different period than the stone buildings. The analyzed Cehpech ceramics show that some 51% of all sherds were from Yokat Striated water jars; another 41% from Muna Slate cooking, serving, and water vessels; and only 2.5% from "fancy" Ticul Thin Slate bowls, with no imports and no censers (Boucher 1984). In sum, the ceramics appear to be a reasonable domestic assemblage.

Architectural style dates from Sayil appear to corroborate the conclusion that most mapped remains are roughly Terminal Classic, but they hint at a possible subdivision. G. Andrews, (1985a) conducted the first inventory of all standing buildings for any single major Puuc site. He was able to assign style dates to 71 stone buildings at Sayil according to the stylistic sequence he worked out during his survey of the whole Puuc region (G. Andrews 1982, 1985a, 1985b). The frequencies of the three styles of Puuc architecture recorded among these 71 structures at Sayil are listed in Table 12.1.

It will be noted that the provisional dates listed in Table 12.1 (G. Andrews 1985b; Ball 1985) indicate that Sayil was perhaps occupied far longer than the conventional dating of the Terminal Classic Period (Cehpech Ceramic Horizon) to a.d. 800–1000 (Brainerd 1958; R. Smith 1971). Since we currently lack other evidence than the admittedly controversial style dates to subdivide the occupation of Sayil, we will not attempt to standardize temporally our population figures.

Furthermore, several lines of evidence suggest that the Early Puuc Style buildings continued in use while new ones in the Classic Puuc styles were added. First, there are several examples of Classic Style rooms, wings, or whole buildings added on to Early Puuc buildings (the Great Palace is the best-known). Second, several building groups differing in their style dates are connected by the same central causeway in the site core, suggesting continuation of old groups after new groups were added. Third, we have no clear examples yet of precociously abandoned or filled-in Early Puuc Style rooms or buildings occurring before general site abandonment.

We therefore think that if we were to make any temporal subdivision of the remains belonging to the expansively dated Terminal Classic Period on the basis of architectural style, the subdivision must be made in the ratio of all to one-third (i.e., the ratio of the number of Classic Puuc *plus* Early Puuc buildings to Early Puuc buildings alone in Table 12.1). This ratio may indicate the direction, and perhaps the timing and magnitude, of elite population change through time at Sayil.

Table 12.1 raises another point concerning periodization and contemporaneity. We can speculate that Sayil was already in premature decline soon after the appearance of the Puuc Mosaic Style buildings about A.D. 840. The Puuc Mosaic Style structures there are only a small proportion (1:6) of the Puuc Colonnette Style, despite the fact that the two styles have roughly equal proportions (7:10) within the Puuc region as a whole (G. Andrews 1985a:3). In addition, the overlapping provisional date ranges for the two styles—the Mosaic Style first appearing some 70 years after the start of Colonnette Style constructions—could be taken to indicate that most of the Colonnette Style buildings might already have been built before Mosaic Style buildings were added. The few Mosaic Style buildings might then require only a decade or two to be added before all construction ceased, perhaps 200 years before these two Classic Puuc styles died out in the region as a whole. This speculation seems like a logical if unexpected twist on time-standardization methods examined in this volume. Without other lines of documentation, is this curtailment not as reasonable as assuming that an average number of structures were spread throughout a phase (or in each century), or that their numbers had peaked at the chronological midpoint? If this speculation were correct, then obviously the question of contemporaneity (and population numbers) during the later facet also would be reduced from dealing with hundreds of years to only a much more manageable 80 or 90 years.

POPULATION ESTIMATION FORMULA

Now that we have anticipated in the foregoing discussion of data some of the factors necessary to make an estimation of the population once resident at Sayil, it is time to spell them all out. There are numerous ways to estimate past population numbers (although few that will provide real demographic information such as sex ratios, age distributions, mortality, morbidity, etc.). Here we shall resort to the analysis of a particularly revealing sort of artifact consumption—namely, the putative dwelling structures built at Sayil (see McAnany, this volume, for a parallel study of Sayil based on water consumption).

Structures have been the focus of attention because they are relatively large and mappable artifacts, not tradeable or movable, and permanent (although this last aspect raises problems of reuse and periodization). In addition to this traditional focus, however, the marvelous visibility of building plans (and the more frequent use of foundation braces) typical of some northern lowland sites permits us to refine straight structure counts by considering room counts. In effect, we shall provisionally extrapolate to an entire settlement the type of room-by-room analysis of individual structures and clusters exemplified by Folan (1969) and R. E. W. Adams (1974).

The basic form of the computation to estimate population is: $A \times B \times C \times D$ where $A =$ the census unit, here structure or room counts; $B =$ the proportion of units that were dwellings; $C =$ the proportion of units occupied contemporaneously (including periodization and disuse factors); and $D =$ family size. As is so often the case in archaeology, a straightforward calculation will inevitably be wrong, and a calculation more sensitive to the realities of human behavior and the archaeological record will be controversial. The preliminary results for Sayil are presented in Table 12.2.

The types of mapped structures ($=$ mapped A) discussed earlier can be arranged in descending order by the reliability with which we think they can be identified as dwellings: foundation braces, stone buildings, bare platforms, levelings, chiches ($= B$). We have mapped 70.72% of the total built-up settlement area, from which a multiplier of $1.00 \div 0.72 = 1.41$ is obtained to estimate the projected total ($=$ full A) for the whole settlement. We have also shown why we think all these structures derive from a single period of occupation ($= C = 1$) *or* can be heuristically subdivided into an earlier facet when only one-third of the structures were occupied ($= C/3$) versus a later facet when all were occupied ($= C = 1$ again). Before running the calculation, we need a figure for D, the number of people per structure or room.

Estimation of D depends largely on selecting an average family size appropriate to the nature and size of the census unit. In order to avoid an ambiguity that plagues the published record on Maya house counts, we want to make two fundamental distinctions clear. First, we are counting by individual structures or individual rooms, never by entire clusters, patio groups, or other collective entities. Second, we are attempting to count only those structures that are most likely to have been dwellings, not merely "domestic structures" of all sorts that include ancillaries in which nobody ever lived. In order to keep these distinctions clear we have avoided using the ambiguous term *house mound* (cf. Sabloff 1983). In general, there is no reason to use this term when the actual forms of the structures signified are known, as here at Sayil (or when elsewhere they are inferrable from excavated examples), nor need it be employed when more specific uses of the structures are allegedly known (as they usually should be after excavation of a reasonable sample).

Although a figure of 5.6 people/family (and usually per structure as well) has often been used as the population multiplier *D,* one must be skeptical of the appropriateness and accuracy of this figure (R. E. W. Adams 1974:289; Tourtellot 1983:48). Examination of various historical and modern census documents suggests that the number of inhabitants per "house" was actually considerably higher (e.g., Table 5.5 in Ringle 1985 gives a range of 6.3 to 13.58 persons). Considering that the "house" size in some Maya sites is on the average of 50 m²/platform (Tourtellot 1983:37) and room size at Sayil averages about 8 m² in foundation-brace buildings and 12 m² in stone-walled buildings, it seems reasonable that the number of inhabitants *per room* at Sayil would not much exceed a nuclear family of 4 persons (the completed size necessary to ensure replacement). The preliminary figure for the average number of rooms per structure at Sayil is 1.65 rooms/foundation brace (range 1–5) and 3.38 rooms/stone building (including here the 22-room South and 94-room Great palaces). Therefore, a multiplier of 4 persons/room will produce average family sizes per structure (= "house?") equivalent to 6.6 persons/foundation brace and 13.52 persons/stone building, remarkably similar to the range of historical averages cited above.

Two more conservative procedures for estimating the number of people from architectural plans are (1) assuming that only one family occupied each *structure* rather than each room and (2) assuming that only one family occupied each entire feature cluster (for only those feature clusters that contain dwelling-type structures). Neither alternative is applied here, although the necessary structure counts are provided in Table 12.2 to calculate alternative 1. Alternative 1 has the advantage of obviating the question whether rooms within particular buildings had different uses, but it probably underestimates the number of people in all the structures with above-average numbers of rooms. We have not finished the codification of feature-cluster types necessary to execute alternative 2 but would expect the resulting population estimate to be grossly low unless a larger (extended) family size was used in the equation.

Before estimating the number of people who need to be added for the 29.28% of the urban settlement area whose features have not yet been mapped, we will make one justifiable correction to the stone-building count. Because the nonmapped area is in the periphery and we know that the size of stone buildings usually decreases with distance from the site core, we shall exclude from the count the five multistory stone buildings, all located in the site core and containing 10 to 94 rooms each (149 total rooms). This exclusion lowers the average number of rooms per structure for the remaining 209 single-story stone buildings to 2.62 (= average of 10.48 persons/single-story stone building). Consequently, 209 × 2.62 × 4 × 0.41 = 898 is our estimate of the additional people living in unmapped stone buildings. These are the only basic figures that need to be changed for the calculation of the preliminary estimate of total community population (the population estimates that include this downward adjustment are marked with an asterisk in Table 12.2).

CONCLUSIONS

First, the population estimates listed in Table 12.2 for five types of potential dwellings and two site areas within Sayil are rather mechanical estimates whose sources and limitations have been presented above. These preliminary estimates make no allowance for the use of some structures (and rooms?) as something other than dwellings. In lieu of anything more concrete, one could take precedents from analyses of southern lowland sites and apply a 15% discount for nondwelling domestic structures (Haviland 1965; Tourtellot 1983) against the structure counts in Table 12.2 (see note 3). At present we suspect that nondwelling use is a more regular or serious consideration for the buildings of entirely perishable construction that may have been erected on the platforms, levelings, and chiches separately listed toward the bottom of the table. Also, no allowance has been made for disoccupancy rates, either temporary or permanent, or for rates of possible change in the function of the rooms or structures while in use. Realistically, these rates may also have covaried with the particular types and uses of the buildings, characteristics that should be more fully established once excavations are completed.

Second, as part of the excavation program, we will investigate all types of features at Sayil in an attempt to determine their uses and positively date and sequence them. Excavations across open areas will search for additional classes of structures, features, and activities and will relate them to the mapped features enumerated in Table 12.2. Data for a more sensitive estimation of population should be acquired through these excavations.

As part of this effort, Smyth (1988) has conducted an ethnoarchaeological investigation of Yucatec Maya households in order to study the spatial relations of activities carried on in house yards and the types of disposal practices and residues they engender. This work provides specific categories of data that may enable us positively to identify ancient dry storage locations and activities, as well as abandonments, among the structures and rooms counted here as dwellings and in other currently enigmatic features. It may also help us to find concrete grounds for a detailed reconciliation between the population estimate made here on the basis of room counts and the two estimates for Sayil obtained by McAnany (this volume) from a substantially independent analysis of the chultunes that are believed to have stored the supply of water essential to year-round survival at Sayil.

Third, the counts present rather startling data on the question of "palaces" as residences. Frequently considered elite residences, stone buildings at Sayil constitute 37% of the most likely dwelling structures (stone buildings and foundation braces with definable rooms), 55% of all definable rooms, and 53% of the estimated population in those rooms. Even deducting the 596 persons estimated for the 149 rooms in the multistory stone buildings, on the argument that those rooms were only for administration, the population in single-story stone buildings still constitutes more than 48% of the revised total population. Or perhaps only the people living in the multistory stone buildings ("real palaces?") should be considered the elite, their numbers (596) then representing only 8.3% of the total living in definable rooms (7159), or 5.5% if we use the maximum population of 10,858. Even this latter percentage is markedly higher than one would expect from other studies (e.g., R. E. W. Adams 1974; Tourtellot, this volume). Clearly, there is something odd going on; we hope the study of our collections from numerous refuse areas associated with a variety of structures will help clarify the purpose of Puuc "palaces."

Finally, various manipulations are possible with the data in Table 12.2, the first map-based structure counts and estimates ever made for a Puuc site. The maximum calculated population for Sayil is 10,858 (3147 persons/km²), far above the densities typical of southern lowland sites and higher than densities over 2000 that are calculable for other northern lowland sites such as Mayapan, Chunchucmil, or perhaps Dzibilchaltun (Kurjack and Garza T. 1981:304). The chiches are included in this high estimate: if they really were dwellings (recall that the border of the Sayil settlement as specified above does not coincide with their limit), the ones that may fan out beyond Sayil proper would add many more people to the community.

Alternatively, the estimate for foundation-brace and stone buildings could be taken as a minimum reasonable determination of Sayil population. This figure of 7159 persons converts to a density of 2075 persons/km², perhaps more in line with estimates for other northern sites but still double or triple the estimates for southern sites. These masonry-foundation braces and stone buildings are not the sorts of ruins that could easily be missed in the south, despite the heavier forest and soil covers there. Sayil really is more densely occupied than some other Maya sites, with observed densities of up to 3.5 feature clusters on basal platforms/ha, not counting chiches.

ACKNOWLEDGMENTS

We are most grateful to the National Science Foundation for supporting our work at Sayil under grant BNS-8302016. Throughout we have had the splendid cooperation of the personnel of the Instituto Nacional de Antropología e Historia in Mexico. We wish to single out the direct assistance we have received from Arqlgos, Tomás Gallareta Negrón, Carlos Pérez Alvarez, Sylviane Boucher, and Alfredo Barrera Rubio of the Centro Regional de Yucatán (INAH); the guidance of the guardian at Sayil, Don Miguel Uc and his family; and the dozen Maya assistants who struggled through the forest with us. George Andrews deserves praise for the skill and speed with which he conducted the valuable architectural survey. The following students and former students have made important contributions to the data and ideas we have on Sayil: Diana Christensen, Bernd Fahmel Beyer, Thomas R. Killion, Signa L. Larralde, Patricia A. McAnany, Stanley L. Walling, LuAnn Wandsnider, and L. Val Whitley. At the University of New Mexico we owe our gratitude to many individuals who have helped our work with their time and facilities, and to the Latin American Institute for all their assistance along the way.

NOTES

1. Results from excavations and intensive surface collection during 1987–88, not yet fully analyzed, have been used here only to avoid definitely erroneous statements.

2. Continued reconnaissance in 1987, by Nicholas P. Dunning, confirmed the projected southeastern border in Map 12.1 but added a narrow lobe of settlement along the valley margin in the southwest corner, extending beyond the Column Group. This lobe may add another 1 km^2 to the urban area of Sayil. Thus the population estimates made in Table 12.2 may have to be increased by an additional multiplier factor of 1.29 to account for a 22.5% increase in settlement area.

3. If we extrapolate from the recent excavation of a foundation brace at Sayil, a deduction of 0 to 25% could be taken from the Table 12.2 estimates to account for possible nondwelling uses for certain mapped rooms.

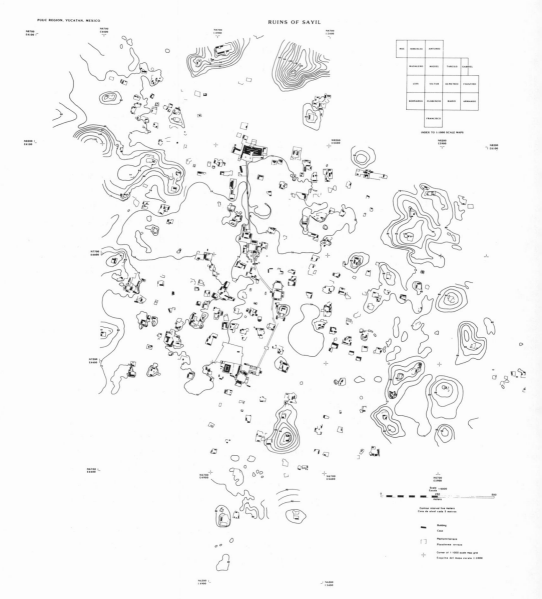

Map 12.1   The ruins of Sayil (courtesy Sayil Archaeological Project).

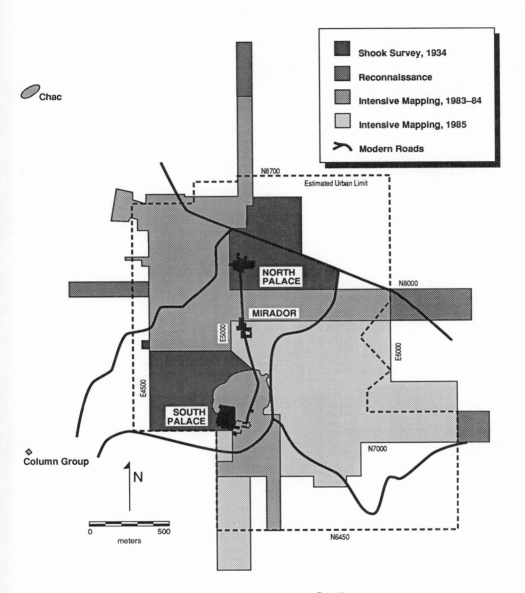

Map 12.2   Mapped and surveyed areas at Sayil.

Table 12.1   Style Dates for 71 Stone Buildings at Sayil

Classic Puuc Architectural Complex	A.D. 770–1050	67.6%
Style	Date	% of Structures
Puuc Mosaic Style	A.D. 840–1050	5.6
Puuc Mosaic or Colonnette		29.6
Puuc Colonnette Style	770–1050	32.4

Early Puuc Architectural Complex	A.D. 550–770	32.4%
Style	Date	% of Structures
Early Puuc Style	650–770	32.4
Protopuuc Style	600–650	0
Early Oxkintok Style	550–600	0

Source: G. Andrews 1985a

Table 12.2 Preliminary Population Estimate for Terminal Classic Sayil (3.45 km²)

Feature Type	No. of Structures	Rooms/ Structure (Average)	People/ Room	Population/ Type	Site Area Multiplier	Site Population/ Type	Cumulative Site Population
Foundation brace	362	1.65	4	2,389	1.41	3,368	3,368
Stone building	214	3.38	4	2,893	1.41	3,791[a]	7,159[a]
Bare platform < 51 m²	177	1.65?	4	1,168	1.41	1,647	8,806
Side levelings	7	1.00	4	28	1.41	39	8,845
Chich mound	357	1.00?	4	1,428	1.41	2,013	10,858

[a]See text for discount taken against multistory stone buildings.

13 /

Water Storage in the Puuc Region of the Northern Maya Lowlands: A Key to Population Estimates and Architectural Variability

Patricia A. McAnany

Questions regarding population size and room function are fundamental issues archaeologists would like to resolve. Difficulties arise partly because of substantive gaps in the archaeological record and partly because of a near absence of methodological linkages between data observations and both demographic estimates and the determination of room function. Increased archaeological survey throughout the Maya lowlands (reflected in this volume) is quickly closing the substantive gap. The methodological challenge remains.

In Mesoamerica, demographic estimates in both the highlands and the lowlands have been based traditionally on one of three methods: ceramic chronology, "mound" counts, or an assessment of agricultural potential; innovative examples of the first two techniques can be found in this volume. In this chapter, however, I employ a fourth technique based on water-storage potential. Here a quantitative assessment of prehistoric water-storage facilities provides the key to a derivation of population estimates and an examination of room function.

The importance of water availability to settlement location has been addressed by Haberland (1983). Few researchers, however, have documented the presence and significance of water-storage facilities in areas that lack suitable available water. Although a pronounced dry season is present in many portions of the Maya lowlands, it is in the Puuc Hills that conditions of rainfall, local hydrology, and geomorphology collectively result in an acute seasonal water deficit.

Despite the presence of rich agricultural soils in the Puuc Hills (Dunning 1988), this seasonal water deficit effectively dampened population growth until the Terminal Classic (ca. A.D. 800), when there was an explosive rate of population increase, particularly in the valley of Sayil. This growth is probably the result of population movements in response to both a deteriorating political and economic situation to the south and a climatic shift to wetter conditions in the northern Lowlands (Dahlin 1983; Folan et al. 1983).

This analysis of water-storage facilities and their association with architectural features is based primarily on settlement data from the Terminal Classic city of Sayil. In many respects the settlement map of Sayil (covering 2.44 km²; Tourtellot et al., this volume, Map 12.1) is unique for the Maya lowlands. Owing to the semiarid climate and proximity of the limestone bedrock to the surface, there has been little soil accumulation over the ancient architectural features of Sayil. It has been possible to map wall alignments, foundation braces, room entrances, platform retaining walls, and water-storage chambers without excavation (Tourtellot et al., this volume). Additionally, Sayil has a relatively short occupational span, probably 200 years or less. This temporal span, abbreviated for a Maya settlement, ameliorates (but does not negate) the problem of structure noncontemporaneity. In sum, Sayil research provides a wealth of settlement data that are both extensive and fine-grained and are ideal for the analysis of architectural variability.

WATER IN THE PUUC HILLS

In contrast to the wet, eastern side of the Yucatan Peninsula, the western portion has vegetation described as tropophytic and classified in the Dry Evergreen Formation Series (Wagner 1964:221–23). In fact, desertlike conditions exist in the Puuc Hills for six months of the year.

In the northern portion of the Yucatan Peninsula the flat, limestone plains are dotted with cenotes, or natural wells, many of which, prehistorically and today, are magnets for population aggregations (Garza T. and Kurjack 1980). Except for shallow basins (*sartenejas*) that sometimes hold water through the dry season, there is *no surface water* in the tropical cone-karst topography of the Puuc Hills. This region can be classified geomorphologically as an actively eroding Phase III karst system (Jakucs

1977:133). The water table is 40 to 90 m below the land surface (E. W. Andrews IV 1964:19)—precluding the construction of prehistoric wells. From Sayil the nearest source of water during the dry season requires a 3.6-km trip to the opening of a cave, the Gruta de Chac. The journey to water entails a 65-m vertical descent followed by a tortuous crawl through a narrow passageway (Andrews IV 1964:11; Stephens 1962b:19).

Total annual rainfall in the Puuc Hills is more than 1000 mm, roughly half the amount that falls on the central Peten. As in many parts of the Maya lowlands, the rainfall shows a pronounced seasonality. Precipitation data from a meteorological station 26 km northwest of Sayil are presented in the lower chart of Figure 13.1. These monthly rainfall tallies have been averaged over a nine-year period and thus encapsulate only a portion of the total variability in annual rainfall, which is estimated to be as high as 30% (Dunning, personal communication 1987). Eighty-seven percent of the mean annual precipitation occurs within six months—from May to October.

Furthermore, there is significant annual variation in the mean monthly rainfall. The tendency for dry-season rainfall to deviate widely from the average values is illustrated in the upper chart of Figure 13.1 using the coefficient of variation (CV). The coefficient of variation is a simple calculation of the standard deviation divided by the mean and multiplied by 100. The resulting statistic is a unitless measure of the dispersion of individual monthly rainfall amounts about the average rainfall value. Expressed in percentages, the CV can be compared among months, since the calculation controls for the higher mean of the wet months. There are no statistical guidelines for interpreting CV values; D. Thomas (1986:84) suggests that values greater than 10% indicate an underlying multimodal distribution or wide dispersion of individual values around the mean. As shown in Figure 13.1 months of high rainfall have low CVs and vice versa. From December to April the CV exceeds 100%, and it is only during the height of the wet season (June–October) that the CV falls below 50%. Thus, the mean monthly rainfall during the dry season represents not a predictable average, but rather a central tendency around which there is dramatic variation from year to year. In short, the problem confronting residents of the Puuc Hills was not only how to deal with predictably less rainfall during the dry season, but also how to buffer against periods of extremely low or nonexistent rainfall.

These environmental conditions not only posed a challenge to colonizing populations, but resulted in a solution that provides a key to the complexities of archaeological demography. Lacking the cenotes of the northern Yucatecan plains or the aguadas of the Peten, the populations colonizing the Puuc Hills constructed water-storage facilities (here referred to by the Mayan term *chultun* [plural, *chultunes*]) in order to "even out" the seasonal periodicity in rainfall.

In this chapter the demographic profile of Sayil will be examined by (1) establishing a quantitative relationship between water-storage facilities and human water requirements, (2) employing chultun frequency as a basis for population estimates, (3) identifying patterns of variability in structure types in relation to chultun frequency, and (4) comparing population estimates based on chultun support capacity with estimates derived from a count of habitable units with associated chultunes.

WATER STORAGE, SETTLEMENT GROWTH, AND SPACING

J. Eric Thompson described the chultunes of the Puuc region as "water-proofed ... underground chambers shaped rather like giant Chianti flasks" (1975:xv). Although bell-shaped subterranean pits are common throughout the Maya lowlands, particularly in the Peten (Ford 1986; D. Puleston 1965, 1968, 1973), the bell-shaped pits of northern Yucatan differ fundamentally with regard to location, features of construction, and function. The Peten chultunes are located adjacent to habitation platforms; in the northern region, however, platforms were constructed on top of the majority of chultun cavities. Furthermore, the northern-style chultunes were waterproofed with several thick coats of plaster, and their necks opened onto rainfall catchments constructed by contouring the platform surface. The opening for the chultun was generally punched through a hard limestone caprock, and the body of the "flask" was excavated into the softer, underlying sascab deposits.

These water cisterns are ubiquitous features at major cities and minor settlements throughout the Puuc zone—for example, Labna, Sayil, Kabah, Uxmal, and Oxkintok (Barrera R. 1982; Brainerd 1958; Gonzalez F. 1981; Pollock 1980; Stephens 1962a; E. Thompson 1897). Pollock (1980:561) has noted that "almost every paved area, from plaza, to courtyard, to simple dwelling platform, seems to have had one or more of these underground cisterns." They have also been recorded in the Chenes region to the southwest, at Santa Rosa Xtampak and Xcalumkin (DeBloois 1970), and as far northeast as Chichen Itza (Morley 1928).

The limestone caprock occurring in outcrops located on valley side slopes and peaks of the Puuc Hills is a fundamental prerequisite for the construction of these water cisterns. Monroe (1981:271) has studied the process of caprock formation in similar tropical cone-karst topography in Puerto Rico and suggests that the indurated layer results "from partial solution of the soft, powdery limestone ... followed by an almost immediate reprecipitation of crystalline calcium carbonate." In the Puerto Rican study the caprock layer varied in thickness from a few cm to 10, the latter occurring on the tops and sides of mogotes—remnant hills of the tropical cone karst referred to as *uitz* in Yucatecan Mayan.

The presence and thickness of this caprock layer may be the single most powerful determinant of the distribution and density of the settlement at Sayil. Where the bedrock is inaccessible (such as on the deeply alluviated valley floor), several meters thick (on the summits of the cone karsts), or highly fractured, there are few residential complexes. The majority of the settlement at Sayil is situated on the side slopes of the valley floor where rocky outcrops alternate with flatter surfaces suitable for agriculture (Dunning 1988).

Figure 13.2 is a schematic cross-section of a chultun-residential complex. As shown, chultunes generally open onto a plaza surface. Thus, chultun construction can be thought of as analogous to the construction of a basement or foundation under a house. Initially, bedrock outcrops without deep fractures would be selected as potential locations for future chultunes. In all likelihood, the caprock was punctured and the texture and permeability of the underlying sascab tested before construction of a residential unit commenced. Strength and impermeability are two critical specifications for a completed chultun: strength, because a contoured platform was constructed over the hollow chamber (Figure 13.2), and impermeability, naturally, because the cist must be capable of holding water.

At a promising location, a subconical underground chamber was then excavated. The interiors of these chambers often have smoothly undulating surfaces and are not perfectly symmetrical. Excavation of the sidewalls appears to have stopped when more resistant bedrock was encountered. The soft limestone sascab extracted from the pit was used for construction as mortar and plaster, possibly to line the chamber interior itself. (In recent times abandoned chultunes adjacent to restored architecture at Sayil have been used invariably as quarries for mortar material.) After the cist was completed, the neck was lined with a circular wall of stones behind which a layer of platform fill was deposited and contoured so as to slope toward the opening.

Chultun construction involved several stages of structural engineering. Excavation of a chultun through an existing basal platform, with no prior evaluation of caprock strength and sascab impermeability, would have posed a unique, if not insurmountable, construction challenge. This fact has interesting demographic implications. Since these facilities supplied water for a finite number of people, a doubling or tripling of the size of a residential unit had to be accommodated either by construction of additional ancillary chultun platforms or by fissioning of the family unit and construction of new chultun-platform complexes wherever suitable outcrops occurred. Thus, the physical determinant of chultun construction (location of suitable caprock) was a significant factor influencing the growth and spacing of residential units. On a more general level, the residential location of the water cisterns is important because it represents storage of a critical resource at the level of the family rather than of the community.

Chultun Capacity

Although none of the chultunes from Sayil has been excavated, E. Thompson (1897) excavated 30 of these facilities in the central area of Labna (about 6 km east of Sayil). Published plans and profiles from this research were used to calculate chultun capacity. Diameter was found to be remarkably constant, hovering about a mean of 4.6 m (standard deviation = 0.47 m). There was, however, tremendous variability in chultun height, the average height being 3 m with a standard deviation of 0.90 m. The constancy of the measured diameters indicates that the horizontal extent of excavation was minimized, possibly to avoid collapse of the overlying platforms and structures. If we use the equation for calculating the volume of a cone

$$v = [(\tfrac{2}{3}\pi r^2 h]$$

the resultant chultun capacities, in liters, are found to be highly variable, with a continuous distribution ranging from 7000 to 75,000 l. The multimodal nature of this distribution is illustrated in Figure 13.3. One extremely large chultun reaches a capacity of 94,725 l. Excluding this outlier, mean capacity at Labna is 35,860 l, which coincides with the central mode of the essentially trimodal distribution of chultun capacity (Figure 13.3). Using an identical method for calculating volume, Brainerd (1958:30) computed an average capacity of only 28,387 l for the same Labna chultunes. Evidently, he deleted more than one larger-than-average chultun from his calculated average and in doing so lowered the average capacity estimate. The capacity of the underground cists, however, reflects only the passive potential for storage. The size of the water catchment area is the variable that actually determines the amount of rainwater funneled into the cisterns.

A catchment surface, sloping toward the opening of a chultun, is schematically illustrated in Figure 13.2 An archaeological example of a platform with two well-preserved catchment rings is shown in the plan view of Figure 13.4. The four *chultunes* in this residential complex are indicated with solid black circles and the arc of stones defining the catchment basin with a single dashed line. Not surprisingly, measurement of thirteen prehistoric catchment areas identified at Sayil indicates a rather uniform catchment area with a mean of 44.2 m² and a standard deviation of 9.1 m².

DEMOGRAPHIC IMPLICATIONS OF A SEASONAL WATER DEFICIT

Using the average catchment area of 44.2 m², we can estimate the average amount of rainwater a chultun could collect by means of the following equation:

$$w = \sum_{i=1}^{12} m_i[(44.2)0.75]$$

where w is the sum of the net rainfall capture possible during a year, m is the sum of average monthly rainfall (converted from mm to m^3), 44.2 is the average catchment area, and 0.75 is a 25% reduction factor. Admittedly, the magnitude of this reduction factor is chosen arbitrarily in order to provide some allowance for evaporation, transpiration, and other factors that reduce the net amount of water captured in the catchment basins. Calculation of this expression yields a figure of 35,858 l of water, only 2 l shy of average chultun capacity for Labna. If monthly water consumption is taken into account, however, it becomes clear that most cisterns were probably never filled to capacity, perhaps an intentional part of chultun engineering. An overflowing cistern in the middle of a residential platform would pose a health, not to mention a traffic, problem rivaling that of dehydration.

Water-storage capacity can be converted into numbers of parched throats by using the generally accepted, minimal human water-consumption figure of 2.4 l/day (*World Book Encyclopedia*). For comparative purposes a more generous, and perhaps more realistic, consumption estimate of twice the minimal, or 4.8 l/person/day, will also be employed, to allow for the use of water for purposes other than human consumption, that is, for washing, ceramic production, pot irrigation, or construction activities such as mixing lime plaster and mortar. An arbitrary number of 30 individuals/chultun was chosen in order to calculate a running average of chultun level through the dry season. Rates of water depletion would be applicable for 30 people/chultun at minimal water consumption, or for 15 people/chultun at maximum water consumption.

The monthly cycle of water usage by household members and refill through average monthly rainfall can be expressed by the following equation:

$$r = [a(0.90) + (m - 2160)]$$

where m represents the net monthly water capture, 2160 is the constant monthly water demand (30 days $\times$ 2.4 l/day $\times$ 30 people = 2160 l, or 30 days $\times$ 4.8 l/day $\times$ 15 people = 2160 l), and a equals the amount of water remaining from the previous month. A 10% reduction factor (0.90) has been applied to the net water storage from the previous month. Although Pollock (1980:561) states that a properly maintained chultun should have no leakage or evaporation, there is simply no way to evaluate what percentage of these cisterns were well maintained at any one point in time. In an effort to deal with this ambiguity I will assume that all cisterns had a modest rate of leakage and lost 10% of their stored water during any given month. The value of r equals the remaining, or net surplus, water storage at the end of the month.

To arrive at a conservative estimate of chultun support capacity one can model a worst-case scenario. Consider the following situation: it is the middle of the wet season (August) and, owing to an unseasonably late onset of the rainy season or an inopportune chultun replastering episode, the cistern is empty. The calculations for a monthly sequence of filling through rainfall capture and depletion through consumption from August to April are shown in Table 13.1. During the month of August the chultun captures 5304 l of water (m), 2160 l are consumed, and there is a net water balance of 3144 l (r). During each month of the remaining wet season the net balance grows until the dry season arrives and the net amount of stored water begins to shrink. By the end of the dry season (end of April) the chultun is dry (Table 13.1).

If a more optimistic scenario is modeled with the chultun dry at the *beginning* rather than the *middle* of the wet season, the calculations are similar but 1207 l of water would remain at the end of April. This amount is less than what 30 people, at minimum intake, would need for a single month and would be consumed quickly if the onset of the wet season were delayed by only one month (not an uncommon situation in the Puuc Hills). To further exacerbate this precarious situation, a dry season of less than average rainfall would additionally decrease water reserves. In short, in the Puuc Hills the real challenge was to make it through the dry season without exhausting all water reserves.

The demographic implication of this deterministic relationship between chultun support capacity and the population of Sayil is that the number of cisterns should be related directly to the size of the dry-season population. To date, approximately 70.7% (2.44 km²) of the total settlement area around Sayil has been mapped (Tourtellot et al., this volume). Within the mapped area, 256 on-platform chultunes and 51 off-platform chultunes have been recorded. This count is conservative, since there are undoubtedly chultun openings that have been sealed or otherwise rendered invisible to surface survey. Because only the on-platform cisterns have the plastered interiors and catchment areas that ensure that they were water-storage facilities, they alone are used in population estimates. At this point, population estimates based purely on chultun support capacity can be derived. The low (15) and high (30) estimates of persons/*chultun* multiplied by the number of recorded cisterns (256) yields a population range of 3840 to 7680. Assuming the same density of cisterns in the unmapped portion of Sayil (29.3%), we arrive at a population range for the entire site of 5431 to 10,863. The average of this range (8147) is probably the most realistic estimate; 30 people/*chultun* would yield a total population of 120 people for the residential complex (only 900 m²) which is illustrated in Figure 13.4.

These population estimates are based on three fundamental assumptions. The first—which is untestable—is that nearly all the cisterns have been recorded. The second, that all segments of the population were supplied with water from chultunes, and the third, that chultunes were always built in residential compounds, are examined in further detail below.

CHULTUNES AND ARCHITECTURAL VARIABILITY

With an understanding of the relationship between chultun capacity and human water requirements, the variability in Sayil architectural units vis-à-vis chultun frequency can now be examined. The residential unit, or feature cluster, of Figure 13.4 consists of structures and features built atop a basal platform ($N = 281$). The structures with interior room divisions are foundation braces (an outline of single-coursed stones over which a perishable structure was constructed). Stone buildings, usually with core-veneer masonry and corbelled vaults or perishable roofs, are the only other type of structure with internal room divisions. Room size in stone buildings is larger, on the average ($\bar{x} = 16m^2$, $N = 214$), than the room size of foundation braces ($\bar{x} = 12m^2$; $N = 362$). The particular platform complex of Figure 13.4 contains two smaller platforms. Somewhat enigmatic in function, such small platforms are common features at Sayil ($N = 663$). In the analysis below, the character and frequency of each of four feature types (foundation braces, stone buildings, small platforms, and basal platforms) are examined in relation to chultun frequency.

Chultunes and Roomed Structures

The sample of foundation braces and stone buildings was tabulated separately by feature cluster according to the frequency of on-platform cisterns within each feature cluster. This grouping created eight classes, with 0–7 chultunes per feature cluster, respectively. The average number of rooms per feature cluster within each of the eight classes was calculated (Table 13.2). Additionally, quartile values at the 25th and 75th quartiles indicate the extent to which the frequency distribution is tightly clustered or highly dispersed around the mean value or is even multimodal (Table 13.2).

FOUNDATION BRACES
As indicated in Table 13.2, feature clusters with foundation braces that lack chultunes altogether have the lowest average number of rooms ($\bar{x} = 2.3$). This fact, together with the small basal platform size of feature clusters in this class (discussed in further detail below) suggests that these feature clusters may be ancillary and not representative of focal residential units. An analysis of the spatial distribution of this class will be necessary in

order to identify whether it tends to occur (a) adjacent to larger basal platforms with multiple chultunes—suggesting growth of the residential unit without complete fissioning—or (b) in more isolated contexts indicating a seasonal or task-specific occupation.

There is a steady incremental growth in the number of rooms per feature cluster for foundation braces associated with 0, 1, and 2 chultunes. The average number of rooms increases from 2.3 to 2.9 to 4.8, respectively. Within each chultun class the closeness of the 25th and 75th quartile values indicates a narrow range of values, or a unimodal frequency distribution. Selected histograms of room frequencies associated with 1 and 2 chultunes are presented in Figure 13.5. Clearly, both distributions are skewed to the right; the mode, however, shifts from 2 rooms/1 chultun (A) to 4 rooms/2 chultunes (B). Based on this correlative increase, 2–3 rooms/chultun can be thought of as a prime domestic ratio of rooms to chultunes at Sayil. That is, on the average there will be 1 water storage facility for every 2 to 3 foundation-brace rooms, and the number of rooms can be expected to double in proportion to the increase in chultunes. This pattern is consistent with the imputed function of foundation braces as residential units and the implied direct relationship between size of the residential unit and water-storage capacity.

When chultun frequency per feature cluster exceeds 2, however, the data do not indicate proportional increases in number of rooms. In fact, foundation braces with 3 or more chultunes exhibit basically the same frequency distribution as those foundation braces with one or two chultunes. Moreover, there is a slight decline in the average number of rooms, although it should be noted that the smaller sample size of these classes contributes to a "flat" frequency distribution. Despite the small sample size, this pattern suggests an upper threshold for the size of the domestic unit and warrants further investigation. This threshold would be based on a doubling, but not a tripling or quadrupling, of the prime domestic ratio of foundation-brace rooms per chultun. In short, few domestic units grew beyond 4–6 rooms and 2 chultunes. Units with more favorable ratios of chultunes per room number may be sharing stored water with nearby "chultunless" residential units or otherwise engaged in an activity with high water demands, such as pot irrigation.

STONE BUILDING

An examination of the number of rooms in stone buildings per feature cluster (also classified by chultun frequency [Table 13.2]) reveals a different pattern from that of foundation braces. First of all, stone buildings with no associated chultunes have, on the average, one more room per feature cluster than foundation braces in the same chultun frequency class. Second, unlike foundation braces, there is no proportional increase in number of rooms between stone buildings with 1 and 2 chultunes. In fact, the mean and the 75th quartile values are nearly identical in chultun classes 1 and 2. Histograms of these two classes (Figure 13.6) highlight this contrast. Two rooms per one chultun is the dominant pattern of Figure 13.6A almost to the exclusion of all other room-number classes. This peak in the frequency distribution is simply depressed in Figure 13.6B—suggesting that the 2:1 ratio of rooms with core-veneer masonry to chultunes is a constant rather than a multiplicand (as was the 2:1 ratio of foundation-brace rooms to chultunes). Third, the frequency distribution of the small sample of stone building rooms associated with 3 or more chultunes appears to exhibit a multimodal distribution; that is, there are feature clusters with 2–5 rooms and others with more than 13 rooms (Table 13.2).

The fact that stone buildings and chultunes do not have the same linear relationship that is displayed by the foundation-brace rooms can be illustrated using Spearman's rank-order correlation coefficient. A correlation coefficient (r) is a measure of the linear relationship between two variables. If one variable is a perfect linear function of another, the correlation coefficient will be 1.0 or -1.0. A value of 0 indicates that there is no bivariate linear relationship. Foundation braces and chultunes, though not highly correlated, yield an r value of 0.54 (probability value < 0.01); the r value for stone buildings and chultunes is even lower ($r = 0.47$, probability value < 0.01). The lower correlation coefficient and the nonproportional increase in stone building rooms with increased chultun frequency cast doubt on the functional assignation of all stone buildings as the nexus of domestic units. Though this analysis does not prove that stone buildings were strictly nonresidential, it does demonstrate a more complex and somewhat erratic patterning between chultunes and stone buildings and the absence of anything resembling the prime domestic ratio that exists between foundation braces and chultunes.

Chultunes and Small Platforms

In certain "neighborhoods" of Sayil, particularly on the periphery of the settlement, there is a high density of small, somewhat amorphous platforms. These structures may have served as foundations for perishable structures lacking internal room divisions, as open-air work surfaces, or for some other agricultural or task-oriented function. Most of the platforms are built at ground level and have no associated features, particularly chultunes. There are two categories of platforms. The first, termed *Bak Chich,* is built of exceptionally small stones, is amorphous in outline, and tends to cover less than 25 m². The location and stratigraphy of these features is described by Tourtellot et al. (this volume). The other category includes bordered platforms that are very regular in outline, have clearly defined retaining walls, and are constructed either at ground level or atop basal platforms.

The most striking characteristic of the relationship between small platforms and chultun frequency is its static nature (Table 13.3). More than 75% of the platforms lacking associated chultunes are single platforms; this class numerically outweighs all other classes. With 1 or more associated chultunes there is little change in the average number of platforms per feature cluster. The value at the 75th quartile also remains relatively constant. Platforms associated with 3 chultunes deviate from this pattern. Closer inspection of this class revealed a frequency distribution that is skewed by the presence of a single outlier with eight platforms. Spearman's rank-order correlation coefficient (calculated separately for the Bak Chich and the well-defined platforms) indicates a weak inverse correlation ($r = -0.33$, probability value < 0.01) between Bak Chich and chultunes and a weak positive correlation ($r = 0.36$, probability value < 0.01) between other platforms and chultunes.

In summary, Table 13.3 and Spearman's rank-order correlation coefficient indicate that the frequency of chultunes is not positively associated with platform frequency. That is, as the number of chultunes increases, the number of platforms remains constant or decreases. The severity of the seasonal water deficit at Sayil strongly argues against the identification of single platforms lacking associated chultunes as a class of domestic structures with year-round occupation. Given the locational pattern of these features, seasonal occupation or task-specific use are possible options. The bordered platforms that *are* associated with chultunes tend to occur with other feature types, such as foundation braces and stone buildings. This co-occurrence suggests that these platforms are components of feature clusters but that their presence and frequency may not determine the population size of the residential unit. Specifically, feature clusters are likely to have one or two bordered platforms regardless of the overall number of foundation braces or stone buildings in the cluster. The bordered platforms may have been used in a functionally specific manner, perhaps as kitchens or grain-storage areas.

Chultunes and Basal Platforms

As mentioned above, many residential units at Sayil were constructed over bedrock outcrops that were judged suitable for water containment. During and after chultun construction, the undulating surface of the limestone caprock was leveled to create the basal platform (Figure 13.2). Part of this surface was used for rainfall catchment; other portions supported superstructures. In a general sense basal platform area is a good predictor of chultun frequency (Table 13.4). As basal platform area increases, so does the frequency of chultunes. The tandem increase of the platform area value at the 75th quartile of Table 13.4 indicates a stepwise increase in platform area in relation to chultun frequency. With each additional chultun there is nearly a doubling of basal platform area.

There are basal platforms of all sizes, however, that lack associated chultunes, and this pattern may have a locational explanation. That is, if these platforms are contiguous to feature clusters with a high frequency of chultunes, then they may be satellite residences or a subset of an extended family unit. Furthermore, basal platforms contiguous to the sacbe invariably lack associated chultunes, and this absence is undoubtedly a function of their nonresidential character (Sabloff et al. 1984).

The proportional increase in basal platform area relative to chultun frequency follows a pattern similar to the increase in the number of foundation-brace rooms relative to chultun frequency. This correlation indicates that basal platform size, like room number, is conditioned by domestic considerations and water-storage needs.

POPULATION ESTIMATES: CHULTUN FREQUENCY VERSUS HABITABLE UNITS

In this section population estimates derived from chultun frequency are contrasted with estimates based on the average number of habitable units per feature cluster. Once again, the platforms are classified by chultun frequency. Based on the above analyses, structure classes with no associated chultunes are eliminated from the population estimates and all structures associated with chultunes are included.

Feature clusters were analyzed in terms of habitable units—the sum total of room and small-platform counts per feature cluster (generally those structures built atop basal platforms) (Table 13.5). The two large structural complexes, known as the North and South palaces, were excluded from the analysis. Because estimates of the number of individuals per habitable unit vary widely (Ringle and Andrews, this volume), and as Tourtellot et al. (this volume) point out, room size at Sayil averages only 8 m² for foundation braces and 12 m² for stone buildings, I prefer a low figure of 4 individuals/habitable unit. This figure is doubled for a "high-end" estimate. The minimum and maximum estimates derived for chultun support capacity (at 15 and 30 individuals) are also included in the table. Results for the 70.7% of the site mapped can be extrapolated to the unmapped area to give total site estimates, conservatively, of 4750 to 5431 and, liberally, of 9485 to 10,863. Although the population estimate based on habitable units is slightly lower, there is a striking concordance between the two methods.

An arithmetic average of these four estimates (7632) divided by total settlement area (3.45 km²) yields a population density of 2212 people/km², a high density even by northern Maya lowlands standards (Culbert 1988). Owing to the extremely patchy distribution of arable land in the northern lowlands, however, future survey of intersite areas will probably bear out Culbert's (1988) prediction that, in contrast to the south, there was more overall population clustering in the north and a lower density of residential units between large centers.

This approach to the prehistoric demographic profile of Sayil can be compared to that taken by Tourtellot et al. (this volume). Basing their projection of the population of Sayil on the average number of rooms per structure (regardless of chultun presence) and using an estimate of 4 individuals/room, they arrive at an estimated population of 9990. This estimate falls between my more liberal estimates, which are based on 30 people/chultun (10,863) and 8 people/habitable unit (9485) *after* structure lacking associated chultunes were excluded. If nonchultun-associated structures were also residential, then their exclusion from my "habitable units" calculation has the effect of depressing the population estimates. These structures may have been residential but were not equipped with water cisterns because (a) they were occupied only during the wet season, (b) they were occupied by individuals who were not able to make such a capital investment, or (c) they represent a stage in a residential and or family developmental cycle.

SUMMARY AND CONCLUSIONS

Within complex societies variability in structure use results, in large part, from the proliferation of social roles and the construction of places at which these roles are enacted. In the archaeological record this translates into structures that deviate in some way from residential structures. The quest to identify nonresidential structures and to address their functional implications is a long-standing one in the Maya lowlands (see Harrison 1970 for a historical review).

In this study four types of structures (foundation braces, stone buildings, platforms, and basal platforms) have been analyzed; although these structure types may co-occur in feature clusters, each type relates independently to chultun presence and frequency. For instance, at low chultun frequencies foundation braces display a tendency for room number to increase proportionally to chultun frequency. This relationship has been termed a prime domestic ratio. Stone buildings, on the other hand, do not display a proportional increase at lower chultun frequencies and exhibit a tendency toward multimodality in the number of rooms per chultun at higher chultun frequencies. This contrastive pattern suggests a complex, multifunctional nature for stone structures. Small platforms usually lack associated chultunes, and when they have chultunes, platform frequency is not correlated with chultun frequency. Instead, there is often one platform per feature cluster, suggesting that these structures were used in a manner that did not fluctuate with family size—as, for example, for storage or kitchens. The high frequency of small, single platforms lacking chultunes suggests seasonal habitations or functionally specific structures. Finally, there is a positive relationship between basal platform area and chultun frequency, once again indicating the important role that cisterns played in the finished size of the residential unit.

In a larger sense, Sayil is but one of a host of comparable Terminal Classic cities located in the Puuc Hills, all of which probably had populations ranging between 6000 and 12,000. Conceivably, these late but relatively dense settlements (approximately 2000/km² at Sayil) were augmented by populations that radiated out of the Classic Period core areas to settle one of the last underpopulated areas of the Maya lowlands. The advantage of the Puuc Region was the fertile soils; the disadvantage was the lack of available water. Contrary to the epithet commonly used in reference to the Maya, there is nothing mysterious about the process of population radiation. It is common among agriculturalists living under conditions of population packing, for which there is increasing evidence in the central Peten (Culbert 1988; Turner, this volume). The adaptation of the Maya to the Puuc was, however, remarkable from the standpoint of hydraulic engineering. The customization of underground pits for the purpose of water storage allowed dense settlement to cover one of the last Maya "frontiers," the land of the uitz.

ACKNOWLEDGMENTS

Research at Sayil has been supported by the National Science Foundation (grant BNS-8302016). I gratefully acknowledge the enthusiasm and support received from the project directors, Jeremy A. Sabloff and Gair Tourtellot. The following individuals read drafts of this chapter, offered helpful criticisms, and were kind enough to point out imponderable sections, which I hope I rendered more ponderable in the rewrite: Anthony P. Andrews, E. Wyllys Andrews, Philip J. Arnold III, George L. Cowgill, T. Patrick Culbert, Thomas W. Killion, Bernd Fahmel Beyer, Don S. Rice, Robert S. Santley, Gordon R. Willey, and an anonymous reviewer.

Table 13.1 Net Water-Storage Capacity of Chultunes Through the
Dry-Season (In Liters)

Month	Initial Volume (a)	10% Reduction (0.90)	Average Monthly Capture (m)	Remaining after Monthly Consumption (−2,160)	Net Storage (r)
Aug.	0	0	5,304	3,144	3,144
Sept.	3,144	2,830	7,259	5,099	7,929
Oct.	7,929	7,136	5,118	2,958	10,094
Nov.	10,094	9,085	1,345	−815	8,270
Dec.	8,270	7,443	871	−1,289	6,154
Jan.	6,154	5,539	534	−1,626	3,913
Feb.	3,913	3,522	610	−1,550	1,972
Mar.	1,972	1,775	563	−1,597	178
Apr.	178	160	616	−1,554	—

Table 13.2 Room Numbers and
Chultun Frequency

Chultunes/ Feature Cluster	No. of Feature Clusters	Rooms/Feature Cluster		
		Average x̄	Quartiles 25th	75th
		Foundation Braces		
0	63	2.3	1	3
1	55	2.9	2	4
2	19	4.8	2	7
3	9	3.9	1.5	6
4	4	4	2.25	5.75
5	3	2.6	1	4
6	2	6	4	8
7	1	9	−	−
		Stone Buildings		
0	35	3.2	2	4
1	41	4.2	2	3.5
2	11	4.2	2	5
3	5	3.6	2	5.5
4	4	14.2	3.75	23
5	2	9.5	2	17
6	2	9.5	5	14
7	1	9	−	−

Table 13.3 Platform Numbers and Chultun Frequency

Chultunes/ Feature Cluster	No. of Feature Clusters	Platforms/Feature Cluster: Average x̄	Quartiles 25th	Quartiles 75th
0	568	1.1	1	1
1	44	1.7	1	2
2	18	1.8	1	2
3	7	3.7	3	4
4	4	2	1	3
5	2	1	–	–

(Platforms)

Table 13.4 Basal Platform Area and Chultun Frequency

Chultunes/ Basal Platform	No. of Basal Platforms	Basal Platform Area: Average (m²)	Basal Platform Area: 75th Quartile
0	126	232	318
1	103	379	544
2	31	679	959
3	10	1,063	1,833
4	5	3,005	6,418
5	3	1,767	—
6	2	3,388	—
7	1	2,762	—

Table 13.5 Population Estimates Based on Chultun Support Capacity and Habitable Units

No. of Feature Clusters	Chultunes/ Feature Clusters	Chultun Support Capacity × Feature Clusters: Min. (15)	Max. (30)	Habitable Units/ Feature Cluster: Average	SD	Individual/Unit: Min. (4)	Max. (8)
110	1	1,650	3,300	3.7	4.1	1,628	3,256
31	2	930	1,860	5.5	4.3	682	1,364
10	3	450	900	7.9	3.1	316	632
5	4	300	600	20.2	10.1	404	808
3	5	225	450	9.6	8.3	115	230
2	6	180	360	15.5	9.2	124	248
1	7	105	210	21.0	–	84	168
Total		3,840	7,680			3,353	6,706
Extrapolated to 29.3% unsurveyed section		1,591	3,183			1,397	2,779
Total		5,431	10,863			4,750	9,485

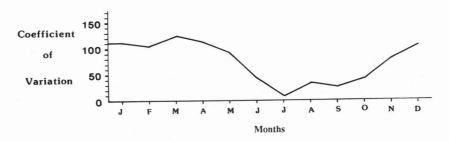

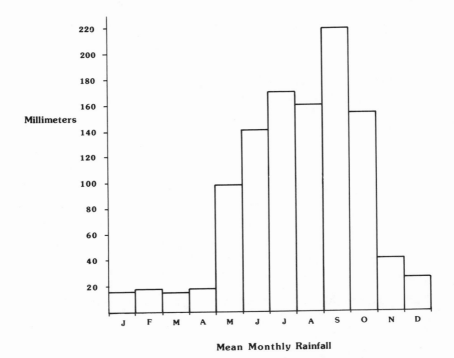

Figure 13.1   Histogram and chart of coefficient of variation for
average monthly rainfall data based on nine years of
complete records from C.I.A.P.Y. (Uxmal). Source:
División Hidrométrica, Secretária de Agricultura y
Recursos Hildraúlicos, Mérida, Yucatán, México.

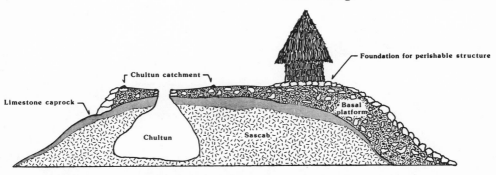

Figure 13.2 Schematic cross-section of Sayil feature cluster with chultun.

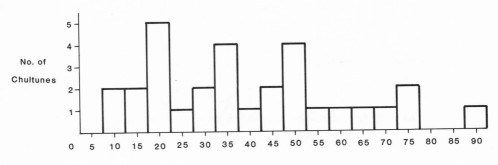

Figure 13.3 Chultun capacities based on excavated samples from Labna (E. Thompson 1897).

281

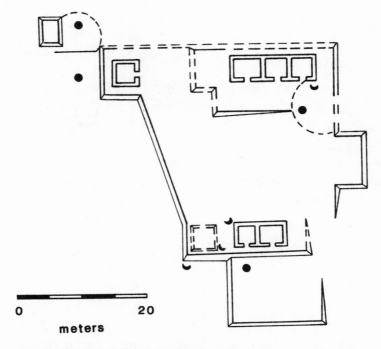

Figure 13.4 Sayil feature cluster with well-preserved chultun catchment rings.

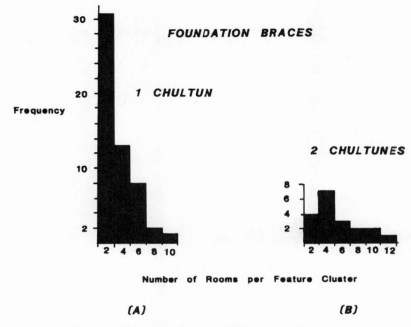

Figure 13.5   Foundation-brace rooms per feature cluster and in association with (A) one and (B) two chultunes.

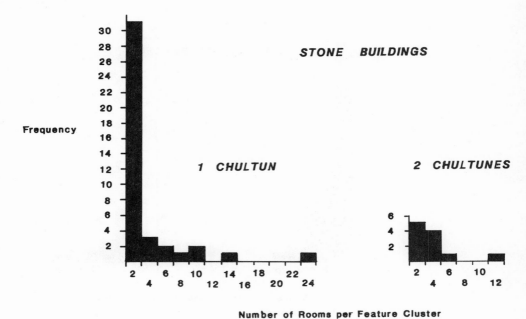

Figure 13.6   Stone building rooms per feature cluster and in
association with (A) one and (B) two chultunes.

14 /

Disjunctive Growth in the Maya Lowlands

ROBERT E. FRY

Only since the 1970s have we begun to get an understanding of the structure of regional demographic patterns in the southern and central Maya lowlands. Most settlement studies in the Maya lowlands have concentrated on sites rather than regions. The largest surveyed areas, centered on Tikal (Coe 1967; Haviland et al. 1968) or Edzna (Matheny et al. 1983), are affected by the historical developments at these major centers. At present there are no completed programs of regional analysis on the central or southern lowlands comparable to the Copan Project in the southeast periphery (Webster and Freter, this volume), the Kaminaljuyu Project in the Guatemalan highlands (Michels 1979), or the regional settlement programs in the Valleys of Mexico (Sanders et al. 1979) or Oaxaca (Blanton et al. 1982; Kowaleski et al. 1989). Nevertheless, information from a number of settlement pattern programs can be assembled to provide an approximation of a regional analysis. These programs provide data on differing levels of settlement hierarchy and economic specialization. I will also examine some of the problems affecting the comparability of settlement data from differing archaeological programs.

The goal of this chapter is to see if rates of population change correlate with agricultural intensification and political centralization. Demographic profiles from four separate zones with differing positions in the southern and central lowlands will be compared. The four areas chosen for comparison include central and peripheral Tikal, Guatemala; Becan, Campeche; the Pulltrouser Swamp zone, Belize; and Barton Ramie, Belize. The sites form a hierarchy of degrees of centralization, with Tikal a primar center, Becan a smaller primary center, and Pulltrouser Swamp and Barton Ramie at the lower end of the settlement hierarchy. Two of the four regions, Pulltrouser Swamp (B. Turner and Harrison 1983) and Becan (B. Turner 1974, 1983a), show definite evidence of large-scale agricultural intensification. Pulltrouser Swamp has the best-documented raised-field system in the lowlands, and Becan has an elaborate system of terraces. Although there has been speculation about the presence of intensification in the bajos surrounding Tikal (Harrison 1978; Dahlin et al. 1980), the presence of large-scale systems comparable to those documented for Campeche and Quintana Roo (B. Turner 1974; Harrison 1978) has not yet been documented. The same is true of the Belize River Valley settlements near Barton Ramie. Thus the four sites provide a comparison of the effects of centrality and intensification on population.

The zones differ in degree of economic specialization as well. The systems of agricultural intensification at Becan and the Pulltrouser zone could have produced agricultural items for exchange. The Pulltrouser data indicate possible production of maize and cotton (B. Turner and Harrison 1983). Although there is speculation that the raised fields of northern Belize could have been used to produce cacao (Hammond 1974b; Dahlin 1979), neither palynological or artifactual data support such a conclusion (B. Turner and Harrison 1983). Some degree of stockpiling of chert nodules and production of chert tools is evident at Becan (Stoltman 1978; P. Thomas 1981) and in certain parts of the Tikal peripheral areas (Fry 1969). Tikal may also have produced various finished products, including wooden items (O. Puleston 1969; Fry 1969). No evidence for any major occupational specialization in craft production has been demonstrated for Pulltrouser or Barton Ramie.

DEMOGRAPHIC AND DEVELOPMENTAL PROFILES

Methodology

In this section I summarize the methods used in constructing the demographic profiles used in this analysis. I have calculated figures for maximum structure occupancy using principles similar to those outlined by Culbert et al. (this volume). All figures are based on counts per phase of mounded structures assumed to be residences. Since I was directly involved in the research design and collection of data from peripheral Tikal and Pulltrouser Swamp, the data from these programs are probably more reliable than my recalculation of figures from Becan (P. Thomas 1981) and

Barton Ramie (Willey et al. 1965). Sampling of areas between mounds at Tikal by Bronson (1968) indicated that earlier phases were underrepresented. A program of rapid shovel testing and small test excavations in unmounded areas at Pulltrouser showed that there are similar biases in that zone (McQuarrie 1982). However, for the sake of comparability this nonmounded occupation is not included in calculations.

All of the programs except those from central Tikal and Barton Ramie used some variation of stratified random sampling in choosing units. However, the fact that the central Tikal program came up with results remarkably similar to those of the random sampling program in peripheral Tikal gives us confidence in the central Tikal figures. The Barton Ramie program excavated almost 25% of the 262 structures mapped, and the overall dispersal of units chosen superficially resembles a random distribution.

Excavations were made in approximately 33% of the mound groups in peripheral Tikal. A total of 719 structures clustered into 283 groups was mapped in the north and south survey strips. Thus we sampled about 13% of the structures. At Becan 35 of the 665 structures were sampled using a stratified random sampling research design involving four major classes of residential structures. This sample of slightly over 5% was supplemented by dating of surface collections from another 364 structures. The two sets of figures are quite similar. In my calculations I have used only the evidence from excavated structures to make the data more comparable. Finally, at Pulltrouser Swamp a total of 253 structures was mapped in four separate settlement zones. These exclude the mapped structures from the site of Kokeal, which was excavated using a nonrandom sampling research design. The 253 structures include mounds that appear to be too small to be residences as well as obvious public architecture, so only the 173 probable residential structures were included in the sampling procedure. A total of 35 structures (about 20%) was chosen using a stratified random sampling research design.

In the studies on which the present research is based, several differing excavation methods were used to ascertain the occupational sequence, though none involved extensive excavation. In peripheral Tikal, posthole sampling was used to locate midden deposits associated with structures (Fry 1972). No excavation into structure fills was attempted unless the midden was superimposed on earlier construction. Because of the dense, undisturbed forest cover, surface collection was possible in only a few cases. Puleston pointed out that sampling was not random within a group, and this may be a biasing factor (D. Puleston 1973). The densest middens were often associated with the largest structure of the group, which in many cases was the oldest structure. This would skew the sample toward the structures with the longest occupation and thus would tend to lead toward overestimation of early population. The problem is greatest in large groups with complex occupational histories. Other work at Tikal (Haviland 1985; Culbert et al., this volume) indicates that the earliest structures in the group continued to be occupied as other residences and structures were added. This allows us to be confident that such midden sampling units are likely to represent the maximum occupation of a group.

A major question about the midden sampling procedure is its adequacy in reconstructing the total occupation of a group or structure. Critics note that the use of midden deposits as a source of fill would tend to remove evidence of earlier occupation. As Culbert et al. (this volume) point out, although cross-lot fits between middens and fills confirm that such practices existed, in most cases some of the original midden was left behind. This pattern has been assumed in the present study, and the presence of a small number of examples of an earlier ceramic complex at the bottom of a midden has been used to indicate an occupation for that time span. This problem would be most serious in larger structures with repeated occupation. However, in many cases it was possible to locate the midden pits on top of the substructure platforms and thus sample both occupation and earlier fill debris at the same time.

The problems of continuity of occupation and finding its traces may also be less problematic at the margins of major sites. Testing and more extensive excavation at structures in peripheral Tikal showed that the practice of using occupation debris in fills was not common. Possibly because of distance among structures or a slower rate of addition to mounded construction, fills in the Tikal peripheral zone were relatively free of significant quantities of occupation debris. Indeed, this paucity of datable material in fill samples discovered during the early stages of the peripheral area excavation program was the prime driving force in the decision to use the posthole sampling approach. Finally, more thorough excavation at four of the small residential structures randomly sampled in the south survey strip confirmed the excavation sequence derived from the test-pit sample. In addition, random test pits placed in larger constructions excavated at the small nucleated site of Navajuelal (Green 1970) confirmed or predicted accurately the construction and occupational sequence at those loci sampled.

The Pulltrouser Swamp program used a combination of in-structure testing and midden sampling based on posthole exploration because there was evidence of extensive use of middens as fills. Extensive surface collection of most of the structure was also possible, owing to recent cultivation for sugarcane. This strategy enabled us to find evidence of shorter-term or less intensive occupation in terminal phases which might be missed by the more restricted testing program.

The excavation program at Becan used the traditional method of in-structure test-pitting. Additionally, surface collections, possible because of more extensive ground-surface disturbance, allowed for more accurate recording of short-term terminal occupation. The Barton Ramie program used extensive in-structure test-pitting combined with more intensive excavation at several locations. The complex pattern of mound construction and occupation at Barton Ramie is quite distinctive compared to small and medium-sized residential structures at other sites.

Adjustment Factors

One of the major issues in the discussion of Maya settlement patterns and demography is the question of continuity of occupation (Haviland 1970; Sanders and Price 1968; Culbert et al., this volume; Tourtellot, this volume). Short-term occupation of structures would reduce population sizes significantly. Since we now have more information from several decades of intensive excavation and sampling, it has become clear that there is no uniform pattern at all southern and central lowland Maya sites. Some sites and regions show greater continuity of occupation than others. Central locations of major sites tend to show greater continuity than peripheral regions. Above all, local political and economic factors have created a variety of patterns.

For the present study I decided to try to deal with this situation in all its complexity rather than simply assume either continuous or shifting occupation. If the results of an excavation indicated occupation through several phases, then the structure occupation was counted as continuous and not divided by a time factor. The same procedure was followed if there was a major series of rebuildings compatible with a phase-long occupation. On the other hand, structures with small quantities of associated artifactual debris and minimal constructional sequences were counted as short-term occupations and divided by a time factor. Culbert et al. (this volume) estimate occupation using a 150-year use-life. I have chosen to use 100 years, since in many cases in peripheral Tikal the quantity of cultural material is not great and little remodeling took place.

I have used this approach in calculating the figures on relative population for peripheral Tikal, the Pulltrouser Swamp settlements, Becan, and Barton Ramie. In the last two cases I recalculated figures after evaluating the excavation data from the tested structures in the published site reports. The central Tikal data are from Culbert et al. (this volume) and are used for illustrative purposes only, since the assumption of cyclical occupation is made in that chapter.

Comparison of Demographic Profiles

The closest match of demographic profiles is, as expected, between central and peripheral Tikal (Tables 5.1, 5.2, and 14.1; Figure 14.1). The slightly lower presence of Preclassic occupation in peripheral Tikal, especially in the pre-Cauac complexes, may simply be a reflection of the differing testing approaches. In some cases small constructions or debris from Middle and early Late Preclassic occupation may be buried under later construction. Since Cimi complex diagnostics are relatively rare in collections from peripheral Tikal, I have combined Cauac and Cimi into one longer ceramic complex. The differences in the Early Classic are the most significant, since several areas in peripheral Tikal show only earlier Early Classic occupation, a situation not noted in central Tikal. Although the profiles are similar in the Late Classic, distributional data show a shift toward occupation north of central Tikal through the Late Classic. There is also evidence of greater compaction of population in the same span of time. The Terminal Classic is marked by the tendency to occupy larger complexes with range structures, but the peripheral areas see some occupation of smaller structures as well. Overall, the two profiles show a marked similarity throughout the sequence.

By contrast, the demographic profile for the settlement around Becan (Table 14.2, Figure 14.1) shows marked differences. This flatter profile indicates a proportionately higher population in the Late Preclassic and a slight slump in the Early Classic. The profile is not that different from those at sites such as Pulltrouser Swamp or Barton Ramie (Tables 14.3 and 14.4, Figure 14.2) The main dissimilarity is the more rapid falloff in population in the later Late Classic and Terminal Classic.

The Belizean sites are quite similar to each other. Starting in the Late Preclassic and Protoclassic, the demographic profiles vary sharply from those of the central area major centers. Population for the later Preclassic and Protoclassic is relatively higher in comparison to maximum occupation in the Late Classic. Both zones show extensive occupation in the Floral Park sphere and a dip in either the Protoclassic or earlier Early Classic. Pulltrouser rises to its peak occupation earlier than most other sites, with a strong late Early Classic occupation, and remains at a high plateau for three phases. Barton Ramie peaks somewhat later but also continues at a broad plateau for an extended period of time. Both zones showed continued high occupation into the Terminal Classic, and Barton Ramie also had a significant Late Postclassic occupation.

Both zones, of course, had lower absolute maximum populations than the estimated figure of 92,000 for the combined central and peripheral Tikal areas and the much lower but significant Becan population of approximately 2800 (P. Thomas 1981:182). Rough estimates for Pulltrouser indicate a maximum population for all four communities in the swamp zone at under 800 (if a figure of 5.6 people/residence is used). Barton Ramie may have had a maximum population of about 1400 during the Spanish Lookout phase.

DEMOGRAPHIC PROFILES OF THE CENTRAL SITES

The Tikal and Becan zones have indications of initial significant settlement in the Middle Preclassic. Actual density of occupation is hard to estimate since many of the constructions were not mounded and thus are not visible on the surface. Most settlements were small, relatively dispersed, and concentrated on the areas closest to good land for slash-and-burn cultivation. In the upland areas or areas distant from permanent water, settlement appears to have shifted over time. However, relatively continuous use of small ritual structures suggests that populations did not travel great distances and that they maintained their use of existing public architecture.

The Late Preclassic shows continuity with the earlier patterns but with a significant increase in population size, though perhaps no major increase in the rate of population growth. At central Tikal and Becan there was additional investment in private housing, as seen in the development of mounded bases for residential construction. This activity also indicates greater stability of population. Significant increments were added to public architecture, and the time interval between major additions appears to have been shortened. Although populations were larger, they still seem to have concentrated in and around the same areas used during the Middle Preclassic. These areas were just more densely and permanently occupied.

There is clear evidence of significant conflict in at least the later part of the Late Preclassic at Becan. The fortifications there appear to date to this period (Webster 1976). Although no direct evidence exists for defensive features in the Tikal zone during this time span, a Protoclassic fortification at the site of Muralla de Leon (D. Rice and P. Rice 1981), southeast of Tikal, also indicates patterns of conflict. The increasing density of population in the Late Preclassic may be in part a response to the compaction of settlement generally associated with intensive raiding of warfare, at least in the central portions of the peninsula. Or the pattern may reflect increasing pressures by regional elites consolidating their powers in the central part of the peninsula. These factors may explain the relatively higher population of Becan compared to Tikal at this time.

The Protoclassic is a difficult time period to discuss, since its manifestations are so variable. The Protoclassic is strongly in evidence at the Belizean sites studied but not at Becan or Tikal. At the latter sites there is a greater shift between Preclassic and Classic ceramics and only a minor representation of types associated with the Floral Park sphere. At Tikal the time is marked by the Cimi ceramic complex and appears to be one of notable population growth, comparable to that recorded at Pulltrouser and Barton Ramie. At Becan there is an even less strong division between the Preclassic and Classic, though it is again likely that population increased throughout the Late Preclassic. P. Thomas (1981) notes that the largest structure at the site was probably constructed late in the Late Pre-classic Pakluum phase.

The second major disparity in demographic curves comes in the earlier Early Classic. This period is a problematic one for most people working on population estimates in much of the Maya lowlands. Originally, it was thought that there was a decrease in occupation at many sites since the numbers of structures occupied seemed to decrease. A radical recent position even proposes that the disparity may be due to increased differentiation in archaeological ceramics, with "Early Classic" ceramics actually a socially distinctive subcomplex used by elites, with the remainder of the population still using Late Preclassic ceramics (Lincoln 1985). This position is highly questionable, given the discovery of Early Classic ceramics in a wide variety of household contexts at a large number of sites. In addition, studies that control for phase length have determined that there was a total population increase at many sites, although not a sharp increase in rate of population growth. What appears to be most striking in this period is a tendency for residential structures to become more dispersed.

In peripheral Tikal there is evidence for an increased total population in the earlier Early Classic, with additional mound groups added to established communities or segments of regional settlement. New groups were also constructed in areas previously unused but favorable for slash-and-burn agriculture. This phenomenon of dispersed settlements in peripheral Tikal was first noted by the Tikal Sustaining Area Project's survey program along the north and south survey strips in areas 4 to 8 km from the site center. Ford's Tikal-Yaxha transect data also indicate increasing occupation of the Tikal half of the transect in the Early Classic, with a decline in the Yaxha half (Ford 1986). Part of this settlement increase may have come from population resettled from areas such as the Yaxha-Sacnab and other lacustrine environments (D. Rice and P. Rice 1981).

Tikal seems to have reached its largest physical size in terms of continuous settlement in the earlier Early Classic, though density might have been quite low in areas remote from older centers of nucleation. In this time period the northern Tikal earthworks was constructed (D. Puleston and Callender 1967). The construction of the earthworks does not seem to be correlated with any trend toward population nucleation within the fortification, a pattern also noted at Becan.

Significant population shifts occurred during the Manik complex at Tikal. Those settlements in new zones dating to the Early Classic are from the earlier part of the Manik phase. On the other hand, there is evidence of significant construction of small, nucleated sites in the peripheral zones, such as Navajuelal (Green 1970), which date to the latter portion of the Early Classic. Later Early Classic sherds were encountered at the base of middens associated with larger clusters of mounds outside the northern defensive earthworks. If there is a shift toward denser population and also a shift in rate of population growth in the Tikal region, I tend to place the take-off period in the later portion of the Manik phase rather than in the succeeding Ik phase, when both peripheral and central Tikal show close to their maximum population size.

At Becan the Early Classic Period is one of population retrenchment. Although there is not a deep dip in population during the Chacsik phase, population was concentrated near the fortifications and major public architecture. On the other hand, areas farther from the site center of Becan began to be heavily occupied during the Sabucan phase after a much lighter occupation in the Pakluum and Chacsik phases, partly due to the establishment of new nuclei of population (Chicanna).

Of special interest is the lack of significant construction of new houses or new construction levels in existing residences during the Early Classic at Becan. This is surprising, considering the much higher frequency of ceramics associated with the Early Classic. It seems that labor investment in housing decreased during the Early Classic.

The Becan evidence supports an increase in population perhaps beginning in the Sabucan phase but peaking in the Bejuco phase. At Becan this relatively rapid increase is associated with the development of the intensive system of terracing documented by B. Turner (1974, 1978b, 1983a). This is the same period in which stockpiling of chert in mounds, begun in the earlier Sabucan phase, reached its peak (P. Thomas 1981). The population profile parallels the demographic pattern at Tikal. However, there is no evidence at this time that the population upsurge at Tikal during the Late Classic is correlated with any shift toward intensification of food production. At Becan the development of more complex agronomic systems is marked by a significant increase in agricultural implements such as worn biface ovates used as hoes. In peripheral Tikal there is no evidence for increased numbers of agricultural tools in Late Manik or Ik phase occupation debris.

Population appears to have peaked in the total zone near Tikal and Becan in the earlier phase of the Late Classic. In the later, precollapse phase of the Late Classic, total population may have declined somewhat, particularly at Becan. At both sites there is evidence of increasing nucleation of population, with filling in of areas close to the major ceremonial centers. Although population nucleation is sometimes considered a response to turbulent political climates, no evidence exists of reuse of the defensive earthworks at either site. Although occupation may have actually decreased in peripheral Becan, construction of larger and more substantial residential structures and plazuela groups seems to have increased (P. Thomas 1981:102–3). In addition, at Tikal there is evidence that population grew faster to the north of central Tikal, especially in the area near the growing Late Classic center of Jimbal.

The Terminal Classic sees a rapid and drastic decline in population at both Tikal and Becan. There is little evidence of major constructional activity either in the centers or in peripheral settlement areas. Settlement is either concentrated in old elite residential zones or scattered in small groups in the surrounding countryside. The more generalized tool kits and presence of more agricultural tools in peripheral Tikal indicate that the residents may have been full-time agriculturalists. Houses in peripheral areas were much poorer, with little labor investment in these zones.

Both Tikal and Becan show sparse Late Postclassic activity. At Becan there is only a censer complex for the Lobo phase and thus no evidence of actual habitation. Areas near aguadas or water in central and peripheral Tikal show some scanty occupation, along with activities at older abandoned temples in central Tikal, Uolantun, and Navajuelal.

DEMOGRAPHIC PROFILES OF THE BELIZEAN SITES

The demographic profiles from the Pulltrouser zone and Barton Ramie show significant differences from the central places previously discussed. These sites have a markedly higher occupancy rate in the Preclassic compared to Tikal. They also show bimodal peaks, compared to the unimodal peak at Tikal. Finally, there is greater continuity between the Late Classic and Terminal Classic and more significant Late Postclassic occupation.

Both zones show occupation as early as or earlier than the central sites, with some ceramics of the early Middle Preclassic Bladen complex recovered from the Pulltrouser excavations. Both zones show evidence of more continuous and possibly denser occupation through the Middle and Late Preclassic than at the central sites. Occupation is directly on the ground surface with no investment in mounded domestic architecture. The Late Preclassic peak of occupation at Pulltrouser is marked by incorporation into a more tightly integrated regional economy, as seen in the regional dominance of lithics produced by the Colha workshops (McAnany 1986; Shafer 1983; Shafer and Hester 1983) and in the distributional patterns of regionally produced ceramics (Fry 1989).

Both Barton Ramie and Pulltrouser show a strong Floral Park component, although it is marked by heavier population density at Barton Ramie. The earlier Early Classic (Nuevo Tzakol) at Pulltrouser shows continuing and even growing occupation, while the same period at Barton Ramie shows a slightly lower population. Pulltrouser Swamp has a pattern familiar for much of northern Belize. Population, after growing continually in the Preclassic through the Protoclassic, appears to decline in the Early Classic. There is construction in some of the larger plazuela groupings but little evidence of addition to existing structures or the construction of new structures. Population may have simply become more dispersed or may have clustered closer to the New River. Dahlin (1977) indicates that population on Albion Island in the Hondo River Valley peaked during the Early Classic and declined in the Late and Terminal Classic. However, my recent examination of type collections from the Albion Island surveys reveals a preponderance of Terminal Classic ceramics.

Population increases sharply in the latter portion of the Early Classic and into the beginning of the Late Classic at Pulltrouser. There is a significant Middle Classic component in the Pulltrouser zone with relatively abundant cylindrical tripod vessels. In addition, tradewares come from as far away as the Campeche coast. A whole new settlement area, Ti Baat, was occupied intensively for the first time and became one of the major loci of population in the zone. Older areas also show occupation, but they do not show the almost explosive growth as seen at Ti Baat. Lacking a complete regional survey, we cannot as yet determine if this growth is due to internal dynamics or to shifts in the distribution of regional population.

Although the earliest evidence of raised-field construction dates to the Late Preclassic (Fry 1983; B. Turner and Harrison 1983), more than half of the securely dated fields are Late Classic. Thus the maximum in population is correlated with the largest scale of the Pulltrouser Swamp raised-field system, an obvious parallel to the situation at Becan. Unlike at Becan, however, population size and density at Pulltrouser remained high through the Late Classic and Terminal Classic. As I have observed, one reason that population declined so rapidly in the Terminal Classic Eznab phase at Tikal was the lack of investment in agricultural systems that allowed for more fluidity in population movement (Fry 1970). Certainly one reason for continued occupation of the Pulltrouser zone may well have been the accumulated labor investment in the raised-field system, with its potential for multicropping. On the other hand, population remains higher in Belize in the Terminal Classic than in the central portions of the peninsula, reflecting political as well as economic factors.

The Late Classic is the population peak at Barton Ramie, with relatively equally high population in the Tiger Run and Spanish Lookout phases. It is difficult to determine whether there was significant falloff in population in the later part of the Spanish Lookout complex equivalent to that of the Terminal Classic at Pulltrouser or the central sites. The evidence from continuous construction indicates a strong continuity into the Terminal Classic. Thus population does not show the rapid decline experienced in the central sites. It is possible that settlements not so intimately tied to the Classic political system were less disrupted by the political and economic changes of the turbulent Late Classic-Terminal Classic boundary.

Both sites show later Postclassic occupation. There may have been continuous occupation at Barton Ramie, whereas the evidence for Pulltrouser indicates depopulation and new colonization. The Waterbank complex material is a thin veneer in most situations and very localized on top of earlier constructions. The greater scale of population at Barton Ramie is distinctive for the Late Postclassic.

CONCLUSIONS

The information on demographic trends in selected lowland Maya sites shows the most striking difference when the history of occupation of smaller settlements and smaller centers is compared to that of major centers like Tikal. These smaller sites do not show the extreme swings in population characteristic of the major central places, and the small centers show greater continuity in occupation. The tendency of Maya archaeologists to concentrate on settlement areas close to major centers may thus exaggerate the magnitude of population shifts. Some of the problems in lowland Maya chronology, therefore, such as the Early Classic decline at some sites, may simply reflect the more volatile population shifts at regional capitals or major central places. The heterogeneity of demographic trends should make us cautious in seeing pan-lowland patterns, and it reinforces the need for surveys and programs of regional scope.

It appears that the building of strong polities involved both warfare (Webster 1976) and the recruitment and maintenance of large populations. The decline of population at the Belizean sites and Becan in the Early Classic may reflect the failure of the emerging polity or linked polities in the area in comparison with the emerging central-zone sites. The growth of Tikal in the Early Classic along with evidence of fortifications show a later phase of polity building and one that seems to have been more successful. The rebound in the later Early Classic in the case of Pulltrouser and Becan, and the early Late Classic in the case of Barton Ramie, may well have been correlated with the increasing involvement of the central part of the lowlands in an integrated politicoeconomic system. The Belizean sites weathered the breakup of this system demographically, and the Pulltrouser zone may have been involved in a Terminal Classic system based in northern Belize.

ACKNOWLEDGMENTS

I would like to thank Pat Culbert for the continuing dialogue on lowland Maya demography and critical comments. Data from peripheral Tikal were gathered while I was a member of the Tikal Sustaining Area Project, with William A. Haviland, director, and the late Dennis E. Puleston, field director. This project was supported by National Science Foundation grant GS 1409. The Pulltrouser Swamp Project was founded by National Science

Foundation grants BNS 78-12537 and BNS 80-24516. I am indebted to Peter Harrison and B. L. Turner II, project directors, for the opportunity to study the settlement systems at Pulltrouser Swamp, and to Leah Minc, Stan Walling, Patricia McAnany, who conducted the survey and excavation of the Pulltrouser communities. Any errors in interpretation of the Tikal and Pulltrouser data are, of course, my own.

Table 14.1   Relative Population Figures for Peripheral Tikal

| Date | Complex | Cases | | Adjust-ment Factor | Adjusted Cases | Relative Popu-lation |
		Con-tinuous	Shift-ing			
A.D. 930–1130(?)	Caban	0	1	1/2	0.5	1
A.D. 830–930(?)	Eznab	14	1	1/1	15	29.4
A.D. 700–830	Imix	45	4	10/13	48	94
A.D. 600–700	Ik	51	0	1/1	51	100
A.D. 250–600	Manik	17	59	10/35	34	45
100 B.C.–A.D. 250	Cauac & Cimi	11	0	10/35	3	6
250–100 B.C.	Chuen	1	0	10/15	0.7	1
500–250 B.C.	Tzec	1	0	10/25	0.4	1
750–500 B.C.	Eb	1	0	10/25	0.4	1

Table 14.2   Relative Population Figures for Becan

| Date | Complex | Cases | | Adjust-ment Factor | Adjusted Cases | Relative Popu-lation |
		Contin-uous	Shift-ing			
A.D 830–1050	Xcocom	5	5	1/2.2	7.3	22.9
A.D 730–830	Chintok	12	8	1/1	20.0	62.7
A.D 600–730	Bejuco	25	9	1/1.3	31.9	100.0
A.D 500–600	Sabucan	6	19	1/1	25.0	78.4
A.D 250–500	Chacsik	9	23	1/2.5	18.2	57.1
200 B.C.–A.D 250	Pakluum	18	14	1/4.5	21.1	66.1
400–200 B.C.	Acachen	2	1	1/2	2.5	6.6

Table 14.3   Relative Population Figures for Pulltrouser Swamp

| | | Case | | Adjust- | | Relative |
| | | Contin- | Shift- | ment | Adjusted | Popu- |
Date	Complex	uous	ing	Factor	Cases	lation
A.D. 1300–1500(?)	Waterbank	1	5	1/2	3.5	15.9
A.D. 800–950(?)	Rancho	20	0	10/15	20.0	90.9
A.D. 650–800	Santana	22	0	10/15	22.0	100.0
A.D. 500–650	Yo	18	0	10/15	18.0	81.8
A.D. 300–500	Nuevo	13	3	1/2	14.5	66.0
A.D. 150–300	Freshwater	9	1	10/15	9.7	44.1
100 B.C.–A.D. 150	Late Cocos	9	5	10/25	11.0	50.0
300–100 B.C.	Early Cocos	2	0	1/2	2.0	9.1
600–300 B.C.	Lopez	1	3	1/3	2.0	9.1

Table 14.4   Relative Population Figures for Barton Ramie

| | | Cases | | Adjust- | | Relative |
| | | Contin- | Shift- | ment | Adjusted | Popu- |
Date	Complex	uous	ing	Factor	Cases	lation
A.D. 950–1150	New Town Spanish	51	9	1/2	55.5	86
A.D. 700–950	Lookout	65	1	10/25	65.4	100
A.D. 600–700	Tiger Run	50	0	1/1	50.0	77
A.D. 300–600	Hermitage	35	6	1/3	37.0	57
A.D. 150–300	Floral Park	33	16	10/15	43.7	67
300 B.C.–A.D. 150	Mt. Hope	8	13	10/45	10.9	17
600–300 B.C.	Barton Creek	7	9	1/3	10.0	15
900–600 B.C.	Jenny Creek	4	15	1/3	9.0	14

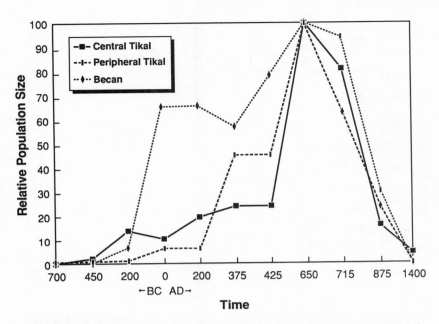

Figure 14.1 Demographic profiles for central Tikal, peripheral Tikal, and Becan.

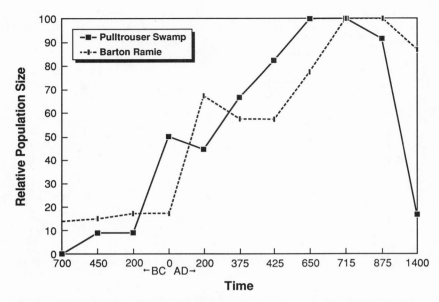

Figure 14.2 Demographic profiles for Pulltrouser Swamp and Barton
Ramie.

15 /

Population Reconstruction of the Central Maya Lowlands: 1000 B.C. to A.D. 1500

B. L. TURNER II

Reconstructing human populations for prehistoric times is a hazardous endeavor because of problems of data and methodology, and the resulting population estimates, typically with large degrees of error, must be viewed with caution. Nevertheless, such reconstructions cannot be avoided, because of the important and peculiar attributes of population that diminish the utility of qualitative assessments or surrogate measures (e.g., number of settlements).

Population is not only a component of the landscape—as is soil, vegetation, or climate—and therefore fundamental to the description of places or regions, aspects of it can intentionally and radically transform the landscape. Although these transformations are more fully understood in terms of nature-society interactions, broad trends can be detected between changes in population and landscape transformation as they develop in place. Population size is also directly linked to the nature of the economy and, therefore, must be considered in analyses of economic change. Indeed, population has been used to explain various aspects of the economy (and political economy), either as a deterministic variable or as a component of more complex, systemic interactions.

For these reasons alone, it is interesting that so little attention has been paid to reconstructions of lowland Maya populations at regional levels, especially by way of comparison to the Basin of Mexico (e.g., S. Cook and

Borah 1960; Denevan 1976; Sanders et al. 1979). When we consider the scholarly interest in the Maya and the number of population-resource explanations of the collapse of the Classic civilization (see Culbert, ed., 1973; Lowe 1985; B. Turner 1989), this paucity is downright puzzling. Prior to the 1960s, several "dead reckoning" estimates had been made for the entire lowlands in Classic times (Table 15.1). These ranged from about 3 to 13 million people and typically involved subjective evaluations of pan-lowland carrying capacities or agricultural systems. Since that time, considerable effort has been expended to settlement studies from which population or population-density estimates were developed for individual sites or small areas (e.g., Ashmore, ed., 1981; Haviland 1969; 1970; D. Puleston 1973; Willey et al. 1965). Well into the 1970s, however, regional assessments were limited to qualitative assessments of general population densities (e.g., Coe 1965; Sanders 1973).

R. E. W. Adams (1981:250) cautiously advanced a regional reconstruction with rather startling zenith population estimates, ranging from 13.7 to 26.1 million for an enlarged central zone, some 51,000 km². Such reconstructions are not only controversial (e.g., Petersen 1975; Sanders 1981); they emphasize the need for thorough examinations of the demographic implications and the assumptions behind the estimating procedures. An appropriate criticism of much of the population work dealing with the ancient Maya, including my own, has been its parochialism and the minimal attention given to comparisons and to the larger body of knowledge in demography, population history, and population geography.

This study provides a *trial procedure* for calculating regional populations based on house-sites and settlement-hierarchy data, and uses it to reconstruct the populations of the central Maya lowlands from 300 B.C. to A.D. 1500. It is a recalculation of a reconstruction of the same regional population (extending to 1985) that was prepared as part of a larger project dealing with comparative, long-term population trends (B. Turner 1986; Whitmore et al. 1990). The original study was undertaken previous to the development of this volume and to the publication of certain complementary material, such as Lowe's (1985) assessment of the Classic collapse in the southern Maya lowlands, Ford's (1986) residential survey between Tikal and Yaxha, and Culbert et al.'s occupational treatment in this volume. It is noteworthy that several of the temporal and spatial implications found by Lowe are supported in this reconstruction.

THE STUDY AREA

The central Maya lowland region is located at the base of the Yucatan Peninsula and encompasses southeastern Campeche and southwestern

Quintana Roo, Mexico, and the northeastern quadrant of Peten, Guatemala. This region is not "naturally" delimited and can be demarcated in a number of ways (Map 15.1) (see B. Turner 1983:a7–10). The approach taken here follows that of B. Turner (1983a), in which physiographic and archaeological characteristics are combined to define a spatial unit. To facilitate calculations in this study, I have limited the central Maya lowland region to the interior ridge land or rolling terrain of the southern Yucatan-northern Peten area as it relates to culturally defined units. This ridge land ranges in elevation from about 50 to 300 m above sea level, has no permanent or navigable rivers, and maintains an average of about 65% uplands (as opposed to seasonally inundated depressions or bajos). The elevation and the ratio of upland to depression are significant in distinguishing this sector of the central Maya lowlands from its eastern and western sectors (see B. Turner 1983a:1–10). The latter are low in elevation (fewer than 50 m above sea level), and as much as 50% of the landscape is composed of depressions.

The core of this physiographic unit corresponds rather well with three archaeological regions, defined architecturally and demonstrated by use of the nearest-neighbor statistic (R. E. W. Adams and Jones 1981). From north to south, these are the Rio Bec, Calakmul, and Tikal "regions" (here, subregions) (Map 15.1). Based on the distribution of known sites, the subregions measure about 4780 km², 5335 km², and 12,600 km², respectively. (The precise demarcation of each subregion is somewhat arbitrary. The rectilinear boundaries in Map 15.1 have been used to facilitate the ease of area calculations.) The central Maya lowland region as used here— the so-called core zone—is some 22,715 km² in area, constituting about 6–10% of the entire lowland Maya area, depending on delimitations. Its north-south axis is about 360 km long, beginning in east-central Campeche and extending to the edge of the savanna zone in south-central Peten. Its east-west width is variable, from about 80 to 120 km.

Archeologically, the Calakmul and Tikal subregions are apparently much more similar to one another than they are to the Rio Bec subregion (R. E. W. Adams 1981). Differences between the former and latter include the characteristics of settlement patterns and chronologies. For these reasons, this study explores reconstructions for both the regional and subregional levels.

DATA AND RECONSTRUCTION PROCEDURES

Regional reconstructions for the prehistoric period are stymied because of logistical problems involved in surveying and excavating in the forest (large tracts are inaccessible by plane or automobile). Fortunately, lengthy investigations have taken place at Tikal (e.g., Coe 1965), many of them devoted to questions of population (Haviland 1969, 1970, 1972a,b). Other major sites have not been investigated in such detail, with the focus of study on survey and excavations of site acropolises. El Mirador (Dahlin 1984; Matheny 1986) has been examined recently, and Rio Azul (R. E. W. Adams et al. 1984) and Calakmul were under investigation at the time that this reconstruction was developed. Rural and intersite surveys of the Tikal subregion have been undertaken (W. Bullard 1960; Ford 1982, 1986; D. Puleston 1973, 1974; D. Rice 1978; D. Rice and P. Rice 1980, 1981). To my knowledge, no such studies exist for the Calakmul subregion, although surveys report civic-ceremonial centers and rural structural remains similar to those of the Tikal subregion (e.g., Ruppert and Denison 1943; Schufeldt 1950). The Rio Bec subregion has had the benefit of detailed studies at the fortified site of Becan and its immediate hinterlands (R. E. W. Adams 1974, 1981; P. Thomas 1974, 1981). In addition, information on rural population has been obtained by sampling procedures and surveys (Eaton 1975; B. Turner 1976, 1983a).

This regional reconstruction relies largely on the data generated in these studies, knowledge of site locations and approximate size (e.g., R. E. W. Adams 1981; I. Graham 1967; D. Rice and Puleston 1981), and attempts to place sites in rank orders (R. E. W. Adams and Jones 1981; W. L. Fash 1977). The results obviously have a considerable degree of error in terms of "raw" population figures. Nevertheless, the general trends in population through time are most probably correct (see Lowe 1985; Willey 1982).

The contributions in this volume have detailed the basic means by which data are generated and manipulated to produce population estimates for Maya sites and locales. These need not be reiterated. Rather, the estimation procedures used in this reconstruction are described, with details limited to those aspects that are original to this study.

The settlement, or house-count, method of estimation has become virtually standardized, and it is used here to produce "rural" population estimates. The basic formula is

(a) number of structures [in a defined area]

× (b) % of structures dating to a chronological phase of occupation

× (c) % of time structures occupied in that phase [phase-occupancy rate]

× (d) % of structures that were occupational dwellings [dwelling rate]

= (e) number of structures occupied at any moment in time

× (f) average number of occupants per structure

= (g) total population at any moment.

If the structure count (a) is based on a sampling procedure, the results are converted to a population-density figure and multiplied by the area involved.

Few "intensive" studies of rural house sites have been made in the central lowlands (and none for the Calakmul subregion) which include systematic sampling of a large number of mounds (e.g., Ford 1986). Because of the detail paid to the Preclassic phases of occupation, the figures derived from the work on rural settlements around the central lakes of Peten (D. Rice 1978; D. Rice and P. Rice 1981) have been used here for variables *a* and *b* as they apply to the Tikal and Calakmul subregions. For the Rio Bec subregion, these variables have been taken from work dealing with the "environs" of Becan (P. Thomas 1981), as modified by rural studies conducted by the Rio Bec ecological project (Ball 1983; B. Turner 1983a).

Variables *c* and *d* require extensive and detailed excavations that have been associated with only a few studies focusing on major sites or "urban" areas. Therefore, it is common to adopt "standard" figures for them. In this case, work at Tikal suggests a phase-occupancy rate (*c*) of 93% and a dwelling rate (*d*) of 84% (Haviland 1970:193; 1972b). These figures have been used in this study because of the sheer paucity of alternatives. Further work will undoubtedly find that the "standard" figures vary by region, time period, and rural-urban settlement type.

Finally, the common figures for the average number of occupants per dwelling (*f*) are 5.4–5.6. These figures are based on ethnographic work in Yucatan and compared to Naroll's (1962) formula for relating floor space to population (D. Puleston 1974).[1] They are also consistent, if not conservative, for paleotechnic, agrarian economies. The lower figure is used in this study.

A major problem with regional population reconstructions derived solely from the house-count procedure is the failure to account for intraregional spatial variation in house remains, particularly as manifested in nucleated versus rural settlements (Ford 1986). A rural-based density figure would underestimate regional populations, and a site-based figure would overestimate them. One approach seeks some average density of the two methods. To my knowledge, no one has accounted for this discrepancy quantitatively. A trial procedure using settlement rank orders is developed here to explore the problem.

R. E. W. Adams (1981; also Adams and Jones 1981; E. Turner et al 1981) has "rank ordered" sites in the central Maya lowlands based on plaza and acropolis sizes. This information can be used in a modified, rank-size formula:

(a) the population size of the largest site
÷ (b) the rank order of any other site
× (c) the occupational-chronological phase rate
= (d) total population of the site for a chronological phase.

The results of all sites are summed by chronological phase to produce a total "site-population estimate."

For regional reconstructions it is also necessary to calculate the area with which this rank-order population is associated. This is achieved following a similar formula:

(A) the areal size of the largest site
÷ (B) the rank order of any other site
× (C) the area chronological phase rate
= (D) total area of site.

These procedures assume that site-population size and area roughly corresponded to the rank order.[2] Although the applicability of this assumption requires careful testing, R. E. W. Adams's incipient work suggests that at least a "loose" rank ordering of sites was highly plausible. Tikal is invariably conceded to have been the largest site in the central lowlands (rank order 1). Its smallest maximum population has been estimated at 40,000 (variable a) with an area of 122.0 km² (variable A). The rank orders (variables b and B) are modifications of R. E. W. Adams (1981) and range from 2 to 7 (Table 15.2). Any site not rank ordered by Adams has been assigned the lowest rank (7). The occupational-chronological phase rate (c) refers to the percentage of structures occupied by time phase, while that for area (C) refers to the space consumed by those structures.

The regional and subregional reconstructions are produced by combining the two procedures (house count and rank order):

(1) subregional area
− (2) area of ranked sites in the subregion
= (3) subregional rural area
× (4) % of habitable land
= (5) habitable rural area of the subregion
× (6) subregional rural population density
= (7) total subregional rural population
+ (8) total subregional rank-order site population
= (9) total subregional population.

The three subregional population totals are summed to create a regional estimate for any particular time phase.

The new, "critical" variable in this procedure is the percentage of habitable land (4). This variable refers to the proportion of well-drained land (not seasonally or permanently inundated) on which the ancient Maya built the great preponderance of their structures. Perhaps 65% of the central lowlands, on average, is well-drained land.

Key Data and Procedural Problems.

The appropriate sections of this volume, B. Turner (1986), and Whitmore and Turner (1986) should be consulted for details of the problems inherent in these procedures and population reconstructions for the Maya region and elsewhere in Mesoamerica. Several "larger" problems inherent, or potentially inherent, in the data and assumptions are discussed here, however.

Poorly drained depressions (bajos, akalches, swamps) comprise much of the central lowlands. It is generally thought that building structures of any kind do not occur within them, and in most cases this assumption may be correct. In 1980, however, the rubble of stone structures was found atop a series of raised or wetland fields deep within Bajo de Morocoy, Quintana Roo (Gliessman et al. 1985; B. Turner 1986). Their functions are not known, but the discovery suggests that some sort of occupation may have taken place within some bajos. I suspect, however, that this occupation was probably never large and, therefore, had minimal influence on regional population reconstructions.

Mayanists have been prone to rely on ethnographic analogies from the greater Maya area for clues about the past. The problem with this approach is that the analogy for the central lowlands is based on a land-extensive economy, not the land-intensive economy that undoubtedly existed during the ascendancy of the Classic Maya. This potential error underlies the use of ethnographic evidence from the Maya region for reconstructions of the past, such as J. E. S. Thompson's (1971) evidence of house abandonment among nineteenth- and twentieth-century Maya swidden cultivators.[3] Land-extensive conditions existed throughout the central lowlands sometime before 300 B.C. and after A.D. 800–1000; for these periods the Thompson analogy, or other arguments about periodic use of dwellings, may be appropriate. From at least 300 B.C. until the collapse, however, varying land-intensive conditions existed throughout much of the central area; the analogy is probably not applicable for such conditions. Some of the well-drained uplands, for example, contain so many structures that a significant portion of the prime agricultural land is literally consumed by them. Presumably, in land-intensive conditions a large proportion of abandoned structures (dwellings) would constitute a rather inefficient method of land use.

Another analogue problem (detailed in this volume) involves the number of structures that constitute a single dwelling and the average number of people who occupied a single dwelling (e.g., Ford 1982, 1986).[4] These issues may never be resolved by way of analogy; direct "tests" by way of excavations are needed. A significant number of structures (the size of house mounds) may have been used for other purposes. In this case the estimates in this reconstruction would be inflated. If groups of structures (two to three) constituted a single dwelling, however, the occupants of each dwelling might have been a larger group than a nuclear family (Ford 1986). Interestingly, those who would reduce the multipliers in the standard procedures tend to ignore the ethnographic and archival data suggesting that the number of occupants per dwelling (number of structures uncertain) may have been significantly larger than 5.4 (e.g., Hellmuth 1977).

The rank-order procedure explored here has numerous problems and requires further assessment and tests. For example, the assumption that the masses of acropolises or areas of courtyards correspond positively with past population size seems a reasonable one. Usually, the larger the site, the more wealth and power that was concentrated there, as manifested in these features (and sheer monumental architecture). Unfortunately, a sufficient range of site populations has not been established by surveys and excavations to assess the correspondence. It may well have varied by subregion, as suggested by the differences in settlement patterns and density of structures between the Rio Bec subregion and other two subregions. Also, studies of various sites are sufficiently small in number and lacking in detail to create major errors in the data used to establish the subregional rank order.

Another important issue involves the temporal invariance of our rank-order procedures. Although general growth (phasing) patterns existed throughout each subregion, individual sites maintained individual patterns of growth and decline, and each site was not in harmonious phase with the others. (This is also a problem in house-count procedure). Tikal was probably the largest site in the central Maya lowlands in the Late Classic Period, but not necessarily in the Preclassic Period or in each phase of a period. Significantly, recent studies at El Mirador (Dahlin 1984; Matheny 1986) and at Cerros (outside the central region; Robertson and Freidel, eds., 1986) indicate that these sites were abandoned after the Preclassic, or A.D. 300. If future studies uphold site abandonment for a large number of sites previous to the Classic collapse, then major adjustments must be made in assessing regional populations. Since the data simply do not allow phasing assessments per site, errors in this reconstruction are compounded. These errors are probably reduced, however, by the use of subregional phasing (i.e., Tikal compared to Rio Bec).

Finally, in merging the two procedures, it is necessary to distinguish between "rural" and "urban," a difficult problem in that many large sites have no clear demarcations, and settlement density simply tapers off into "rural" conditions. The use of rank-order areas to establish "urban areas" involves all the problems noted for rank-order population assessment.

Recognizing the problems inherent in any regional reconstruction, I have made an attempt to err on the side of caution in order to produce low estimates. This policy was followed because not to do so produces staggering results that are controversial and difficult to justify, particularly given the data problems. D. Puleston (1973), for example, made a strong case that the 40,000 maximum population for Tikal can be derived only by artificially limiting the size of the site. He argued that 60,000 people is a more likely figure. If this is true, then the rank-order estimates increase accordingly, unless Tikal was a primate city—an unlikely circumstance given the evidence to date.

By "dead reckoning," the error factor for the prehistoric estimates could be as high as ± 50%. The percentage probably decreases for the Classic Period (A.D. 300–800/1000) and increases before and after that period. This is so not only because of the paucity of evidence for Preclassic times, but also because the land-extensive economies that existed may have involved more frequent vacating of structures than was the practice in the Classic Period. Despite the potentially large error factor, the broad pattern of prehistoric population growth and decline seems valid. The growth and decline was so dramatic that even a 50% degree of error does not eliminate the pattern. This assessment is supported by estimates of the percentages of prehistoric population independently derived by Culbert et al. (this volume; also Lowe 1985).[5]

POPULATION RECONSTRUCTION

Recent evidence indicates the existence of a Paleolithic population in the Maya lowlands (MacNeish et al. 1980), but its relationship to the Neolithic Maya civilization is not understood at this time. The Maya may have appeared in the lowlands as a full-blown agricultural society by about 3000–2000 B.C. (Hammond 1986). Regional population reconstructions cannot be traced back this far, however, because of the paucity of data for these early times and the limited phasing of the record. Indeed, most published house counts provide an initial phasing no earlier than 1000–300 B.C., which by convention means that the first date is the latter.

The initial population density for the central Maya lowlands, excluding the Rio Bec region, is 14.6 people/km^2 for 300 B.C., and that for the end of the prehistoric period is about 4.1 people/km^2 (A.D. 1500). Between these two figures exists at least one dramatic wave of population growth and decline in which the zenith population and its density may have approached 3 million and 150/km^2, respectively (Figure 15.1; Table 15.3). This wave lasts longer than 1800 years in prehistory (and continues another 400 years into historic times). The wave is apparent regardless of the form of analysis (arithmetic or logarithmic) and is evident at all spatial scales (Figure 15.1; Tables 15.3–15.6).

The Rio Bec subregion is not precisely in phase with the other two

(Table 15.6), and as a result, the population curve is more complex than a single wave of growth and decline. From 300 B.C., the population of the central lowlands grew slowly during a 600-year period and peaked at a little over 1 million people. The following 300 years may have witnessed a stabilization of this growth, or even a slight decline. This result, however, is created by the estimates for the Rio Bec subregion alone, which suggest a population loss of nearly 180,000 during the 300 B.C.–A.D. 300 phase (Table 15.6). Neither of the two southern subregions displayed this trend; their populations grew.[6] The fact that the larger trend coincides with the so-called hiatus (Willey 1974) of the Maya civilization suggests that much of the period was marked by slow growth or stabilization of the regional population.[7]

From A.D. 600, the three subregional curve trends correspond. A population explosion ensued until about A.D. 800. For this 200-year period the regional growth rate was 0.45–0.58%/annum, reaching a maximum population ranging between 2.6 and 3.4 million. This range is created by the phasing of the Rio Bec data—indicating that a maximum population was reached in A.D. 700, not A.D. 800 as per the other two subregions—and by discrepancies for the degree of decline of the Rio Bec population from A.D. 700–800. P. Thomas (1981) records a substantial population decline at Becan which, if projected for the Rio Bec subregion, creates a substantial subregional decline of about 1 million people in 100 years. The evidence from rural structures in that subregion does not suggest such a decline (Ball 1983; B. Turner 1983a).[8]

The famed regional depopulation (and civilization collapse) follows sometime after A.D. 800. By A.D. 1000, the population had dropped to less than 1 million or so, generating depopulation rates of 0.53–0.65. This trend continues, such that by the dawn of European contact the regional population of less than 75,000 is only a shadow of its former size.[9]

COMMENTS

The broader pattern of the rise and fall of the prehistoric population in the central Maya lowlands of at least 2500 years duration (1000 B.C. to A.D. 1500) is difficult to refute. Controversy has focused on the actual size of population before its decline and on the eve of Spanish penetration of the region (e.g., Sidrys and Berger 1979). The latter dispute may be largely semantical. The population estimates of those arguing for an "unvacated" region are so low by comparison to those experienced in the eighth and ninth centuries that the region was indeed comparatively "vacant" (e.g., A. Andrews 1984; S. Cook and Borah 1974; Gerhard 1979; Jakeman 1938; G. Jones 1983; Lange 1971; Roys 1965:660; J. E. S. Thompson 1967).

Related to this controversy is the implication that the maximum prehistoric populations were not nearly as large as suggested here; hence the magnitude of the population losses between A.D. 800–1000 and 1500 are exaggerated. For example, Hellmuth (1977:438) refers to populations of the central lake area of Peten in the late 1500s and follows with the observation that "this population probably approaches the maximum for this region [central Peten lake area] in the Classic Period, so observations of this region are particularly appropriate for understanding the earlier situation in the eighth century." Most interpretations of the archaeological evidence contradict this assessment.

A significant number of Mayanists appear to conclude that the continuing high survey counts of house sites cannot be dismissed because they are too large (for whatever reasons) and that tests for such variables as rates of structural occupation per phase indicate that major reductions in the population estimates may not be warranted. As in the case of the Basin of Mexico, skeptics apparently want comparisons from the prehistoric Old World or the tropics in general. For example, Sanders's (1973, 1977, 1981) criticisms of the higher population estimates for the Maya draw on analogues from elsewhere. Interestingly, numerous examples exist of large population densities in the tropics, both past and present (e.g., Netting 1977), and as shall be shown, the densities obtained in the central Maya lowlands are not excessive compared to those of other Mesoamerican cultural core zones.

Here I have attempted to produce a low estimate range while remaining true to the procedures employed. Two interpretations that appear to contradict the first part of this statement are the rate of structural occupancy per phase (0.93) and the rank-order phase conversions. The former is based on few tests; many more are needed, particularly in rural situations. For example, given the number of structures found in various "rural" studies, maximum *upland* population densities of 162/km² and 420/km² are calculated for the Tikal and Rio Bec regions, respectively. I am suspicious of these figures, particularly the one for the Rio Bec region, although the density of "rural" structures in that region is high indeed. "Random" and complete surveys indicate structure densities of 130–140/km² (P. Thomas 1981; B. Turner 1983).[10] I have decided, however, to remain true to the calculation procedures in terms of the multipliers used for the number of these structures that are residences and their rates of occupation. Spatial and temporal variations in the occupancy rate obviously occurred, but we as yet have no way to estimate these changes.

The rank-order conversions require considerable examination. Undoubtedly, the results are "inflated" by the uniform phasing used for each subregion and the inability to grapple with the problems of variable site sizes through time. But these problems may be offset somewhat by the use of the "rock bottom" maximum population for Tikal (rank order 1 = 40,000) as the basis for estimating other site populations.

A comparison of population densities between the central Maya lowlands and the Basin of Mexico reveals that the densities generated in this study are not extravagant. For the large majority of the time before A.D. 300, density figures for the central Maya lowlands apparently did not exceed 15 people/km². From about A.D. 300 to 600, the figure rose to the mid-40–50 range, and by A.D. 800 it had reached no more than about 145 people/km². This high density fell considerably, to the low-40 range by A.D. 1000. The density continued to fall, such that sometime after 1500 (and continuing until about 1950) the figure was below 1 person/km² (B. Turner 1989). For comparison, the average populations per km² for the Basin of Mexico for 300 B.C., A.D. 650, and A.D. 1500 were 11.3, 37.6, and 180.4, respectively (Sanders et al. 1979:217–18). The maximum densities resulting from the population reconstruction here do not exceed those of the basin, although higher densities were apparently obtained at an earlier time in the Maya area (for agricultural explanations see B. Turner and Harrison [1978, 1981, 1983] and B. Turner [1983b, 1985]). Indeed, the zenith densities projected here are consistent with, if not lower than, those projected for other "high civilization" regions in prehistory (Whitmore et al. 1990). It is also noteworthy that the rates of population growth derived from the reconstruction are well within the range of those expected for paleotechnic, agrarian-based societies (Table 15.3).

It must be noted that the densities derived for the Rio Bec subregion are much higher than the total densities, suggesting (1) that major data errors exist, (2) that special conditions existed there which are not accounted for by the estimation method, or (3) that this subregion indeed had very densely settled populations. Survey errors do not seem to be a problem, although more in-depth rural surveys of the subregion would be useful. Reports, from early expeditions into the subregion (Ruppert and Denison 1943) to more recent house counts (B. Turner 1976; P. Thomas 1981), indicate the high density of structural remains of all kinds across the landscape. As yet, no evidence has emerged to suggest that the Rio Bec data should be treated differently than any others in deriving population estimates. Fine-tune phasing of "rural" structures, however, may demonstrate a greater diversity of occupation by time periods than currently exists.

Perhaps the most controversial issue involved with the maximum density estimates is the result obtained by extrapolating them across the entire Maya lowlands, an area of some 300,000 to 500,000 km², depending on the boundaries used. To do so yields astronomical populations (see R. E. W. Adams 1981: 250). I caution against such procedures. The evidence does not yet exist to suggest that the entire lowland area had densities as large as those in the central Maya lowland region. Even within the central region, considerable variations in population characteristics existed through both space (e.g., Ford 1986) and time (Willey 1977, 1982). Presumably, the magnitude of these variations increased at the interregional scale, lowering substantially those estimates based on regional or subregional extrapolations to the entire lowlands.

Finally, I reiterate that the numbers per se are not necessarily the most important element of this reconstruction. Perhaps the more significant finding is the single wave of population growth and decline in which the nadir population on the decline side of the trajectory represents a massive depopulation. In the central Maya lowlands, population appears not to have been resilient; its crash precedes by at least half a century the population holocausts wrought by the European conquest of the western hemisphere. The apparent magnitude of the collapse and the exceedingly long period of no recovery (almost 2000 years) mark this population history as one that is indeed exceptional by world standards (Lee 1987). In this vein, Mayanists must begin to examine carefully the demographic implications of their population estimates and growth-decline trends and how they relate to comparative evidence. These implications involve issues not only of food, fuel, and shelter, but age-sex structure, fertility and mortality rates, migration, and so on (e.g., Petersen 1975).[11] But perhaps most important are the demographic implications of a population collapse without recovery of any significance. Fertile clues for such cases can be found in the seminal work of Lee (1986).

AKNOWLEDGEMENTS
This research was undertaken as part of the Millennial Longwaves of Human Occupance Project, supported by NSF-Geography (grant SES 841–3657). I thank the members of this project (Thomas Whitmore, Douglas Johnson, Robert Kates, and Thomas Gottschang) and the project's lead adviser, Gordon R. Willey, and advisory panel (Robert M. Adams, Karl W. Butzer, and Donald Dumond), and R. E. W. Adams and A. Ford for their comments and discussions. This treatment is my responsibility, and the calculations and figures presented supersede those in project reports and in B. Turner (1989). The project's larger conclusions can be found in Whitmore et al. (1990).

NOTES

1. Naroll's (1962) results have been challenged, and no agreement exists that floor-space comparisons across cultures can be made (e.g., LeBlanc 1971).

2. The validity of the rank-order concept and procedure is argued at length in the geographic literature. The procedure is standard; the reliability of the results is problematic (Szymanski and Agnew 1981). Berry (1961) concluded that, "the simpler the economic and political life of the

[region] and the lower its degree of economic development," the more likely the rank-size rule would apply. Note that Maya sites have been found to follow a rank-size distribution (R. E. W. Adams and Jones 1981).

3. Tolstoy and Fish (1975) suggest that the tradition of lowering by 75% Maya population estimates derived from house counts was based on the notion of generational abandonment of houses as per the ethnographic data in land-extensive economies. If this is so, it is not apparent in the early literature. D. Puleston (1973:43–48) concludes that the Ricketsons (1937) did it to account for the drudgery of cutting the forest with stone tools. I (B. Turner 1978a) suggest that the reduction was an attempt to reduce the high population counts to a range supportable by swidden cultivation.

4. Ford (1982) finds a mound density of 110/km² in central Peten but concludes that mounds cluster as "households" at an average of 2.7 mounds/household. Therefore, potential "house sites" could be 40/km².

5. This reconstruction was undertaken in 1986, at which time Culbert made available to me his calculations of the percentage occupancy of various sites. His figures were used to produce an alternative reconstruction to that provided here (B. Turner 1986). Subsequently, Culbert modified his calculations (Culbert et. al., this volume). I have not had time to produce a new Culbert-based reconstruction, and in fairness to him, I have deleted an alternative reconstruction in this work. It is noteworthy that this alternative produces a curve with a shape very similar to that produced here.

6. Ford (1986) notes a diminution in rural occupancy in the Early Classic period for the Tikal-Yaxha area, not unlike the Rio Bec results. I have not used her results in the calculations because they are based on a small example. Future work may indicate that the diminution of the rural area for this time was a pan-regional phenomenon.

7. The population "lull" and cultural hiatus could be, of course, artifacts of ceramic dating, and changes in ceramic interpretations could alter this phase of the reconstruction particularly.

8. I have only recently noticed the possible incongruency in the population phasing for Becan (outside its moat) and our sample of "rural" structures in the Rio Bec region. A similar incongruency has been noted by Ford (1986) for the Tikal-Yaxha region. It is a subject that begs further study and could lead to results that alter population reconstructions.

9. It is of interest that the nadir of this decline is not reached until the middle or late nineteenth century, when the total population may not have exceeded 6800, with an average density of 0.3 people/km² (B. Turner 1986).

10. This study suggests the possibility of two different patterns of settlement. Comparatively, the Tikal area is marked by a number of highly

ranked sites and low "rural" structure densities. The Rio Bec area, in contrast, has fewer highly ranked sites and a very high rural structure density.

11. Petersen (1975:235) has conjectured that ideological stances have unconsciously affected the studies of prehistoric populations, leading to inflated population estimates. Of course, the same could be said of some demographers' outright rejection of the possibility that large populations existed in the Prehispanic New World without recourse to data.

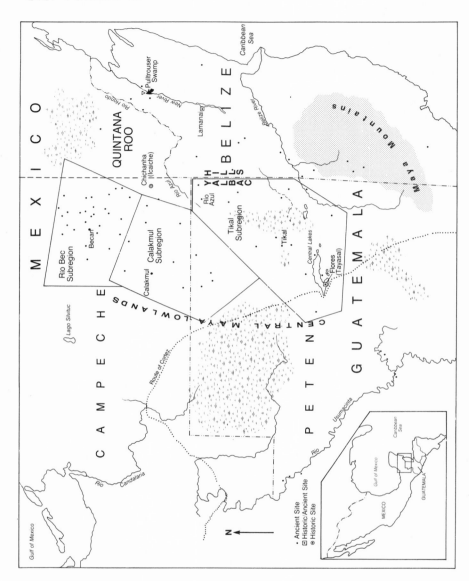

Map 15.1 The central Maya lowlands.

Table 15.1   Population Estimates for the Classic Maya

Source	Density (per km²)	Total Population
Thompson (1954:29)	4.0	1,000,000
Termer (1951:106)	6.6	1,650,000
Stevens (1964:299)	6.6	—
Thompson (1950:17)	12.0	3,000,000
Termer (1953:152)	12.0	—
Morley and Brainerd (1956:47)	12.0	—
J. Hester (1954:121)	23.0	4,500,000
Sanders (1962:95)	30.0	—
Spinden (1928:6511)	31.0	8,000,000
Brainerd (1954:78)	19.0–31.0	5–8,000,000
Ricketson and Ricketson (1937:23)	51.0[a]	13,000,000
Morley (1946:316)	51.0[a]	13,000,000

[a]Based on the assumption that the ancient Maya employed some form of intensive agriculture.

Table 15.2 Subregional Rank-Order Populations and Site Areas

Sites by Subregion			Site Population			
Tikal (12,600 km²)	Calakmul (5335 km²)	Rio Bec (4780 km²)	Rank Order	Low	High	Area (km²)
Tikal			1	40,000	60,000	122.0
Naranjo Rio Azul	Calakmul		2	20,000	30,000	61.0
	Mirador		3	13,000	20,000	40.6
Uaxactun Kinal Yaxha	Naachtun	Rio Bec	4	10,000	15,000	30.5
La Honradez Nakum Ucanal Tayasal	Nakbe La Muñeca Oxpemul	Becan Pechal Peor es Nada	5	8,000	12,000	24.4
Chochkitam Xultun Chunhuitz San Clemente Holmul Ixlu	Uxul Alta Mira Balakbal	Hormiquero Km 132 El Palmar Chicanna Nochebuena Okolhuitz	6	6,667	10,000	20.3
Itzimte El Encanto Uolantun Xmakabatun Yaltitud	La Muralla Pared de los Reyes Pacayal Tintal	Xpuhil 1 Xpuhil 2–4 Km 122 Carmelita Laguna de Zoh	7	5,714	8,571	17.4
Tikinchakan Cenote El Zapote La Pochitoca El Temblor Jimbal El Paraiso El Zotz Ideahz Ideahi Aguacatal Ba 15 Ba 14	Guiro Ing. 1 Ing. 2 Ing. 3 Ing. 4 Ing. 5	Ramonal Porvenir Puerto Rico Buenos Aires Channa Corriental Culucbalom Payan Pueblo Viejo Ceibarico No te Metas Pasion del Cristo Desprecio Halatun Km 183 Namac Noh-Sayab Puch San Lorenzo Tres Marias Tortuga Uaacbal Xaxbil Xuts				

Table 15.2, Subregional Rank-Order Populations and Site Areas (*Continued*)

Sites by Subregion			Site Population			
Tikal (12,600 km²)	Calakmul (5335 km²)	Rio Bec (4780 km²)	Rank Order	Low	High	Area (km²)
Totals	Tikal			284,057	427,286	868.1
	Calakmul			144,476	216,714	440.2
	Rio Bec			239,714	359,571	730.1

Note: Rank orders are based on modifications of R. E. W. Adams (1981) and Adams and Jones (1981). Individual site populations and areas are based on the figures for Tikal as explained in the text.

Table 15.3 Prehistoric Population Reconstructions: Central Maya Lowlands (300 B.C.–A.D. 1500)

Subregion	300 B.C.	A.D. 300	600	800	1000	1200	1500
Tikal	182,413	336,346	404,435	1,520,107	276,504	168,732	51,684
Calakmul	78,835	158,328	174,752	656,960	119,567	72,922	22,336
Rio Bec	N/A	613,192	485,163	473,034 1,214,254	525,592	N/A	N/A
Totals	261,248	1,137,866	1,064,350	2,650,101 3,391,321	921,663	241,654	74,020
Population density (per km^2)	14.6	50.1	46.9	116.7 149.3	40.6	13.5	4.1
Growth/decline rates (%/annum)	N/A	N/A	−0.02	0.46 0.58	−0.53 −0.65	N/A	N/A

Note: Italics signifies the absence of the Rio Bec data for the figure in question.

Table 15.4 Population Reconstruction: Tikal Region (12,600 km²)

Population	900–300 B.C.	300 B.C.–A.D. 300	300–600	600–800	800–1000	1000–1200	1200–1500
% of maximum population	12.0	24.1	26.6	100.0	18.2	11.1	3.4
Civic-ceremonial center population	34,183	68,651	75,772	284,857	51,844	31,619	9,685
Rural-intersite area population	148,230	297,695	328,577	1,235,250	224,816	137,113	41,999
Total population	182,413	366,346	404,348	1,520,107	276,659	168,732	51,684
Population density (per km²)	14.5	29.1	32.1	120.6	22.0	13.4	4.1

Table 15.5 Population Reconstruction: Calakmul Region (5,355 km²)

Population	900–300 B.C.	300 B.C.– A.D. 300	300–600	600–800	800–1000	1000–1200	1200–1500
% of maximum population	12.0	24.1	26.6	100.0	18.2	11.1	3.4
Civic-ceremonial center population	16,977	34,096	37,633	141,476	25,749	15,704	4,810
Rural-intersite area population	61,858	124,232	137,119	515,484	93,818	57,219	17,526
Total population	78,835	158,327	174,751	656,960	119,567	72,923	22,337
Population density (per km²)	14.8	29.7	32.8	123.1	22.4	13.7	4.2

Table 15.6 Population Reconstruction: Rio Bec Region (4,700 km²)

Population	300 B.C.– A.D. 300	300–450	450–600	600–700	700–800	800–1000
% of maximum population	45.5	32.2	36.0	100.0	35.1 90.1	39.0
Civic-ceremonial center population	109,070	77,188	86,297	239,714	84,140 215,982 388,894	93,488
Rural-intersite area population	504,122	356,763	398,866	1,107,960	998,272 473,034	423,104
Total population	613,192	433,951	485,163	1,347,674	1,214,254	525,593
Population density (per km²)	128.3	90.8	101.5	281.9	99.0 254.0	110.0

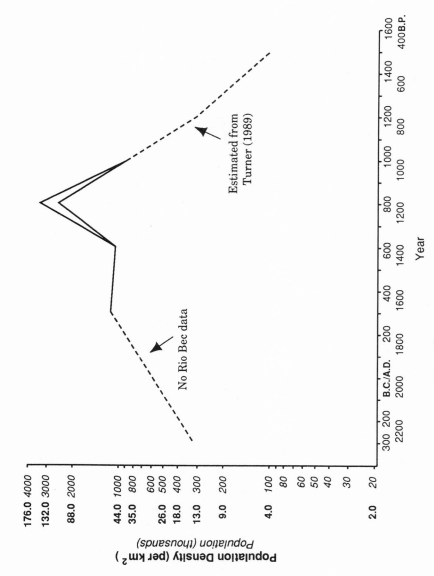

Figure 15.1 Reconstruction of population of the central Maya lowlands.

16 /
Demographic Archaeology in the Maya Lowlands

ROBERT S. SANTLEY

Mayanists have always been interested in population history. Maya sites, for example, were once thought to be "vacant centers" containing comparatively little population, and sociopolitical structure was viewed as being egalitarian, with positions of leadership and power rotated among all adult males regardless of ancestry (Vogt 1961, 1964). This perception of Maya society had great impact on reconstructions of settlement patterns and land use, which were seen as very dispersed, with subsistence based on slash-and-burn agriculture. Although surveys of rural areas indicated that house-mound counts near centers were high in some areas (W. Bullard 1960; Carr and Hazard 1961), it was not until the 1970s that Mayanists recognized that substantial parts of the lowlands were densely settled in Classic times (Ashmore, ed., 1981). Research in the hinterland of major Maya centers quickly led to the discovery of relic agricultural features such as raised fields, terraces, drainage canals, and other evidence of intensive land use, which finally put the swidden hypothesis to rest (Harrison and Turner 1978).

Despite the fact that demographic factors have occasionally loomed large in Maya studies, there has been surprisingly little work on the subject until recently. As this volume illustrates, most of this research has been devoted to describing gross changes in the size, density, and spatial distribution of population at a site or region through time. To place this work in perspective, I will deal with four topics: three models of population growth and decay with different demographic structures and different theoretical implications, current methods used to reconstruct lowland Maya population history, a comparison of the methods Mayanists use with those employed in highland Mexico, and a look at the road ahead.

Like Mayanists, historical demographers have also been concerned with defining long-term population trends. Most of this research, however, has been conducted using census data from urban centers, not from rural areas where farming was the principal means of livelihood. It is precisely here where Maya archaeology has great potential to make a meaningful contribution to our knowledge about long-term patterning in regional and site demography.

MODELS OF POPULATION GROWTH AND LOSS

All populations exhibit a particular demographic structure. This structure may be described in terms of the proportion of the population in different age groups and the sex ratio of each. By and large, growing populations are bottom-heavy, with significant numbers of infants and children, a substantial proportion of whom reach reproductive age. A shrinking population, in contrast, is one in which the number of adults exceeds the number of infants who survive to reproductive age, whereas in stable populations there is a balance between the number of adults removed from the reproductive pool and the frequency of new entries into it. Although stable and shrinking populations may be bottom-heavy, younger cohorts need not constitute the majority. Demographers generally explain population change by means of the relative contributions of birth, death, and migration rates. Fertility and mortality patterns have great impact on the number of new individuals born into a population, the proportion of newborns who attain reproductive age, and the number of offspring a mating pair may have. This information, when combined with knowledge about rates of migration, provides a framework for dealing with changes in demographic structure.

The demographic history of populations varies greatly across space and through time (G. Cowgill 1975a; Hassan 1979; Spooner 1972). In some areas periods of growth are followed first by periods of population decline and then by another growth spurt, often to a higher level (S. Cook 1972; Feinman et al. 1985), whereas in other areas episodes of rapid and sustained increase precede long periods of population stability or near-zero growth (Clarkson 1971; Sanders et al. 1979; Santley and Rose 1979). In still other areas the pattern is one of growth followed by steady population decline over millennia (R. M. Adams 1981; Ammerman et al. 1976; Hollingsworth 1969).

The two simplest forms of population increase are exponential growth and logistic growth (Wilson and Bossert 1971; Whittaker 1975). Under conditions of exponential growth, the rate of reproduction per individual remains more or less constant. Populations undergoing exponential growth therefore reproduce at a uniform rate. Most populations exhibit exponential growth profiles only under special circumstances and only for comparatively short periods of time. Although the number of additional persons is not great when population size is small, any human population allowed to grow at its full exponential rate would become exceedingly large in only a few thousand years. Thus, as populations expand to their limit or carrying capacity (K), compensating factors come into play, curbing growth and sometimes affecting declines in numbers.

Logistic growth is common as populations undergoing unchecked growth approach their carrying capacity. Because population growth increases in rate early in the sequence but is always checked sooner or later, the growth curve is sigmoid in shape. Logistic growth curves may be divided into three phases. During the early phase population is little affected by external constraints and grows at a maximum rate. Phase-one logistic growth often occurs when species discover new habitats, which are subsequently colonized. In the middle phase environmental factors begin to slow growth by decreasing the birth rate, increasing the mortality rate, or both, such that growth involves the addition of a standard number of individuals per unit of time (e.g., 2000 persons/1000 years). In the third phase population approaches and finally stabilizes at carrying capacity. Often as well, populations overshoot carrying capacity and then stabilize. Sometimes there is an initial overshoot, after which the population drops back and increases again, with oscillations of decreasing amplitude until stabilization is achieved at carrying capacity. In other situations the overshoot is followed by fluctuations of constant amplitude, and in others the pattern is one of boom and bust cycles, with each overshoot followed by a crash and population returning to phase-one levels before further growth occurs.

Human populations differ from other biological organisms in their ability to alter food-procurement systems and hence increase the carrying capacity level (Boserup 1965; Sanders and Webster 1978; B. Turner et al. 1977). Although human populations frequently approach carrying capacity and experience declines in numbers due to crop disasters, poor nutrition, and increased disease burden, often they rebound in a few hundred years and reach even higher levels because of improvements in agricultural technology. The resulting "sawtooth" pattern consists of a series of logistic growth spurts interdigited with periods of exponential falloff (Whittaker 1975). The demographic history of China is a case in point (Figure 16.1A). Interestingly, cycle amplitude decreases with time while cycle frequency increases, particularly in the past 500 years, implying that perturbations in later Chinese history were more frequent but had less severe demographic consequences (S. Cook 1972). The demographic history of Egypt is much the same; however, long-term cycles of growth also subsume shorter-term cycles of growth and decline brought about by repeated military conquest and later epidemics (Figure 16.1A) (Hollingsworth 1969). Moreover, changes in the slope of both curves, when graphed logarithmically, indicate long-term shifts in rates of growth and depopulation and by implication fluctuations in fertility and mortality rates.

The demographic history of central Mexico illustrates this pattern of cyclic growth and decay (Figure 16.1B). In the Basin of Mexico, populations generally reached peak levels whenever the region was unified under a single political authority (Sanders et al. 1979). Episodes of growth also associate with developments in agricultural technology: floodwater and diversion-flow irrigation in the Terminal Formative; canal irrigation in Classic times; and drainage or chinampa agriculture in the Aztec Period. Rates of population growth, however, were the greatest very early in the sequence, and the population history varies from subregion to subregion, indicating that a migration process was perhaps in operation (Santley and Rose 1979). Local perturbations also had an impact; ethnohistoric sources suggest that several years of widespread famine preceded the demise of the Toltec Empire, and settlement survey data imply that the Xitle eruption at the end of the Terminal Formative had much the same effect (Davies 1980; Sanders et al. 1979). Cyclic growth and decline also characterize the demographic history of the Valley of Oaxaca (Blanton et al. 1982; Feinman et al. 1985). Except for the Conquest Period, when the valley was split into a number of competing polities, population maxima again associate with periods of political unification and changes in land-use practices. Like the Basin of Mexico, the Valley of Oaxaca has a generally up-trending population curve, with peak levels attained at the time of the Conquest.

The population history of the Maya lowlands is more variable (Figure 16.2A). Areas such as Pulltrouser Swamp and the Belize River Valley show the sawtooth pattern. A period of growth is followed by a population maximum, then decline, and finally subsequent growth to higher levels. The Late Classic collapse also appears to be more attenuated, though Belize does lose population. The pattern in the Tikal, Calakmul, and Rio Bec regions is entirely different (Figure 16.2B). Here growth is moderate but sustained until the Late Classic, after which population levels crash with only limited demographic recovery later on. Although the timing of the collapse and the ensuing episode of demographic loss varies somewhat from site to site, the pattern at most centers is much the same. Growth during the Formative Period conforms to the exponential model, not the logistic model. An exponential curve also describes the collapse, suggesting a mirror-image pattern of population growth and decay. Although the degree of fit with the exponential model is reasonably good, growth rates do vary with time (Figure 16.3). In general, crude growth rates remained relatively stable in the Preclassic but then increased dramatically, reaching a peak in the early Late Classic. Thereafter growth rates rapidly tapered off, and subsequently population levels declined, implying an overshoot phenomenon.

The growth curve for the south-central lowlands is fairly typical of population colonizing new or comparatively unsettled areas. In such settings communities are widely spaced, and the abundance of arable land permits village fissioning. What is unusual is the dramatic increase in rates of growth in the early Late Classic, especially considering the magnitude of the populations involved. The use of bajos for raised-field agriculture may be a major contributory factor here. Production levels on raised fields are two to four times the yields on dryland plots, and if cropping regimes were polycultural early in the history of bajo utilization, then raised-field plots would have provided Maya farmers with a mix of resources rich in most nutrients, thereby allaying stress and reducing mortality. However, as population levels increased further still, monocultural cropping strategies would have become the norm, reducing population nutritional status and enhancing susceptibility to disease. In response to increased mortality and morbidity, Maya populations would have had greater difficulty raising children to reproductive age. If this line of reasoning is followed, population levels near the end of the Late Classic should have fluctuated widely, which would have had dramatic repercussions on the viability of the agrarian support base, dependent as it was on the application of vast amounts of labor to keep the system going. Demographic instability, then, may have sent Maya economies into a power dive, with long-term degradation of the agricultural landscape fueled by increased mortality and ultimately emigration being the result.

Skeletal data from several lowland sites do indicate marked changes in the paleodemographic status of Maya populations through time. Although information on the status of Preclassic populations is still forthcoming, it appears that stress levels increased dramatically in Classic times. At Tikal there was a marked reduction in nonelite adult male stature during the Late Classic (Haviland 1967) in comparison to earlier time periods, a pattern that also occurs at Altar de Sacrificios (Saul 1973), Barton Ramie (Willey et al. 1965), and perhaps Copan (Longyear 1952). At Tikal mortality was particularly high for infants and females entering childbearing age (Haviland 1972a), which also seems to have been the case at Copan in the Late Classic (Sanders, personal communication 1985). At Altar de Sacrificios (Saul 1973) and Copan (Storey, personal communication 1985) the incidence of porotic hyperostosis also increased markedly in Late Classic times. Porotic hyperostosis, most authorities now agree, occurs in populations suffering from chronic anemias that are often caused by inadequate amounts of iron intake, although prolonged breastfeeding, diarrheal infections, and parasitic disease infestations due to population aggregation may also have played a role (Kent 1986; Walker 1985). Moreover, iron and zinc deficiencies should have become more severe if the diet became increasingly maize-dependent as population levels rose throughout the Classic (Santley et al. 1986). In addition, the incidence of linear dental enamel hypoplasia is fairly high for all time periods at Altar and Seibal, indicating that short-term developmental arrests from disease and/or inadequate nutrition were also a common problem (Saul 1973).

Some Maya growth curves are therefore exponential-like, whereas others illustrate a pattern of cyclic growth and decay. The sawtooth pattern characterizes growth profiles in areas where raised-field agriculture was practiced or Maya populations had access to riverine habitats. Exponential-like profiles, in contrast, occur in areas that are landlocked and where agriculture involved a substantial dryland component. Paleodemographic data from certain sites in landlocked areas indicate declines in health and nutritional status in the Late Classic, suggesting that interrelationships among demographic status, nutrition and disease, and prevailing modes of land use may be the key to explaining variability in population histories. The abandonment of the south-central lowlands in Terminal Classic times appears to be related to both increased mortality and emigration to neighboring areas, which may have been brought about by degradation of the agricultural landscape.

Methods of Population Estimation in the Maya Region

Archaeologists reconstruct the population history of a site or region by devising methods to measure properties of the archaeological record said to be responsive to the number of occupants. All the chapters in this volume deal with *archaeodemography:* the systematic study of estimating the number of people who lived in a structure, at a site, or in a region at one or more points in time in the past. The method Maya archaeodemographers employ to estimate past population size has three steps. First, time is compartmentalized into a series of discrete phases encompassing several hundred years of occupation, generally based on quantitative or qualitative changes in ceramics. Counts are then obtained for elements of the archaeological record assumed to be demographically sensitive, such as room number, platform size, or density of remains. These figures are subsequently multiplied by some estimate of modal population per entity or area per site to compute phase-specific population estimates. This operation is repeated for all phases represented in the sequence to produce a reconstruction of site or regional demographic history.

This method has some obvious shortcomings. One problem is the number of occupants per room, structure, or platform and the number of such features per unit area. Although much research relies heavily on a figure of 5.6 persons/residence, derived from ethnohistoric documents, studies in this volume demonstrate considerable variability, depending on the case example and the archaeologist's use of the documentary record, with the modal estimate per house often being much higher (Ringle and Andrews, this volume; McAnany, this volume). Another problem is the number of mounds that physically functioned as habitation structures. Work at Copan (Webster and Freter, this volume), Sayil (McAnany, this volume), and in the Peten (Ford 1986) implies that a much lower frequency of mounds were habitation structures than previously expected. This research suggests that at least 40 to 50% of all structures had functions other than residence and that population estimates based purely on house-mound counts ought to be decreased accordingly.

An even more serious problem is the distorting effect that differential phase duration has on the quantity of archaeological remains produced (Culbert 1988; Culbert et al., this volume). Basically, it is argued that the longer a site is occupied, the greater the number of house mounds or platforms there will be, especially in areas such as the Maya lowlands, where settlement patterns are dispersed and there is sufficient room to move residential structures as conditions dictate. According to Culbert (1988), a better way to compare phases of dramatically different length is to adjust the counts to a standard unit of time: for example, 100 years. Length of mound occupancy, then, is assumed to be constant from one phase to the next. Only unobtrusive house mounds and small platforms are standardized in this fashion, since larger structures show multiple renovations and a labor investment that indicates occupancy for longer periods of time. The effects of this adjustment on phase-specific house-mound counts are sometimes enormous (cf. Willey 1977 and Culbert 1988).

The work of Culbert et al. (this volume) raises an even more significant point: that of the episodic contemporaneity of remains, an issue also considered by other authors in this volume without much consensus other than to assume occupancy duration as a constant. For most archaeologists, contemporaneity refers to the coexistence of objects and elements. Materials found together in the archaeological record are used as a basis for making statements about properties of past systems. Archaeological context, however, is not the same as systemic context, which (following Schiffer [1972, 1976]) can produce serious errors in the magnitude of the population estimates so derived. A closer examination of the procedures Mesoamericanists employ and the assumptions commonly made illustrates how such a situation can come about.

As we have seen, population estimation in the Maya region involves the use of the three-step procedure described above. This method assumes that the number of entities in the universe under study is complete or that an adequate or representative sample of those entities has been obtained, a requirement that has been brought into question by recent work at Nohmul (Pyburn, this volume) and Pulltrouser Swamp. The net effect of this "invisible universe," as Harrison (personal communication 1987) terms it, is to increase the number of structures expected. It seems clear that the population estimates for Maya sites will most certainly also rise, an observation that dovetails nicely with the evidence for intensive land use.

More structures, unfortunately, do not always mean more population. Although there is a general positive relationship between structure density and population density, the relationship may exhibit different slopes and need not necessarily be linear in form. Many archaeologists working in Mesoamerica consider that sites with residential architecture (house mounds) and associated features such as hearths, storage pits, and refuse dumps were sedentary communities occupied on a year-round basis, often throughout all of the phase in question or throughout a constant fraction of it. Mayanists making this assumption ignore the fact that the mobility structure of human groups has obvious implications not only for the number of sites formed but also for the scale of the population estimates derived. Empirical studies have made clear that mobility is a property of human behavior on all levels of sociocultural integration. Two kinds of mobility options are important in this regard: site reoccupation and site reuse.

Reoccupation refers to the redundant use of space without spatial congruence in the location of residential sites (Brooks and Yellen 1987). Particular localities are frequently used for different purposes at different times, a pattern of differential serial use that should be reflected in the character of the assemblages of artifacts and features left at Maya sites and their spatial patterning. *Reuse,* on the other hand, occurs in situations "in which space is organized and used in a pattern which is spatially congruent with previous occupations of the same space" (Brooks and Yellen 1987:69). Often the pattern of reuse involves mobility systems that are residentially constrained or entrenched (M. Graham and Roberts 1986). Entrenched mobility is found in settlement systems in which residential moves are scheduled from point to point over a restricted land area during a seasonal round, with this pattern being repeated year after year (M. Graham 1986). Entrenchment may also take place in longer cycles, with localities occupied as residential sites for a generation or two and then abandoned for a decade or so. Populations return to residential sites because they have invested in facilities and technology left at that site in anticipation of future use.

Prevailing archaeological opinion holds that Classic Period Maya settlement patterns were dispersed, with land-use strategies involving the application of vast amounts of labor to maintain the food-production system, which apparently required that peasants live near agricultural holdings (Ashmore, ed., 1981). Dispersed occupation, however, is not the only settlement-subsistence arrangement in the humid tropics, nor is agriculture the only variable that determines settlement patterns. Residentially entrenched settlement patterns typically occur when there are incongruities in the factors determining residence. Different variables exerting effects on the farmer's behavior at different times and in different places require that he maintain structures at several locations. High-density zones in such systems would represent foci of settlement where elites, their immediate dependents, and craftspeople resided permanently but where farmers lived for only part of the year. Structures would also be erected near agricultural resources, would be used by the farmer and his family during the growing season or when agricultural activities were labor-intensive or required a large labor force, and then would be abandoned. Moreover, individual sites might be deserted on the death of the extended family head, a Postcolumbian Maya custom, or when insect infestations or other pests became particularly bothersome. Thus, it is quite conceivable that within an archaeological phase of 200 years a total of 10 to 15 structures might have been used and abandoned by the same coresidential group. Conventional survey techniques might show all these structures as "house mounds."

Work at Copan implies that some Maya settlement systems may have been organized in just this fashion (Webster and Freter, this volume). Rural settlement in the area around the main nucleus of occupation at Copan fits the pattern common in other parts of the southern lowlands; house mounds occur almost everywhere, although densities are the greatest on bottomlands along stream tracts and especially near the main ceremonial center. The excavation of a set of house-mound clusters in the vicinity of the main acropolis indicates that they were occupied by family groups of different rank; all kinds of domestic refuse are present, as well as great numbers of burials. The assemblages associated with structures in rural settings look quite different. Here domestic refuse is much less abundant and burials are not present, implying a categorically different kind of occupation. According to Sanders (personal communication 1988), many of these structures may have only been seasonally occupied by male cultivators who maintained residences within a few kilometers of the main acropolis. Late Classic Maya settlement in the Copan Valley consequently may have a densely settled core, the urban center per se, surrounded by a large rural hinterland that was occupied on a much more impermanent basis. I am not suggesting that all Maya settlement systems were organized in this fashion, only that we do not know that they were not.

The grossly inflationary effects of entrenchment and reoccupation on Maya house-mound counts should be obvious. If habitation structures went through an occupation/abandonment cycle but were consistently reused at the end of each cycle, house-mound counts would have to be reduced by a factor of 50% to estimate the number of buildings simultaneously occupied by families. Total counts might have to be reduced by a factor of 75 to 90% if structure use-life was short (e.g., 25 years) but the reuse cycle was comparatively long (e.g., 100–125 years). Entrenchment, with each coresidential group maintaining one or more field houses, would require a further 50 to 75% reduction to estimate the number of structures inhabited by family groups on a contemporaneous basis. Finer periodizations will not allow resolution of these problems, as most structure-occupation/abandonment cycles are probably well within the limits of the finest chronologies. Neither will the blanket application of a correction figure help us much, for the mobility requirements of a population are likely to change from one time period to the next if demographic growth occurs and subsistence strategies change.

Clearly, what is needed are investigations of the range of mobility options manifest in different systemic contexts, the conditions under which groups maintain or change their mobility strategies, the interrelationships between mobility patterns and agricultural land-use strategies, and the archaeological consequences of different mixes of mobility strategies in different settings, both urban and rural. Midrange research of this type has the potential of producing powerful methods for assigning meaning to the archaeological record. Only then can we have any confidence, even in a relative sense, in house-mound counts as a source of demographic information.

METHODS OF POPULATION ESTIMATION IN HIGHLAND MEXICO

Research on population history has a much longer history in highland Mesoamerica, particularly in the Basin of Mexico (Blanton 1972; Parsons 1971; Parsons et al. 1982; Sanders et al. 1979) and in the Valley of Oaxaca (Blanton 1978; Blanton et al. 1982; Feinman et al. 1985). Much of this research has employed occupational density as a measure of the number of persons inhabiting sites. Archaeodemographers who use this method assume that the amount of refuse discarded at a settlement varies in direct relation to site population. Twice as many persons deposit twice as much garbage, and if population density is twice as high, the density of surface remains, mainly pottery, is likely to be twice as high also. Variation in occupational density, which can be empirically measured in the field, is thus assumed to be primarily a function of variation in the density of population. Multicomponent sites must be dealt with separately. Here, phase-specific densities must be computed and the absolute densities adjusted based on the frequency of materials from different periods. The area over which different occupation densities are distributed is then calculated and population estimates derived.

Use of this method requires some assumptions about past systemic contexts and the character of the archaeological record in each. First, all time periods from which the materials derive must be of equal duration so that phase length has little impact on the amount of refuse discarded. Second, the method assumes little change in the generic composition of the ceramic assemblage from one time period to the next. In addition, postdepositional processes should not obscure surface deposits, causing underestimates, and specialized activities such as craft production should have little effect on the amount of refuse discarded.

Finally, garbage disposal must involve discard near residences. Refuse disposal, however, varies greatly from one situation to another. In general, the lower the population density, the greater the likelihood that there will be vacant space available for trash middens near the residence and the greater the probability that locations of tool use and tool discard will spatially coincide (J. Clark 1986; Hayden and Cannon 1983; Schiffer 1972, 1976). This seems to be the case on the Gulf Coast (Killion 1987; Santley et al. 1987) and in the Maya lowlands (Ashmore, ed. 1981; McAnany 1986), two regions where a dispersed settlement pattern prevails. Where there should be little spatial congruity between location of use and location of discard is at sites such as Teotihuacan, where structures were built directly adjacent to one another, with little intervening space (Gunnerson 1973; Niemczewski 1977). Consequently, until the interrelationships between type of occupation and refuse densities are worked out in more detail, it seems best to restrict application of this method to cases in which occupation is single-phase, short-term, and not deflated and there are independent archaeological and/or ethnohistoric controls on refuse disposal, specialized ceramic production, and population. In the Basin of Mexico these conditions are met only during the Late Aztec Period.

Roofed-over space is another variable that has been applied to measure population. Methods that use roofed-over space assume that changes in the size of a structure are primarily a function of variation in population size. The first study employing roofed-over space as an indicator of number of occupants was conducted by Naroll (1962), who concluded, after sampling largest settlements in 18 societies, that the population of a structure or site can be predicted as roughly one-tenth of the roofed-over space in square meters. Although this rule of thumb has been widely applied by archaeologists, subsequent research has demonstrated that it works best in egalitarian agricultural societies in which structures are occupied by single family units, where there is little intrahouse storage of goods and raw materials, and where most of the family's domestic activities occur outside the dwelling. In societies in which buildings are not divided into rooms but are occupied by multifamily units, the amount of roofed-over space averages about 6 m²/person (Casselberry 1974), whereas in contexts where there is a substantial amount of storage within buildings, including the penning of domestic animals overnight, the amount of per capita floor space varies from 8 to more than 24 m² and the standard deviations between family units are large (LeBlanc 1971). Settlements containing structures that share partition walls (e.g., room blocks in Southwest pueblos) support even larger numbers of persons per unit area (Hill 1970; Longacre 1976).

Differences in household status present additional variability. Archaeologists have long recognized the fact that elites living in large masonry structures probably had more space per capita than peasants occupying pole-and-thatch huts, but mode of house construction may not always be a useful indicator of household status. For example, at Loma Torremote, a Late Formative village in the Basin of Mexico, all houses were constructed of wattle and daub, with crushed tepetate floors (Santley 1977). Although dwelling size averaged about 35 m², some structures were much larger, implying a greater number of occupants. Since disposal of the dead involved interment under house floors or in the adjacent patios and all house compounds were occupied for more or less the same length of time (ca. 100 years), differences in the number of burials present might be used as a relative indicator of differences in the average number of inhabitants. Interestingly, the number of burials found in different house compounds was about the same, but the average area of floored-over space varied considerably, which indicated that differences in structure size could be attributed to status differentials, a conclusion supported by other lines of evidence. Larger structure size was also linked to a series of specialized activities such as centralized storage, group ritual, and obsidian working, which took place in different areas (rooms?) within the house.

It should be apparent that the relationships among the variables affecting structure size and refuse density still remain largely undefined. We need to know how other independent variables—for example, household activity structure or family status—condition the amount of roofed-over space required. I am in no way suggesting that Mesoamericanists should not worry about archaeodemography, but I do believe that the methods that archaeodemographers currently have at their disposal do not always produce very robust results. This inadequacy requires that archaeologists, Mayanists included, engage in research aimed at understanding the relationships among population, subsistence, mobility, and economic structure, and the kinds of archaeological residues generated in different socioeconomic contexts under different density regimes. As the chapters in this volume illustrate, Mayanists are beginning to make some strides in these directions, but there is still much to do.

THE ROAD AHEAD

What should the road ahead look like? Two research directions show great promise.

First, there should be more research on paleodemography: the study of human skeletal remains as a tool for deriving inferences about prehistoric demographic structure and the factors that influence or condition that structure. Demographers commonly use vital rates of birth and death as measures of the quality of life in contemporary societies. To describe the structure of a human population, demographers construct a life table, an analytic model that generates summary population statistics such as life expectancy, survivorship, and mortality rate (Acsadi and Nemeskeri 1970; Weiss 1973). Life tables may also be constructed using archaeological skeletal series, provided that burial patterns can be defined, members of both sexes and all age groups are represented, and the samples derive from short time periods (Angel 1971; Buikstra 1976; M. N. Cohen and Armelagos 1984; Sattenspiel and Harpending 1983; Ubelaker 1974).

Paleodemographic methods work best in situations in which the deceased was buried under or around the residential structure. Then the paleodemography of different coresidential groups can be defined in some detail and estimates of the average number of persons who lived in the structure derived (Sanders et al. 1979; Santley 1977). Population estimates for different residential groups cannot be computed using the life-table method of estimation in situations in which preservation or past cultural practices skew the sample and in which interment was in cemeteries, though in the latter case computations for sites might be obtained.

The skeletal remains can also supply useful information on paleopathology and paleonutritional status, which have known impacts on paleodemographic structure. The incidence and severity of paleopathologies such as transverse lines, dental hypoplasia, Wilson bands, dental antimere asymmetry, and such lesions as porotic hyperostosis and metacarpal notching allow definition of the amount of nutritional stress experienced by infants, children, and adolescents (El Najjar et al. 1976; Martin et al. 1985; Steinbock 1976). In adults nutritional stress affects stature, the frequency of dental caries and peridontal disease, calcifications, bone texture and curving, as well as other traits, which when taken together with those pathologies affecting younger cohorts, can provide a powerful explanatory framework accounting for variation in population structure and consequently group size (Buikstra and Mielke 1985; M. N. Cohen and Armelagos 1984; Rose et al. 1985).

Skeletal tissues also provide a record of general dietary history. Carbon isotope analysis can be used to establish various plant diets (Wing and Brown 1979). Photosynthesis in plants follows two main biochemical pathways: C_3 and C_4, which can be distinguished by their respective carbon isotope ratios ($^{13}C/^{14}C$) (Lerman and Troughton 1975). Maize is one of the foremost C_4 plants of economic importance whose presence and relative contribution to the diet is reflected in carbon isotope ratios (Vogel and van der Merwe 1977). More widely applied is trace element analysis (Brown 1973; Gilbert 1975; Schoeninger 1979). The amount of different trace elements present in human bone varies as a function of the kind of resource consumed, which permits the reconstruction of general dietary patterns. Of all the elements examined, strontium has been the most often used (Brown 1973; Schoeninger 1979; Szpunar 1977; Wing and Brown 1979; Gilbert 1985).

To my knowledge, techniques of physiochemical analysis have not been applied to skeletal samples from the Maya region, despite the fact that these procedures display tremendous potential for identifying dietary regimes and the effects differences in diet may have had on paleodemography. One problem for which such techniques may have direct relevance is the Classic Maya collapse. I suspect that demographic instability, influenced by declining health status, played a major causal role in the collapse (Santley et al. 1986). Peasant mortality probably increased throughout the Classic Period, especially for infants and females entering childbearing age but also for other age-sex groups as well. Elite life expectancy may have been somewhat better, though perhaps not by a significant margin by the end of the Late Classic. Coastal populations should have fared better because of access to marine and riverine resources and river levee lands.

Second, much work is needed on defining the interrelationships among rises in population density, agricultural intensification, and changes in socioeconomic complexity. The lack of genuine theory-building on this subject is appalling given the volume of literature. Why, for example, should population pressure produce any changes in the institutional fabric of society, or put another way, is there any causal relationship between increases in population density on the one hand and the advent of economic stratification, the rise of the state, and the development of civilization, let alone the characteristics of complex systems at later time periods, on the other?

Almost all work on this subject has followed the lead of Boserup (1965), who pointed out that the degree of intensification is a direct function of population density, at least in the humid tropics. Most archaeological research on this problem has been concerned with demonstrating that there is (or is not) a relationship among rising population density, agricultural intensification, and sociocultural complexity (Ball 1977a; Blanton et al. 1982; Harrison and Turner 1978; Webster 1977; Sanders and Webster 1978; B. Turner et al. 1977). Although Boserup does offer a series of speculations concerning interrelationships between mode of land use and tenure arrangements, she says very little about how intensification produces sociocultural complexity. As a result, it is difficult to have any confidence in theories of state development employing population pressure as a causal agent, because there is no theoretical calculus specifying the conditions that select for complexity given agricultural intensification, the dynamic linkages between variables assigned explanatory import, and the form emergent complex systems take.

Where do we go from here? Two areas of inquiry deserve more attention before there will be much progress in theory-building. First, we have virtually no information on village subsistence organization. Most of the literature on subsistence economies in Mesoamerica consists of descriptions of techniques of land use (Kirkby 1973; Sanders et al. 1979; Stadelman 1940; Steggerda 1941). It is still unclear how farmers organize their subsistence behavior when they have access to different types of land, the array and proportion of different cultigens planted when different land-use strategies are applied, the kinds of storage procedures implemented by individual cultivators and more inclusive village groupings, and the conditions responsible for each. For example, some systems, like the Inca, emphasized the control of large corvee labor forces that cultivated state lands and worked in industries producing goods used for sustaining and enhancing elite power and for redistribution to the populace at large in times of need (Conrad 1981). Other systems, like the Aztec, were supported primarily by tribute in luxury and subsistence goods (Berdan 1982; Hassig 1985). These differences in elite and state power bases probably had major impact on system economic organization. Research investigating the role of storage facilities at Maya sites is planned for the Puuc region (Tourtellot et al., this volume), but except for McAnany's recent work at Sayil (this volume), Mayanists have yet to address this question adequately as well as define its implications.

Another potentially productive line of research concerns the organization of human groups in aggregated environments. Most recent work on the development of complex society has adopted a regional approach emphasizing articulations between communities, but largely unrecognized is a rather substantial literature that suggests that the social dynamics responsible for increasing complexity occur *within* communities. In other words, larger-scale sociopolitical (and presumably economic) complexity is an emergent property of permanent aggregation at one place (Barth 1978; Carneiro 1967; Rapoport 1975; Specht 1973). According to Lekson (1984), the population threshold for complexity within a single settlement is surprisingly low: about 2500 people, based on modern cross-cultural research. If the patterning detected by Lekson is indeed a genuine response to aggregation, then it is likely that other properties of complexity represent an ordered adjustment to living at particular settlements. More work at the community level should allow us to evaluate the degree to which increasing complexity is a function of changing modes of local versus intercommunity articulation. Specification of how households, local kin groups or cooperatives, and villages structure their subsistence organization should give us a better understanding of the interrelationships among mode of production, population distribution, and sociocultural complexity.

A. OLD WORLD

China ————   Egypt - - - - - - -

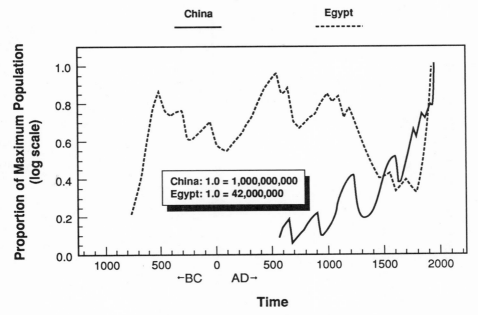

B. HIGHLAND MEXICO

Valley of Oaxaca ————   Basin of Mexico - - - - - - -

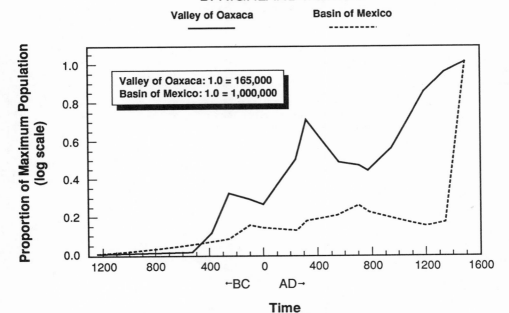

Figure 16.1   Demographic history of China, Egypt, and highland Mexico.

A. MAYA REGIONS

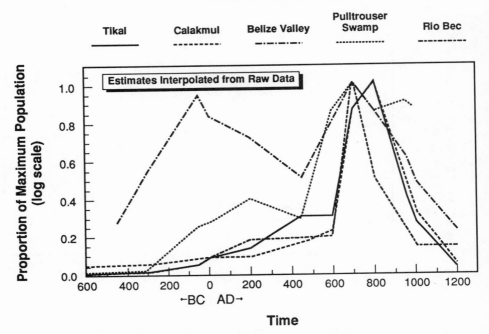

B. TIKAL CURVE FITTING

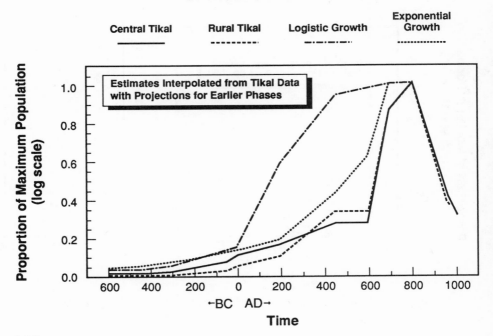

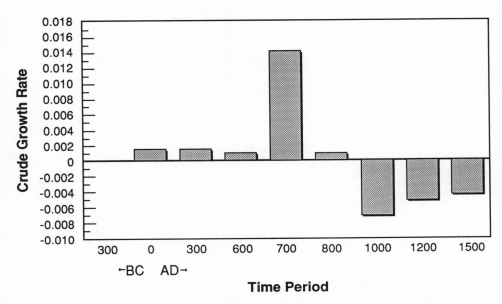

Figure 16.3   Crude growth rates for the south-central Maya lowlands.

◀Figure 16.2   Demographic history of various Maya sites.

Bibliography

ACSADI, G., AND J. NEMESKERI
1970   *History of Human Lifespan and Mortality.* Akademiai Kiado, Budapest.

ADAMS, R. E. W.
1971   *The Ceramics of Altar de Sacrificios, Guatemala.* Papers of the Peabody Museum of American Archaeology and Ethnology, vol. 63, no. 1. Harvard University, Cambridge.
1974   A Trial Estimation of Classic Maya Palace Population at Uaxactun. In *Meso-american Archaeology: New Approaches,* edited by N. Hammond, pp. 285–296. University of Texas Press, Austin.
1977a   Rio Bec Archaeology and the Rise of Maya Civilizaton. In *The Origins of Maya Civilization,* edited by R. E. W. Adams, pp. 77–99. University of New Mexico Press, Albuquerque.
1977b   *Prehistoric Mesoamerica.* Little, Brown, Boston.
1981   Settlement Patterns of the Central Yucatan and Southern Campeche Regions. In *Lowland Maya Settlement Patterns,* edited by W. Ashmore, pp. 211–258. University of New Mexico Press, Albuquerque.
1982   Rank Size Analysis of Northern Belize Maya Sites. In *The Archaeology of Colha, Belize: 1981 Interim Report,* edited by T. Hester, H. Shafer, and J. Eaton, pp. 60–64. Center for Archaeological Research, University of Texas at San Antonio, and Centro Studi e Richerche Ligabue, Venice.

ADAMS, R. E. W. (COMPILER)
1974   *Preliminary Reports on Archaeological Investigations in Rio Bec Area, Campeche, Mexico.* Middle American Research Institute, Publication 31, pp. 103–146. Tulane University, New Orleans.

ADAMS, R. E. W. (EDITOR)
1977   *The Origins of Maya Civilization.* University of New Mexico Press, Albuquerque.

ADAMS, R. E. W., W. E. BROWN, JR., AND T. P. CULBERT
1981   Radar Mapping, Archaeology, and Ancient Maya Land Use. *Science* 213:1457–1463.

ADAMS, R. E. W.,G. D. HALL, I. GRAHAM, F. VALDEZ, S. L. BLACK, D. POTTER, D. J.
CANNELL, AND B. CANNELL
1984   *Rio Azul Project Reports No. 1. Final 1983 Report.* Center for Archaeological Research, University of Texas at San Antonio.

ADAMS, R. E. W., AND R. C. JONES
1981   Spatial Patterns and Regional Growth among Classic Maya Cities. *American Antiquity* 46:301–32.

ADAMS, R. MCC.
1966   *The Evolution of Urban Society: Early Mesopotamia and Prehispanic Mesoamerica.* Aldine, Chicago.
1972   Demography and the Urban Revolution in Lowland Mesopotamia. In *Population Growth: Anthropological Implications,* edited by B. Spooner, pp. 60–63. MIT Press, Cambridge.
1981   *Heartland of Cities.* University of Chicago Press, Chicago.

ADAMS, R. MCC., AND H. J. NISSEN
1972   *The Uruk Countryside: The Natural Setting of Urban Societies.* University of Chicago Press, Chicago.

AMMERMAN, A. J.
1975   Late Pleistocene Population Alternatives. *Human Ecology* 3:219–33.

AMMERMAN, A. J., L. L. CAVALLI-SFORZA, AND D. K. WAGENER
1976   Toward the Estimation of Population Growth in Old World Prehistory. In *Demographic Anthropology,* edited by E. B. W. Zubrow, pp. 27–61. University of New Mexico Press, Albuquerque.

ANDERSON, A. H., AND H. J. COOK
1944   Archaeological Finds near Douglas, British Honduras. Carnegie Institution of Washington, Division of Historical Research. *Notes on Middle American Archaeology and Ethnology,* No. 40. Cambridge, Mass.

ANDREWS, A. P.
1983   *Maya Salt Production and Trade.* University of Arizona Press, Tucson.
1984   The Political Geography of Sixteenth-Century Yucatan Maya: Comments and Revisions. *Journal of Anthropological Research* 40:584–596.

ANDREWS, E. W., IV
1964   *Explorations in the Gruta de Chac, Yucatan, Mexico.* Middle American Research Institute, Publication 31, pp. 1–22. Tulane University, New Orleans.
1965   *Progress Report on the 1960–1964 Field Seasons, National Geographic Society–Tulane University Dzibilchaltun Program.* Middle American Research Institute, Publication 31, pp. 23–67. Tulane University, New Orleans.

ANDREWS, E. W., IV, AND E. W. ANDREWS V
1980   *Excavations at Dzibilchaltun, Yucatan, Mexico.* Middle American Research Institute, Publication 48. Tulane University, New Orleans.

ANDREWS, E. W., V
1981   Dzibilchaltun. In *Supplement to the Handbook of Middle American Indians,* vol. 1, *Archaeology,* edited by V. R. Bricker and J. A. Sabloff, pp. 313–341. University of Texas Press, Austin.
1986   Olmec Jades from Chacsinkin, Yucatan, and Maya Ceramics from La Venta, Tabasco. In *Research and Reflections in Archaeology and History: Essays in Honor of Doris Stone,* edited by E. W. Andrews V, pp. 11–49. Middle American Research Institute, Publication 57. Tulane University, New Orelans.
1990   The Early Ceramic History of the Lowland Maya. In *Vision and Revision in Maya Studies,* edited by F. Clancy and P. D. Harrison. University of New Mexico Press, Albuquerque, in press.

ANDREWS, E. W., V, AND N. HAMMOND
1990   Redefinition of the Swasey Phase at Cuello, Belize. *American Antiquity* 55, in press.

ANDREWS, E. W., V, W. M. RINGLE, P. J. BARNES, A. BARRERA RUBIO, AND T. GALLARETA NEGRÓN
1984   Komchen, an Early Maya Community in Northwest Yucatan. In *Investigaciones recientes en el area Maya,* vol. 1, pp. 73–92. XVII Mesa Redonda, Sociedad Mexicana de Antropologia. Mexico City.

ANDREWS, G. F.
1982   Puuc Architectural Styles: A Reassessment. Paper presented at Symposium on Northern Maya Lowlands: New Data, Syntheses, and Problems. Universidad Autónoma de México, Mexico City.
1985a   The Architectural Survey at Sayil: A Report on the 1985 Field Season. Ms. on file, Sayil Archaeological Project.
1985b   Chenes-Puuc Architecture: Chronology and Cultural Interaction. In *Arquitectura y Arqueología: Metodologías en la Cronología de Yucatán.* Centre d'Etudes Mexicaines et Centramericaines, Etudes Mesoamericaines Serie II, 8:10–39. Mexico City.

ANGEL, J. L.
1971   *The People of Lerna: Analysis of a Prehistoric Aegean Population.* Smithsonian Institution Press, Washington, D.C.

ARNOLD, J.E., AND A. FORD
1980   A Statistical Examination of Settlement Patterns at Tikal, Guatemala. *American Antiquity* 45:713–726.

ASHMORE, W.
1980   The Classic Maya Settlement at Quirigua. *Expedition* 23 (1): 20–27.
1981a   *Precolumbian Occupation at Quirigua, Guatemala: Settlement Patterns in a Classic Maya Center.* Unpublished Ph.D. dissertation, Department of Anthropology, University of Pennsylvania.
1981b   Some Issues of Method and Theory in Lowland Maya Settlement Archaeology. In *Lowland Maya Settlement Patterns,* edited by W. Ashmore, pp. 3–69. University of New Mexico Press, Albuquerque.

1984 Quirigua Archaeology and History Revisited. *Journal of Field Archaeology* 11:365–386.

1986 Peten Cosmology in the Maya Southeast: An Analysis of Architecture and Settlement Patterns at Classic Quirigua. In *The Southeast Maya Periphery,* edited by P. A. Urban and E. M. Schortman, pp. 35–49. University of Texas Press, Austin.

1988 Household and Community at Classic Quirigua. In *Household and Community in the Mesoamerican Past,* edited by R. R. Wilk and W. Ashmore, pp. 153–169. University of New Mexico Press, Albuquerque.

ASHMORE, W. (EDITOR)

1981 *Lowland Maya Settlement Patterns.* University of New Mexico Press, Albuquerque.

ASHMORE, W., AND G. R. WILLEY

1981 A Historical Introduction to the Study of Lowland Maya Settlement Patterns. In *Lowland Maya Settlement Patterns,* edited by W. Ashmore, pp. 3–18. University of New Mexico Press, Albuquerque.

BAKER, P. T., AND W. T. SANDERS

1972 Demographic Studies in Anthropology. *Annual Reviews of Anthropology* 1:151–178.

BALL, J. W.

1977a The Rise of the Northern Maya Chiefdoms: A Socioprocessual Analysis. In *The Origins of Maya Civilization,* edited by R. E. W. Adams, pp. 101–132. University of New Mexico Press, Albuquerque.

1977b *The Archaeological Ceramics of Becan, Campeche.* Middle American Research Institute, Publication 43. Tulane University, New Orleans.

1979 Ceramics, Culture History and the Puuc Tradition: Some Alternative Perspectives. In *The Puuc: New Perspectives,* edited by L. Mills, pp. 18–35. Scholarly Studies in the Liberal Arts, No. 1. Central College, Pella, Iowa.

1983 Typological Identification and Phasing of Ceramics from Terraced Sites. Appendix 4 of B. L. Turner II, *Once Beneath the Forest: Prehistoric Terracing in the Rio Bec Region of the Maya Lowlands.* Dellplain Latin American Studies, No. 13. Westview Press, Boulder.

1985 A Summary view. In *Arquitectura y arqueología: metodologías en la cronología de Yucatán.* Centre d'Etudes Mexicaines et Centramericaines, Etudes Mesoamericaines Series II, 8:85–88. Mexico City.

BALL, J. W., AND E. W. ANDREWS V

1978 *Preclassic Architecture at Becan, Campeche, Mexico.* Middle American Research Institute, Occasional Paper 3. Tulane University, New Orleans.

BARRERA RUBIO, A.

1982 Obras Hidráulicas en la region Puuc, Yucatán, México. Paper presented at Symposium on Northern Maya Lowlands: New Dates, Syntheses, and Problems. Universidad Autónoma de México, Mexico City.

BARRERA RUBIO, A., F. GARCÍA,. F. LLANES C., AND N. ALONZO T.

1983 Salvamento arqueológico y preservación arquitectónica en Sayil, Yucatán.

Boletín de la Escuela de Ciéncias Antropológicas de la Universidad de Yucatán 63:21–30.

BARTH, F. (EDITOR)
1978 *Scale and Social Relations.* Universitetsflorlaget, Oslo.

BAUDEZ, C.
1983 *Introducción a la arquelogía de Copán, Honduras, tomos I–III.* Secretaria de Estado en el Despacho de Cultura y Turismo, Tegucigalpa, Honduras.

BENEDICT, F. G., AND M. STEGGERDA
1936 The Food of the Present-day Maya Indians of Yucatan. *Carnegie Institution of Washington,* Publication 456:155–188.

BERDAN, F. E.
1982 *The Aztecs of Central Mexico: An Imperial Society.* Holt, Rinehart and Winston, New York.

BERRY, B. J. L.
1961 City Size Distributions and Economic Development. *Economic Development and Cultural Change* 9:573–588.

BINFORD, M.
1983 Paleolimnology of the Peten Lake District, Guatemala. I. Erosion and Deposition of Inorganic Sediment as Inferred from Granulometry. *Hydrobiologia* 103:199–203.

BLANTON, R.
1972 *Prehispanic Settlement Patterns of the Ixtapalapa Region, Mexico.* Occasional Papers in Anthropology 6, Department of Anthropology, Pennsylvania State University, University Park.
1978 *Monte Alban: Settlement Patterns at the Zapotec Capital.* Academic Press, New York.

BLANTON, R., S. KOWALEWSKI, G. FEINMAN, AND J. APPEL
1982 *Monte Alban's Hinterland, Part I: Prehispanic Settlement Patterns of the Central and Southern Part of the Valley of Oaxaca, Mexico.* Memoir of the Museum of Anthropology, 15. University of Michigan, Ann Arbor.

BOSERUP, E.
1965 *The Conditions of Agricultural Growth.* Aldine, Chicago.

BOUCHER, S.
1984 Análisis del material cerámico del Proyecto Sayil, Yucatán: Temporada 1984. Ms. on file, Sayil Archaeological Project.

BRAIDWOOD, R., AND C. REED
1957 The Achievement and Early Consequences of Food-Production: A Consideration of the Archaeological and Natural-History Evidence. *Cold Spring Harbor Symposia on Quantitative Biology* 22:19–31.

BRAINERD, G. W.
1954 *The Maya Civilization.* Southwest Museum, Los Angeles.

1956   Changing Living Patterns of the Yucatecan Maya. *American Antiquity* 22:162–164.

1958   *The Archaeological Ceramics of Yucatan.* University of California Anthropological Records, vol. 19. Berkeley and Los Angeles.

BRONSON, B.

1968   Vacant Terrain. Ms. on file, University Museum, University of Pennsylvania.

1975   The Earliest Farming: Demography as Cause and Consequence. In *Population, Ecology, and Social Evolution,* edited by S. Polgar, pp. 53–78. Mouton, the Hague.

BROOKS, A. S., AND J. E. YELLEN

1987   The Preservation of Activity Areas in the Archaeological Work in Northwest Ngamiland, Botswana. In *Method and Theory in Activity Area Research: An Ethnoarchaeological Approach,* edited by S. Kent, pp. 64–106. Columbia University Press, New York.

BROWN, A. B.

1973   *Bone Strontium as a Dietary Indicator in Human Skeletal Populations.* Unpublished Ph.D. dissertation, University of Michigan, Ann Arbor.

BRUSH, S.

1975   The Concept of Carrying Capacity for Systems of Shifting Cultivation. *American Anthropologist* 77:799–811.

BUIKSTRA, J. E.

1976   *Hopewell in the Lower Illionis Valley: A Regional Approach to the Study of Human Biological Variability and Prehistoric Mortuary Behavior.* Northwestern Archaeological Program, Scientific Papers 2. Evanston, Ill.

BUIKSTRA, J. E., AND J. H. MIELKE

1985 Demography, Diet, and Health. In *The Analysis of Prehistoric Diets,* edited by R. I. Gilbert and J. H. Mielke, pp. 360–422. Academic Press, New York.

BULLARD, M. R., AND R. J. SHARER

1988   The Ceramics of Quirigua. Ms. on file, American Section, University Museum, University of Pennsylvania, Philadelphia.

BULLARD, W. R., Jr.

1960   Maya Settlement Patterns in Northeastern Peten, Guatemala. *American Antiquity* 25:355–372.

1970   Topoxte: A Postclassic Maya Site in Peten, Guatemala. In *Monograph and Papers in Maya Archaeology,* edited by W. R. Bullard, Jr. Papers of the Peabody Museum of American Archaeology and Ethnology, vol. 61, pp. 245–308. Harvard University, Cambridge.

BURGHARDT, A.

1959   The Location of River Towns in the Central Lowland United States. *Annals of the Association of American Geographers* 49:305–323.

CALNEK, E. E.

1972   Settlement Patterns and Chinampa Agriculture at Tenochtitlan. *American Antiquity* 37:104–115.

CARNEIRO, R. L.
1967 On the Relationship between Size of Population and Complexity of Social Organization. *Southwestern Journal of Anthropology* 23:234–242.
1970 A Theory of the Origin of the State. *Science* 169:733–738.

CARNERIO, R. L., AND R. HILSE
1966 On Determining the Probable Rate of Population Growth during the Neolithic. *American Anthropologist* 68:177–181.

CARR, R. F., AND J. E. HAZARD
1961 *Map of the Ruins of Tikal, El Peten, Guatemala.* Tikal Reports, No. 11, University Museum Monograph, University Museum, University of Pennsylvania, Philadelphia.

CASSELBERRY, S. E.
1974 Further Refinement of Formulae for Determining Population from Floor Area. *World Archaeology* 6:117–122.

CHASE, A. F.
1979 Regional Development in the Tayasal-Paxcaman Zone, El Peten, Guatemala: A Preliminary Statement. *Cerámica de Cultura Maya* 11:86–119.
1983 *A Contextual Consideration of the Tayasal-Paxcaman Zone, El Peten, Guatelama.* Unpublished Ph.D. dissertation, Department of Anthropology, University of Pennsylvania, Philadelphia.
1985a Postclassic Peten Interaction Spheres: The View from Tayasal. In *The Lowland Maya Postclassic,* edited by A. Chase and P. Rice, pp. 184–205. University of Texas Press, Austin.
1985b Archaeology in the Maya Heartland: The Tayasal-Paxcaman Zone, Lake Peten, Guatemala. *Archaeology* 38(1):32–39.
1986 Time Depth or Vacuum: The 11.3.0.0.0 Correlation and the Lowland Maya Postclassic. In *Late Lowland Maya Civilization: Classic to Postlcassic,* edited by J. A. Sabloff and E. W. Andrews V, pp. 99–140. University of New Mexico Press, Albuquerque.

CHASE, A. F., AND D. Z. CHASE
1983 *La cerámica de la zona Tayasal-Paxcamán, Lago Petén Itzá, Guatemala.* Privately bound and distributed by the University Museum, University of Pennsylvania, Philadelphia.
1985 Postclassic Temporal and Spatial Frames for the Lowland Maya: A Background. In *The Lowland Maya Postclassic,* edited by A. F. Chase and P. M. Rice, pp. 9–22. University of Texas Press, Austin.
1987a *Glimmers of a Forgotten Realm: Maya Archaeology at Caracol, Belize.* University of Central Florida, Orlando.
1987b *Investigations at the Classic Maya City of Caracol, Belize: 1985–1987.* Precolumbian Art Research Institute Monograph 3. San Francisco.
1987c Putting Together the Pieces: Maya Pottery of Northern Belize and Central Peten, Guatemala. In *Maya Ceramics,* edited by P. M. Rice and R. J. Sharer, pp. 47–72. British Archaeological Reports International Series 345(i). Oxford.

CHASE, A., AND P. RICE (EDITORS)
1985   *The Lowland Maya Postclassic: Questions and Answers.* University of Texas Press, Austin.

CHASE, D. Z.
1981   The Maya Postclassic at Santa Rita Corozal. *Archaeology* 34(1):25–33.
1982   *Spatial and Temporal Variability in Postclassic Northern Belize.* Unpublished Ph.D. dissertation, Department of Anthropology, University of Pennsylvania, Philadelphia.
1985   Ganned but Not Forgotten: Late Postclassic Archaeology and Ritual at Santa Rita Corozal, Belize. In *The Lowland Maya Postclassic,* edited by A. F. Chase and P. M. Rice, pp. 104–125. University of Texas Press, Austin.
1986   Social and Political Organization in the Land of Cacao and Honey: Correlating the Archaeology and Ethnohistory of the Postclassic Lowland Maya. In *Late Lowland Maya Civilization: Classic to Postclassic,* edited by J. A. Sabloff and E. W. Andrews V, pp. 347–377. University of New Mexico Press, Albuquerque.

CHASE, D. Z., AND A. F. CHASE
1982   Yucatec Influence in Terminal Classic Northern Belize. *American Antiquity* 47:596–614.
1986a *Offerings to the Gods: Maya Archaeology at Santa Rita Corozal.* University of Central Florida, Orlando.
1986b Archaeological Insights on the Contact Period Lowland Maya. In *Los Mayas de tiempos tardios,* edited by M. Rivera and A. Ciudad, pp. 13–50. Sociedad Española de Estudios Mayas y Instituto de Cooperación Iberoamericana, Madrid.
1988   *A Postclassic Perspective: Excavation at the Maya Site of Santa Rita Corozal, Belize.* Precolumbian Art Research Institute Monograph 4. San Francisco.

CHASE, D. Z., A. F. CHASE, AND W. A. HAVILAND
1990   The Classic Maya City: Reconsidering "The Mesoamerican Urban Tradition." *American Anthropologist* 92, in press.

CHASE, D. Z., AND N. HAMMOND
1982   Excavation of Nohmul Structure 20. *Mexicon* 4(1):7–12.

CHEEK, C.
1982   *Excavations in Group 3, Copan, Honduras.* Submitted to the Instituto Hondureño de Antropología e Historia, Tegucigalpa, Honduras.

CLARK, C., AND M. HASWELL
1964   *The Economics of Subsistence.* Macmillan, London.

CLARK, J. E.
1986   From Mountains to Molehills: A Critical Review of Teotihuacan's Obsidian Industry. In *Economic Aspects of Prehispanic Highland Mexico,* edited by B. L. Isaac, pp. 23–74. Research in Economic Anthropology Supplement 2. JAI Press, Greenwich, Connecticut.

CLARKSON, L. A.
1971   *The Pre-Industrial Economy in England, 1500–1750.* B. T. Batsford, London.

CLIFF, M.
1982   *Lowland Maya Nucleation: A Case Study from Northern Belize.* Unpublished Ph.D. dissertation, Southern Methodist University, Dallas.

COE, W.
1965   Tikal: Ten Years of Study of a Maya Ruin in Lowland Guatemala. *Expedition* 8(1):5–56.
1967   *Tikal: A Handbook of the Ancient Maya Ruins.* University Museum, University of Pennsylvania, Philadelphia.

COE, W. R., AND W. A. HAVILAND
1966   Review of *Prehistoric Maya Settlements in the Belize Valley,* by G. R. Willey, W. R. Bullard, Jr., P. Glass, and J. C. Gifford. *American Journal of Archaeology* 70:309–311.
1982   *Introduction to the Archaeology of Tikal, Guatemala.* Tikal Reports, No. 12, University Museum Monograph 46. University of Pennsylvania, Philadelphia.

COGOLLUDO, D. L. DE
1842–   *Los tres siglos de la dominación española en Yucatán o sea historia de esta*
  45   *provincia.* Campeche-merida.

COHEN, M. N.
1975   Archaeological Evidence for Population Pressure in Pre-agricultural Societies. *American Antiquity* 40:471–475.
1977   *The Food Crisis in Prehistory: Overpopulation and the Origins of Agriculture.* Yale University Press, New Haven.

COHEN, M. N., AND G. J. ARMELAGOS (EDITORS)
1984   *Paleopathology at the Origins of Agriculture.* Academic Press, Orlando.

COHEN, S.
1986   1 × 1's or 2 × 2's: A View from the Pits. Ms. on file with the author.

CONRAD, G. W.
1981   Cultural Materialism, Split Inheritance, and the Expansion of Ancient Peruvian Empires. *American Antiquity* 46:3–26.

COOK, E.
1972   Energy for Millennium Three. *Technology Review* 75:16–23.

COOK, S. F.
1972   *Prehistoric Demography.* McCaleb Module in Anthropology. Addison Wesley Modular Publications, Reading, Pa.

COOK, S. F., AND W. BORAH
1960   The Indian Population of Central Mexico, 1531–1610. *Ibero-Americana* 44. University of California Press, Berkeley.

1974 *Essays in Population History: Mexico and the Caribbean.* University of California Press, Berkeley.

CORDY, R. M.
1986 Relationships between the Extent of Social Stratification and Population in Micronesian Polities at European Contact. *American Anthropologist* 88:136–142.

COWGILL, G.
1963 *Postclassic Period Culture in the Vicinity of Flores, Peten, Guatemala.* Unpublished Ph.D. dissertation, Harvard University, Cambridge.
1975a On Causes and Consequences of Ancient and Modern Population Changes. *American Anthropologist* 77:505–525.
1975b Population Pressures as Non-Explanation. In *Population Studies in Archaeology and Biological Anthropology: A Symposium,* edited by A. C. Swedlund. *Memoirs of the Society for American Archaeology* 30:127–131.

COWGILL, U.
1962 An Agricultural Study of the Southern Maya Lowlands. *American Anthropologist* 64:273–286.

COWGILL, U., AND G. E. HUTCHINSON
1966 The Chemical History of Laguna de Petenxil. *Memoirs of the Connecticut Academy of Arts and Sciences* 17:121–260.

CULBERT, T. P.
1973 The Downfall at Tikal. In *The Classic Maya Collapse,* edited by T. P. Culbert, pp. 63–92. University of New Mexico Press, Albuquerque.
1977 Early Maya Development at Tikal, Guatemala. In *The Origins of Maya Civilization,* edited by R. E. W. Adams, pp. 27–43. University of New Mexico Press, Albuquerque.
1988 The Collapse of Classic Maya Civilization. In *The Collapse of Ancient States and Civilizations,* edited by N. Yoffee and G. Cowgill, pp. 69–101. University of Arizona Press, Tucson.
1989 Polities in the Northeast Peten, Guatemala. In *Classic Maya Political History: Hieroglyphic and Archaeological Evidence,* edited by T. P. Culbert, Cambridge University Press, Cambridge, in press.

CULBERT, T. P. (EDITOR)
1973 *The Classic Maya Collapse.* University of New Mexico Press, Albuquerque.
1989 *Classic Maya Political History: Hieroglyphic and Archaeological Evidence.* Cambridge University Press, Cambridge, in press.

CULBERT, T. P., AND L. J. KOSAKOWSKY
1985 The Demography of Central Tikal. Paper presented at the 50th Annual Meeting of the Society for American Archaeology, Denver.

DAHLIN, B. H.
1977 The Initiation of the Albion Island Settlement Pattern Survey. In *The Rio Hondo Project and Investigation of the Maya of Northern Belize. Journal of Belizean Affairs* 5.

1979   Cropping Cash in the Protoclassic: A Cultural Impact Statement. In *Maya Archaeology and Ethnohistory,* edited by N. Hammond and G. R. Willey, pp. 21–37. University of Texas Press, Austin.

1983   Climate and Prehistory on the Yucatan Peninsula. *Climatic Change* 5:245–263.

1984   A Colossus in Guatemala: The Preclassic Maya City of El Mirador. *Archaeology* 37(5):18–25.

DAHLIN, B. H., J. E. FOSS, AND M. E. CHAMBERS
1980   Project Acalches. In *El Mirador, Peten, Guatemala: An Interim Report,* edited by T. Matheny, pp. 37–58. Papers of the New World Archaeological Foundation, No. 45. Brigham Young University, Provo, Utah.

DAHLIN, B., R. QUIZAR, AND A. DAHLIN
1987   Linguistic Divergence and the Collapse of Preclassic Maya Civilization. *American Antiquity* 52:367–382.

DAVIES, N.
1980   *The Toltec Heritage: From the Fall of Tula to the Rise of Tenochtitlan.* University of Oklahoma Press, Norman.

DEBLOOIS, E. I.
1970   Archaeological Researches in Northern Campeche. Ms. on file, Department of Sociology and Anthropology, Weber State College.

DEEVEY, E. S.
1978   Holocene Forests and Maya Disturbance near Quexil Lake, Peten, Guatemala. *Polskie Archivum Hydrobiologii* 25:117–129.

1984   Stress, Strain, and Stability of Lacustrine Ecosystems. In *Lake Sediments and Environmental History,* edited by E. Hayworth and J. Lund, pp. 203–229. Leicester University Press, Leicester.

DEEVEY, E. S., M. BRENNER, AND M. BINFORD
1983   Paleolimnology of the Peten Lake District, Guatemala. III. Late Pleistocene and Gamblian Environments of the Maya Area. *Hydrobiologia* 103:211–216.

DEEVEY,. E. S., M. BRENNER, M. FLANNERY, AND G. H. YEZDANDI
1980   Lakes Yaxha and Sacnab, Peten, Guatemala: Limnology and Hydrology. *Polskie Archivum Hydrobiologii,* Supplement 57:419–460.

DEEVEY, E. S., AND D. S. RICE
1980   Coluviación y retención de nutrimentos en el distrito lacustre del Petén Central, Guatemala. *Biotica* 5:129–44.

DEEVEY, E. S., D. S. RICE, P. M. RICE, H. VAUGHAN, M. BRENNER, AND M. FLANNERY
1979   Maya Urbanism: Impact on a Tropical Karst Environment. *Science* 206:298–306.

DENEVAN, W. M.
1976   *The Native Population of the Americas in 1492.* University of Wisconsin Press, Madison.

DICKSON, D. B.
1975   Settlement Pattern Stability and Change in the Middle Northern Rio Grande Region, New Mexico: A Test of Some Hypotheses. *American Antiquity* 40:159–171.

DOBYNS, H.
1966   Estimating Aboriginal American Population: An Appraisal of Techniques with a New Hemispheric Estimate. *Current Anthropology* 7:395–416.

DUNNING, N. P.
1988   The Catchment Area of Sayil and Its Carrying Capacity. In *Archaeological Investigations at Sayil, Yucatan, Mexico: Phase II, the 1987 Field Season.* University of Pittsburgh Anthropological Papers, No. 2. Pittsburgh, in press.

DUPAQUIER, J.
1974   *Introduction a la demographie historique.* Gamma, Paris.

DURKHEIM, E.
1893   *Division of Labor in Society.* Translated by G. Simpson. Free Press, New York.

EATON, J. D.
1975   Ancient Agricultural Farmsteads in the Rio Bec Region of Yucatan. *Contributions of the University of California Archaeological Research Facility* 27:56–82.

EATON, J. D., AND J. W. BALL
1978   *Studies in the Archaeology of Coastal Yucatan and Campeche, Mexico.* Middle American Research Institute, Publication 46. Tulane University, New Orleans.

EL NAJJAR, M. Y., D. J. RYAN, C. G. TURNER II, AND B. LOZOFF
1976   The Etiology of Porotic Hyperositosis among Prehistoric and Historic Anasazi Indians of Southwestern United States. *American Journal of Physical Anthropology* 44:477–488.

EMERSON, R. A.
1935   A Preliminary Survey of the Milpa System of Maize Culture as Practiced by the Maya Indians of the Northern Part of the Yucatan Peninsula. Ms. on file, Cornell University.

ERASMUS, C.
1965   Monument Building: Some Field Experiments. *Southwestern Journal of Anthropology* 21:277–301.

EVERSLEY, D. E. C.
1965   A Survey of Population in an Area of Worcestershire from 1660–1850 on the Basis of Parish Registers. In *Population in History: Essays in Historical Demography,* edited by D. V. Glass and D. E. C. Eversley, pp. 394–419. Arnold, London.

FARRISS, N.
1985   *Maya Society under Colonial Rule: The Collective Enterprise of Survival.* Princeton University Press, Princeton.

FASH, W. L.
1977   The Rank Ordering of Maya Centers: A Review and Case Study. Ms. on file at Tozzer Library, Harvard University.
1983a   *Maya State Formation: A Case Study and Its Implications.* Unpublished Ph.D. dissertation, Department of Anthropology, Harvard University, Cambridge.
1983b   Deducing Social Organization from Classic Maya Settlement Patterns. In *Civilizations in the Ancient Americas,* edited by R. M. Leventhal and A. L. Kolata, pp. 261–288. University of New Mexico Press, Albuquerque.
1989   Sociopolitical Evolution in Copan: Correlations and Contradictions in the Material and State Records. Paper presented at the 88th Annual Meeting of the American Anthropological Association, Washington, D.C.

FEDICK, S. L.
1985   Prehistoric Maya Land Use Patterns in the Upper Belize Valley. Paper presented at the 50th Annual Meeting of the Society for American Archaeology, Denver.
1989   The Economics of Agricultural Land Use and Settlement in the Upper Belize River Valley. In *Prehistoric Maya Economies of Northern Belize,* edited by P. McAnany and B. Isaac, pp. 215–253. Research in Economic Anthropology Supplement 4. University Press of America, Lanham, Maryland.

FEINMAN, G. M., S. A. KOWALEWSKI, L. FINSTEN, R. E. BLANTON,. AND L. NICHOLAS
1985   Long-term Demographic Change: A perspective from the Valley of Oaxaca, Mexico. *Journal of Field Archaeology* 12:333–362.

FERRING, C. R.
1986   Rate of Fluvial Sedimentation: Implications for Archaeological Variability. *Geoarchaeology* 1:259–274.

FISH, S., P. FISH, AND J. MADSEN
1987   Perception and Scale in the Evaluation of Dispersed Phenomena. Paper presented at the 52nd Annual Meeting of the Society for American Archaeology, Toronto.

FLANNERY, K. V. (EDITOR)
1976   *The Early Mesoamerican Village.* Academic Press, New York.
1982   *Maya Subsistence: Studies in Memory of Dennis E. Puleston.* Academic Press, New York.

FOGEL, I. L.
1988   Report on Geomorphological Studies in the Vicinity of Quirigua. Ms. in preparation, American Section, University Museum, University of Pennsylvania, Philadelphia.

FOLAN, W. J.
1969   Dzibilchaltun, Yucatan, Mexico: Structures 384, 385, and 386: A Preliminary Interpretation. *American Antiquity* 34:434–461.

FOLAN, W. J., J. GUNN, J. D. EATON, AND R. W. PATCH
1983   Paleoclimatological Patterning in Southern Mesoamerica. *Journal of Field Archaeology* 10:453–468.

FOLAN, W. J., E. R. KINTZ, AND L. A. FLETCHER
1983   *Coba, a Classic Maya Metropolis.* Academic Press, New York.

FORD, A.
1981   *Conditions for the Evolution of Complex Societies: The Development of the Southern Maya Lowlands.* Unpublished Ph.D. dissertation, University of California, Santa Barbara.
1982   Los Mayas en El Petén: Distribución de las poblaciones en el Periodo Clásico. *Mesoamerica* 3:124–144.
1986   *Population Growth and Social Complexity: An Examination of Settlement and Environment in the Central Maya Lowlands.* Anthropological Research Paper No. 35. Arizona State University, Tempe.

FORD, A., AND J. E. ARNOLD
1982   A Reexamination of Labor Investments at Tikal: A Reply to Haviland and Folan et al. *American Antiquity* 47:436–440.

FORD, A., AND K. OLSON
1989   Aspects of Ancient Maya Household Economy: Variation in Chipped Stone Production and Consumption. In *Prehistoric Maya Economies of Northern Belize,* edited by P. McAnany and B. Isaac, pp. 185–214. Research in Economic Anthropology Supplement 4. University Press of America, Lanham, Maryland.

FREIDEL, D. A.
1978   Maritime Adaptation and the Rise of Maya Civilization: The View from Cerros, Belize. In *Prehistoric Coastal Adaptations: The Economy and Ecology of Maritime Middle America,* edited by B. L. Stark and B. Voorhies, pp. 239–265. Academic Press, New York.
1979   Culture Areas and Interaction Spheres: Contrasting Approaches to the Emergence of Civiliation in the Maya Lowlands. *American Antiquity* 44:36–54.

FREIDEL, D. A., R. ROBERTSON, AND M. CLIFF
1982   The Maya City of Cerros. *Archaeology* 35(4):12–21.

FREIDEL, D. A., AND J. A. SABLOFF
1984   *Cozumel: Late Maya Settlement Patterns.* Academic Press, New York.

FRETER, A. C.
1988   *The Classic Maya Collapse at Copan, Honduras: A Regional Settlement Perspective.* Unpublished Ph.D. dissertation, Department of Anthropology, Pennsylvania State University, University Park.

FRIED, M.
1967   *The Evolution of Political Society: An Essay in Political Anthropology.* Random House, New York.

FRY, ROBERT E.
1969   *Ceramics and Settlement in the Periphery of Tikal, Guatemala.* Unpublished Ph.D. dissertation, Department of Anthropology, Unversity of Arizona, Tucson.
1970   Trading Systems and the Lowland Maya Collapse. Paper presented at the 35th Annual Meeting of the Society for American Archaeology, Mexico City.
1972   Manually Operated Posthole Diggers as Sampling Instruments. *American Antiquity* 37:259–261.
1974   Settlement Systems in Southern Quintana Roo, Mexico. Paper presented at the XLI Congreso Internacional de Americanistas, Mexico City.
1979   The Economics of Pottery at Tikal, Guatemala: Models of Exchange for Serving Vessels. *American Antiquity* 44:494–512.
1983   The Ceramics of the Pulltrouser Area: Settlements and Fields. In *Pulltrouser Swamp: Ancient Maya Habitat, Agriculture and Settlement in Northern Belize,* edited by B. L. Turner II and P. D. Harrison, pp. 194–211. University of Texas Press, Austin.
1989   Regional Ceramic Distribution Patterning in Northern Belize: The View from Pulltrouser Swamp. In *Prehistoric Maya Economies of Northern Belize,* edited by P. McAnany and B. L. Isaac, pp. 91–111. Research in Economic Anthropology Supplement 4. University Press of America, Lanham, Maryland.

GALLARETA NEGRÓN, T.
1984   *Cobá: Forma y función de una comunidad Maya prehispanica.* Unpublished Tesis profesional, Universidad de Yucatán, Mérida.

GANN, T.
1897   On the Contents of Some Ancient Mounds in Central America. *Proceedings of the Society of Antiquaries of London, 2d Series* 16:308–317.
1900   Mounds in Northern Honduras. *Nineteenth Annual Report, 1897–1898, Bureau of American Ethnology,* part 2, pp. 661–692. Washington,D.C.
1918   *The Maya Indians of Southern Yucatan and Northern British Honduras.* Bureau of American Ethnology, Bulletin No. 64. Washington, D.C.

GANN, T., AND M. GANN
1939   *Archaeological Investigations in the Corozal District of British Honduras.* Bureau of American Ethnology, Bulletin No. 123. Washington, D.C.

DE LA GARZA, M., A. L. IZQUIERDO, M. DEL CARMEN LEÓN, AND T. FIGUERÓA
1983   *Relaciones histórico-geográficas de la gobernación de Yucatán (Mérida, Valladolid y Tabasco).* 2 vols. Universidad Nacional Autónoma de México, Mexico City.

GARZA TARAZONA DE GONZÁLEZ, S., AND EDWARD B. KURJACK
1980   *Atlas arqueológico del estado de Yucatán.* 2 vols. Instituto Nacional de Antropología e Historia, Centro Regional del Sureste. Mexico City.

1981   El medio ambiente y los asentamientos mayas en época prehispánica. In *Memoria del Congreso Interno 1979.* Instituto Nacional de Antropología e Historía, Centro Regional del Sureste. Mexico City.

GERHARD, P.
1979   *The Southeast Frontier of New Spain.* Princeton University Press, Princeton.

GIFFORD, J.
1976   *Prehistoric Pottery Analysis and Ceramics of Barton Ramie in the Belize Valley.* Memoirs of the Peabody Museum of American Archaeology and Ethnology, vol. 18. Harvard University, Cambridge.

GILBERT, R. I.
1975   *Trace Element Analyses of Three Skeletal Amerindian Populations at Dickson Mounds.* Unpublished Ph.D. dissertation, University of Massachusetts, Amherst.
1985   Stress, Paleonutrition, and Trace Elements. In *The Analysis of Prehistoric Diets,* edited by R. I. Gilbert and J. H. Mielke, pp. 339–358. American Press, New York.

GLIESSMAN, S. R., B. L. TURNER, F. J. ROSADO MAY, AND M. F. AMADOR
1985   Ancient Raised-Field Agriculture in the Maya Lowlands of Southern Mexico. In *Drained Field Agriculture in Central and South America,* edited by J. P. Darch, pp. 91–110. British Archaeological Reports International Series 189. Oxford.

GONZÁLEZ, F. BALTAZAR
1981   Depósitos subterraneos en Uxmal, Yucatán. In *Memoria del Congreso Interno, 1979,* pp. 203–210. Instituto Nacional de Antropología e Historia, Centro Regional del Sureste, Mexico City.

GORDON, G. B.
1896   *Prehistoric Ruins of Copan, Honduras.* Memoirs of the Peabody Museum of American Archaeology and Ethnology, vol. 1, no. 1. Harvard University, Cambridge.

GOVERNMENT INFORMATION SERVICES
1983   *Belize Fact Sheet.* Government Information Services Publication, Belize.

GRAHAM, I.
1967   *Archaeological Explorations in El Peten, Guatemala.* Middle American Research Institute, Publication 33. Tulane University, New Orleans.

GRAHAM, M.
1986   *Tarahumara Mobility and Residence: An Ethnoarchaeological Study of Settlement.* Proposal to the National Science Foundation. Department of Anthropology, University of New Mexico, Albuquerque.

GRAHAM, M., AND A. ROBERTS
1986   Residentially Constrained Mobility: A Preliminary Investigation of Variation in Settlement Organization. *Haliksa'i: University of New Mexico Contributions to Anthropology* 5:104–115.

GRAUNT, J.

1975　*Natural and Political Observations Mentioned in a Following Index and Made Upon the Bills of Mortality.* Reprinted. Arno Press, New York. Originally published 1662.

GREEN, E.

1970　*The Archaeology of Navajuelal, Guatemala.* Unpublished Ph.D. dissertation, Department of Anthropology, University of Pennsylvania, Philadelphia.

1973　Location Analysis of Prehistoric Maya Sites in Northern British Honduras. *American Antiquity* 38:279–293.

GUNNERSON, C. G.

1973　Accumulation of Debris in Cities. *Journal of the Environmental Engineering Divison (ASCE)* 99:229–243.

HAAS, J.

1984　*The Evolution of the Prehistoric State.* Columbia University Press, New York.

HABERLAND., W.

1983　To Quench the Thirst: Water and Settlement in Central America. In *Prehistoric Settlement Patterns: Essays in Honor of Gordon R. Willey,* edited by E. Z. Vogt and R. M. Leventhal, pp. 78–88. University of New Mexico Press, Albuquerque.

HAINLINE-UNDERWOOD, J.

1964　*Human Ecology in Micronesia: Determinants of Population Size.* Unpublished Ph.D. dissertation, University of California, Los Angeles.

1965　Culture and Biological Adaptation. *American Anthropologist* 67:1174–1197.

HAMMOND, N.

1974a　The Distribution of Late Classic Maya Major Ceremonial Centers in the Central Area. In *Mesoamerican Archaeology: New Approaches,* edited by N. Hammond, pp. 313–334. University of Texas Press, Austin.

1974b　Preclassic to Postclassic in Northern Belize. *Antiquity* 48:177–189.

1975　*Lubaantun: A Classic Maya Realm.* Peabody Museum of American Archaeology and Ethnology, Monograph 2. Harvard University, Cambridge.

1977　The Earliest Maya. *Scientific American* 236:116–133.

1978　The Myth of the Milpa: Agricultural Expansion in the Maya Lowlands. In *Pre-Hispanic Maya Agriculture,* edited by P. D. Harrison and B. L. Turner II, pp. 23–34. University of New Mexico Press, Albuquerque.

1981　Settlement Patterns in Belize. In *Lowland Maya Settlement Patterns,* edited by W. Ashmore, pp. 157–186. University of New Mexico Press, Albuquerque.

1982　The Prehistory of Belize. *Journal of Field Archaeology* 9:349–362.

1983　Nohmul, Belize: 1982 Investigations. *Journal of Field Archaeology* 10:245–254.

1985　*Nohmul: A Prehistoric Maya Community in Belize, Excavations 1973–1983.* British Archaeological Reports International Series 250(i). Oxford.

1986　The Emergence of Maya Civilization. *Scientific American* 255:106–115

HAMMOND, N. (EDITOR)

1975　*Archaeology in Northern Belize: 1974–1975 Interim Report of the British*

Museum—Cambridge University Corozal Project. Cambridge Centre of Latin American Studies, Cambridge University Press, Cambridge.

1976   *Archaeology in Northern Belize: Corozal Project 1976 Interim Report.* Cambridge Centre for Latin American Studies, Cambridge University Press, Cambridge.

HAMMOND, N., K. CLARK, M. HORTON, M. HODGES, L. MCNATT, L. KOSAKOWSKY,
AND K. A. PYBURN

1985   Excavation and Survey at Nohmul, Belize, 1983. *Journal of Field Archaeology* 12:177–200.

HAMMOND, N., S. S. DONAGHEY, C. GLEASON, J. C. STANECO, D. VAN TUERENHOUNT,
AND L. KOSAKOWSKY

1987   Excavation and Survey at Nohmul, Belize, 1985. *Journal of Field Archaeology* 14:257–281.

HAMMOND, N., C. HEIGHWAY, D. PRING, R. WILK, AND E. GRAHAM

1973   1973 Operations. In *Cambridge University Corozal Project, 1973 Interim Report,* edited by N. Hammond, pp. 34–73. Cambridge University Press, Cambridge.

HAMMOND, N., K. A. PYBURN, J. ROSE, J. STANEKO, D. MUYSKENS, T. ADDYMAN,
A. JOYCE, C. ROBIN, C. GLEASON, AND M. HODGES

1988   Excavation and Survey at Nohmul, Belize, 1986. *Journal of Field Archaeology* 15:1–15.

HARRISON, P. D.

1970   *The Central Acropolis, Tikal, Guatemala: A Preliminary Study of the Functions of Its Structural Components during the Late Classic Period.* Unpublished Ph.D. dissertation, Department of Anthropology, University of Pennsylvania, Philadelphia.

1978   Bajos Revisited: Visual Evidence for One System of Agriculture. In *Prehispanic Maya Agriculture,* edited by P. D. Harrison and B. L. Turner II, pp. 247–254. University of New Mexico Press, Albuquerque.

1983   The Pulltrouser Swamp Settlement Survey and Map. In *Pulltrouser Swamp: Ancient Maya Habitat, Agriculture, and Settlement in Northern Belize,* edited by B. L. Turner II and P. D. Harrison, pp. 140–157. University of Texas Press, Austin.

1986   Tikal: Selected Topics. In *City-States of the Maya: Art and Architecture,* edited by E. P. Benson, pp. 45–71. Rocky Mountain Institute for Pre-Columbian Studies, Denver.

HARRISON, P. D., AND B. L. TURNER II (EDITORS)

1978   *Pre-Hispanic Maya Agriculture.* University of New Mexico Press, Albuquerque.

HASSAN, F.

1973   On Mechanisms of Pouplation Growth during the Neolithic. *Current Anthropology* 14:535–540.

1978   Demographic Archaeology. In *Advances in Archaeological Method and*

Theory, vol. 1, edited by M. Schiffer, pp. 49–103. Academic Press, New York.

1979 *Demographic Archaeology.* Academic Press, New York.

HASSIG, R.

1985 *Trade, Tribute, and Transportation: The Sixteenth-Century Political Economy of the Valley of Mexico.* University of Oklahoma Press, Norman.

HAVILAND, W.

1963 *Excavation of Small Structures in the Northeast Quadrant of Tikal, Guatemala.* Ph.D. dissertation, Department of Anthropology, University of Pennsylvania, Philadelphia.

1965 Prehistoric Settlement at Tikal, Guatemala. *Expedition* 7(3):14–23.

1967 Stature at Tikal: Implications for Ancient Maya Demography and Social Organization. *American Antiquity* 32:316–325.

1969 A New Population Estimate for Tikal, Guatemala. *American Antiquity* 34:424–433.

1970 Tikal, Guatemala, and Mesoamerican Urbanism. *World Archaeology* 2:186–198.

1972a Family Size, Prehistoric Population Estimates, and the Ancient Maya. *American Antiquity* 37:135–139.

1972b Estimates of Maya Population: Comments on Thompson's Comments. *American Antiquity* 37:261–262.

1981 Dower Houses and Minor Centers at Tikal, Guatemala: An Investigation into the Identification of Valid Units in Settlement Hierarchies. In *Lowland Maya Settlement Patterns,* edited by W. Ashmore, pp. 89–117. University of New Mexico Press, Albuquerque.

1985 *Excavations in Small Residential Groups of Tikal: Groups 4F-1 and 4F-2.* Tikal Reports, No. 19, University Museum Monograph 58. University of Pennsylvania, Philadelphia.

1988 Musical Hammocks at Tikal: Problems with Reconstructing Household Composition. In *Household and Community in the Mesoamerican Past,* edited by R. R. Wilk and W. Ashmore, pp. 121–134. University of New Mexico Press, Albuquerque.

1989 *Excavations in Residential Areas of Tikal: Non-elite Groups Without Shrines.* Tikal Reports, No. 20, University Museum Monograph. University of Pennsylvania, Philadelphia. In preparation.

HAVILAND, W., D. PULESTON, R. FRY, AND E. GREEN

1968 *The Tikal Sustaining Area: Preliminary Report on the 1967 Season.* Report presented to the National Science Foundation (Grant GS-1409), Washington, D.C.

HAYDEN, B., AND A. CANNON

1983 Where the Garbage Goes: Refuse Disposal in the Maya Highlands. *Journal of Anthropological Archaeology* 2:117–163.

HELLMUTH, N.

1971 Some Notes on the Ytza, Quijache, Verapaz Chol, and Toqueque Maya—A Progress Report on Ethnohistory Research Conducted in Seville, Spain,

June–August, 1971. Mimeographed paper, Foundation for Latin American Anthropological Research, New Haven, Connecticut.

1972a Excavations Begin at Maya Site in Guatemala. *Archaeology* 25:148–149.

1972b Progreso y notas sobre la investigación ethnohistórica de las tierras bajas de los siglos XVI a XIX. *América Indígena* 32:179–244.

1977 Cholti-Lacandon (Chiapas) and Peten-Ytza Agriculture, Settlement Pattern and Population. In *Social Process in Maya Prehistory,* edited by N. Hammond, pp. 421–428. Academic Press, New York.

HENRY, L.

1967 Some Data on Natural Fertility. *Eugenics Quarterly* 18:81–91.

HESTER, J. A.

1954 *Natural and Cultural Bases of Ancient Maya Subsistence Economy.* Unpublished Ph.D. dissertation, Department of Anthropology, University of California, Los Angeles.

HESTER, T., H. SHAFER, AND J. EATON (EDITORS)

1982 *The Archaeology of Colha, Belize: 1981 Interim Report.* Center for Archaeological Research, University of Texas at San Antonio.

HEWETT, E. L.

1916 Latest Work of the School of American Archaeology at Quirigua. In *Holmes Anniversary Volume,* edited by E. A. Ayer et al., pp. 157–162. Washington, D.C.

HILL, J. N.

1970 *Broken K Pueblo.* Anthropological Papers 18. University of Arizona, Tucson.

HOHMANN, H., AND A. VOGRIN

1982 *Die Architektur von Copan.* Akademische Druck Verlagsanstalt, Graz, Austria.

HOLLINGSWORTH, T.

1969 *Historical Demography.* Cornell University Press, Ithaca.

HULL, C. H. (EDITOR)

1963-64 *The Economic Writings of Sir William Petty.* Reprinted A. M. Kelley, New York. Originally published 1899.

JAKEMAN, M. W.

1938 *The Maya States of Yucatan (1441–1545).* Unpublished Ph.D. dissertation, University of California, Berkeley.

JAKUCS, D. L.

1977 *Morphogenetics of Karst Regions: Variants of Karst Evolution.* John Wiley, New York.

JENKINS, R. N., R. INNES, J. R. DUNSMORE, S. H. WALKER, C. J. BIRCHALL, AND J. S. BRIGGS

1976 *The Agricultural Development of Potential of the Belize Valley.* Land Resource Study 24, Land Resource Division. Ministry of Overseas Development, England.

JONES, C., W. ASHMORE, AND R. J. SHARER
1983   The Quirigua Project: The 1977 Season. In *Quirigua Reports, Volume II,* edited by E. M. Schortman and P. A. Urban, pp. 1–38. University Museum Monograph 49. University of Pennsylvania, Philadelphia.

JONES, C., AND R. J. SHARER
1986   Archaeological Investigations in the Site Core of Quirigua. In *The Southeast Maya Periphery,* edited by P. A. Urban and E. M. Schortman, pp. 27–34. University of Texas Press, Austin.

JONES, G. D.
1979   Southern Lowland Maya Political Organization: A Model of Change from Protohistoric through Colonial Times. *Actes du XLII Congres International des Americanistes* 8:83–94.
1983   The Last Maya Frontiers of Colonial Yucatan. In *Spaniards and Indians in Southeastern Mesoamerica: Essays on the History of Ethnic Relations,* edited by M. J. MacLeod and R. Wassertrom, pp. 65–91. University of Nebraska Press, Lincoln.

KAPLAN, D.
1963   Men, Monuments, and Political Systems. *Southwestern Journal of Anthropology* 19:397–410.

KENT, S.
1986   The Influence of Sedentism and Aggregation on Porotic Hyperostosis and Anaemia: A Case Study. *Man* 21:605–636.

KIDDER, A. V.
1950   Introduction. In A. L. Smith, *Uaxactun, Guatemala: Excavations of 1931–1937.* Carnegie Institution of Washington, Publication No. 588. Washington, D.C.

KILLION, T. W.
1987   *Agriculture and Residential Site Structure among Contemporary Campesinos in Southern Veracruz, Mexico: A Foundation for Archaeological Inference.* Unpublished Ph.D. dissertation, Department of Anthropology, University of New Mexico, Albuquerque.

KIRKBY, A. V. T.
1973   *The Use of Land and Water Resources in the Past and Present Valley of Oaxaca, Mexico.* Memoirs of the Museum of Anthropology 5. University of Michigan, Ann Arbor.

KOSAKOWSKY, L., AND F. VALDEZ
1982   Rethinking the Northern Belize Formative Ceramic Chronology. Paper presented at the 47th Annual Meeting of the Society for American Archaeology, Minneapolis.

KOWALESKI, S. A., G. FEINMAN, L. FINSTEN, R. E. BLANTON, AND L. M. NICHOLAS
1989   *Monte Alban's Hinterland, Part II: Prehispanic Settlement Patterns in Tlacolula, Etla, and Ocotlan, the Valley of Oaxaca, Mexico.* Memoirs of the Museum of Anthropology 25. University of Michigan, Ann Arbor.

KURJACK, E. B.

1974   *Prehistoric Lowland Maya Community and Social Organization: A Case Study at Dzibilchaltun, Yucatan, Mexico.* Middle American Research Institute, Publication 38. Tulane University, New Orleans.

1979   *Introduction to the Map of the Ruins of Dzibilchaltun, Yucatan, Mexico.* Middle American Research Institute, Publication 47. Tulane University, New Orleans.

KURJACK, E. B., AND S. GARZA TARAZONA DE GONZÁLEZ

1981   Pre-Columbian Community Form and Distribution in the Northern Maya Area. In *Lowland Maya Settlement Patterns,* edited by W. Ashmore, pp. 287–309. University of New Mexico Press, Albuquerque.

LANGE, F. W.

1971   Una reevaluación de la población del norte de Yucatán en el tiempo del contacto español: 1528. *América Indígena* 31:117–139.

LEBLANC, S.

1971   An Addition to Naroll's Suggested Floor Area and Settlement Population Relationship. *American Anthropologist* 36:210–211.

LEE, R. D.

1986   Malthus and Boserup: A Dynamic Synthesis. In *The State of Population Theory: Forward From Malthus,* edited by D. Coleman and R. Schofield, pp. 96–130. Basil Blackwell, London.

1987   Population Dynamics of Humans and Other Animals. *Demography* 24:443–465.

LEKSON, S. H.

1984   Largest Settlement Size and the Interpretation of Sociopolitical Complexity. Paper presented at the 49th Meeting of the Society for American Archaeology, Portland.

LEOPOLD, L. B., M. G. WOLMAN, AND J. P. MILLER

1964   *Fluvial Processes in Geomorphology.* Freeman, San Francisco.

LERMAN, J. C., AND J. H. TROUGHTON

1975   Carbon Isotope Discrimination by Photosynthesis: Implications for the Bio- and Geosciences. In *Proceedings of the Second International Conference on Stable Isotopes,* edited by E. R. Klein and P. D. Klein. Washington, D.C.

LEVENTHAL, R. M.

1979   *Settlement Patterns at Copan, Honduras.* Unpublished Ph.D. dissertation, Department of Anthropology, Harvard University, Cambridge.

LINCOLN, C.

1985   Ceramics and Ceramic Chronology. In *A Consideration of the Early Classic Period in the Maya Lowlands,* edited by G. R. Willey and P. Mathews, pp. 55–94. Institute for Mesoamerican Studies, State University of New York at Albany.

LONGACRE, W. A.
1976 Population Dynamics at Grasshopper Pueblo, Arizona. In *Demographic Archaeology,* edited by E. B. W. Zubrow, pp. 169–184. University of New Mexico Press, Albuquerque.

LONGYEAR, J. M., III
1952 *Copan Ceramics: A Study of Southeastern Maya Pottery.* Carnegie Institution, Publication 597. Washington, D.C.

LOWE, J. W. G.
1985 *Dynamics of Apocalpyse: A Systems Simulation of the Classic Maya Collapse.* University of New Mexico Press, Albuquerque.

MCANANY, P. A.
1986 *Lithic Technology and Exchange among Wetland Farmers of the Eastern Maya Lowlands.* Unpublished Ph.D. dissertation, Department of Anthropology, University of New Mexico, Albuquerque.

MCGUIRE, R. H.
1983 Breaking Down Cultural Complexity: Inequality and Heterogeneity. *Advances in Archaeological Method and Theory,* vol. 6, edited by M. B. Schiffer, pp. 91–142.

MACNEISH, R. S., S. J. K. WILKERSON, AND A. NELKEN-TERNER
1980 *First Annual Report of the Belize Archaeological Reconnaisance.* Robert F. Peabody Foundation for Archaeology, Philips Academy, Andover, Massachusetts.

McQUARRIE, H.
1982 Buried Structures. Ms. on file, University of New Mexico, Albuquerque.

MALLORY, J. K., III
1984 *Late Classic Maya Economic Specialization: Evidence From the Copan Obsidian Assemblage.* Unpublished Ph.D. dissertation, Department of Anthropology, Pennsylvania State University, University Park.

MALTHUS, T. R.
1960 *On Population: Thomas Robert Malthus.* Edited by G. Himmelfarb. Random House, New York.

MARCUS, J.
1976 *Emblem and State in the Classic Maya Lowlands.* Dumbarton Oaks, Washington, D.C.

MARSHALL, J. F., S. MORRIS, AND S. POLGAR
1972 Culture and Natality: A Preliminary Classified Bibliography. *Current Anthropology* 13:268–277.

MARX, K.
1967 *Capital: A Critique of Political Economy.* International, New York.
1974 *Grundrisse: Foundations of the Critique of Political Economy.* Penguin, Harmondsworth.

MATHENY, R.
1986 Investigations at El Mirador, Peten, Guatemala. *National Geographic Research* 2:332–353.

MATHENY, R. T., D. L. GURR, D. W. FORSYTH, AND F. R. HAUCK
1983 *Investigations at Edzna, Campeche, Mexico, Volume 1, Part 1: The Hydraulic System.* Papers of the New World Archaeological Foundation, No. 46. Brigham Young University, Provo, Utah.

MATHEWS, P.
1985 Maya Early Classic Monuments and Inscriptions. In *A Consideration of the Early Classic Period in the Maya Lowlands,* edited by G. R. Willey and P. Mathews, pp. 5–54. Institute for Mesoamerican Studies, State University of New York at Albany.

MARTIN, D. L., A. H. GOODMAN, AND G. J. ARMELAGOS
1985 Skeletal Pathologies as Indicators of Quality and Quantity of Diet. In *The Analysis of Prehistoric Diets,* edited by R. I. Gilbert and J. H. Mielke, pp. 227–279. Academic Press, New York.

MEGGERS, B. J.
1954 Environmental Limitation on the Development of Culture. *American Anthropologist* 56:801–824.

MICHELS, J. W.
1979 *The Kaminaljuyu Chiefdom.* Monograph Series on Kaminaljuyu. Pennsylvania State University Press, University Park.

MILLON, R.
1973 *Urbanization at Teotihuacan, Mexico, Vol. 1: The Teotihuacan Map, Part One: Text.* University of Texas Press, Austin.
1976 Social Relations in Ancient Teotihuacan. In *The Valley of Mexico,* edited by E. Wolf, pp. 205–248. University of New Mexico Press, Albuquerque.

MONROE, W. H.
1981 Formation of Tropical Karst Topography by Limestone Solution and Reprecipitation. In *Karst Geomorphology,* edited by M. M. Sweeting, pp. 266–273. Hutchinson Ross, Stroudsburg, Pennsylvania.

MONTMILLON, O. DE
1988 Tenam Rosario—A Political Microcosm. *American Antiquity* 53:351–370.

MORLEY, S. G.
1923 Report. *Carnegie Institution of Washington, Yearbook* 22:267–272.
1928 Report of Karl Ruppert on the Outlying Sections of Chichen Itza. *Carnegie Institution of Washington, Yearbook* 27:305–307.
1937–38 *The Inscriptions of Peten.* Carnegie Institution of Washington, Publication 437. Washington, D.C.
1946 *The Ancient Maya.* Stanford University Press, Stanford.

MORLEY, S. G., AND G. W. BRAINERD
1956 *The Ancient Maya,* 2d ed. Stanford University Press, Stanford.

MUYSKINS, DEBORAH
1985   Surface Collection Analysis. Ms. on file with the author.

NAROLL, R.
1962   Floor Area and Settlement Population. *American Antiquity* 27: 587–589.

NETTING, R. MCC.
1974   Agrarian Ecology. *Annual Review of Anthropology* 3:21–56.
1977   Maya Subsistence: Mythologies, Analogies, Possibilities. In *The Origins of Maya Civilization,* edited by R. E. W. Adams, pp. 299–333. University of New Mexico Press, Albuquerque.
1982   Some Truths about Household Size and Wealth. In *Archaeology of the Household,* edited by R. R. Wilk and W. L. Rathje, pp. 641–662. *American Behavioral Scientist* 25.

NETTING, R. MCC., R. R. WILK, AND E. ARNOULD (EDITORS)
1985   *Households: Comparative and Historical Studies of the Domestic Group.* University of California Press, Berkeley.

NIEMCZEWSKI, C.
1977   History of Solid Waste Management. In *The Organization and Efficiency of Solid Waste Collection,* edited by E. S. Savas, pp. 11–24. D. C. Heath, Lexington, Massachusetts.

NUTINI, H.
1967   A Synoptic Comparison of Mesoamerican Marriage and Family Structure. *Southwestern Journal of Anthropology* 23:838–404.

ODUM, H. T.
1971   *Environment, Power, and Society.* Wiley, New York.

OVIEDO Y VALDÉS. G. F. DE
1851–55 *Historia general y natural de las Indias, íslas y tierra firme del Mar Oceano,* 4 vols. Real Academia de la Historia, Madrid.

PALERM, ANGEL, AND ERIC WOLF
1957   Ecological Potential and Cultural Development in Mesoamerica. In *Studies in Human Ecology.* Social Science Monographs No. 3, pp. 1–37. Pan American Union, Washington, D.C.

PARSONS, J.
1971   *Prehistoric Settlement Patterns in the Texcoco Region, Mexico.* Memoirs of the Museum of Anthropology No. 3. University of Michigan, Ann Arbor.

PARSONS, J. R.; E. BRUMFIEL, M. H. PARSONS, AND D. J. WILSON
1982   *Prehistoric Settlement Patterns in the Southern Valley of Mexico: The Chalco Xochimilco Region.* Memoirs of the Museum of Anthropology 14. University of Michigan, Ann Arbor.

PENDERGAST, DAVID
1981   Lamanai, Belize: Summary of Excavation Results, 1974–1980. *Journal of Field Archaeology* 8:29–53.

1986   Stability through Change: Lamanai, Belize, from the Ninth to the Seventeenth Century. In *Late Lowland Maya Civilization: Classic to Postclassic,* edited by J. A. Sabloff and E. W. Andrews V, pp. 223–249. University of New Mexico Press, Albuquerque.

PETERSEN, W.
1975   A Demographer's View of Prehistoric Demography. *Current Anthropology* 16:227–245.

PLOG, F.
1968   *Archaeological Surveys: A New Perspective.* Unpublished Master's thesis, University of Chicago, Chicago.
1973   Diachronic Archaeology. In *Research and Theory in Current Archaeology,* edited by C. Redman, pp. 181–198. John Wiley, New York.

PLOG, S., F. PLOG, AND W. WAIT
1978   Decision-Making in Modern Surveys. In *Advances in Archaeological Method and Theory,* vol. 1, edited by M. B. Schiffer, pp. 383–421. Academic Press, New York.

POHL, M. (EDITOR)
1985   *Prehistoric Lowland Maya Environment and Subsistence Economy.* Papers of the Peabody Museum of American Archaeology and Ethnology, vol. 77.

POLGAR, S.
1972   Population History and Population Policies from an Anthropological Perspective. *Current Anthropology* 13:203–211, 260–262.
1975   Population Evolution, and Theoretical Paradigms. In *Population, Ecology, and Social Evolution,* edited by S. Polgar, pp. 1–25. Mouton, The Hague.

POLLOCK, H. E. D.
1962   Introduction. In H. Pollock, R. Roys, T. Proskouriakoff, and A. Smith, *Mayapan, Yucatan, Mexico,* pp. 1–22. Carnegie Institution of Washington, Publication 619. Washington, D.C.
1980   *The Puuc: An Architectural Survey of the Hill Country of Yucatan and Northern Campeche, Mexico.* Memoirs of the Peabody Museum of American Archaeology and Ethnology, vol. 19. Harvard University, Cambridge.

POLLOCK, H. E. D., R. L. ROYS, T. PROSKOURIAKOFF, AND A. L. SMITH
1962   *Mayapan, Yucatan, Mexico.* Carnegie Institution of Washington, Publication 619. Washington, D.C.

PRESSAT, R.
1972   *Demographic Analysis: Methods, Results, Applications.* Aldine-Atherton, Chicago.

PRICE, B.
1973   Prehispanic Irrigation Agriculture in Nuclear America. In *Explorations in Anthropology: Readings in Culture, Man, and Nature,* edited by M. Fried, pp. 216–246. Thomas Y. Crowell, New York.

PRING, D.
1973   Op 8—Santa Rita. In *British Museum—Cambridge University Corozal Project, 1973 Interim Report,* edited by N. Hammond, pp. 62–67. Cambridge Centre of Latin American Studies, Cambridge University Press, Cambridge.
1977   *The Preclassic Ceramics of Northern Belize.* Unpublished Ph.D. dissertation, University of London.

PRING, D., AND N. HAMMOND
1975   Investigation of a Possible Installation at Nohmul. In *Archaeology of Northern Belize: 1974–1975 Interim Report of the British Museum—Cambridge University Corozal Project,* edited by N. Hammond, pp. 116–127. Cambridge Centre of Latin American Studies, Cambridge University Press, Cambridge.

PULESTON, D.
1965   The Chultuns of Tikal. *Expedition* 7(3):24–29.
1968   *Brosimum alicastrum as a Subsistence Alternative for the Classic Maya of the Central South Lowlands.* Unpublished Master's thesis, University of Pennsylvania, Philadelphia.
1973   *Ancient Maya Settlement Patterns and Environment at Tikal, Guatemala: Implications for Subsistence Models.* Unpublished Ph.D. dissertation, University of Pennsylvania, Philadelphia.
1974   Intersite Areas in the Vicinity of Tikal and Uaxactun. In *Mesoamerican Archaeology: New Approaches,* edited by N. Hammond, pp. 301–311. Duckworth, London.
1983   *The Settlement Survey of Tikal.* Tikal Reports No. 13. University Museum Monograph 48, University of Pennsylvania, Philadelphia.

PULESTON, D ., AND D. CALLENDER
1967   Defensive Earthworks at Tikal. *Expedition* 9(3):40–48.

PULESTON, O. S.
1969   *Functional Analysis of a Functional Tool Kit from Tikal.* Unpublished Master's thesis, University of Pennsylvania, Philadelphia.

PULESTON, O. S., AND D. E. PULESTON
1971   Ecological Approach to the Origins of Maya civilization. *Archaeology* 24:330–337.
1972   A Processual Model for the Rise of Classic Maya civilization in the Southern Lowlands. *Proceedings of the XL International Congress of Americanists,* Rome 1972, pp. 119–124. Tilgher, Geneva.

PYBURN, K. A.
1986   The Functional Interpretation of Prehistoric Lowland Maya Non-mound Features. Paper presented at the 51st Annual Meeting of the Society for American Archaeology, New Orleans.
1988   *The Settlement of Nohmul: Development of a Prehispanic Maya Community in Northern Belize.* Unpublished Ph.D. dissertation, Department of Anthropology, University of Arizona, Tucson.

1989 Maya Cuisine: Hearths and the Lowland Maya Economy. In *Prehistoric Maya Economies of Northern Belize,* edited by P. A. McAnany and B. L. Isaac, pp. 325–344. Research in Economic Anthropology Supplement 4. University Press of America, Lanham, Maryland.

RAPOPORT, A.
1975 Towards a Redefinition of Density. *Environment and Behavior* 7:133–157.

RATHJE, W. L.
1970 Socio-political Implication of Lowland Maya Burials: Methodology and Tentative Hypotheses. *World Archaeology* 1:359–374.

REDFIELD, R., AND A. VILLA ROJAS
1934 *Chan Kom: A Maya Village.* Carnegie Institution of Washington, Publication 448. Washington, D.C.

REINA, R.
1967 Milpas and Milperos. *American Anthropologist* 69:1–20.

REINA, R. E., C. F. WARD III, AND R. M. MAXWELL
1984 Molab in 1727 Chinautla, Guatemala: A Case Study in Cultural Continuity. Paper presented at the Annual Meeting of the American Society for Ethnohistory, New Orleans.

RICE, D. S.
1976 *The Historical Ecology of Lakes Yaxha and Sacnab, El Peten, Guatemala.* Unpublished Ph.D. dissertation, Pennsylvania State University, University Park.
1978 Population Growth and Subsistence Alternatives in a Tropical Lacustrine Environment. In *Pre-Hispanic Maya Agriculture,* edited by P. D. Harrison and B. L. Turner II, pp. 35–61. University of New Mexico Press, Albuquerque.
1986 The Peten Postclassic: A Settlement Perspective. In *Late Lowland Maya Civilization: Classic to Postclassic,* edited by J. Sabloff and E. W. Andrews V, pp. 301–344. University of New Mexico Press, Albuquerque.
1988 Classic to Postclassic Maya Household Transitions in the Central Peten, Guatemala. In *Household and Community in the Mesoamerican Past,* edited by R. R. Wilk and W. Ashmore, pp. 227–247. University of New Mexico Press, Albuquerque.

RICE, D. S., AND D. E. PULESTON
1981 Ancient Maya Settlement Patterns in the Peten, Guatemala. In *Lowland Maya Settlement Patterns,* edited by W. Ashmore, pp. 121–156. University of New Mexico Press, Albuquerque.

RICE, D. S., AND P. M. RICE
1980 The Northeast Peten Revisited. *American Antiquity* 45:432–454.
1981 Muralla de Leon: A Lowland Maya Fortification. *Journal of Field Archaeology* 8:273–288.
1982a Informe preliminar de "Proyecto Lacustre," Petén, Guatemala: La segunda

temporada, 1980. *Boletín de la Escuela de Ciencias Antropológicas de la Universidad de Yucatán* 10:17–39.

1982b Informe preliminar de "Proyecto Lacustre," Petén, Guatemala: La tercera temporada, 1981. *Boletín de la Escuela de Ciencias Antropológicas de la Universidad de Yucatán* 10:39–42.

1983 El impacto de los Mayas en el ambiente tropical de la cuenca de los Lagos Yaxhá y Sacnab, el Petén, Guatemala. *América Indígena* 43:261–297.

1984a Lessons from the Maya. *Latin American Research Review* 19:7–34.

1984b Collapse to Contact: Postclassic Archaeology of the Peten Maya. *Archaeology* 37(2):46–51.

RICE, D., P. RICE, AND E. S. DEEVEY, JR.

1985 Paradise Lost: Classic Maya Impact on a Lacustrine Environment. In *Prehistoric Lowland Maya Environment and Subsistence Economy,* edited by M. Pohl, pp. 91–105. Papers of the Peabody Museum of American Archaeology and Ethnology, vol. 77. Harvard University Press, Cambridge.

RICE, P. M.

1979a The Ceramic and Non-ceramic Artifacts of Yaxha-Sacnab, El Peten, Guatemala. Part I—The Ceramics: Section A, Middle Preclassic. *Cerámica de Cultura Maya* 10:1–36.

1979b The Ceramic and Non-ceramic Artifacts of Yaxha-Sacnab, El Peten, Guatemala. Part I—The Ceramics: Section B, Postclassic Pottery From Topoxte. *Cerámica de Cultura Maya* 11:1–85.

1986a The Peten Postclassic: Perspectives from the Central Peten Lakes. In *Late Lowland Maya Civilization: Classic to Postclassic,* edited by J. Sabloff and E. W. Andrews V, pp. 251–299. University of New Mexico Press, Albuquerque.

1986b An Obsidian Hydration Dating Sequence in the Southern Maya Lowlands. *Journal of New World Archaeology,* in press.

1987 *Macanche Island, El Peten, Guatemala: Excavations, Pottery and Artifacts.* University Presses of Florida, Gainesville.

RICE, P. M., AND D. S. RICE

1985 Topoxte, Macanche, and the Central Peten Postclassic. In *The Lowland Maya Postclassic,* edited by A. F. Chase and P. M. Rice, pp. 166–183. University of Texas Press, Austin.

RICKETSON, O., AND E. B. RICKETSON

1937 *Uaxactun, Guatemala, Group E. 1926–1931.* Carnegie Institution of Washington, Publication 477. Washington, D.C.

RINGLE, W. M.

1985 *The Settlement Patterns of Komchen, Yucatan, Mexico.* Unpublished Ph.D. dissertation, Department of Anthropology, Tulane University, New Orleans.

RINGLE, W. M., AND E. W. ANDREWS V

1988 Formative Residences at Komchen, Yucatan, Mexico. In *House and Household in the Mesoamerican Past,* edited by R. R. Wilk and W. Ashmore, pp. 171–197. University of New Mexico Press, Albuquerque.

ROBERTSON-FREIDEL, R. A.
1980 *The Ceramics from Cerros: A Late Preclassic site in Northern Belize.* Unpublished Ph.D. dissertation, Department of Anthropology, Harvard University, Cambridge.

ROBERTSON, R. A., AND D. A. FREIDEL (EDITORS)
1986 *Archaeology at Cerros, Belize, Central America. Volume I. An Interim Report.* Southern Methodist University Press, Dallas.

ROBIN, C. A.
1985 Surface Collection Analysis at Nohmul. Ms. on file with the author.

ROSE, J. C., K. W. CONDON, AND A. H. GOODMAN
1985 Diet and Dentition: Development Disturbances. In *The Analysis of Prehistoric Diets,* edited by R. I. Gilbert and J. H. Mielke, pp. 281–305. Academic Press, New York.

ROYS, R. L.
1965 Lowland Maya Native Society at Spanish Contact. In *Archaeology of Southern Mesoamerica, Part 2,* edited by G. R. Willey, pp. 659–678. Handbook of Middle American Indians, vol. 3, R. Wauchope, general editor. University of Texas Press, Austin.

ROYS, R. L., F. V. SCHOLES, AND E. B. ADAMS
1940 *Report and Census of the Indians of Cozumel, 1570.* Contributions to American Anthropology and History, No. 30. Carnegie Institution of Washington, Publication 523. Washington, D.C.
1959 Census and Inspection of the Town of Pencuyut, Yucatan, in 1583 by Diego García de Palacio, Oidor of the Audiencia of Guatemala. *Ethnohistory* 6:195–225.

RUE, D.
1986 *A Palynological Analysis of Pre-Hispanic Human Impact in the Copan Valley,* Honduras. Unpublished Ph.D. dissertation, Department of Anthropology, Pennsylvania State University, University Park.

RUPPERT, K., AND J. H. DENISON
1943 *Archaeological Reconnaissance in Campeche, Quintana Roo, and Peten.* Carnegie Institution of Washington, Publication 543. Washington, D.C.

SABLOFF, J. A.
1975 *Excavations at Seibal: Ceramics.* Memoirs of the Peabody Museum of American Archaeology and Ethnology, vol. 13, no. 2. Harvard University, Cambridge.
1983 Classic Maya Settlement Pattern Studies: Past Problems, Future Prospects. In *Prehistoric Settlement Patterns: Essays in Honor of Gordon R. Willey,* edited by E. Z. Vogt and R. M. Leventhal, pp. 413–422. University of New Mexico Press, Albuquerque.

SABLOFF, J., AND E. W. ANDREWS V (EDITORS)
1986 *Late Lowland Maya Civilization: Classic to Postclassic.* University of New Mexico Press, Albuquerque.

SABLOFF, J. A., P. A. MCANANY, N. FAHMEL BEYER, T. GALLARETA NEGRON, S. L. LARRALDE, AND L. WANDSNIDER

1984   *Ancient Maya Settlement Patterns at the Site of Sayil, Puuc Region, Yucatan, Mexico: Initial Reconnaissance (1983).* Latin American Institute Research Paper Series, No. 14. University of New Mexico, Albuquerque.

SABLOFF, J. A., G. TOURTELLOT, B. FAHMEL BEYER., P. A. MCANANY, D. CHRISTENSEN, S. BOUCHER, AND T. R. KILLION

1985   *Settlement and Community Patterns at Sayil, Yucatan, Mexico: The 1984 Season.* Latin American Institute Research Paper Series, No. 17. University of New Mexico, Albuquerque.

SANDERS, W. T.

1960   *Prehistoric Ceramics and Settlement Patterns in Quintana Roo, Mexico.* Carnegie Institution of Washington, Publication 606, Contributions to American Anthropology and History, No. 6. Washington, D.C.

1962–63   Cultural Ecology of the Maya Lowlands. *Estudios de Cultura Maya* 2:79–121, 3:203–241.

1965   The Cultural Ecology of the Teotihuacan Valley. Ms. on file, Department of Anthropology, Pennsylvania State University, University Park.

1973   The Cultural Ecology of the Lowland Maya: A Reevaluation. In *The Classic Maya Collapse,* edited by T. P. Culbert, pp. 325–365. University of New Mexico Press, Albuquerque.

1974   Chiefdom to State: Political Evolution at Kaminaljuyu, Guatemala. In *Reconstructing Complex Societies,* edited by C. Moore, pp. 97–121. American Schools of Oriental Research, Cambridge, Massachusetts.

1977   Environmental Heterogeneity and the Evolution of Lowland Maya Civilization. In *The Origins of Maya Civilization,* edited by R. E. W. Adams, pp. 287–297. University of New Mexico Press, Albuquerque.

1981   Classic Maya Settlement Patterns and Ethnographic Analogy. In *Lowland Maya Settlement Patterns,* edited by W. Ashmore, pp. 351–369. University of New Mexico Press, Albuquerque.

1984   Preindustrial Demography and Social Evolution. In *Essays in Honor of Harry Hojier,* edited by T. Earle, pp. 8–39. Undeva Press, Malibu.

1989   Household, Lineage and State in Eighth-Century Copan, Honduras. In *The House of the Bacabs,* edited by D. Webster, pp. 89–105. Studies in Precolumbian Art and Archaeology, no. 29, Dumbarton Oaks, Washington, D.C.

SANDERS. W. T. (COMPILER)

1986   *Excavaciones en la zona urbana de Copán, tomo I.* Instituto Hondureño de Antropología e Historia, Tegucigalpa, Honduras.

SANDERS, W. T., A. KOVAR, T. CHARLTON, AND R. DIEHL

1970   *The Natural Environment, Contemporary Occupation and 16th Century Population of the Valley.* Occasional Papers in Anthropology, No. 3. Department of Anthropology, Pennsylvania State University, University Park.

SANDERS, W. T., J. PARSONS, AND R. SANTLEY

1979   *The Basin of Mexico: Ecological Processes in the Evolution of a Civilization.* Academic Press, New York.

SANDERS, W. T., AND B. PRICE
1968 *Mesoamerica: The Evolution of a Civilization*. Random House, New York.

SANDERS, W. T., AND R. SANTLEY
1978 A Mesoamerican Capital. *Science* 202:303–304.

SANDERS, W. T., AND L. L. WEBSTER
1978 Unilinealism, Multilinealism, and the Evolution of Complex Society. In *Social Archaeology: Beyond Subsistence and Dating,* edited by C. L. Redman, M. J. Berman, E. V. Curtin, W. T. Langhorne, Jr., N. M. Versaggi, and J. C. Wanser, pp. 249–302. Academic Press, New York.

SANTLEY, R. S.
1977 *Intra-Site Settlement Patterns at Loma Torremote and Their Relationship to Formative Prehistory in the Cuauhtitlan Region, State of Mexico*. Unpublished Ph.D. dissertation, Pennsylvania State University, University Park.
1980 Disembedded Capitals Reconsidered. *American Antiquity* 45:132–144.

SANTLEY, R. S., T. W. KILLION, AND M. T. LYCETT
1986 On the Maya Collapse. *Journal of Anthropological Research* 42:123–159.

SANTLEY, R. S., P. ORTIZ CEBALLOS, AND C. A. POOL
1987 Recent Archaeological Research at Matacapan, Veracruz: A Summary of the Results of the 1982 to 1986 Field Seasons. *Mexicon* 9:41–48.

SANTLEY. R., AND E. ROSE
1979 Diet, Nutrition, and Population Dynamics in the Basin of Mexico. *World Archaeology* 11:185–207.

SATTENSPIEL, L., AND H. HARPENDING
1983 Stable Populations and Skeletal Age. *American Antiquity* 48:489–498.

SATTERTHWAITE, L.
1951 Reconnaissance in British Honduras. *University of Pennsylvania Museum Bulletin* 16:21–37.

SAUL, F. P.
1973 Disease in the Maya Area: The Pre-Columbian Evidence. In *The Classic Maya Collapse,* edited by T. P. Culbert, pp. 301–324. University of New Mexico Press, Albuquerque.

SCARBOROUGH, V. L.
1980 *The Settlement System in a Late Preclassic Maya Community: Cerros, Northern Belize*. Unpublished Ph.D. dissertation, Department of Anthropology, Southern Methodist University, Dallas.

SCARBOROUGH, V., AND R. ROBERTSON
1986 Civic and Residential Settlement at a Late Preclassic Maya Center. *Journal of Field Archaeology* 13:155–175.

SCHACHT, R. M.
1980 Two Models of Population Growth. *American Anthropologist* 82:782–798.
1984 The Contemporaneity Problem. *American Antiquity* 49:678–695.

SCHIFFER, M. B.
1972   Archaeological Context and Systemic Context. *American Antiquity* 37:156–165.
1976   *Behavioral Archaeology.* Academic Press, New York.

SCHIFFER, M. B., A. SULLIVAN, AND T. C. KLINGER
1978   The Design of Archaeological Surveys. *World Archaeology* 10:1–29.

SCHOENINGER, M. J.
1979   *Dietary Reconstruction at Chalcatzingo, a Formative Period Site in Morelos, Mexico.* Technical Reports of the Museum of Anthropology 9. University of Michigan, Ann Arbor.

SCHOLES, F. V., AND R. L. ROYS
1948   *The Maya Chontal Indians of Acalan-Tixchel: A Contribution to the History and Ethnography of the Yucatan Peninsula.* Carnegie Institution of Washington, Publication 560. Washington, D.C.

SCHORTMAN, E. M.
1980   Archaeological Investigations in the Lower Motagua Valley. *Expedition* 23(1):28–34.
1984   *Archaeological Investigations in the Lower Motagua Valley, Department of Izabal, Guatemala: A Study in Monumental Site Function and Interaction.* Unpublished Ph.D. dissertation, University of Pennsylvania, Philadelphia.
1986   Maya/Non-Maya Interaction along the Late Classic Southeast Maya Periphery. In *The Southeast Maya Periphery,* edited by P. A. Urban and E. M. Schortman, pp. 114–137. University of Texas Press, Austin.

SCHUFELDT, P. W.
1950   Reminiscence of a Chiclero. In *Morleyana, A Collection of Writings in Memoriam, Sylvanus Griswold Morley—1883–1948,* pp. 224–229. School of American Research and the Museum of New Mexico, Santa Fe.

SHAFER, H. J.
1983   The Lithic Artifacts of the Pulltrouser Area: Settlements and Fields. In *Pulltrouser Swamp: Ancient Maya Habitat, Agriculture and Settlement in Northern Belize,* edited by B. L. Turner II and P. D. Harrison, pp. 212–245. University of Texas Press, Austin.

SCHAFER, H. J., AND T. R. HESTER
1983   Ancient Maya Chert Workshops in Northern Belize, Central America. *American Antiquity* 48:519–543.

SHARER, R. J.
1978   Archaeology and History at Quirigua, Guatemala. *Journal of Field Archaeology* 5:51–70.
1985   Terminal Events in the Southeastern Lowlands: A View from Quirigua. In *The Lowland Maya Postclassic,* edited by A. F. Chase and P. M. Rice, pp. 245–253. University of Texas Press, Austin.
1988   Quirigua as a Classic Maya Center. In *The Classic Maya Southeast,* edited by E. H. Boone and G. R. Willey, pp. 31–65. Dumbarton Oaks, Washington, D.C.

1989 Diversity and Continuity in Maya Civilization: Quirigua as a Case Study. In *Classic Maya Political History: Hieroglyphic and Archaeological Evidence,* edited by T. P. Culbert. Cambridge University Press, Cambridge, in press.

SHEETS, P. D. (EDITOR)
1983 *Archaeology and Volcanism in Central America: The Zapotitlan Valley of El Salvador.* University of Texas Press, Austin.

SHOOK, E. M.
1955 Yucatan and Chiapas. *Carnegie Institution of Washington, Yearbook* 54:289–295. Washington, D.C.

SHUMAN, M. K.
1974 *The Town Where Luck Fell: The Economics of Life in a Henequen Zone Pueblo.* Unpublished Ph.D. dissertation, Department of Anthropology, Tulane University, New Orleans.

SIDRYS, R.
1976 *Mesoamerica: An Archaeological Analysis of Low-Energy Civilization.* Unpublished Ph.D. dissertation, Department of Anthropology, University of California, Los Angeles.
1983 *Archaeological Excavations in Northern Belize, Central America.* Monograph 17, Institute of Archaeology, University of California, Los Angeles.

SIDRYS, R., AND R. BERGER
1979 Lowland Maya Radiocarbon Dates and the Classic Maya Collapse. *Nature* 277:269–274.

SIMMONS, C., S. TARANO, AND J. PINTO
1959 *Clasificación de reconocimiento de los suelos de la República de Guatemala.* Ministerio de Agricultura, Instituto Agro-Pecuaria, Guatemala.

SMITH, A. L.
1962 Residential Associated Structures at Mayapan. In *Mayapan, Yucatan, Mexico,* edited by H. E. D. Pollock, pp. 165–320. Carnegie Institution of Washington, Publication 619. Washington, D.C.
1982 *Excavations at Seibal. Major Architecture and Caches.* Memoirs of the Peabody Museum of American Archaeology and Ethnology, vol. 15, no. 1. Harvard University, Cambridge.

SMITH, M. E.
1987 Household Possessions and Wealth in Agrarian States: Implications for Archaeology. *Journal of Anthropological Archaeology* 6:297–335.

SMITH, R. E.
1955 *Ceramic Sequence at Uaxactun, 2 vols.* Middle American Research Institute, Publication 20. Tulane University, New Orleans.
1971 *The Pottery of Mayapan.* Papers of the Peabody Museum of American Archaeology and Ethnology, vol. 66. Harvard University, Cambridge.

SMYTH, M. P.
1988 *Storage Behavior in the Puuc Region of Yucatan: An Ethnoarchaeological*

Investigation. Unpublished Ph.D. dissertation, Department of Anthropology, University of New Mexico, Albuquerque.

SPECHT, D. A.
1973   System Size and Structural Differentiation in Formal Organizations: An Alternative Base-Line Generator. *American Sociological Review* 38:479–480.

SPINDEN, H. J.
1928   *The Ancient Civilizations of Mexico and Central America*. American Museum of Natural History, Handbook Series, No. 3. New York.

SPOONER, B. (EDITOR)
1972   *Population Growth: Anthropological Implications*. MIT Press, Cambridge.

STADELMAN, R.
1940   *Maize Cultivation in Northwestern Guatemala*. Carnegie Institution of Washington, Publication 523. Washington, D.C.

STEGGERDA, M.
1941   *Maya Indians of Yucatan*. Carnegie Institution of Washington, Publication 531. Washington, D.C.

STEINBOCK, R. T.
1976   *Paleopathological Diagnosis and Interpretation: Bone Diseases in Ancient Human Populations*. Charles C. Thomas, Springfield, Ill.

STENHOLM, N. A.
1973   *Identification of House Structures in Mayan Archaeology: A Case Study of Kaminaljuyu*. Unpublished Ph.D. dissertation, University of Washington, Seattle.

STEPHENS, J. L.
1962a *Incidents of Travel in Yucatan, Volume One*. University of Oklahoma Press, Norman.
1962b *Incidents of Travel in Yucatan, Volume Two*. University of Oklahoma Press, Norman.

STEVENS, R. L.
1964   The Soils of Middle America and Their Relations to Indian Peoples and Culture. In *Natural Environment and Early Cultures,* edited by R. C. West, pp. 265–315. Handbook of Middle American Indians, vol. 1, P. Wauchope, general editor. University of Texas Press, Austin.

STOLTMAN, J. B.
1978   *Lithic Artifacts from a Complex Society: The Chipped Stone Tools of Becan, Campeche, Mexico*. Middle American Research Institute, Occasional Paper 2. Tulane University, New Orleans.

STRAUSS, E.
1954   *Sir William Petty: Portrait of a Genius*. Free Press, Glencoe.

STUART, G. E., J. C. SCHEFFLER, E. B. KURJACK, AND J. W. COTTIER

1979   *Map of the Ruins of Dzibilchaltun, Yucatan, Mexico.* Middle American Research Institute, Publication 47. Tulane University, New Orleans.

STUIVER, M., AND P. J. REIMER

1986   A Computer Program for Radiocarbon Age Calibration. *Radiocarbon* 23:1022–1030. (Rev. 1.3, Radiocarbon Calibration Program [CALIB], 1/09/87, Quarternary Isotope Laboratory, Quaternary Research Center AK-60, University of Washington, Seattle.)

SZPUNAR, C.

1977   *Atomic Absorption Analysis of Archaeological Remains: Human Ribs from Woodland Mortuary Sites.* Unpublished Ph.D. dissertation, Department of Anthropology, Northwestern University, Evanston, Ill.

SZYMANSKI, R., AND J. A. AGNEW

1981   *Order and Skepticism: Human Geography and the Dialectic of Science.* Association of American Geographers, Washington, D.C.

TAINTER, J. A.

1988   *The Collapse of Complex Societies.* Cambridge University Press, New York.

TERMER, F.

1951   *The Destiny of Population in the Southern and Northern Maya Empires as an Archaeological and Geographical Problem.* Proceedings of the 29th International Congress of Americanists, vol. 1, pp. 101–107. Chicago.

1953   Die Hochkultur der Maya und ihre Erforschung durch die moderne Amerikanistik. *Universitas* 8:149–159.

THIEN, L. B., A. S. BRADBURN, AND A. L. WELDEN

1982   *The Woody Vegetation of Dzibilchaltun: A Maya Archaeological Site in Northwest Yucatan, Mexico.* Middle American Research Institute, Occasional Paper 5. Tulane University, New Orleans.

THOMAS, D. H.

1986   *Refiguring Anthropology.* Waveland Press, Prospect Heights, Illinois.

THOMAS, P. M., JR.

1974   Prehistoric Settlement at Becan: A Preliminary Report. In *Preliminary Reports on the Archaeology of the Rio Bec Area, Campeche, Mexico,* compiled by R. E. W. Adams, pp. 139–146. Middle American Research Institute, Publication 31. Tulane University, New Orleans.

1981   *Prehistoric Maya Settlement Patterns at Becan, Campeche, Mexico.* Middle American Research Institute, Publication 45. Tulane University, New Orleans.

THOMPSON, E. H.

1897   *The Chultunes of Labna, Yucatan.* Memoirs of the Peabody Museum of American Archaeology and Ethnology, vol. 1. Harvard University, Cambridge.

THOMPSON, J. E. S.

1950 *Maya Hieroglyphic Writing: Introduction.* Carnegie Institution of Washington, Publication 589. Washington, D.C.

1951 The Itza of Tayasal, Peten. In *Homenaje al Doctor Alfonso Caso,* edited by J. Comas, pp. 389–400. Imprenta Nueva, Mexico.

1954 *The Rise and Fall of Maya Civilization.* University of Oklahoma Press, Norman.

1967 The Maya Central Area at the Spanish Conquest and Later: A Problem in Demography. In *Proceedings of the Royal Anthropological Institute of Great Britain and Ireland for 1966,* pp. 23–37.

1971 Estimates of Maya Population: Deranging Factors. *American Antiquity* 36:214–216.

1972 *The Maya of Belize: Historical Chapters Since Columbus.* Benex Press, Belize.

1975 Introduction. In *The Hill-Caves of Yucatan,* by Henry C. Mercer. University of Oklahoma Press, Norman.

TOLSTOY, P., AND S. K. FISH

1975 Surface and Subsurface Evidence for Community Size at Coapexco, Mexico. *Journal of Field Archaeology* 2:97–104.

TOURTELLOT, G., III

1970 The Peripheries of Seibal: An Interim Report. In *Monographs and Papers in Maya Archaeology,* edited by W. R. Bullard, Jr., pp. 405–419. Papers of the Peabody Museum of American Archaeology and Ethnology, vol. 61. Harvard University, Cambridge.

1976 Patterns of Domestic Architecture at a Maya Garden City: Seibal. Paper presented at the 41st Annual Meeting of the Society for American Archaeology, St. Louis, Mo.

1982 *Ancient Maya Settlements at Seibal, Peten, Guatemala: Peripheral Survey and Excavation.* Ph.D. dissertation, Harvard University, Cambridge.

1983 An Assessment of Classic Maya Household Composition. In *Prehistoric Settlement Patterns: Essays in Honor of Gordon R. Willey,* edited by E. Z. Vogt and R. M. Leventhal, pp. 35–54. University of New Mexico Press, Albuquerque.

1988a Developmental Cycles of Households and Houses at Seibal. In *House and Household in the Mesoamerican Past,* edited by R. R. Wilk and W. Ashmore, pp. 97–120. University of New Mexico Press, Albuquerque.

1988b *Excavations at Seibal: Peripheral Survey and Excavations.* Memoirs of the Peabody Museum of American Archaeology and Ethnology, No. 16. Harvard University, Cambridge.

TOURTELLOT, G., J. A., SABLOFF, M. P. SMYTH, L. V. WHITLEY., S. L. WALLING, T. GALLERETA N., C. PEREZ A., G. F. ANDREWS, AND N. P. DUNNING

1988 Mapping Community Patterns at Sayil, Yucatan, Mexico: The 1985 Season. *Journal of New World Archaeology* 8:1–24.

TOZZER, A. M. (EDITOR AND TRANSLATOR)

1941 *Landa's Relación de las Cosas de Yucatán.* Papers of the Peabody Museum of American Archaeology and Ethnology, vol. 18. Harvard University, Cambridge.

TRIK, A. S.

1939   Temple XXII at Copan. *Contributions to American Anthropology and History,* no. 27. Carnegie Institution of Washington, Publication 509. Washington, D.C.

TURNER, B. L., II

1974   Prehistoric Intensive Agriculture in the Maya Lowlands. *Science* 185:118–124.

1976   Prehistoric Population Density in the Maya Lowlands: New Evidence for Old Approaches. *Geographical Review* 66:73–82.

1978a   The Development and Demise of the Swidden Thesis of Maya Agriculture. In *Pre-Hispanic Maya Agriculture,* edited by P. D. Harrison and B. L. Turner II, pp. 13–22. University of New Mexico Press, Albuquerque.

1978b   Ancient Agricultural Land Use in the Central Maya Lowlands. In *Pre-Hispanic Maya Agriculture,* edited by P. D. Harrison and B. L. Turner II, pp. 163–182. University of New Mexico Press, Albuquerque.

1983a   *Once Beneath the Forest: Prehistoric Terracing in the Rio Bec Region of the Maya Lowlands.* Dellplain Latin American Studies, No. 13. Westview Press, Boulder.

1983b   Comparison of Agrotechnologies in the Basin of Mexico and the Central Maya Lowlands: Formative to the Classic Maya Collapse. In *Interdisciplinary Approaches to the Study of Mesoamerican Highland-Lowland Interaction,* edited by A. Miller, pp. 13–45. Dumbarton Oaks/Harvard University, Washington, D.C.

1985   Issues Related to Subsistence and Environment among the Ancient Maya. In *Prehistoric Lowland Maya Environment and Subsistence Economy,* edited by M. Pohl, pp. 195–209. Papers of the Peabody Museum of American Archaeology and Ethnology, vol. 77. Harvard University, Cambridge.

1986   *Population Reconstruction of the Central Maya Lowlands: 1000 B.C. to Present.* Technical Paper no. 2, Millennial Long Waves of Human Occupance Project. CENTED, Clark University.

1989   The Rise and Fall of Maya Population and Agriculture, 1000 B.C. to Present: The Malthusian Perspective Reconsidered. In *Hunger and History: Food Shortages, Poverty and Deprivation,* edited by L. Newman, et al. Basil Blackwell, Oxford.

TURNER, B. L., II, R. Q. HANHAM, AND A. V. PORTARARO

1977   Population Pressure and Agricultural Intensity. *Annals of the Association of American Geographers* 67:384–396.

TURNER, B. L., II, AND P. D. HARRISON

1978   Implications from Agriculture for Maya Prehistory. In *Pre-Hispanic Maya Agriculture,* edited by P. D. Harrison and B. L. Turner II, pp. 337–373. University of New Mexico Press, Albuquerque.

1981   Prehistoric Raised-Field Agriculture in the Maya Lowlands. *Science* 213:399–405.

TURNER,B. L., II, AND P. D. HARRISON (EDITORS)
1983   *Pulltrouser Swamp: Ancient Maya Habitat, Agriculture, and Settlement in Northern Belize.* University of Texas Press, Austin.

TURNER, E. S., N. I., TURNER, AND R. E. W. ADAMS
1981   Volumetric Assessment, Rank Ordering, and Maya Civic Centers. In *Lowland Mayan Settlement Patterns,* edited by W. Ashmore, pp. 71–88. University of New Mexico Press, Albuquerque.

UBELAKER, D.
1974   *Reconstruction of Demographic Profiles from Ossuary Skeletal Samples: A Case Study from the Tidewater Potomac.* Smithsonian Contributions to Anthropology 18. Smithsonian Institution, Washington, D.C.

VAILLANT, G.
1940   Patterns in Middle American Archaeology. In *The Maya and Their Neighbors,* edited by G. Hay, pp. 295–305. Appelton-Century, New York.

VAUGHAN, H., E. S., DEEVEY, AND S. GARRETT-JONES
1985   Pollen Stratigraphy of Two Cores from the Peten Lake District, with an Appendix of Two Deep-Water Cores. In *Prehistoric Lowland Environment and Subsistence Economy,* edited by M. Pohl, pp. 73–90. Papers of the Peabody Museum of American Archaeology and Ethnology, vol. 77. Harvard University, Cambridge.

VILLA ROJAS, A.
1945   *The Maya of East Central Quintana Roo.* Carnegie Institution of Washington, Publication 559. Washington, D.C.
1969   The Maya of Yucatan. In *Ethnology, Part 1,* edited by E. Z. Vogt, pp. 244–297. Handbook of Middle American Indians, R. Wauchope, general editor. University of Texas Press, Austin.

VILLAGUTIERRE SOTO-MAYOR, J. DE
1933   *Historia de la conquista de la provincia de el Itzá.* Reprinted. Biblioteca Guatemala, Guatemala. Originally published 1701, Madrid.

VILQUIN, E.
1975   Vauban: Inventeur des recensements. *Annales de Demographie Historique* 11:207–257.

VLACEK, D. T., S. GARZA DE GONZALEZ, AND E. B. KURJACK
1978   Contemporary Farming and Ancient Maya Settlements: Some Disconcerting Evidence. In *Pre-Hispanic Maya Agriculture,* edited by P. D. Harrison and B. L. Turner II, pp. 211–223. University of New Mexico Press, Albuquerque.

VLECK, D. T., AND W. L. FASH
1986   Survey in the Outlying Areas of the Copan Region, and the Copan-Quirigua Connection. In *The Southeast Maya Periphery,* edited by P. Urban and E. Schortman, pp. 102–113. University of Texas Press, Austin.

VOGEL, J. C., AND N. J. VAN DER MERWE
1977   Isotopic Evidence for Early Maize Cultivation in New York State. *American Antiquity* 42:238–242.

VOGT, E.
1961   Some Aspects of Zinacantan Settlement Patterns and Ceremonial Organization. *Estudios de Cultura Maya* 1:131–145.
1964   Some Implications of Zinacantan Social Structure for the Study of the Ancient Maya. 35th International Congress of Americanists, *Actas* 1:307–319. Mexico City.

VOORHIES, B.
1982   An Ecological Model of the Early Maya of the Central Lowlands. In *Maya Subsistence,* edited by K. V. Flannery, pp. 65–95. Academic Press, New York.

WAGNER, P. L.
1964   Natural Vegetation of Middle America. In *Natural Environment and Early Cultures,* edited by R. C. West, pp. 216–264. Handbook of Middle American Indians, vol. 1, R. Wauchope, general editor. University of Texas Press, Austin.

WALKER, P. L.
1985   Anemia among Prehistoric Indians of the American Southwest. In *Health and Disease in the Prehistoric Southwest,* edited by C. F. Merbs and R. J. Miller, pp. 139–164. Anthropological Research Papers 34. Arizona State University, Tempe.

WAUCHOPE, R.
1934   House Mounds of Uaxactun, Guatemala. *Contributions to American Anthropology and History,* no. 7. Carnegie Institution of Washington, Publication No. 436. Washington, D.C.
1938   *Modern Maya Houses: A Study of Their Archaeological Significance.* Carnegie Institution of Washington, Publication 502. Washington, D.C.

WEBSTER, D. L.
1976   *Defensive Earthworks at Becan, Campeche, Mexico.* Middle American Research Institute, Publication 41. Tulane University, New Orleans.
1977   Warfare and the Evolution of Maya Civilization. In *The Origins of Maya Civilization,* edited by R. E. W. Adams, pp. 335–372. University of New Mexico Press, Albuquerque.
1985   Recent Settlement Survey in the Copan Valley, Honduras. *Journal of World Archaeology* 5:39–51.
1988   Copan as a Classic Maya Center. In *The Classic Maya Southeast,* edited by E. H. Boone and G. R. Willey, pp. 8–14. Dumbarton Oaks, Washington, D.C.

WEBSTER, D., AND ABRAMS, E.
1983   An Elite Compound at Copan, Honduras. *Journal of Field Archaeology* 10:285–296.

WEBSTER, D., AND N. GONLIN
1988   Households of the Humblest Maya. *Journal of Field Archaeology* 15:169–190.

WEEKS, J. M.

1988   Residential and Local Group Organization in the Lowlands of Southwestern Campeche, Mexico: Evidence from the Mission Census of 1615. In *House and Household in the Mesoamerican Past,* edited by R. R. Wilk and W. Ashmore, pp. 73–96. University of New Mexico Press, Albuquerque.

WEISS, K.

1973   *Demographic Models for Anthropology.* Memoirs of the Society for American Archaeology, 27.

1976   Demographic Theory and Anthropological Inference. *Annual Review of Anthropology* 5:351–381.

WHITE, L.

1949   *The Science of Culture.* Farrar, Strauss and Giroux, New York.

1959   *The Evolution of Culture: Civilization to the Fall of Rome.* McGraw-Hill, New York.

WHITMORE, T. M., AND B. L. TURNER, II

1986   *Population Reconstruction of the Basin of Mexico: 1150 B.C. to Present.* Technical paper no. 1, Millennial Long Waves of Human Occupance Project. CENTED, Clark University.

WHITMORE, T. M., B. L. TURNER, II, D. L. JOHNSON, R. W. KATES, AND T. R. GOTTSCHANGE

1990   Long-term Population Change. In *The Earth as Transformed by Human Action,* edited by B. L. Turner II, R. W. Kates, W. C. Clark, J. R. Richards, J. Mathews, and W. M. Meyer. Cambridge University Press, Cambridge.

WHITTAKER, R.

1975   *Communities and Ecosystems.* Macmillan, New York.

WILK, R. R.

1975   Survey and Excavation at Colha. In *Archaeology in Northern Belize: 1974– 1975 Interim Report of the British Museum–Cambridge University Corozal Project,* edited by N. Hammond, pp. 152–184. Cambridge Centre of Latin American Studies, Cambridge University Press, Cambridge.

1976   Work in Progress at Colha, 1976. In *Maya Lithic Studies,* edited by T. Hester and N. Hammond, pp. 35–40. Center for Archaeological Research, University of Texas at San Antonio.

1984   Households in Process: Agricultural Change and Domestic Transformation among the Kekchi Maya of Belize. In *Households: Comparative and Historical Studies of the Domestic Group,* edited by R. McC. Netting, R. Wilk, and E. Arnould, pp. 217–244. University of California Press, Berkeley.

WILK, R. R., AND W. ASHMORE

1988   *Household and Community in the Mesoamerican Past,* University of New Mexico Press, Albuquerque.

WILK, R. R., D. PRING, AND N. HAMMOND

1975   Settlement Pattern Excavations in the Northern Sector of Nohmul. In *Archaeology in Northern Belize: 1974–1975 Interim Report of the British Museum–Cambridge University Corozal Project,* edited by N. Hammond, pp.

72–108. Cambridge Centre of Latin American Studies, Cambridge University Press, Cambridge.

WILK, R. R., L. REYNOLDS, AND H. WILHITE
1980   The Settlement Area Sampling Project at Cuello. Paper presented at the 45th Annual Meeting of the Society for American Archaeology, Philadelphia.

WILK, R. R., AND H. WILHITE
1982   The Settlement Area Sampling Program at Cuello. Ms. on file with the author.
1989   Patterns of Household and Settlement Change at Cuello. In *Cuello: A Prehistoric Maya Settlement in Northern Belize,* edited by N. Hammond. Cambridge University Press, Cambridge, in press.

WILLEY, G. R.
1973   *The Altar de Sacrificios Excavations: General Summary and Conclusions.* Papers of the Peabody Museum of American Archaeology and Ethnology, vol. 64, no. 3. Harvard University, Cambridge.
1974   The Classic Maya Hiatus: A "Rehearsal" for the Collapse? In *Mesoamerican Archaeology: New Approaches,* edited by N. Hammond, pp. 417–433. University of Texas Press, Austin.
1977   The Rise of Maya Civilization: A Summary View. In *The Origins of Maya Civilization,* edited by R. E. W. Adams, pp. 383–423. University of New Mexico Press, Albuquerque.
1982   Maya Archaeology. *Science* 215:260–267.

WILLEY, G. R., AND W. R. BULLARD
1965   Prehistoric Settlement Patterns in the Maya Lowlands. In *Archaeology of Southern Mesoamerica, part 1,* edited by G. R. Willey, pp. 360–371. Handbook of Middle American Indians, R. Wauchope, general editor. University of Texas Press, Austin.

WILLEY, G. R., W. R. BULLARD, J. GLASS, AND J. GIFFORD
1965   *Prehistoric Maya Settlements in the Belize Valley.* Papers of the Peabody Museum of American Archaeology and Ethnology, vol. 54. Harvard University, Cambridge.

WILLEY, G. R., AND R. LEVENTHAL
1979   Prehistoric Settlement at Copan. In *Maya Archaeology and Ethnohistory,* edited by N. Hammond, pp. 75–102. University of Texas Press, Austin.

WILLEY, G. R., R. LEVENTHAL, AND W. FASH
1978   Maya Settlement in the Copan Valley. *Archaeology* 31(4):32–43.

WILLEY, G. R., AND P. MATHEWS (EDITORS)
1985   *A Consideration of the Early Classic Period in the Maya Lowlands.* Institute for Mesoamerican Studies, Publication 10. State University of New York at Albany.

WILLEY, G. R., A. L. SMITH, G. TOURTELLOT, AND I. GRAHAM
1975   *Excavations at Seibal. Introduction: The Site and Its Setting.* Memoirs of the

Peabody Museum of American Archaeology and Ethnology, vol. 13, no. 1. Harvard University, Cambridge.

WILLEY, G. R., AND D. B. SHIMKIN
1973   The Maya Collapse: A Summary View. In *The Classic Maya Collapse,* edited by T. P. Culbert, pp. 457–502. University of New Mexico Press, Albuquerque.

WILLIGAN, J. D., AND K. LYNCH
1982   *Sources and Methods of Historical Demography.* Academic Press, New York.

WILSON, E. M.
1980   Physical Geography of the Yucatan Peninsula. In *Yucatan: A World Apart,* edited by E. H. Moseley and E. D. Terry, pp. 5–40. University of Alabama Press, Tuscaloosa.

WILSON, E. O., AND W. BOSSERT
1971   *A Primer on Population Biology.* Sinauer Associates, Sunderland, Massachusetts.

WING, E. S., AND A. B. BROWN
1979   *Paleonutrition: Method and Theory in Prehistoric Foodways.* Academic Press, New York.

WISDOM, C.
1940   *The Chorti Indians of Guatemala.* University of Chicago Press, Chicago.

WITTFOGEL, K. A.
1957   *Oriental Despotism: A Study in Total Power.* Yale University Press, New Haven.

WOLMAN, M. G., AND L. B. LEOPOLD
1970   Flood Plains. In *Rivers and River Terraces,* edited by G. H. Dury, pp. 166–196. Praeger, New York.

WRIGHT, A. C. S., D. H. ROMNEY, R. H. ARBUCKLE, AND V. E. VIAL
1959   *Land in British Honduras: Report of the British Honduras Land Use Survey Team.* Colonial Research Publication 24. Colonial Office, London.

ZUBROW, E.
1971   Carrying Capacity and Dynamic Equilibrium in the Prehistoric Southwest. *American Antiquity* 36:127–138.
1975   *Prehistoric Carrying Capacity: A Model.* Cummings, Menlo Park.

Index